The Global Dynamics of News:
Studies in International News Coverage
and News Agendas

Contemporary Studies in International Political Communication

Abbas Malek, Series Editor

Spoken and Written Discourse: A Multi-disciplinary Perspective
by Khosrow Jahandarie, 1999

The Global Dynamics of News: Studies in International News Coverage and News Agendas
edited by Abbas Malek and Anandam P. Kavoori, 1999

The Global Dynamics of News: Studies in International News Coverage and News Agendas

edited by

Abbas Malek
Howard University

and

Anandam P. Kavoori
University of Georgia

Ablex Publishing Corporation
Stamford, Connecticut

Printed in the United States of America

Library of Congress Cataloguing-in-Publication Data

The global dynamics of news: studies of international news coverage and news agendas / edited by Abbas Malek, Anandam P. Kavoori.
  p. cm.—(Contemporary studies in international political communication)
  Includes bibliographical references and index.
  ISBN 1-56750-462-0 (cloth)—ISBN 1-56750-463-9 (pbk.)
  1. Foreign news. 2. Communication, International. 3. Journalism—Political aspects. I. Malek, Abbas. II. Kavoori, Anandam P. III. Series.
Pn4784.F6G58 2000
070.4'332—dc21   99-29339
                                  CIP

Ablex Publishing Corporation
100 Prospect Street
P.O. Box 811
Stamford, Connecticut 06904-0811

Contents

Part IV. Transnational Perspectives

Acknowledgments

We would like to thank the following people for their editorial assistance on this book: Dawn Pick, Seok Kang, James Rada, Christina Joseph, and Larisa Bosma.

Introduction

Abbas Malek
Howard University

Anandam P. Kavoori
University of Georgia

This book is an attempt to locate the study of news—perhaps the genre best epitomizing the process of media globalization—within contemporary debates about news flow, transnational media cultures, and globalization. The book seeks to fill a considerable gap in the literature of international communication and transnational media studies, which have focused on issues of media culture, especially popular culture (soaps, music), but have left news mostly underexplored. While there have been piecemeal attempts to understand the role of news globally in different journal-length articles and large single projects (see, for example, Cohen, Adoni, & Bantz, 1990; Malik, 1992; Sreberny-Mohammadi, 1995; and the ongoing NewsFlow project being coordinated by Annabelle Sreberny Mohammadi and Robert Stevenson), no collections that theorize the role of news and present a range of empirical studies from a comparative, national, and transnational perspective have yet been published. This book brings together both theoretical essays and case studies that are informed by historical and contemporary debates about issues of media flow and media imperialism specifically, and those of media globalization generally.

The book is organized into four interconnected parts. Each part contains chapters that theoretically and empirically inform the global dynamics of news—understood from a variety of perspectives. We have intentionally not divided the book by region or type of institution, but rather by the specific kind of dynamic that informs different aspects of news seen globally.

The first part, Theorizing News, presents theoretical/empirical chapters that attempt to provide a conceptual map for understanding news as one aspect of media globalization and global media culture, written by scholars who attempt to locate news within different conceptual vectors. Chapter 1, "Transnational Cultural Studies and International News: Some Research Questions," by Anandam Kavoori, Kalyani Chadha, and Christina Joseph, argues that news needs to be framed within the four global grids of modernity, postmodernity, nationalism, and globalization. It offers sample questions based on such a perspective and uses examples from the nation of India to ground their questions. Chapter 2, "A Matrix Model for Framing News Media Reality," by Naren Chitty, develops a model for global/local culture within a matrix model of perception. This model for processing social reality then is applied to the case of how the news media constructs "corridors of meanings" around the sites of Singapore and Sydney. Peter Oehlkers's chapter, "Mediating News: The 'International Media Echo' and Symbolic International Relations," develops the notion of international media echo as a way to theorize news as a form of staged symbolic communication that structures relations between the public, journalists, and nations. Each of these chapters draws on different bodies of literature to inform our understanding of the dynamics of news globally.

While this first section provides overall theoretical frames, the other sections in this book use specific sites (comparative analysis of news, national news agendas, and news agencies) to approach the understanding of news as a global dynamic. The combination of both theory and empirical data provides the conceptual unity to the chapters that follow.

Part II, Comparative Perspectives, provides examples of the emergent commonalties and differences in news agendas across countries. The chapters in this section approach this from a variety of perspectives and research methodologies—all aimed at examining the *comparative* dynamics of news coverage and agendas. Chapter 4, "Ideological Manipulation via Newspaper Accounts of Political Conflict: A Cross-national Comparative News Analysis of the 1991 Moscow Coup," by Li-Ning Huang and Katherine McAdams, draws on a media hegemony perspective to examine the ideological bias in newspaper coverage of the 1991 Moscow coup in the United States, China, and Taiwan. Chapter 5, "International News in the Latin American Press," by Jose-Carlos Lozano and colleagues, examines issues of comparative news coverage and content from a cultural imperialism and dependency perspective and suggests that there are multiple sets of referencing/coverage taking place across the seven countries examined. Carolina Acosta-Alzuru and Elizabeth Lester's chapter, "A War by Any Other Name: A Textual Analysis of Falklands/Malvinas War Coverage in United States and Latin American Newspapers," draws on the textual analysis/cultural studies tradition and suggests that news accounts are structured in dominance and work to maintain "preferred" discourses about the "other" and in the process do ideological work, rather than just providing neutral news coverage.

Part III, National Perspectives, is the most comprehensive and grows out of contemporary debates about media globalization, which focus on processes of both transnationalization and localization—especially the resurgence of the discourse of nationalism. This section examines in detail how the national perspective is constructed and formed through multiple mediations of the international, and explores different aspects of this process (from varying theoretical/empirical perspectives). Chapter 7, "Hegemonic Frames and International News Reporting: A

Comparative Study of *The New York Times* Coverage of the 1996 Indian and Israeli Elections," by Ritu and Krishna Jayakar, and Chapter 8, "Medusa's Gaze: North American Press Coverage of the Peruvian Hostage Crises," by Gina Bailey, examine this process from an American perspective. Both chapters are informed by a news discourse/thematic analysis perspective and deal with debates about media hegemony and the cultural function of news coverage. Charles Quist Adade's chapter, "In the Shadows of the Kremlin: Africa's Media Image from Communism to Post-Communism," examines a little-known discourse that has global relevance: the changing/unchanged image of Africa in the Soviet Union. Framed by an intercultural communication perspective, Adade's work examines the cultural, historical, and politico-ideological factors behind the formation, reinforcement and dissemination of specific images of Africa in the Russian media. Chapter 10, "Covering the South Caucasus and Bosnian Conflicts, Or How the Jihad Model Appears and Disappears," by Karim H. Karim, focuses on Canadian news coverage of the conflict in Bosnia and argues that the reporting reinforced historically constituted modes of discourse and underlie what he calls "a Jihad model" of reporting and journalism. Tsan-Kuo Chang and Chen Yanru's chapter, "Constructing International Spectacle on Television: CCTV News and China's Window on the World, 1992–1996," provides a much needed "Chinese" perspective on how the outside has been constructed.

The last three chapters in Part III focus on specific sites where the key processes of post-cold war transition have taken place (these include globalized capitalism, political liberalism, media-centrism) and show how news can be seen as part of this process. Chapter 12, "Looking East, Heading West: Images of Former Friends and Foes in the Bulgarian Communist/Socialist Party Press," by Anelia Dimitrova, shows how the reinvention of ideology has taken place within a specific formerly propagandist press outlet. Arnold de Beer's chapter, "New Mirror in a New South Africa? International News Flow and News Selection at *Beeld*, an Afrikaans Daily," and Chapter 14, "South Africa's Miracle Cure: A Stage-managed Television Spectacular?," by Eric Louw and Naren Chitty, focus on two aspects of this process in South Africa. De Beer's chapter examines the news agenda of a traditional Afrikaans daily, while the chapter by Louw and Chitty points to how the political establishment in South Africa stage-managed a television performance to establish its place in the global market as well as to establish political legitimacy.

The last part, Transnational Perspectives, focuses on one of the key aspects of the global news system: international and national news agencies. Chapter 15, "Constructing the Global, Constructing the Local: News Agencies Re-present the World," by Oliver Boyd Barrett, locates the study of news services within the larger sets of debates around globalization, modernity, and nationalism and examines the specific roles that the Internet and national news agencies perform within the world system. Daya Kishan Thussu's chapter, "Development News versus Globalized Infotainment?," provides a theoretical link with both the older literatures on news agencies and contemporary debates about media globalization by focusing on the role of Gemini News, one news agency that is oriented to the Third World. Chapter 17, "Flows of News from the Middle Kingdom: An Analysis of International News Releases from Xinhua," by Charles Elliot, examines the Chinese news agency and relates how its transnational coverage is related to specific national and political aims. The final chapter, by Anthony Giffard ("International Agencies and Global Issues: The Decline of the Cold War News Frame"), examines how a North–South class-based frame of reporting has come to dominate news coverage, as opposed to the East–West narrative framework.

We urge that this book be used both as a research and as a teaching resource. To that end, we have added a list of questions to facilitate discussion in an appendix at the end of the book. This collection should be of general interest to scholars teaching courses in media studies and mass communication and would be of direct interest to instructors teaching courses such as International Communication, Political Communication, News and Society, Issues in Media Globalization, and so on. Degree programs that emphasize print and broadcast news and international communication would find this collection especially suitable.

REFERENCES

Cohen, A., Adoni, H., & Bantz, C. (1990). *Social conflict and television news*. Newbury Park, CA: Sage.

Malik, R. (1992). The global news agenda. *Intermedia, 20*(1), 12–29.

Sreberny-Mohammadi, A. (1995). International news flows in the post cold war world. *Electronic Journal of Communication, 5*, 7–17.

I

Theorizing News

1

Transnational Cultural Studies and International News: Some Research Questions

Anandam P. Kavoori
University of Georgia

Kalyani Chadha
University of Maryland

Christina Joseph
University of Georgia

This chapter provides a theoretical agenda for the study of international news from a transnational cultural studies perspective. It is not a literature review of the field of transnational cultural studies, nor is it based on an empirical analysis of news texts. Our goals are rather to provide some research questions to better understand the cultural function of international news. This chapter draws from research proposals and pilot papers (Kavoori & Chadha, 1998) from an ongoing project in the nation of India. We do not offer a summary of the findings from those papers here, but we use them as reference points to suggest that the theoretical questions being addressed in the Indian context are of relevance for news outlets throughout the Third World, as they function under contemporary conditions of market liberalization and media globalization. In sum, we offer the research questions in our ongoing study as a theoretical guideline for news-based projects in different countries.

This chapter is organized as follows. We suggest that an understanding of international news has to go beyond traditional concerns of development and dependency theory to locating news within four "global grids"—those of modernity, postmodernity, nationalism, and capitalism. These "grids" are common reference points in the transnational cultural studies approach. We then provide a working definition of each of these global grids. The section ends with the delineation of a cultural studies approach to news—that is, it sees news in a cultural and sociopolitical context—and suggests that there are three kinds of news broadcasts emergent in India. These are termed "state-based news," "liberal state news," and "Western-style populist news."

Then, we discuss state-based news and liberal state news by examining the development of these two genres on Indian television and link their development to the four global grids identified above. We then suggest a series of research questions that is guiding our research in India and can be applied to other Third World sites. A discussion of Western-style populist news follows, with examples from two news stations in India. This section also concludes with a similar set of research questions. Finally, we summarize our major points in the conclusion.

Our overall argument is that international news functions as a general arbitrator of cultural values cross-culturally (Kavoori, 1994) structured by the four global dynamics of modernity, postmodernity, capitalism, and nationalism. We see the function of this chapter in a collection such as this is to complement the wealth of empirical studies and to add to the diversity of theoretical perspectives open to current and future researchers of international news.

A GLOBAL GRIDS MODEL FOR INTERNATIONAL NEWS

Transnational cultural studies is an interdisciplinary concern that draws on the fields of cultural studies, anthropology, comparative literature, history, and postcolonial studies to theorize current conditions of globality. Current research in international communication has been dominated by paradigms of modernization and dependency. Periodic reviews of the field of international communication over the last two decades by Hamid Mowlana (1973, 1986) have shown a persistence of a limited conceptual model for understanding complex global relations. In his latest such review (1994), he calls for a conceptual framework that moves beyond the "sense of international communication as interaction's amongst states or policy making elite's" (p. 15), which has undergirded both modernization and dependency frameworks. Mowlana calls for an increased understanding of a cultural approach to global issues both at the "topical, substantive level as well as the epistemological level" (p. 27). In a similar vein, Sreberny-Mohammadi (1992) identifies an emergent paradigm of "cultural revisionism" as the direction of the future—a future that she points out is still searching for a coherent theoretical shape.

We believe part of that coherence can come by drawing on the transnational cultural studies literature that has focused on four globally occurring dynamics (or what we term "grids") that can be applied to the study of any cultural text or institutional practice. These dynamics are those of modernity, postmodernity, nationalism, and capitalism. Each of the grids has a complex, contested, and rich history and a review of the literature in each field is outside the purview of this chapter. What does follow is our use specific of these terms.

Modernity. By modernity, we mean the specific locus of institutional practices that emerge within the socioeconomic space of European industrial and urban growth and then become transmuted as a vocabulary for social excellence. The benchmarks of that excellence include those of industrial enterprise, economic valuation, political accountability, and cultural freedom. In our use of it, modernity then retains its traditional use as a term of periodization and its wider use as a prescription for societal development.

Postmodernity. By postmodernity, we mean the emergence of not only a new kind of social and economic accounting (culture as consumption) but a specific semiotic universe (a globally interconnected, rapidly mobile landscape of signifiers) and new vocabularies for mediation (such as in emergent genres of infotainment).

Nationalism. By nationalism, we mean both its traditional signifier for the ethos of new states (and those yet to be born) and the emergent values of "renewal" in Third World states as they grapple with current conditions of globality.

Capitalism. Finally, capitalism is used both in the sense of a globally connected matrix of economic relations and in its current "naturalization" by nation states for social and economic development.

In examining news, we move away from recent revisionist scholarship, which has struggled to problematize meaning in a postmodern world, often falling back on economic determinism (Ferguson, 1992) or using older notions of cultural pluralism seen globally (Sreberny-Mohammadi, 1992). A beginning point for us is that news (in its programming, narrative, and institutional contexts) is less about providing information than about socialization. To treat news as an agency of socialization means that we are concerned with its function as a "social teacher" across time. The most significant features lie in its recurring themes rather than in its informational content and in the contextual location of news, the idea that programming is produced under special social and cultural circumstances (Dahlgren, 1982).

In developing our study of television news in India, we examined news on Doordarshan (hereafter referred to as DD) and Rupert Mudoch's Star Channel. These two channels have the highest viewership in Indian television. Four broadcasts were examined—*DD Hindi News* and *Aaj Tak (Until Today)*, both airing on DD, and *Zee News* and *Star News*, which air on the Star Channel. We analyzed sample news programming, read literature in the print news media, and studied the advertising on each channel (Kavoori & Chadha, 1998). Based on this research, we identified a typology of news termed "state based news" and "Western-style popular news." This typology then was related to the global grids model and guided the development of a theoretical hypothesis for each station. The theoretical hypothesis was in turn used to develop specific research questions.

The two sections that follow now detail the typology in the Indian case, followed by a theoretical hypothesis for each station and a set of corresponding research questions.

DOORDARSHAN HINDI NEWS: STATE-BASED NEWS

Doordarshan was conceived in 1959 as a rural development oriented medium. Over time, it assumed its primary role as a state broadcaster with the explicit aim of articulating a specific vision of the national (and of the state apparatus of the dominant Congress party). For the better part of its life (from the 1960s to the 1980s), DD's Hindi news broadcast came to stand for a number of things—poor technical quality, the substandard quality of its programs, its partisan handling of political issues, and its strong establishment orientation. Most critically, it became the voice of the national government reaching out to millions of viewers.

Most metropolitan areas in India get at least two channels of the state broadcaster—DD1, or the "national" channel, and DD2, which is aimed at "entertainment," competing with private national and transnational media programming. Of the two, the "national" channel has been the preeminent source of news and entertainment since the advent of satellite and microwave connections and then in the 1980s and 1990s as part of "must-carry" regulations in the burgeoning cable industry (Mitra, 1993).

The international coverage on *DD Hindi News* is heavily based in favor of visits by Indian officials abroad and similar visits by international visitors to India; stories about regional and national development plans; stories on ASEAN (Association of South East Asian Nations) and the Non-Aligned Movement; and meetings of Indian government officials with Western aid and governmental organizations (Kavoori & Chadha, 1998).

What makes each of these stories state centered is not just content, but their narrative format. The stories are read by a talking head (that is, a news reader and not a journalist). The reading style is formal—very dry in tone and highly literary in style. The language used is a highly enunciated form of formal Hindi. In short, *DD Hindi News* mimics a traditional, high culture style (the kind of culture in fact that the state often sponsors). For Indian viewers, *DD Hindi News* is thus inextricably tied up with their identities as citizens, their stance toward the news bearing within it, a stance toward the state (Jayasankar & Monteiro, 1994).

Our theoretical hypothesis, then, is that news coverage on *DD Hindi News* performs a specific kind of socialization—one grounded in a traditional sense of nationalism and regionalism—and a specific vision of "modernity." In DD's international news, the nation state is constructed both internally (via stories about various national development projects and their achievements, often comparing India's development favorably with other Third World countries) and externally (through its role in the international arena and as a global/regional political and economic player). Equally crucial is the extensive coverage given to news of Indian achievements abroad (especially news of artists, musicians, sportsmen, and scientists) If there is a vision of the nation state that emerges from DD's international news, it is this: The nation state is strong, resurgent, and honorable. Such coverage is in tune with the rhetoric of nationhood that first surfaced in the 1940s with the independence movement. It has retained that essentialized, unabashed articulation of the state's interests by centering the state with the nation. Appadurai (1990) has pointed out that "one important new feature of global cultural politics is that state and nation are at each other's throats, and the hyphen that links them now is less an icon of conjuncture than an index of disjuncture" (p. 304). However, no such disjuncture exists in DD's vision of the Indian nation state. Part of the reason for this lack of conflict comes from the broadcasts negotiation of "modernity." To be "modern" on DD implies adherence to the benchmarks of Euro-industrial and urban growth and those of cultural renewal, especially in the "high" arts and that of political secularism (as long as it does not endanger the dominant political party). Hence, modernity is represented by a multitude of stories about national achievement—of industrial and technological growth; stories about cooperation and collaboration with other countries; and regional and development plans. In each case, the state's role is that of an international arbitrator of modernity.

With this overall theoretical hypothesis in mind, the following research questions (structured by nationalism-modernity) are guiding our analysis of *DD Hindi News* and can be applied to any other state-based news in the Third World.

1. What changes in "national" discourse take place as state media deal with contemporary conditions of globalization?
2. What kinds of modernist undertakings are articulated by international news and which are undervalued? This is of special relevance in the case of transitional and mixed economies, where differing models of modernity are often at work—those drawing from Western capitalism and those from socialism.
3. What is the extent of news coverage of state-sponsored economic internationalism (for example, organizations like ASEAN) as it encounters global capitalism, with its agenda driven by market economics?
4. What happens to news coverage of state-sponsored political internationalism (for example, organizations like the Non-Aligned Movement and NATO)? In

what terms is contemporary, state-sponsored, economic internationalism (such as NAFTA) covered?

5. How is the relationship between "state" and "nation" articulated in its rapid devolution globally? How were events such as the breakup of Yugoslavia and the former Soviet Union covered? How are the events in Kosovo being covered?

DOORDARSHAN'S *AAJ TAK*: STATE-BASED LIBERAL NEWS

As the process of economic liberalization expanded into the media marketplace, DD was forced by viewer loss to rethink its strategy of state based news. In a short span of time (between 1993 and 1996), various news and entertainment programs were developed. Journalist Amit Agarwal puts this succinctly:

> What DD is allowing today was unthinkable earlier. After years of current affairs discussion on topics like water conservation and the virtues of India's non-aligned policy, today DD viewers can hope to view programs that really qualify as current affairs.... As one of its programs ran a story on Lorena Bobbit, it was as though DD itself was Bobbitising its past (1994, p. 113)

One of the most successful programs has been the Hindi news bulletin *Aaj Tak (Until Today)*. Produced by an independent production company for DD, *Aaj Tak* has followed the narrative model of Western commercial television: tight editing, moving between studio and field reports, extensive use of visuals and live reports. It uses a narrative formula that constructs national and international news through individuals who are framed as protagonists in a conflict—conflicts over national development, regional politics, and, most often, national and international economic policy and practices (Kavoori & Chadha, 1998).

Our theoretical hypothesis is that the *Aaj Tak* broadcast represents an indigenous vocabulary for modernity, nationalism, and capitalism. The nation here is presented with the muted voice of the state and with the focus of the news squarely on an urban-industrial model of modernity. For example, news stories present the nexus between the nation state and national and international business interests as unproblematic. The state, in other words, is not presented as morally upright (as in *DD Hindi News*), but as a rational, coherent agent of industrial development. The editing and placement of certain individuals (state business leaders, international bankers) is done with the aim of developing a new identity for the nation state as an active member of the global marketplace. By contrast, *DD Hindi News* usually presents global and regional political/economic news within the vectors of colonial culpability and post-colonial guilt (by the West) and by morally correct nationalism (by the nation state). What is crucially different for *Aaj Tak* is its explicit acceptance of the nation state as controlled by modernism. Its acceptance of modernity's economic parameters also allows it to negotiate the presence of contemporary conditions of capitalism. Unlike *DD Hindi News*, which rarely recognizes the impact and role of global capital, *Aaj Tak* both accepts it and utilizes it as a framework for mediating nationhood and modernity. The differences are important. In DD news, the nation state is rarely an arbitrator of transnational capitalism. Rather, the news focuses on opposition to capitalism via an overemphasis on nationalism. These include stories on national economic policies, indigenous development plans, and so on. The nation state on *DD Hindi News* is thus disengaged with capitalism. In contrast, the nation state is directly engaged with international capital on *Aaj Tak*'s broadcasts—both as a rational mediator of this process and as the arbitrator of differences between global and local capital.

With this overall theoretical hypothesis in mind, the following research questions are framing our analysis of *Aaj Tak* news and can be applied to any other state-based liberal news.

Here are some general research questions for liberal state news (structured by nationalism-modernity-capitalism):

1. What are the specific conjunctions (for example, media and political events) that allow for an uncritical acceptance of modernity by liberal state news?
2. What kinds of economic liberalization policies (by different developing countries) allow for the uncritical acceptance of capitalist modernity by liberal state news? How are such economic liberalization policies covered by liberal state news outlets?
3. How is the content of international news in liberal state media balanced between the needs of state-sponsored capitalism and the older policy/rhetoric of state-centered socialism?
4. What kinds of public personalities are most commonly featured in state-based liberal news? How do politicians that do not know the vocabulary of public relations and a conflict model of news fare under state-based liberal news?
5. How are stories about economic development presented when there is indigenous opposition to such development? In the Indian context, this is especially relevant in the case of minority, tribal, and women's movements.

ZEE TV AND *STAR NEWS*: WESTERN-STYLE POPULIST NEWS

Beginning in 1991, Rupert Murdoch's Star TV network has offered Indian viewers a range of English language programming, including the BBC world service. What was missing was a Hindi language service, which was added in 1992 through Zee TV—an Indian-owned television company.

An English language news service focused on India was introduced in 1996. A leading Indian production house—NDTV (New Delhi Television), which used to produce the English news broadcast for DD2, runs *Star News*. Following conflict over content control (and low ratings), NDTV's head (who is also the anchor) made the leap from the state-controlled commercial network to Murdoch's media conglomerate.

The international news coverage on Zee TV and *Star News* is skewed in favor of economic news based on the activities of the state and by international development agencies (an agenda it shares with DD and *Aaj Tak*), but covers in greater depth major global business corporations. Both run "business news" programs and have frequent business features on the nightly broadcast. Other common stories include those of fashion, music, film, food, and health. Political reporting closely follows a conflict model with individual protagonists (Kavoori & Chadha, 1998).

Our theoretical hypothesis is that both Zee TV and *Star News* present a specific conjunction between international television news and the production of a specific collective socialization—one oriented to western commodity capitalism. Star News extends the narratological conventions adapted by Aaj Tak to their logical conclusion by closely imitating the storytelling techniques of Western commercial news broadcasts. Political news is unambiguously approached as having commodity value (to bring in viewers) with a marked emphasis on stories about disorder and conflict. In terms of their cultural function, both *Star News* and Zee TV are fundamentally different from DD and *Aaj Tak*. For DD and *Aaj Tak*, the kinds of discourses drawn on remain chained to a specific vision of modernity and nationalism and a narrow opening to capitalism (in the case of *Aaj Tak*); Zee TV and *Star News* represent an uncomplicated referencing to capitalism and postmodernity. Their referencing of capitalism is two-fold: One, it is unabashedly oriented to a contemporary vision of capitalism, as determined by a postmodern vision of consumption; two, national identities are intimately connected to the development of capitalist/postmodern identities.

The international news stories on these stations can be expected to articulate a deterministic model of society that equates economic worth with cultural and social development (much like American television's coverage of international events, narrowly focused on issues of freedom and democracy). The political referencing of the nation state is dramatically different from that of DD and *Aaj Tak*. The nation state remains the primary focus of the mediation of modernity for both DD and *Aaj Tak*. For Zee TV and *Star News*, the traditional container of modernity (the nation state) is bypassed in favor of a globally constituted, postmodern culture of consumption as the benchmark for reconstituting national identity.

With these overall theoretical issues in mind, the following research questions are framing our analysis of Zee TV and *Star News* and can be applied to any western style populist news broadcast in the Third World.

Here are some general research questions for Western-style populist news (structured by capitalism-postmodernism):

1. What are the thematic differences between Western populist news (in both its transnational and indigenous forms) and liberal state news? In what ways do

these differences articulate specific disjunctions along lines of modernism, postmodernism, and nationalism?

2. What are the specific vocabularies of production and narrativization that transnational capitalism brings to the news text?
3. What are the ways in which postmodern news (based on the first principle of consumption) articulates the needs of the nation state?
4. What are the modalities of identity progression in news reception as audiences' progress from being hailed as citizens (via state media and liberal state media) to that of consumer (by Western-style populist media).

CONCLUSION

In this chapter, we have identified a set of research questions we are using to examine the television news landscape in India. We suggest that these questions begin the task of rethinking the agenda of international news research, which has traditionally focused on theoretical perspectives drawing on dependency or modernization theory. Our aims were to frame international news as a cultural text and to locate it as an agent of socialization framed within the four global grids of modernity, postmodernity, nationalism, and capitalism. We hope our framework will allow other scholars to restrategize both their content-analytic frameworks and their theoretical orientation toward the global grids model of international news.

REFERENCES

Agarawal, A. (1994, April 14). Media report. *India Today*, 113.

Appadurai, A. (1990). Disjuncture and difference in the global cultural economy. *Theory, Culture and Society*, *7*, 295–310.

Dahlgren, P. (1982). The third world on TV news: Western ways of seeing the other. In W. C. Adams (Ed), *Television coverage of international affairs* (pp. 45–67). Norwood, NJ: Ablex.

Ferguson, M. (1992). The mythology about globalization. *European Journal of Communication*, *7*, 69–93.

Jayasankar, K., & Monteiro, A. (1994, July). *The news, the state, and the spectator.* Paper presented at the International Association of Mass Communication Research, Seoul, Korea.

Kavoori, A. (1994). *Globalization, media audiences, and television news: A comparative study of American, British, Israeli, German, and French audiences.* Unpublished doctoral dissertation, University of Maryland, College Park.

Kavoori, A., & Chadha, K. (1998). Constructing the national on Indian television news. *Journal for Journalism in South Africa, 19*, 34–46.

Mitra, A. (1993). Television and the nation: Doordarshan's India. *Media Asia, 20*, 39–58.

Mowlana, H. (1973). Trends in research on international communication in the United States. *International Journal for Mass Communication Studies, 19*, 2.

Mowlana, H. (1986). *Global information and world communication: New frontiers in international relations.* White Plains, NY: Longman.

Mowlana, H. (1993). From technology to culture. In G. Gerbner, H. Mowlana, & K. Nordenstreng (Eds.), *The global media debate: Its rise, fall, and renewal* (pp. 161–166). Norwood, NJ: Ablex.

Mowlana, H. (1994). Shapes of the future: International communication in the 21st century. *The Journal of International Communication, 1,* 14–32.

Sreberny-Mohammadi, A. (1992). The global and the local in international communication. In J. Curran & M. Gurevitch (Eds.), *Mass media and society.* London: Edward Arnold.

2

A Matrix Model for Framing News Media Reality

Naren Chitty
Macquarie University, Australia

Media scholars have long been aware that news media reality is a world of smoke and mirrors, of sleight of mind. If the gravity of industrial-age reportage dulled the critical faculty and suspended disbelief in the minds of millions of ordinary people, what can be said of the footloose and fancy-free swirl of images and words in a postmodern world? Patterns of smoke are reflected instantaneously as conflagrations in a million media mirrors. Media frenzies ignore the possibility of smouldering. Electronic smoke signals seem to incite journalists into embarking on a scalping expedition.

Sex-related political/legal/media jousting, in the closing years of the 20th century in the United States, is a political soap opera for the international news market. American media variously report, overreport, and misreport the political present and speculate about political futures. But not all stories that capture global attention originate from the U.S. The Asian currency crisis showed the increasing importance of stock markets in Asia. It also showed the expensive (or profitable, as the case may be) outcome of the relationship between currency speculators and media as economic speculum.

The Pauline Hanson story from Australia, discussed later in the chapter, captured the attention of Asia and other parts of the world. The end of colonialism in Hong Kong was a planned media event that also captured global attention.

Stories about the U.S. presidency, Asian currency crisis, Pauline Hanson, and Hong Kong are matters of interest outside their countries of origin. Increasingly, globalization has made analysis of the reality of news media more of a challenge than before. We can no longer confine ourselves to a single level of analysis. Globalization has made the local explode in the global and the global implode in the local. Convergence of elite technologies has altered the nature of elite control of social order. Elite operations have moved from national to global systems. At the same time, the peripherals to computer systems are more affordable for individuals. Global elites produce and distribute the hardware and software of communication for massive global markets; lesser elites have more modest shares of the market.

A framework for analysis of news media in the context of globalization needs to incorporate the global as well as the local, the political-economic as well as the cultural. Vincent Mosco (1996) recognizes the need for political economy to have a systematic dialogue with cultural studies, but finds it expedient "to situate the discipline opposite cultural studies, on the one side, and policy studies, on the other" (pp. 246–247). Staniland (1983) was dissatisfied with the economism and politicism of non-Marxist political economy and called for a holistic approach. Mowlana (1994) has noted: "[I]n the field of international mass communication and information technology, the subject of culture has been only dealt with in the realm of cultural industries and their impact on society and as part of broader cultural studies" (p. 18).

Wallerstein's World System model (1990) comes close to being a holistic model, in that it has a profit-driven world market at the global center that creates a center-periphery division of labor, the inequities of which are justified by cultures of racism and sexism. Realism and balance of power is the ideology of the system, which changes from time to time after wars have been fought and won. In his organization of social life, the predominant "economic" pressures are "international" points and the predominant "political" pressures are "national" points. The capitalist world economy functions by means of a pattern of 50- to 60-year cycles, and is propelled by endless accumulation of capital.

The problem presented by Wallerstein's (1990) model is that it tends to emphasize the role of economics in world structuration and social change at the expense of culture. Additionally, it is not a model that is consistent with postmodern conditions. A model that builds corridors between political economy and culture must be able to make credible connections between the international and the individual, between world politics and personal insecurity, to borrow from Harold Lasswell (1963). I try to achieve this in the "matrix model" through a digitization of social reality into social pixels—values, attitudes, and beliefs. These pixels are embedded in individual matrices, which in turn are embedded in administrative, regional, and political-economic matrices.

This chapter develops a political economy/cultural framework (matrix model), from which it draws categories for headline analysis of news media reporting in Singapore and Australia on competitive movements toward economic and cultural security in those countries.

THE MATRIX MODEL

Matrices are like folders on a computer desktop. Each folder is a matrix within which other folders can be placed, each in turn a nest for other folders, representing values, attitudes, and beliefs. These may be conceived of as pixels, which together produce images of individuality or coloration. Individuals are embedded in one or more ethnohistorical matrices (e-matrices). E-matrices are concerned with cultural reproduction and preservation. They may have begun as groups concerned with economic production and distribution. A family is an example of an e-matrix, which even to this day performs some of both of these functions. So is a nation state. Members of an e-matrix inhabit an ethnohistorical space in which a particular ethnohistorical vocabulary has currency. The primary motivation of an ethno-historical group is survival of cultural identity of the collectivity. Behavior that defies the explanatory power of an individual self-interest-based political economic model can originate in an e-matrix. An example might be behavior such as the voluntary self-immolation of Buddhist monks in Vietnam in protest against the United States. Ethnohistorical vocabularies are related to Benedict Anderson's (1990) "sacred languages," and e-matrices are not unlike Marshall Singer's (1987) "perceptual groups."

When several e-matrices must share resources, either through domination of others by one e-matrix or some other arrangement, they become embedded in an administrative matrix (a-matrix) of their creation. An administrative vocabulary arises, possibly influenced strongly by a dominant e-matrix. A-matrices are locations where state, business, and media are to be found. The rules of self-interest operate here in the conventional manner of individual interest maximization.

Several a-matrices, if they interact, will give rise to a political-economic matrix (p-matrix), either based on the values and vocabulary of a dominant a-matrix or through some other mixture of values and vocabularies. The a-matrices will be embedded in a p-matrix. Before Europe began to colonize the rest of the world, one might say there were many p-matrices. Today, there is but one overall p-matrix, the deterritorialized space of the so-called world market, global culture, and international system. The international vocabularies of this p-matrix include science, mathematics, Western popular music, United Nations officialese, and journalism. A-matrices may also group together in regional political-economic matrices, or r-matrices.

The particular combination of pixels in an individual will provide that individual's coloration and the combination of colorations of individuals in an e-matrix will provide the cultural coloration of that e-matrix. We may conceive of the p-matrix as white, e-matrices as having a variety of hues, and a-matrices being pastel shades of the colorations of their dominant e-matrices.

The p-matrix may be likened to a vast urban area, a "city," where state and market hold sway. Within this city, embedded in a-matrices, are hundreds of thousands of cultural precincts of various sizes, which we may call "ethnicities." Ethnicities are places where ethnohistorical forces are salient, even dominant, and may on occasion prevail over state or market forces.

The city and ethnicities are two separate kingdoms demanding different coin. "International space" is a global city and "ethnohistorical spaces" are ethnicities. Whether the city-ethnicity relationship is seen as hierarchical or nonhierarchical, as center–periphery or center–center, depends on one's perspective. "City" is an administrative connective tissue between "ethnicities." It is the dispersed global "city" that is the site of the world market, the international system, and global culture.

Today, the "city" is coterminous with a global telecommunication web that links humans to machine peripherals. "There is an inter-linking of individuals, institutions, societies and the network called the world computer which gives the whole a cyborg nature. In that sense 'we are the world, we are the cyborg.' Collectively, society and the world computer may be viewed as Terra Cyborg. We are, then, individual cells in this cyborg, we are cyborganisms" (Chitty, 1997, p. 2). Cyborganizations, whether states, intergovernmental organizations, firms, or associations, are linked to the telematic web to a lesser or greater extent. At the same time, there are e-matrices in the ethnicity where some groups and individuals may be at a greater distance from and use the telematic web much less, if at all, than those in the city.

I differentiate between Global Culture and global culture. "Global Culture" (capital G and C) is viewed by me as the sum of "global culture" (lowercase g and c) and "local cultures."

$$GC = (cg + lc_1 + lc_2 + lc_3 + lc_4 + lc_5 + lc_n)$$

The material, economic, and political-cultural aspects of the p-matrix (p), arising from the international system and world market, are what I would call "global culture" (gc). As Mowlana (1994) points out, globalization includes "forces of production/delivery, and consumption of goods and services," which are largely Western, but which do not necessarily obliterate existing "values, attitudes, and morals," in non-Western societies (p. 18). Local values, attitudes, and beliefs are to be found within local cultures, or e-matrices (e).

$$GC = (p + e_1 + e_2 + e_3 + e_4 + e_5 + e_n)$$

Global and local societies are shaped not by one or the other of these matrices, but by the state of flux of their complex relationship. There are corridors between the p-matrix and e-matrices, between city and ethnicities, which allow for the conversion of one kind of power to the other.

$$p \times e_1 + e_2 + e_3 + e_4 + e_5 + e_n$$

The matrix framework may be applied to world politics as well as in a national context.

Things found in the political economic realm can be owned by us, individually and through institutions, to a greater or lesser extent. On the other hand, cultural things can own us, in the sense that we belong to a language group, an ethnohistorical group, an organization, a race, a culture. When we are owned by a cultural thing, we feel we own it, too. To be owned by an e-matrix is to share a perceptual world with other members; these are property rites.

As Singer (1987) argues, sharing a perceptual world quickly becomes belonging to an identity group, where there is a consciousness of like-mindedness. An identity group is a tinder box that can easily become inflamed as an action group, one that seeks to translate cultural power to political economic power. Elites controlling a-matrices will often seek to hasten the process through which political economic leadership leads to cultural hegemony, thus perpetuating a cost-effective political economic power—one that incurs relatively low transaction costs.

Social change and stability are functions of the state of flux of the complex relationship between the political economic (p-matrix) and ethnohistorical (e-matrices), as mediated by a-matrices. For lengths of time, powerful messages and rules emanating from the p-matrix and a-matrices, driven by dominant a-matrices, shape and control the vitality of nondominant a-matrices and e-matrices. But every so often—as seen in the Christian, British, and American e-matrices, transformation of the pagan Roman—Holy Roman and British p-matrices, respectively, which controlled them—empires seem to strike back (Chitty, 1996). Another example is of the Buddhist capture of Hindu India in the time of Emperor Ashoka. Using the computer desktop again as an example, subfolders nested inside many folders could become the folders in which others are nested.

CATEGORIES OF MEDIATED REALITY

I formed my media view of the world through the Singaporean and Sydney media, particularly the principal newspapers of these cities, during my presence in each of them. I looked at copies of *The Strait Times* and the Saturday issue of *The Sydney Morning Herald* regularly, keeping track of news items, columns, and editorial commentary that were related to *economic* and *cultural races* (competitive movements toward security) in Singapore and Australia.

Both of these cities belong to young post-colonial societies, sharing at least one e-matrix, that of former British colonies. Belonging to this e-matrix makes them and many of their people corridors between Europe and Asia. Their a-matrices are embedded in some r-matrices and, along with those of everyone else, in a common p-matrix. At the same time, their a-matrices seek to mediate between individual e-matrices.

Tolerance in an a-matrix of the existence of many e-matrices within can lead to questions of identity, particularly when the tolerance is a result of a relatively large or dominant ethnic majority opting for a pluralist route to success in the economic race. Both Singapore and Australia, industrialized nations with polyglot populations led by Chinese and Anglo-Celtic majorities, respectively, are concerned with the issue of *national identity* as well as *economic ranking*. As do other societies, Singapore and Australia seek to maximize their economic rankings in the world, while retaining their identities. Singapore and Australia have both adopted multiculturalism, which is essentially an abandonment of cultural race.

Newspapers, as channels of political communication, are viewed in this study from a symbolic interactionist perspective as offering avenues for cyborganisms and cyborganizations to shape their identity. Groups do this by speaking to themselves and to the outside world (Mead, 1934). Changes in the p-matrix will result in varying reactions in e-matrices.

The p-matrix makes similar demands of Singapore and Australia. There are demands on both countries to train and educate their labor forces to be more productive, to open their markets to the world and compete in others' markets. It is the safety of the ethnohistorical group (or safety of race), which is the dominant concern within e-matrices. Within international space, the concern is for safety of the community of states in a culture of wealth maximization for individual states and groups of states.

In the case of both economic and cultural races toward security, power is important. Realism argues that there can be no safety or security without power to prevent intervention by others. In the final analysis, denizens of an e-matrix do not wish to feel disadvantaged within the larger p- or a-matrix. P- and a-matrices are shaped by influential e- and a-matrices, respectively, and those with similar ethnohistorical and administrative vocabularies to the dominant groups will be at an advantage.

The market-oriented, democratic, multicultural a-matrix is one in which a historically dominant ethnohistorical group accepts the separate identities of constituent e-matrices and accepts diversity in order to ensure unity for the purpose of succeeding in the global economic race. The dominant e-matrix feels sufficiently secure culturally to encourage equal participation by other e-matrices in the a-matrix and indeed offer others cultural security in order that the a-matrix will be secure in relation to the p-matrix.

There is a perceived connection between social order and attraction of investment in relation to the economic race. There is also a nexus between the pecking order of e-matrices and group perceptions of cultural security. The higher up in the pecking order, the greater the cultural security.

Internationally, the p-matrix has been shaped, through European colonialism and the influence of American power, by an Euro-American e-matrix. However, with other inputs into the p-matrix, including the international vocabularies of nonalignment, environmentalism, feminism, and the material output of factories in regions such as East Asia, the p-matrix has been transformed. We are constantly reading news reports and hearing scholars speak about the rise of China as an economic superpower, of the next century being the "Asian century." There is the perception that the p-matrix will be transformed in such a way that European societies will no longer feel secure. The United States is preoccupied with making the world safe for America, for a time when it will no longer be World Policeman.

On my way back to Sydney at the end of February 1997, I had formed the view that the return of Hong Kong to China, and what it signified, was casting a brilliance as well as a "shadow of the future" over the region. In May 1997, a Krygsman cartoon, depicting the skyline of Hong Kong casting a shadow over Australia, illustrated an article by Greg Sheridan entitled "Shadows of Regional Identity" (p. 15). This was in the same week that Professor Stephen FitzGerald launched his book *Is Australia an Asian Country?* Interestingly, and perhaps unintentionally, the cartoon could have been seen to depict a lighter (democratic) Australian skyline being thrown across the darker (nondemocratic) South China Sea.

Whether what was seen was light or shadow depended very much on whether one was comfortable about declining European influence in the p-matrix or not. It is an ascendant Chinese star, propelled by expatriate Chinese and East Asian capital and the energy of the Chinese people that is responsible for the political chiaroscuro. The change of guard in Hong Kong is reflected in the media as a transition from one Lasswellian (1963) symbolic plateau to another, with all the attendant insecurities.

Feelings of security in European e-matrices within an Australian multicultural a-matrix must surely be challenged if there is a perception of the possibility of the p-matrix being dominated in the future by the Chinese and Japanese in particular and East Asians in general. By the same token, feelings of security in Chinese e-matrices throughout the world, including in Singapore, are increasing. Sheridan (1997) writes that he has friends in Australia who have told him "of those who are one-eighth Chinese now being proud of that Chinese heritage. It has to do with the rise of East Asia" (p. 15).

Additionally, those within any e-matrix who have been disadvantaged by the economic restructuring required by the p-matrix will feel insecure. The combination in Australia of groups within the Anglo-Celtic e-matrix, who have felt disadvantaged by the process of restructuring within Australia and fearful of the geopolitical changes taking place around Australia, does not make for tolerance of multiculturalism and immigration.

This differential preoccupation with security is reflected in the articles in the Australian (Anglo-Celtic) and Singaporean (Chinese-led multicultural) newspapers.

We might say that the two "races" have their own ethnohistorical and political economic goals. Table 2.1 outlines the e and p goals of cultural and economic races.

The notion of "security" or "safety" is important for both cultural and economic races. In the cultural race, it is important to ensure the safety of the culture and cultural group. Perceived threats from national or international quarters to the culture are ways in which those who profess ownership of a culture define its borders. There is the notion that all that is "within" the culture is safe and part of the nation. That which is unsafe is foreign, or a contamination, to the culture.

At the same time, it can be argued that the economic race requires the projection of an image of safety and stability to attract investment and investors. This is an argument that needs some comment. The United States at all times and the Philippines under Marcos attracted and continues to attract investment, despite the former's hypermediation of very real social violence and the latter's dependence on the military for legitimacy. Safety of investment is linked more with political stability than social safety.

Chinese-dominated societies do place a high value on social order, and particularly in Singapore, maintaining a safe, "low crime" environment is viewed as a necessary condition for the attraction of investment. In recent times, Governor Patten of Hong Kong has argued that the "Rule of Law" will be a necessary condition if Singapore is to continue to attract investors after it returns to Chinese rule.

We may take the policy-driven devices of Rule of Law and Political and Economic Freedom, as well as Crime as a resultant, and attempt to plot each of these as high, medium, or low, based on what may be regarded as my perception of an "Australian" public opinion, unquestionably a subjective exercise. However, it reveals that the connection between safety and economic race is not easy to pin down.

TABLE 2.1.
Goals of Cultural and Economic Race

Type of race	Ethnohistorical goal	Political-economic goal
Cultural race	Cultural security of ethnohistorical group.	> Translation of cultural power to political power for ethnohistorical group.
Economic race	Cultural domination for the purpose of ensuring economic and cultural security at low cost.	< Economic advancement of group through economic and political means.

TABLE 2.2.
Factors Contributing to Safety in Four Countries

	Australia	China	Singapore	U.S.
Rule of law	High	Medium	High	High
Openness to political opposition	High	Low	Medium	High
Economic freedom	High	Medium	High	High
Crime	Medium	Low	Low	High

RESEARCH

This chapter examines mediated reality in Sydney and Singapore at an important corridor of time in the contemporary political history of Australia and Singapore, centering the discussion on particular political economic and cultural issues. The corridor of time connects the maiden speech of Pauline Hanson in the Australian parliament and the Hanson retractions of May 30, 1997. I visited Singapore twice and its mediated reality was examined in January 1997. I returned from Singapore to Sydney at the end of February 1997, after spending two weeks in January and three days in February in that city, with a fortnight's interlude in Sydney.

In Singapore, January was a month in which the newly reelected government set its new agenda. This moment brought into focus important features of Singaporean values. Political economic issues will include the issues of changing power relationships in the Asia-Pacific region, education, and trade.

The visit of the U.S. president to Australia at the end of 1996 and the visit of the Japanese prime minister in May 1997, as well as visits by Prime Minister Howard to Singapore and China are important in relation to the Australian self-image. How significant others see us and how we describe ourselves is important. By telling the world who we are, we are also telling *ourselves* who we are (Mead, 1934). National image has become something of a preoccupation in the Australian media after Pauline Hanson made comments about Aboriginals, Asians, and migration, because of Australia's historical image in Asia as a racist society, as a result of the White Australia policy. The matter was of interest in Singapore as well as elsewhere in Asia.

If Ted Turner had wished to choreograph a mega media event for 1997, he could have done no better than the invisible hand of happenstance. The ascendancy of the Liberal Party in Australia, espousing free speech and questioning political correctness, in March 1996, was accompanied by the perhaps hypermediated candor of the independent member of Parliament representing Oxley, Pauline Hanson. When Chinese migrants first came to Australia to work in the gold mines, the Chinese dragon mother had been wounded and weakened by St. George. In July 1997, a greatly diminished St. George was to leave Hong Kong, somewhat unwillingly, to a fully recovered and growing Chinese dragon.

Selected issues and events were analyzed, as mediated by over 100 news reports in the months between October 1996 and May 1997. The headline analysis focuses largely on the Saturday editions of *The Sydney Morning Herald*. However, on occasion, articles from other days and newspapers, namely *The Australian* and *The Daily Telegraph*, were included in the study. Additionally, *The Strait Times* of the weeks in January 1997 when I was in Singapore, were included. The issues selected are related to the economic and cultural races, through the metaconcerns with geopolitical, economic, cultural, and individual security, as reflected in issue areas such as human rights, crime, racism, immigration, image abroad, education, investment, and international alliances.

Headlines are classified under the following categories:

Geopolitical security

Issues: Hong Kong, Taiwan, China

Security in the economic race

Issues: Class, education, immigration, the Australian image abroad, investment, tourism

Security in the cultural race

the Australian self-image, Pauline Hanson, immigration, racism

Individual security

Crime, free speech

There were 71 articles dealing with geopolitical security concerning China among the articles selected from *The Sydney Morning Herald (SMH)*, in mostly Saturday issues. In this period, 32 percent of these articles were in November 1996. The November headlines about China are about Chinese actions in the prelude to the return of Hong Kong, Governor Patten's admonitions, Australia's misreading of China, human rights diplomacy, and China's manifest destiny as an economic superpower. By December 1996, the Howard government is reported to have been showing greater sensitivity to China's sensibilities in the areas of internal politics and human rights. In March 1997, Prime Minister Howard's visit to Beijing is depicted as "Howard sits for his diplomatic test" (p. 13). Also, "Howard denies China visit is fence-mending" (p. 4), confirming thereby that it was. In April, there is recognition: "[W]hen it comes to pressure, Beijing has the (trade) numbers (p. 23). Apparently having passed his diplomatic test, we are told: "Howard is beginning to understand the atlas" (p. 43). By May, there is some voicing again of Australia's sense of displacement: "Home alone: Why Australia is not yet welcome in Asia—and may never be" (p. 1).

The headlines in *The Straits Times (TST)* on matters of geopolitics in relation to China did not reflect the kind of angst evident in *The Sydney Morning Herald*. In January 1997, we read that "China's rise will contribute to world peace, not pose threat to neighbours" (p. 36). In relation to geopolitics, there is also an interest in the *TST* in highlighting weaknesses in the United States. Reporting on President

Clinton's lackluster state-of-the-union message, *The Straits Times* asks "[W]hy does the U.S.'s brilliant run seem to be over?" (p. 40).

In relation to security in the economic race (Australia's image abroad), in October 1996, we note that parliamentary "[l]eaders unite for tolerance: Asian backlash prompts vote against racism (*The Australian*, p. 1). In November, we are informed: "Howard hit by wave of Asian indignation" (*SMH*, p. 8). There is a preoccupation with "[W]hat our neighbours really think of us: Through Asian eyes" (*SMH*, p. 1). We are also told: "Mahathir stings Howard over race" (*SMH*, p. 24) and that "Malaysia warns: racism 'big issue' (*The Australian*, p. 3). It is revealed that "[T]he Hanson factor is repelling Asian business immigrants" (*SMH*, p. 1). We are concerned about our image as Australians and ask the question: "[S]ophisticated Australians? It's just an old wives tale" (*SMH*, p. 4). We are pleased with the comment of that most significant other when the visiting U.S. president "Clinton says thanks to a 'remarkable nation'" (*SMH*, p. 7). Clinton congratulates Australia's multiculturalism.

Other areas that are treated under security in the economic race are education, Aboriginal land claims, immigration, and class. Very little was found on Aboriginal land claims, immigration and class in the newspapers reviewed. This is partly because some of these issues are subsumed by the Hanson reportage. April and May 1997 see a larger number of reports on the Aboriginal land issue. Recognizing some of the class origins of the Hanson ideology, we are reminded: "[I]t's time to look at the uptrodden" (*SMH*, p. 2) and "[S]ocial class, not race, is at the heart of the Hanson debate (*SMH*, p. 15).

Reports about Australian education are about fees going up and resources being withdrawn. We learn that the "[C]lever country slips in rankings" (*SMH*, 1997, p. 15) and that "Asian educators are in a class of their own" (*SMH*, 1997, p. 39). At the same time, our "[S]howpiece schools may face the axe" (*SMH*, 1997, p. 1). We are told that "[H]alf of our science and math teachers would quit if they could" (*SMH*, 1996, p. 10) and "[O]ur students are lagging behind those in Asia" (*SMH*, 1996, p. 10). The result of policies that are meant to secure the Australian economy in the longer term is increased insecurity for students, parents, and teaching staff. On the other hand, in Singapore in the aftermath of the January election, the cabinet places investment in education at the top of *The Strait Times* agenda, envisaging "S'pore as the Boston of the East" (*SMH*, 1997, p. 2).

Security in the cultural race, as presented in the Australian newspapers, focuses very much on Pauline Hanson. As a result of her pronouncements and the Aboriginal land claims, there is some concern about "Australia's racist past" (*SMH*, 1996, p. 42). In an article entitled "Let's look on the bright side, says PM: How little Johnny learnt about race" (*SMH*, 1996, p. 6), there is an account of Prime Minister Howard's schooling in Australianness. The "PM's view of history" (*SMH*, 1996, p. 44) gets an airing. As a consequence of Howard's expressed aversion to bleeding-heart political correctness, we see stories with headlines such as: "[O]ur history rewritten with a politically correct bent" (*SMH*, 1996, p. 13). We learn that "[O]ne in four teachers worries about Asians" (*The Australian*, 1996, p. 3) and that "Hanson activates a cottage industry" (*The Australian*, 1996, p. 8). By December 1996, we learn: "[H]ow Hanson lost her minder" (*The Australian*, p. 33) a disengagement that was inevitable if the MP was to broaden her support.

By January 1997, Australian diplomats are active in deploring Hanson's statements to the regional press. "Asia is our bread ticket: Aussie DPM: Race remarks misunderstood, we want to boost exports, says Fischer" (*TST*, p. 6). Singaporeans are also told that according to "Downer: Few Australians share Hanson's racist views" (*TST*, p. 4). In April, there are reports of increased racism that are linked to Hanson: "Hanson forms party as racism complaints soar" (*SMH*, p. 10). Without much ado, "Howard nails Hanson's lies" (*SMH*, p. 44). But "Hanson rolls on as PM's support falls" (*The Australian*, pp. 1, 2). Opposition leader Beasley makes a "[p]lea for a honey-coloured society" (Stephen, 1997, p. 6). After Australia anti-Hansonites come out in protest against her views and party, we hear that "Hobart protesters silence Hanson" (*SMH*, p. 1).

In terms of security and the individual (free speech), there were a few articles in Australia on "[T]hreats to free speech" (*SMH*, 1996, p. 18): One named an Australian metropolis as "Defamation city" (*The Australian*, 1996, pp. 1, 6). In Singapore, the Tang case was well reported in January and February. On the one hand, Brigadier General Lee said that "Tang was sued to get to the bottom of the matter" (*TST*, 1997, p. 42); and on the other, Tang wanted the Singapore government to "[S]top politicians suing on slightest ground" (*TST*, 1997, p. 42).

In relation to security of the individual (crime), there is a tendency in Singapore to present the island state as a safe place, but as a public campaign warns, "Low crime doesn't mean no crime." In Australia, reporting suggests that crime is on the increase and that "[J]ail's value questioned as crime rate soars" (*SMH*, 1997, p. 9). However, you are also told that in Australia you are "[S]afer than you think" (*SMH*, 1997, p. 37). Singapore reports on the honesty of its own people, such as: "[M]other turns in son who stole from maid (*TST*, 1997, p. 3).

DISCUSSION

At the level of response to geopolitical changes, we might say that the headlines suggest that Singapore is not unhappy about the portended rise of China and decline of the U.S. in the p-matrix, where Singapore has been so successful in the past 25 years. Australia does not appear to be enthusiastic about, or even on occasion recognize, the rise of China and decline of the U.S. There are individual voices that call for sensitivity to China's expectations for reasons of national interest in relation to success in the p-matrix.

Howard himself, like Hanson, seems to have used the rhetoric of a cultural realist in opposition. Both Hanson and Howard begin by sharing a "cultural realism," a gut feeling that a European-Australian majority was not keen on being swallowed by a Chinese migrant dragon, one which had been whelped in Australia. Despite Howard's economic rationalism, in opposition he was within earshot of the voices of an older Anglo-Celtic e-matrix. This cultural realism is fed by a particular e-matrix that will not accept geographical realism. The question of whether Australia is within or without Asia is one of imagined lifespace. After Howard assumed the central position in the Australian a-matrix, it became necessary for him to mediate between e-matrices and also to look after Australia's "national interest" in relation to the p-matrix. The sensationalist reporting of Hanson comments and the consequent economic threats from Asia led to Howard coming to the view that Hanson's pronouncements were not in the national interest. He migrated from a public position that gave considerable weight to cultural realism, to one of p-matrix-driven political-economic realism. Interestingly, he is so p-matrix driven, particularly in relation to China, that he has eschewed the larger, Anglo-Celtic, liberal e-matrix, particularly the U.S. and the U.K., in developing his own pragmatic foreign policy toward China.

Interestingly, while both Singapore and Howard's Australia are driven by economic rationalists, the two countries place different emphases on education. Singapore prioritizes education as a primary area for government investment, seeking to expand both quantitatively and qualitatively. Australia is pruning the tree of knowledge.

Hansonite cultural realism is based on the power of local culture, the magic of the e-matrices. Hanson seeks to appeal to Anglo-Celtic culture in "Country Australia." Her personal strategy as a political entrepreneur is to trade parliamentary and media voice for the votes of as many interest groups as she can gather into a loose coalition of forces.

In doing so, she already has demonstrated that close to 10 percent of Australians are not deterred from supporting her and her views of a more monocultural Australia. Six months after her maiden speech in parliament, Hanson's message seems to have attracted 9 percent of the primary vote to her One Nation party, according to Newspoll figures (*The Australian*, 1997, p. 2). (The figure is for May 9–11, up by 2 percent on May 2–4, by 5 percent on April 18–20, and by 8 percent on April 4–6.)

The figure has stopped climbing. The pro-Hanson corps, as it spilled out of the closet (where it was an imagined Middle Australia) into the opinion polls, proved to be slighter than it had made itself out to be. There are contending speculations about Middle Australia. A more liberal Middle Australia has made the "spiral of silence"— which refers to the increasing pressure of mediated public opinion on individuals to hide their nonmainstream views—work on its behalf. Public opinion consists of opinions that individuals may express about controversial issues without feeling isolated from their communities (Noelle-Neumann, 1991). Policy retreats in 1997 by Hanson suggest that she is making a claim to a wider Middle Australia by pruning her policies of antiracial content. Hanson seems to be responding to her new position within the Australian a-matrix and her consequent familiarization with p-matrix issues.

We might presume that 50 years ago, because of the largely monocultural nature of the society, closer to 100 percent of Australians would have subscribed to Hanson-type views, if they were published at that time. However, based on figures in 1967, we know that only 10.2 percent of those voting in a referendum refrained from endorsing the constitutional recognition of Aboriginal political rights (Ramsey, 1997). One could read into this result a basic liberal democratic instinct in the modern Australian. The 10.2 percent who refrained from endorsing the liberal policy would certainly identify with the Hanson ideology today.

Now that the Hanson closet has been emptied, we see the relative strengths of two Anglo-Celtic e-matrices in Australia. What we saw in 1997 was a death struggle for ownership of the term "mainstream" and Middle Australia. The fact that Howard shares some views with Hanson increased her supporters' belief in their ownership of Middle Australia. But the urban mainstream appears to have absorbed multicultural values to a greater or lesser extent.

Hanson, along with other cultural realists, took the view that if migrants were to choose Australia as their home, they should adopt the culture of Australia, arguing that she would do the same if she went to another country. The opposing argument was stated, in geographic and political economic terms, best perhaps by Stephen FitzGerald (1997). Australia can either choose to become a member of East Asia or to be excluded from "an embryonic Asian confederation with China calling the shots" and Australia becoming something of an impoverished colony (Stephen, 1997, p. 6).

Harold Crouch, in a book review of Stephen FitzGerald's *Is Australia an Asian nation?* (1997), quotes Malaysian prime minister Mahathir as saying that if Australia wants to become Asian it should not rely purely on geography, but also exhibit Asian culture and mentality. The review is illustrated with a cartoon by Mucci depicting a kangaroo dressed in a tiger-striped dinner jacket, wearing sunglasses and holding his chopsticks like a fork and spoon, dining with four plain suited tigers, who look at the kangaroo with a measure of disapproval.

Understandably there have been no arguments made within Australia in similar cultural-realist terms that Australia is in the Asian cultural region and should adjust to those ways. The external influence is presented as political-economic rather than cultural, perhaps because of a historical fear of cultural influence from Asia among some non-Asian Australians. Pauline Hanson's mother told an Australian television audience in 1996 that her generation had always been warned about the yellow races, and now that the yellow races were ahead, it was necessary to do something.

Within Australia, there has been a long history of China. The Dragon's breath inflames the ordinary, unlettered Australian's neck when he is unemployed or underemployed and feels that the Australian economy is not performing in a way that improves his life. In an ironic revolution of the wheel of fortune, whereas Chinese migrated to Australia during the Gold Rush to escape from domestic poverty, the gold rush of the 1990s was one in which investors, producers, and distributors sought Asian investments, partners, and markets. Globalized investment, production, and marketing practices have led to unprecedented economic success in many hitherto slumbering societies, including every nation state that is dominated by Chinese people, giving rise to a revival of interest in new versions of notions like that of Weber's Protestant ethic (Bellah, 1975).

The Hanson phenomenon is fueled by the changing economic relationships among Chinese and other Australians and among China and "Western" states. In turn, the Hanson phenomenon is a political cultural fuel that is ignited by the rays of the ascendant Chinese sun. There are geopolitical and international-political economic changes as well as local cultural and political economic changes that influence the Hanson phenomenon.

It even appeared to me that Paramount Leader Deng passed away almost on cue, to provide a curtain-raiser for the designated mega media event of 1997, the return of Hong Kong—as well as to win the attention of the global Chinese diaspora at this time of renaissance of Chinese civilization. The islands, the sovereignty over which is disputed by China and Japan and that have become theaters for the enactment of Chinese nationalist dramas by Taiwanese and Hong Kong activists, also play a role here.

We might speak of two other cities, China's Hong Kong and Hanson's Ipswich, as metaphors for the hopes and fears of elements of the Anglo and Chinese communities in Australia. Hong Kong and Ipswich are symbols with multiple meanings. Hong Kong may be viewed as an urban testament to the industry and fair-mindedness of the British, one that will fall into disrepair under China. Alternatively, it may be viewed as a testament to the industry of Chinese people under British rule, one that will flourish under the Chinese. Several other possibilities might be located between these two views. Similarly, Ipswich may be viewed as the city that responds to heavy concentrations of migrants by supporting Pauline Hanson's ideology. Alternatively, it may be viewed as a multicultural city that has expressed its support for multiculturalism through community events led by the mayor.

Hanson herself has been transfigured as a 'woman for all reasons.' For some, her face is the tribal taboo sign placed at the border so that members of other tribes would think twice before crossing. To others, it is a mask behind which lurks colonial thinking, a mask that can be used to rally the peoples of East Asia around an Asian identity, in the wake of the *Brittania* carrying the last governor of Hong Kong back to the green and sceptred isle. She reminds Asians of Australia's displacement in Asia and some older Anglo-Celtic Australians that their center seems not to have held. Her flag-wrapped figure evokes national pride in those who see her as a plucky, working-class mother who is willing to do battle with all those dragons from the murky p-matrix.

The matrix model—because it includes the global in the form of p-matrix and varying degrees of local from regional, or r-matrix, through administrative to ethnohistorical and final individual matrices—is suited for comparative analysis of news media reporting on the same events/period in more than one country. Additionally, it may be employed for analysis of news within one country, anchoring content analysis in a holistic, political-economic view of the world.

REFERENCES

Anderson, B. (1990). *Imagined communities*. London: Verso.

Asia is our bread ticket: Aussie DPM: Remarks misunderstood, we want to boost exports, says Fischer. (1997, January 22). *The Straits Times*, p. 6.

Asian educators are in a class of their own. (1997, February 5). *Sydney Morning Herald*, p. 39.

Australia's racist past. (1996, October 26). *Sydney Morning Herald*, p. 42.

Bellah, R. (1971). Reflections on the Protestant ethic analogy in Asia. In K. Thompson & J. Tunstall (Eds.), *Sociological perspectives: Selected readings* (pp. 431–439). Harmondsworth, England: Penguin Education.

Boey, K. C. (1997, June–July). Hanson factor in cultural gulf with Asia. *The Asian Editor*, 91.

Blumer, H. (1969). *Symbolic interactionism: Perspective and method*. Englewood Cliffs, NJ: Prentice Hall.

China's rise will contribute to world peace, not pose threat to neighbours. (1997, January 21). *The Straits Times*, p. 36.

Chitty, N. (1994). Communicating world order. *The Journal of International Communication, 1*, 100–119.

Chitty, N. (1996). Tempestuous times: Unmasking the twentieth century. *The Journal of International Communication, 3*.

Chitty, N. (1997). *Telecommunication and world order: Terra cyborg*. Paper presented at the Asia-Pacific Media Information Centre Annual Conference.

Clever country slips in rankings. (1997, February 8). *Sydney Morning Herald*, p. 15.

Clinton says thanks to a "remarkable nation." (1996, November 22). *Sydney Morning Herald*, p. 7.

Crouch, H. (1997, May 24). Feasting with tigers. *Sydney Morning Herald*, p. 10.

Davidson, K. (1996–97). Howard's choice [Editorial]. In K. Davidson (Ed). *The Australian Rationalist, 42*, 2–5.

Defamation city. (1996, December 21). *The Australian*, pp. 1, 6.

Downer: Few Australians share Hanson's racist views. (1997, January 31). *The Straits Times*, p. 4.

FitzGerald, S. (1997). *Is Australia an Asian country? Can Australia survive in an East Asian future?* St. Leonards, NSW, Australia: Allen & Unwin.

Half of our science and math teachers would quit if they could. (1996, November 22). *Sydney Morning Herald*, p. 10.

Hanson activates a cottage industry. (1996, November 2). *The Australian*, p. 8.

The Hanson factor is repelling Asian business immigrants. (1996, November 30). *Sydney Morning Herald*, p. 1.

Hanson forms party as racism complaints soar. (1997, April 12). *Sydney Morning Herald,* p. 10.

Hanson rolls on as PM's support falls. (1997, May 13). *The Australian,* pp. 1, 2.

Hobart protesters silence Hanson (1997, May 10). *Sydney Morning Herald,* p. 1.

Home alone: Why Australia is not yet welcome in Asia—and may never be. (1997, May 3). *Sydney Morning Herald,* p. 1.

How Hanson lost her minder. (1996, December 14). *The Australian,* p. 33.

Howard is beginning to understand the atlas. (1997, April 5). *Sydney Morning Herald,* p. 43.

Howard denies China visit is fence-mending. (1997, March 29). *Sydney Morning Herald,* p. 4.

Howard hit by wave of Asian indignation. (1996, November 2). *Sydney Morning Herald,* p. 8.

Howard nails Hanson's lies. (1997, May 10). *Sydney Morning Herald,* p. 44.

Howard sits for his diplomatic test. (1997, March 28). *Sydney Morning Herald,* p. 13.

It's time to look at the uptrodden. (1996, November 2). *Sydney Morning Herald,* p. 2.

Jail's value questioned as crime rate soars. (1997, May 3). *Sydney Morning Herald,* p. 9.

Jakubowicz, A. (1996–97). Fear and loathing in Ipswich. *The Australian Rationalist, 42,* 6–13.

Lasswell, H. (1963). *World politics and personal insecurity.* Glencoe, IL: The Free Press.

Leaders unite for tolerance, Asian backlash prompts vote against racism. (1996, October 31). *The Australian,* p. 1.

Let's look on the bright side, says PM. How little Johnny learnt about race. (1996, October 26). *Sydney Morning Herald,* p. 6.

Mahathir stings Howard over race. (1996, November 30). *Sydney Morning Herald,* p. 24.

Malaysia warns: Racism "big issue." (1996, November 23). *The Australian,* p. 3.

Mead, G. H. (1934). *Mind, self, and society.* Chicago IL: University of Chicago Press.

Mosco, V. (1996). *The political economy of communication.* London: Sage.

Mother turns in son who stole from maid. (1997, January 30). *The Straits Times,* p. 3.

Mowlana, H. (1994). Shapes of the future. *The Journal of International Communication 1,* 14–32.

Noelle-Neumann, E. (1991). The theory of public opinion: The concept of the spiral of silence. In J. A. Anderson (Ed.), *Communication yearbook, 14* (pp. 256–287). Newbury Park, CA: Sage.

One in four teachers worries about Asians. (1996, November 23). *The Australian,* p. 3.

Our history rewritten with a politically correct bent (1996, October 26). *Sydney Morning Herald,* p. 13.

Our students are lagging behind those in Asia. (1996, November 22). *Sydney Morning Herald,* p. 10.

The PM's view of history. (1996, November 23). *Sydney Morning Herald,* p. 44.

Ramsey, A. (1997, May 24). 30 years on, and the fuse burns. *Sydney Morning Herald,* p. 41.

Robertson, R. (1994). Globalization and glocalization. *The Journal of International Communication. 1,* 33–52.

Safer than you think. (1997, March 1). *Sydney Morning Herald,* p. 37.

Sheridan, G. (1997, May 13). Shadows of regional identity. *The Australian,* p. 15.

Showpiece schools may face the axe. (1997, January 11). *Sydney Morning Herald,* p. 1.

Singer, M. (1987). *Intercultural communication: A perceptual approach.* Englewood Cliffs, NJ: Prentice Hall.

Social class, not race, is at the heart of the Hanson debate. (1996, December 9). *Sydney Morning Herald*, p. 15.

Sophisticated Australians? It's just an old wives tale. (1996, November 16). *Sydney Morning Herald*, p. 4.

S'pore as the Boston of the East. (1997, January 29). *Sydney Morning Herald*, p. 2.

Staniland, M. (1983). *What is political economy?* New Haven, CT: Yale University Press.

Stephen, T. (1997, May 10). Plea for a honey-coloured society. *Syndey Morning Herald*, p. 6.

Stop politicians suing on slightest ground. (1997, January 31). *The Straits Times*, p. 42.

Tang was sued to get to the bottom of the matter. (1997, January 31). *The Straits Times*, p. 42.

Threats to free speech. (1996, November 29). *Sydney Morning Herald*, p. 18.

Wallerstein, I. (1990). Culture as the ideological battlefield. *Theory, Culture and Society 7*, 31–56.

What our neighbours really think of us: Through Asian eyes. (1996, November 2). *Sydney Morning Herald*, p. 1.

When it comes to pressure, Beijing has the numbers. (1997, April 12). *Sydney Morning Herald*, p. 23.

Why does the U.S.'s brilliant run seem to be over? (1997, January 29). *The Straits Times*, p. 40.

3

Mediating News: The "International Media Echo" and Symbolic International Relations *

Peter W. Oehlkers
Emerson College

News about international relations symbolically mediates relations between nations. To some extent, it is known that audiences are dependent upon the news for their knowledge and understanding of international affairs. The news, therefore, is a stage on which international relations can be played out dramatically—it is a spectacle (Carey, 1989). There are a number of modes through which international relations may be dramatized. For example, Shapiro (1989) considers the sports and war intertext and these modes influence the kinds of stories that are told, the kind of news that is reported, and the kinds of opinions that are generated. One important

*The author would like to thank the following people: Jim Ettema, Susan Herbst, Peter Miller, and Bob Entman for their suggestions and encouragement; Yuji Ijiri for his reading and translation assistance; Hayashi-sensei and Tokinoya-sensei of Tokai University for the opportunity to learn about Japan first-hand.

31

mode is that of the socioemotional, interpersonal relationship, the story of the nation in its civil and sometimes "intimate" relations with other nations (Oehlkers, 1996).

Scholars who study the role of the news in international politics sometimes remark about the "international media echo" (Frederick, 1993); news reported in foreign newspapers and news broadcasts is commonly monitored by government officials and journalists. This news may then be incorporated into news texts in another nation, used to represent attitudes and perspectives in the reported nation toward the events being reported. This process becomes symbolically potent when such news is about the other nation or reports public attitudes toward the other nation; in the dramatic mode of the socioemotional, interpersonal relationship, such news serves to articulate national points of view. The international media echo, therefore, mediates international relations by allowing the construction of a symbolic dialogue between nations.

Arno (1984), in a useful essay introducing his volume on the news media and conflict, suggests that the media echo is a means of international communication—providing the public of one nation access to the public mood of another nation. It opens a channel between publics, allowing a kind of "interpublic" communication. Whether it's American news agencies capturing and reusing footage of Iranian students protesting into the cameras of Iranian news agencies (as in Arno's example) or poll results from one country reported in another country, it would seem that the media echo allows for a kind of international communication based on exchanges between peoples, not states.

This chapter investigates this process in the context of U.S.–Japan relations: Both nations are "media-saturated" and the news agencies of each nation support ample crews of correspondents. In addition, growth in satellite and cable also enable almost direct access to news images produced in the context of the other nation. The recent past has also provided a set of meaningful examples of the news in U.S.–Japan conflict, from controversies over the purchases of "symbolic international assets," to issues of fair trade, to violence against Japanese citizens visiting the United States (see Krauss, 1996). Within Japanese academic/professional journalistic discourse, the role of the news media as a player in U.S.–Japan relations has been addressed, by and large, under the term "*joho masatsu*," or "news friction," and a number of semi-academic books have been published about the issue (see, for example, Ando, 1991; Asano, Okabe, & Miyamoto, 1988; Suzuki, 1992).

Within the context of U.S.–Japan relations, but hopefully in respect to other international relationships as well, this chapter argues that the international media echo is a means less of displaying publics to each other than a means of "staging" relations between publics. The news media do not offer a transparent communication medium between nations, but one that is textually mediated as well as being technologically mediated. Thus, in order to understand the international media echo, it is important to understand the kinds of intertextual transformations that occur between each stage of the process, and to understand the echo as something produced, rather than simply something that occurs. Furthermore, recent critical discussion indicates that the public represented in the news itself is highly symbolic. This suggests that the representations of publics incorporated into the international media echo are less empirical facts and more resources for domestic and international symbolic politics.

THEORIZING THE INTERNATIONAL MEDIA ECHO

The mass media of a particular nation, at a linguistic level, encode a national perspective in news texts. Indeed, the news media allow for the imagination of community constitutive of the nation (Anderson, 1983/1991). While the subject position encoded in news text (the "we") often excludes certain national minority groups (see Hartley, 1992), it speaks for the nation in general. From the point of view of the reader, of course, this subject position is really a text that can be accepted, negotiated, or rejected. We don't have to accept the "we" represented in news text. In practice, however, it is generally accepted as a symbolic representation of what the nation thinks, sees, and says, especially from the perspective of those outside of the national context. Because a nationally defined point of view is present in such a text, it is fairly easy to recode it in another context as an example of "what they think." This kind of use, of course, does hindrance to the variety of points of view that might be present in the other national context that are not represented in such news accounts. Nevertheless, the symbolic connection between the news/press and the national public, and the existence of a stable, documented set of texts makes such accounts compelling approximations of national attitudes.

Hallin and Mancini (1989), in their account of the staging of the Reagan-Gorbachev summits, provide a neat example of the ways in which media images can be used to symbolize an international relationship. The day after the agreement, journalists from the U.S. and the Soviet Union appearing on American and Soviet television via a joint satellite feed hold up newspapers from their respective press—each has the same headline. Hallin and Mancini describe it as a utopian moment—the sign of communion between two putative enemies, mediated, literally, by the media. The underlying symbolic principle behind this particular representation might lie in shared opinions, or in shared attention to the same thing. Nevertheless, it displays a commonality symbolized by news accounts, not simply by the agreement between Reagan and Gorbachev.

An increasingly common theme among critical scholars of the news media and politics is the "symbolic" nature of the public represented in media accounts (see Glasser & Salmon, 1995). In a media saturated political environment, images of the public influence one's political strategies and news analysis. The public, in the form of public opinion polls or radio talk-show transcripts, is often present, expressing opinion about the events and political actions taking place. Some scholars go so far as to suggest the (actual) public has been removed from the political process altogether, replaced by a kind of textual simulacrum; others point out the powerful effect such representations must have on the public themselves (see Peters, 1995). In either case, the public is not naively present in the news, it is a "product" in some sense, of its own mediation. The news may, therefore, be seen as "ventriloquizing" the public (Reeves, 1994) and these representations influence domestic politics and, of course, the international media echo.

The national voice seems to be most purely represented by the voice of "the people"—embodied most efficiently in "public opinion." It is common within elite circles to disregard the public, even fear its effect on international politics. Nevertheless, given the basis of the legitimacy of the modern nation state in the wishes of the people (Wight, 1972), the national voice, when accessed, is the most legitimate representative of the nation. To represent the people of the nation in the form of either the "man-on-the-street," or the public opinion poll, is to offer a voice emanating from the national subject. The rhetoric of Gallup "America speaks" and *USA TODAY*, in its front-page statistics telling its readers what Americans like, both employ this figure. The public opinion poll, because it is scientifically legitimated (Herbst, 1992), provides a particularly powerful resource for invoking and producing national utterances. In the context of international relations, polls are regularly generated displaying the level of "friendliness," for example, what people in one country feel toward another (see Ladd & Bowman, 1996). Changes in this friendly feeling over time are often used to narrate the story of the socioemotional relationship between the nations; often, polls displaying this "friendliness" factor for each nation in question are juxtaposed, purporting to show the "perspective" of each party in the relationship.

This is important to the extent that the symbolic public thus produced has specific domestic political utility, which needs to be understood within the context of local, not global, politics. In the same way that the rhetoric of political leaders is designed in response to local contingencies and may be misunderstood outside that context, the symbolic public is generated for a host of specific purposes. It is the contextual nature of mediated representations of public opinion that is often not appreciated fully in discussion about the international media echo. It is not simply a matter of taking an utterance in one place, and reporting it in another. There is an impressive amount of interpretation, recontextualization, and transformation that must be done.

An additional fact that is relevant to the ways in which the public and national perspectives are interpreted out of news text is the fact that the international media echo is a form of "metajournalism"—journalism about journalism. There are powerful myths in most modern democracies about the power of the media to affect public opinion, the most common story being the "Yellow Press" and its role in spurring the public to demand war against Spain in 1895, are often taken as fact even by media scholars. Schudson (1995) ably dismisses the historical accuracy of such myths.

If media power is assumed among journalists, citizens, and the elite alike, representations of phenomena like "public outcry" become self-fulfilling prophecies, producing symbolically that which they are claiming to simply represent. Stories of media effects and public response constitute a genre of compelling, dramatic narratives, which function to manage and direct the course of news-mediated politics themselves. It is a well-known tenet of both international relations and in-group/out-group theorizing that a group seems more homogeneous from without than from within; thus, myths about media power are likely to be even more powerful when regarded from outside the national political context.

This does not necessarily mark metajournalism as a sensationalistic factor in international relations; while it might, in some cases, exaggerate the monolithicity of a nation's public–press relations, it also opens the opportunity for real self-criticism—of a more relativized journalism that can see the contingencies of storytelling and the fact that multiple stories can be told legitimately about the same thing. From a symbolic point of view, this may have the effect of loosening the tight categories of national public opinions, displaying their own historically contingent conditions.

In summary, the international media echo is not merely a technological phenomenon that allows for publics to see each other; it is a resource for staging symbolic communication episodes between nations. Such relations are always mediated through multiple interpretive frameworks; journalists appropriate news text from other nations that may have been generated originally for specific symbolic purposes. In the case study to follow, there is an attempt to demonstrate the interpretive processes at work, with an emphasis on the ways in which the metaphor of interpersonal relations is used to guide journalistic discourse about international relations.

CASE STUDY: THE SONY-COLUMBIA DEAL

The following case study, based on an analysis of news reports constituting a controversy over Sony's acquisition of Columbia Pictures in 1989, is a portion of a much larger study on that and other news mediated controversies between the United States and Japan (Oehlkers, 1996). The texts selected for this piece were chosen for the way in which they demonstrated the aspects of the international media echo discussed previously. They are not necessarily representative of the overall character of news coverage in the U.S. and Japan about Sony-Columbia. Furthermore, the analysis is restricted to the print media for the sake of ease in transcription and translation.

It is important to understand the political context in which the Sony-Columbia controversy took place to get a better sense of the kinds of interests at work, and the political dynamics in general. At the same time, it is important to understand the cultural context, indeed, the "textual" context informing the controversy—the kinds of "packages" (Gamson & Modigliani, 1989) that had emerged in the news and other areas of public discourse about U.S.–Japan relations. These texts are presuppositions of American and Japanese discourse comprising the controversy.

On September 25, 1989, Columbia Pictures Entertainment announced that it was in the process of completing a deal that would give Sony ownership of its two film and television studios (Columbia and Tri-Star) as well as its extensive film and television library. The Sony-Columbia deal officially announced by Sony two days later, was, at that time, the largest case of Japanese investment into an American corporation to date.

The year 1989 is commonly seen as a turning point in U.S.–Japan relations. The end of the cold war and the end of the urgent necessity for a U.S.–Japan security relationship provided an opening for officials in the United States and Japan to criticize the state of the relationship. A prominent group of critics in U.S. politics and academe (labeled "The Revisionists" in a 1989 *Business Week* cover story; see Neff, Magnusson, & Holstein, 1989) began to express doubts publicly about the nature of the Japanese economy and political system, and whether or not "fair" trade between the United States and Japan was a possibility or not. If not, fundamental changes would be needed in what was perceived as a *laissez-faire* relationship. In the Japanese context, critics emerged and argued for fundamental adjustments in the relationship. Whatever the underlying interests of the actors involved, the politics employed the symbolic relationship between the U.S. and Japan.

In fact, these publications provide interesting examples of the international media echo itself. Revisionist books and articles were translated, published, and bought in great quantities in Japan. Akio Morita and Shintaro Ishihara's book, *A Japan that Can Say No* (1989), was unofficially translated and distributed among members of the United States government and press. In each case, the reception of the book was evaluated not simply in terms of the arguments voiced, but in terms of public acceptance. *A Japan that Can Say No* was on the best-seller list in Japan, and thus widely judged to have public sympathy. Likewise, in Japan, translations of revisionist texts, pointed, ultimately, at the people they were written to influence. Would Americans be carried along in this wind of opinion?

Several U.S.–Japan controversies symbolize this growth of tension: there had been controversy over the FSX deal earlier in the year; Japan had been named an "unfair trader" by the Bush administration under the Super 301 rule; and representatives from both nations were meeting in a set of talks designed to discuss the "structural impediments" to trade between the U.S. and Japan. A particularly visible issue in the late 1980s, was the issue of Japanese investments in the United States. Because of the engineered decline in the dollar in relation to the yen and the inflated land values in Tokyo, giving companies and banks immense collateral for borrowing, there was an intensification of Japanese investment in American real estate and business.

That Japan was "buying up," even "taking over," the U.S. was a common story told in the United States. This story signaled a number of shifts in the way the

U.S.–Japan relationship was narrated. Previously, the U.S. had dominated Japan both economically and culturally in the postwar world. Japan was now superior to the United States, and perhaps even in a position to dominate its former teacher/parent. When Sony announced it was going to acquire Columbia, the fact that this acquisition fit the story of the Japanese buyout of America was immediately recognized by members of the news media in the U.S. and Japan.

On October 9, 1989, one week after the announcement, *Newsweek* published a cover story on American reaction to the deal (Schwartz & Hammer, 1989). While the bulk of American reporting about the deal to that point had been rather neutral in respect to the deal's political implications, the magazine article offered a clear image of American outcry, one that was immediately "echoed" to the Japanese press, and that continues to be an icon in discussions of the destructive role of the media in U.S.–Japan relations. The *Newsweek* cover depicted an image of the "Columbia lady" logo dressed as a Geisha, next to the headline: "Japan Invades Hollywood."

While the cover image was powerful, and reproduced again and again in Japanese contexts, the *Newsweek* article itself had a strong impact, not for its shock value as much as the fact that it provided a clear, coherent, monolithic image of the American public. *Newsweek* had commissioned a poll to measure American responses to questions about the deal, and U.S.–Japan relations in general. The results of the poll legitimized discussion in *Newsweek* about what Americans were thinking and saying in respect to the deal.

Thus, it is important to explore how this monolithic public voice was produced. In a passage later much-quoted in Japanese accounts, this voice received its clearest articulation:

> The news rippled quickly through TV and radio talk shows across the country: this time the Japanese hadn't just snapped up another building; they had bought a piece of America's soul.... (Schwartz & Hammer, 1989, p. 62)

Through the use of free indirect discourse, *Newsweek* adopts a putative American perspective to narrate the story. This perspective was apparently gathered by the magazine through observations of the news media, and is narrated like a natural phenomenon—the news "ripples" through the media. The "news" (hence the public) cries, "the Japanese have bought a piece of America's soul." This becomes the official interpretation of the deal, and legitimizes the sensationalistic cover image. The acquisition is an invasion:

> The Sony deal marks the biggest advance so far in a Japanese invasion of Holly-wood—an influx of yen-rich investors looking to back movies.... It's also the latest in a steady accumulation of headlines over the past few years that all seem to carry the same subliminal message: America is slowly ceding its economic destiny to Japan.... (Schwartz & Hammer, 1989, p. 62)

As in the previous passage, the American experience of the Japanese takeover is portrayed as mediated through the news, fostering the identity of that perspective and the news itself. Thus, *Newsweek*, when reporting the poll results, speaks for an America that cannot speak clearly for itself:

> Although most Americans probably can't articulate exactly why they feel so threatened by Japan's growing economic power, they clearly do. Despite Sony's assurances about American control, a *Newsweek* poll conducted last week found that 43 percent of people surveyed about the Columbia purchase think it's a bad thing, compared with only 19 percent who approve. More than half now consider Japan's economy might be a bigger threat than the military power of the Soviet Union.... (Schwartz & Hammer, 1989, p. 62)

The public is represented, explicitly, as being "unable to articulate" their opinions—*Newsweek* can thus legitimately intervene and mediate the public's thoughts through its own poll questions. The poll takes a plurality of responses and reduces it to a single dimension—approval or disapproval of the deal. Because poll results are represented in terms of percentages of a whole, public opinion becomes monolithic, linked to the majority response, not the variety of responses. The poll can be made to stand for America as a whole, and America, in this case, is fearful.

A second article in the same issue displays the political dynamics behind this voicing of American opinion. Entitled "Five Ways to Fight Back" (see Powell, Martin, Thomas, & Barry, 1989), it compares "Sony Shock," to "*Sputnik* Shock," arguing that the Sony-Columbia deal also has the potential to mobilize the public and the government to fight back economically in the spirit of competition. By producing a "public" that is up in arms, *Newsweek* has made a first step to mobilization, which now can be channeled into the five specific suggestions. Members of the decision-making elite might be convinced, as might the public itself.

It is important to understand that the *Newsweek* representation of American reaction did not reflect a consensus among American news magazines. There were accounts of Sony-Columbia in the American media that did not display American outcry, which could have formed the basis of Japanese accounts as well, but did not. *U.S. News & World Report* (Egan, 1989) provides a remarkably direct contrast to *Newsweek*.

> If any other Japanese firm had snapped up one of America's leading movie and television studios, the deal would have raised howls of protest. Yet when the Sony Corporation announced last week that it was buying Columbia Pictures Entertainment for nearly $5 billion—the biggest U.S. acquisition to date by any Japanese company—the purchase elicited barely a protectionist peep. (Egan, 1989, p. 35)

To *U.S. News & World Report*, the surprising fact about Sony-Columbia was the lack of public outcry against it (which it attributes to the communication skill of Akio Morita). Nevertheless, either because the magazine has no international edition, or because it is considered a minor force in American public life from a Japanese perspective, this account was not publicized in Japan.

The media echo mainly "echoed" *Newsweek*, generating the following texts: the invasion, the buying of the soul, "The Columbia Geisha," "Sony Shock," "Five Ways to Fight Back," and the poll results themselves pervaded subsequent Japanese press coverage of the American reaction against the deal. Americans were agitated over the deal, and in many cases, were portrayed as unjustly so—as if the overreaction to the deal constituted an offense against the relationship as large as the Sony-Columbia deal itself. While the reaction was not always directly attributed to "Americans"—sometimes it was attributed to a sensationalistic media—the notion that Americans had "rejected" Sony's advance became an important story in Japanese public discourse.

Evidence about this effect can be displayed through a short analysis of individual articles. Note that a portrayal of an America up in arms is a symbol of great use within the Japanese establishment—given the importance of *gaiatsu*, or foreign pressure, in the Japanese political system.

THE RECEPTION OF AMERICAN OUTCRY
IN THE JAPANESE PRESS

Before discussing the actual reception of American outcry in the Japanese press, it is worth considering the complex interpretive processes involved in such reception. *Newsweek* magazine provided the bulk of the textual material that would be used in the Japanese media to construct and enact American reaction. *Newsweek* provided the quantified, authoritative account of American public reaction through its poll data, and also provided several short summarizing phrases: "the Sony shock," "Japan bought a piece of America's soul," "Japan invades Hollywood," and so on, that were used in the Japanese press for efficiently articulating American reaction, as these were the things that the American public "said." The cover image of *Newsweek*—Columbia-turned-geisha—was also reproduced many times in the Japanese press. Indeed, the visual imagery of American media representations of Sony-Columbia/Japan provided the backdrop to a number of stories appearing in the Japanese press.

In the realm of broadcast news, the use (and overuse) of the "sound bite" has drawn the attention of many critics. The sound bite offers a text that seems to speak for itself, especially when it has the actual voice or image of the speaker behind it. It shouldn't be surprising that a text that seems to speak for itself crosses language barriers very poorly. The densely coded nature of sound bites is one of the features that makes them effective. Therefore, it would be strange for sound bites to fail to attract different meanings in a different semiotic system. The image of Columbia-turned-Geisha is, even within the American context, a potent image with a variety of possible meanings involving power, gender, and sexuality. In the Japanese semiotic space, the potential meanings become even more powerful, to the point of constituting a direct insult to Japan. The Japanese journalist and media critic, Hiroshi Ando (1991), in a reference to the *Newsweek* cover image, remarks that it signifies the Japanese pollution of Columbia. He explains that the particular flashy garb the image wears is the kind of costume typically worn by the prostitute class of geishas. The image itself is known in Japan, but not as Columbia, rather as the *"Jiyu no megami,"* or "Goddess of Liberty" (the Japanese name for the widely revered Statue of Liberty). The cover image, therefore, charges that the Japanese ownership of Columbia is equivalent to the transformation of the Goddess of Liberty into a prostitute. While the image may not have actually been read this way by the majority of Japanese, it is a meaning that was readily available. This may account both for the perceived intensity of the American reaction in the Japanese sphere and the reception of that image as an insult to Japan.

It should also be noted that the meaning of *Newsweek* itself is different within Japanese circles than in the American media. Most weekly magazines in Japan have reputations as sensationalistic, irresponsible news organs, or as having "cultural" rather than news orientations. When *Newsweek*'s first Japanese-language edition was published during the 1980s, this heralded a seemingly new era of weekly news reporting, and produced a very popular competitor in Asahi's AERA (Sawada, 1990). Thus, *Newsweek* had a good reputation in Japanese circles (and, given its cost, a high class one as well); this contrasts somewhat with American circles in which it might be argued that *Newsweek* has a mildly sensationalistic reputation. (*Time* magazine does not have a Japanese-language edition, although its international edition is well-distributed throughout Japan.) To have this article and cover image appear in *Newsweek* gave more legitimacy to the story than might be expected from an American point of view.

There were, in fact, three different versions of the same issue of *Newsweek* magazine published. There were two different English-language versions, one for an American audience and one for an international audience. (The Japanese-language version of *Newsweek* appears by license with the Japanese firm TBS-Britannica and is not published by the magazine itself.) Unlike the American audience, the international audience did not witness an invasion on the cover of *Newsweek*, they witnessed Japan "moving into Hollywood." The motivational language in the American edition was changed to factual language in the international edition. In its domestic edition, *Newsweek* employed "we" throughout its account of American reaction against Sony-Columbia, thus joining with the reader, and claiming the same identity as the reader. This "we" was replaced, in international editions, with "Americans." What was a call to arms, from an American perspective, became a news story about angry Americans from the international perspective.

Nevertheless, it was the international edition, the one that was readily available in Japan to be bought at the local English-language bookstore, that was photographed for Japanese news stories on the *Newsweek* issue and enacted as American reaction. The later discovery that the magazine had published two different cover headlines generated a minor controversy. To the newspaper *Yomiuri Shinbun* (Okamoto, 1989), reporting in the wake of Mitsubishi's acquisition of Rockefeller Center, it was clear evidence of sensationalism that *Newsweek* should use more emotional language in its American edition and then soften the rhetoric (as if hiding its sensationalism) for the world in general.

There were two waves of response to the *Newsweek* issue in the Japanese press. The first wave simply reported about particular aspects of the issue, focusing on specific "text bites." The second wave was more interpretive, locating the American reaction portrayed therein within the larger context of U.S.–Japan relations.

On the evening of October 2, *Yomiuri Shinbun* had the headline: "Five Ways to Strike Back Against Japan/American Magazine Makes Suggestions in Connection with 'Sony Shock.'" The report simply describes the text of the *Newsweek* article, enacting it as an utterance within the Japanese context, with a fairly unambiguous negative relational message. Likewise, on October 2, another newspaper, *Asahi Shinbun*, ran a report on the *Newsweek* poll that focused on the poll result that had Americans fearing the Japanese more than the Russians. Then on October 4, it introduced the phrase, "Sony bought a piece of America's soul" into the Japanese political sphere. The headline read "'American soul bought' says American Magazine," and the story reports:

> In its issue published on October 2, the American magazine Newsweek ran a cover story about the Sony takeover of Columbia Pictures, titling it "Japan moves into Hollywood," and [calling] the acquisition, "the same as buying a piece of America's soul...." (Okonogi, 1989, p. 13)

The story is brief and unelaborated, but it serves as an announcement of another anti-Japanese text in the sphere of American discourse, an event in the U.S.–Japan relationship. This time a specific vision of the Sony-Columbia deal is displayed: it is like "buying a piece of America's soul."

The second wave of coverage took more detailed versions of these speech events and elaborated their relational meaning. There were a number of such responses, so it is worthwhile to make a few generalizations about them, instead of examining each one separately. A number of important discursive developments run through these responses. First, the phrase in Japanese, *"Bei no hanpatsu"* ("America's negative reaction/repulsion")[1] became institutionalized in respect to the Sony-Columbia deal. Hanpatsu is typically, in such accounts, contrasted to *"kangei,"* a welcoming, or an invitation. Sony-Columbia signaled a shift in American receptiveness of "Japan money" (a synecdoche for Japan in general) from invitation to rejection. Ando (1991), in his analysis of the coverage, makes this rejection narrative explicit. This rejection of Japan can be understood in socioemotional terms as an American rejection of the collective Japanese self. The goal, then, was to find something to attribute this surprising rejection to, and to determine an appropriate response. The second discursive development was the institutionalization of the phrase *"bunka masatsu"* ("culture friction") to describe the relational situation facing the U.S. and Japan. *Masatsu* is a common word in the Japanese context, and it works to essentialize difference to the extent that it strongly and resignedly predicts problems associated with difference. Finally, as indicated above, the American reaction became standardized as identical to the *Newsweek* account. On the one hand, the text bites (such as "Sony shock" and "Japan bought America's soul") were appropriated to "speak" the American reaction. On the other hand, *Newsweek* itself became an icon; its cover and interior images were institutionalized as the image of anti-Japanese American discourse in photos accompanying many news reports.

A report in the *Yomiuri Shinbun* on October 5 (Nishizawa, 1989) is a good example of the way in which the Japanese press constructed monolithic representations of negative American reaction against Sony-Columbia and, by implication, Japan. It reproduced the *Newsweek* cover (international edition) and proclaimed—with the large horizontal headline: *"Kyorestu! Bei no hanpatsu!"* ("Strong Negative American Reaction!"). The dramatic quality of this way of presenting the story rivals *Newsweek*'s cover itself: this may be a call to arms for Americans, but it is a blow, even an insult, to Japan. The American reaction, furthermore, is portrayed as monolithic, coming from three different sources: the public, the media, and politicians alike.

> An intense response from America to this large-scale, $650 billion buyout was more or less anticipated, but the response from the media and Congress was much worse than imagined.... Also, in reference to the advances of Japanese capital, *Newsweek* ran a report titled, "Five Ways for America to Counter Attack." On the one hand, it called for a tough stance, in regard to policy against Japan. It also said that it was more significant than *"Sputnik* Shock," which occurred after the Soviet Union beat the U.S. in the competition over satellites. This is a sign that from now on, these kinds of criticisms of Japan, which have been run in major newspapers such as *The Wall Street Journal*, are likely to escalate. (Nishizawa, 1989, p. 13).

The *Yomiuri* pulls together all "text bites" offered by the *Newsweek* issue: the cover, the "soul" line, the poll results, as well as the previously mentioned—all elements that worked to form the monolithic representation of American reaction that the *Yomiuri* depicts as the "strong negative reaction."

An editorial in the *Asahi Shinbun* on October 5 provides another account of the relational crisis. Like the *Yomiuri* article, it is an attempt to diagnose the source of the conflict and suggest lessons that can be drawn from it. Unlike the *Yomiuri*, however, the *Asahi* locates its diagnosis and suggestions squarely within the context of symbolic U.S.–Japan communication. The editorial begins its narrative with Sony's action of buying Columbia—an act of communication to the American people. The headline reads: "Sony Misread America's Heart." The fundamental conflict, according to the editorial, lies in a misunderstanding. Sony's imagined romance with America has been met with rejection. The *Asahi* quotes *Newsweek* to represent American reaction: "They bought a piece of America's soul" ("Japan-Is-Different," 1989b, p. 2). The *Asahi* then goes on to elaborate the *Newsweek* assertion, taking it as an accurate depiction of inevitable American feelings:

> Columbia is a major film producer, which has made such hits as "Lawrence of Arabia" and "Close Encounters." The films, which are representative of Hollywood, comprise one industry that has a place of affection for the American people. Many Americans probably feel that Japan "money" may have gone too far, in going to such a place. It is probably natural that this kind of response emerged, since there is a way in which Sony's takeover touched an American nerve. (p. 2)

The editorial then attempts to make its own "reading" of the American heart, to understand why, exactly, Americans are so angry toward and/or fearful of Japan. Implicitly, Japan, in the person of Sony, has been rejected. Now it is up to Japan to understand the reasons for such outcry, and to respond in some fashion.

To contextualize its explanation, the *Asahi* draws upon a well-known story: the fable of the grasshopper and the ant. In terms of overall blame, America is clearly in the wrong. It has become dependent upon Japanese capital to fund its "good times," and is unwilling to protect its own future.

> It is not just that Sony is investing in America. Japanese enterprises, in addition to buying real estate and stocks, also buy between 30 and 40 percent of the national bonds the American government issues. It is America who must take the trouble to stop this investment.
>
> The fabled locust looked askance at the assiduous ants as they worked during the summer, but when winter came the grasshopper cried. America, right now, which continues to spend more than it brings in, and weakening its own currency faces the raids of foreign investors, resembles that grasshopper in places. ("Sony Misread," 1989a, p. 2)

Thus, in the larger scheme of things, the American reaction is not Japan's fault, but the result, rather, of certain sensitivities that Sony did not pay sufficient consideration to. On the other hand, Japanese economists need to put more thinking into why such a strong negative reaction came about.

> A Japan that, as a defeated nation received military and economic aid from America, is now rising over America as an economic power. If they thought the products Japan exported were overflowing, now Japanese concerns are hunting high and low for purchases, from buildings to farmland, from high-tech businesses to banks. Compared to the Soviet Union, where there have been advances in mitigating tensions, the scary one is now, rather, Japan. Such an outcry is linked to a growing fear and discomfort in America. ("Sony Misread," 1989a, p. 2)

This attribution of American outcry to American fear reproduces the *Newsweek* account. It also reproduces the myth of Japanese economic dominance. The outcry is embedded in the narrative of the turnaround—Japan is a threat to America precisely because it has so long been America's subordinate. Thus, America is sensitive to the appearance of being dominated. This sensitivity requires consideration in terms of communication.

> This is why it is important for Japanese businesses to not act in such a way to draw out such feelings. When there is investment, they should want to learn the local customs and understand the people. ("Sony Misread," 1989a, p. 2)

The *Asahi* is advocating "friendly" investments, linked with a real understanding of Americans. The *Asahi* offers a mild criticism of Sony for playing into these American sensitivities; Sony has failed to realize how much of a threat Japan appears to America, and for giving Americans something new to feel hurt about.

> On this point, in the case of Sony, there was a certain lack of consideration, as the fact that the president's press conference to announce the deal was held exclusively for Japanese news services. ("Sony Misread," 1989a, p. 2)

The *Asahi* editorial bases its account around the discourse of communication competence. In a sense, it serves as an act of mediation—an attempt to direct the flow of U.S.–Japan communication into more productive paths.

There were also less "productive" utterances enacted in the Japanese press. While most Japanese accounts attributed the American reaction variously to "sensitivity," "fear," or "perceptions of unfairness," some accounts went further and charged the American reaction with racism. The *Asahi Shinbun* published one such account on October 9, a direct negative reaction to a perceived negative relational message. The unsigned article drew from *Newsweek* for its headline, "Sony Shock," and attributed *Newsweek*'s utterances to its ethnocentrism. "With this article, one also becomes aware that, in America as well as Japan, there exists an economic nationalism that discriminates" ("Sony Shock," 1989b, p. 9). It quickly moved to a more central issue, the perceived fact that Americans were rejecting Japan money, while apparently accepting European money. This was displayed as blatant prejudice, and this required comment. "Of course, it is tangled up in racism. There is no outcry when the advances come from Canada, England, Germany, and France—any of the white European nations" ("Sony Shock," 1989b, p. 9).

At the same time, there is an element of pessimism in such an utterance. American prejudice, it seems, is natural and to be expected. The particularly political and symbolic context of Sony-Columbia (the context the *Asahi* editorial attempted to elucidate) was less important as an explanation of American reaction than a deeply-rooted American racism. This is the pessimistic side of culture friction—the proposition that neither side will ever understand the other.

In contrast, in the *Yomiuri Shinbun*, a column by *Washington Post* columnist Hobart Rowen (1989b) that criticized American outcry against the deal, ran, in translation, on the editorial page. Whereas the column was framed as negative and critical in *Washington Post* (the term "Japanophobia" implied an element of racism in negative coverage of Sony-Columbia; see Rowen, 1989a), it was framed, in the translated version, as a positive relational message. While the overall message of the piece remained intact, reinforcing the sense of overemotional American public outcry, it was contextualized as an act of affiliation: Rowen symbolized support of Japan within the American elite. The headline read: "Sony's Acquisition of Columbia Will Enable America to Improve Its Competitive Position/A Japan, Whose Hostile Intentions are Weak, Will Help Resuscitate [America] as Well." Rowen, speaking for an American position, utters words of welcome to Japan money (back to "kangei" from "hanpatsu"), and is noted as reading Sony-Columbia as rooted in "nonhostile intentions." This has the effect of weakening the image of a monolithic negative American reaction. Rowen, and perhaps other Americans, are critical of American press coverage of Sony-Columbia, and are still Japan's friends.

However, most accounts during this time were oriented toward finding adequate responses to the American outcry. A separate article in the *Asahi Shinbun* on October 9 provides a particularly good example of this orientation. The American reaction to Sony-Columbia was contextualized as part of a larger tendency in the U.S. to regard the Japanese as "aliens." The *Newsweek* cover and inside images were used to present this American perception. The Foreign Ministry, the site of official communicative responses to international tension, was the focus of the article, allowed to describe its plans for counteracting this "alien" perception. It reads:

> The foreign ministry searches for a response to the thinking in American that Japan is different. Alarmed at the development of culture friction, it backs intellectual exchange. The atmosphere of such Japan criticism is caused by ignorance and prejudice in America. ("Japan-Is-Different," 1989b, p. 2)

The image of the *Newsweek* cover, in this context, is an expression of America's "ignorance and prejudice." The Ministry criticizes *Newsweek* specifically:

> [I]n reference to criticism in *Newsweek* magazine of the Sony-Columbia deal—"Japan's economic might is a bigger threat than Soviet military power" and "It was like buying a piece of America's soul." [Foreign Ministry spokesperson, Taizo Watanabe] said: "Even in economic activity, one must pay sufficient consideration to the feelings of people in the other country." But, at the same time, he began to get his nerves on edge with a strong tone of criticism toward the *Newsweek* report—"by being emotional, it made the problem bigger than was necessary" ("Japan-Is-Different," 1989b, p. 2).

Watanabe acknowledges the validity of American reaction, implicitly blaming Sony like the Asahi editorial above for insensitivity. At the same time, *Newsweek* is identified like Morita in the American press as a destructive force in U.S.–Japan relations, inappropriately emotional in its coverage. Watanabe, fulfilling his official function, mediates and proposes action. The action he proposes is essentially "better communication." The solution, according to the Foreign Ministry, is to educate Americans to the "real" Japan, by offering such opportunities as journalistic exchange programs.

AMERICAN RESPONSES TO THE JAPANESE RESPONSE (TO AMERICAN REACTION)

In general, there was relatively little attention in the American press to the Sony-Columbia controversy in the weeks following the deal. What reports did exist, however, are interesting for the way they construct U.S.–Japan communication in respect to the news-mediated Japanese response to the news-mediated American response. This section will examine two such articles, the first of which narrates Japanese response in monolithic, martial terms, and the second of which reports Japanese response in dialogic terms.

On October 8, the *Chicago Tribune* ran an article, written by their Tokyo correspondent, relating the story of Japanese reaction to *Newsweek* (Yates, 1989). The *Tribune* provides a particularly good example of the ways in which existing media text can be reworked. The *Tribune* correspondent draws a monolithic Japanese response, and figures the response with pugilistic metaphors. The story begins:

> Japan's Sony Corp., joined by the government and news media, launched a counter-offensive last week to convince U.S. critics that its [buyout of Columbia] is not the beginning of a Japanese propaganda siege.
> "This is not a Japanese invasion," Sony founder and chairman Akio Morita told a handful of American reporters in a hastily convened press conference in Tokyo...
> Then an indignant Japanese government jumped into the fray, followed by an equally annoyed Japanese media. (Yates, 1989, p. 3)

The three Japanese spheres—government, business, and the media—are represented as working as one. Each is responding to the putative American reaction as represented, especially, by *Newsweek* (and American outcry is due to a Japanese communication threat). Mirroring the supposed irritation of Americans against Sony-Columbia, the Japanese media is also annoyed. The Japanese media are not simply reporters of the official Japanese response—they constitute much of the response itself: "Japan's media, always ready to defend Japanese mercantilism, dismissed...critics of the Sony deal..." (Yates, 1989, p. 3). The *Asahi* editorial is invoked and enacted as a "lecture" directed toward Americans, and a concrete example of American annoyance:

> The *Asahi Shinbun* newspaper even went so far as to lecture Washington with the Aesop's fable of the grasshopper and the ant...

> "We see the grasshopper in the present day United States, a country that spent more than it earned and allowed its deficit to accumulate and is now faced with an onslaught of foreign investors, " the paper said in an editorial. (Yates, 1989, p. 3)

Thus, the *Asahi* editorial was uttered, in the American context, as an insult—ironically, a violation of American sensitivities of a kind the editorial itself counseled Japanese to avoid. This insult, in turn, gave rise to the *Tribune* rebuke.

In direct contrast, a *Christian Science Monitor* report on October 24 adopted a dialogic perspective, reporting Japanese response that was geared to understanding, not criticizing, American response, thus offering positive instead of negative relational meanings. Like the *Tribune* account, the *CSM* constructed its account around the central *Newsweek* image. Its headline read: "Inside the Japanese 'Invasion.'" The invasion is literally in quotation marks, invoked as a meaning of the deal in discourse, but not "for real," unlike the *Tribune*, which casts Morita's denial of the "invasion" as another effort in his putative propaganda campaign. The American response, as in Japanese accounts, is constructed entirely around *Newsweek*'s account.

The *Monitor* reports Japanese criticism of Sony-Columbia, thus breaking open the predefined categories of "American" thought and "Japanese" thought.

> A number of Japanese have publicly, and privately, joined the criticism of Sony's deal. The American reaction is understandable, a Japanese businessman said, comparing it to how the Japanese might feel if an American firm bought Kinkakuji, a treasured Buddhist temple.
>
> Buying into Hollywood "enters into a realm where the colors of the heart overwhelm the calculated blacks and whites of legal contracts," writes Yoshio Matsui, economics editor of the leading daily *Yomiuri Shinbun*. (Sneider, 1989, p. 1)

The *Yomiuri*, just like the *Asahi*, had attributed the American reaction to a lack of sensitivity, on Sony's part, to American feelings.

In summary, the Sony-Columbia episode featured at least three turns of the international media echo. Indeed, later Japanese accounts that referred to later American accounts might constitute a four-turn exchange. The echo, however, was not simply the same message bouncing from one media system to another; news messages were consistently interpreted in relational terms. There was a real sense, in other words, that the appropriation of news text from one country to the other constituted a symbolic communicative exchange.

CONCLUSION

As seen in this case study, the news is not a neutral reporter of international affairs but a participant in the process of international relations. It is drawn into the drama of the international relationship as both a representative of the public and a stimulator of public opinion. In either case, cross-reporting may have the effect of effacing the actual public in favor of the public's representation. To general audiences and political elites alike, the relational dramas thus told may affect interpretations of the state of the relationship and influence what sort of actions need to be taken in regard to the relationship. In the case above, a great deal of discourse in the Japanese press involved the question of what practical and symbolic moves could be made to assuage the putatively outraged American public. In many cases, the answer was more communication or better public relations. The international media echo is a reminder, as well, that in the contemporary period, identifiable national public spheres may be maintained, but that they are always interpenetrated; in-group discourse will find its way outside the group, with unpredictable consequences.

The extent to which the media echo was used in the service of the drama of the socioemotional relationship points to some larger issues in regard to common thought about international communication. This study presented the news media as a channel through which images of international communication are constructed and not as a channel for international communication per se. In other words, the news media provide texts that can be interpreted as messages, and contextualized within symbolic relationships. It was only in rare instances that these texts were actually addressed to the other public, and even in those instances the address to the other was largely rhetorical, designed to symbolize dialogue but not enact it. It was within the paradigm of interpersonal relations that the individual texts could be taken as more or less positive or negative, affiliative or alienating relational messages. From this perspective, international communication is a potent symbol, not an actual process of information transmission between national entities. The imagination of the national speaking subject, for example, is an element in the ideological construction of the "nation" itself. The naturalization of national voices may work to suppress differences in perspectives within nations and reify national boundaries in terms of such perspectives.

As previously noted above, representations of nations in relationships are common in public discourse about international politics. Certain nations are called "long time friends," others are "recent enemies." While judgments about friendship or hostility often derive from security judgments at the governmental level, these terms are commonly used at the public level to symbolically manage relations. It is a common political strategy to legitimize war or international competition by reference to a preexisting enmity that has in fact been carefully cultivated (Shapiro, 1989). The same processes are true in respect to the construction of international friendship.

International relations constructed as interpersonal relations assumes communication between two subjects. While nations do not comprise subjects in the literal sense of the word, they do symbolically through the construction of collective identity. Collective identity, a necessary feature of the processes of nation-building (Bloom, 1990), does more than draw borders between in-groups and out-groups, it constructs a symbolic collective subjectivity, a differentiation between Self and Other. We know, thanks to an immense scholarship on "the Other," that this relationship is often based in ideas about power difference, purity, and morality. The differentiation between national Self and national Other creates a symbolic gap that can be crossed by means of communication.

The image of communicating nations is a common one in literature about international communication following World War II. The new medium of communication was conceived as the key to a new global peace, and the image of national entities communicating was used as a key rhetorical figure in proposals for communication policy. White and Leigh (1946/1972), for example, in a book entitled *Peoples Speaking to Peoples*, advocated the end of propagandistic uses of national media and the commencement of a truly internationalized system.

> The government and the people of the United States should recognize the importance of a mutual understanding of each other's true character and purposes and should be prepared not only to communicate to others a truthful and comprehensive account of our own national life and purposes, but to receive and to circulate in the same spirit reciprocal communications with regard to other nations and peoples.

At the heart of this statement, and other statements from the same approximate period, such as Buchanan and Cantril's (1953) study of international opinion and Boulding's (1959) seminal work on international images, lies a central metaphor— the dialogue. Nations are represented as individuals situated across from each other, able to "see" one another. These nations, endowed with characters and purposes, can send and receive messages to and from their counterpart nations about themselves; these messages can be regarded as more or less sincere, honest, and truthful.

The dialogue might be best described as a symbolic structure that opens up dual subject positions for sending and receiving messages; the subjects are seen as bounded, unified subjectivities separated by a gap that can be closed by means of communication. The dialogic metaphor is powerful to the extent that it is generally unexamined, unquestioned, taken as the natural state of things, rather than a convention through which the world operates. Recent work by Der Derian and Shapiro (1989) seeks to apply the insights of post-structuralism to discourse about international relations. Their work suggests that a critical examination of the representation of international communication as dialogue may be in order. Taking White and Leigh's (1972) statement above as a text, for example, one can identify several elements that a critical account would problematize—in particular, its reliance on the figure of unified subjectivities, the figure of communication between these subjectivities, and the notion of "authenticity" in general. These elements are problematic not because of their divergence from an empirical reality, but because of their role in producing natural-seeming representations of political reality itself.

In Shapiro's (1988) discussion of "Guatemala" within American foreign policy discourse, he suggests that images of speaking nations have long populated the "international system," and that such thinking naturalizes the units in question.

> Guatemala is part of what we think of as the international system, a historically produced set of relations among nations. The predominant grammar of this international system has all of the individual nations performing as subjects and objects in the practice of international speech, a set of statements, regarded as intelligible, which

issues from national units. But these units, which are consolidated both in the recognized system of territorialized boundaries and in speech practices, embody histories of struggles over how those unities are to be represented and understood. The ordinary grammar employed in contemporary discourses, whether of national leaders, journalists, or social scientists, constitutes a forgetting of those struggles, which, if they had ended in other ways, might have engendered other grammars and categories. The use of the dominant, intelligible grammar and category-set of international speech thus helps to reinforce a consolidated understanding of these national units, an understanding that accepts both the importance of existing national boundaries and the dominance of whatever person or group (regime, class, ethnic group, and so on) manages to control domestic relations and attract recognition from the international community. (p. 92)

References to a national subject, for Shapiro, amount to complicity in the repression of minority subject positions within that inscribed national space. Indeed, the act of voicing the "name" of the nation itself makes one complicit in the perpetuation of unjust power relations.

For example, to speak about communication between Japan and the United States, one must first assume the presence of the communicating actors, Japan and the United States. This may seem to be a trivially obvious point. From the perspective of Shapiro (1988), however, it is precisely the a priori given-ness of these actors that is put in question. To talk about "mutual understanding" between the U.S. and Japan is problematic not because it means, as some commentators have asserted, that one of the nations succumbs to the understanding of the other; it is problematic because it essentializes a form of understanding as an aspect of nationness to begin with.

The naturalization of nationness, and the corresponding naturalization of the international dialogue, can serve useful, practical political functions. Just as national identity has been an important force in anti-imperialist movements (Eagleton, 1990), the international dialogue, institutionalized in efforts to maintain the rights of nations to have a voice in the international arena (McBride, 1980), is important for the assertion of these identities as important sources of resistance. The international dialogue may be used as a resource of relativization, as a way to contest particular understandings of the world, by setting them against understandings putatively held by other people. To refer to the Japanese as expressing disdain for American society provides a position from which a critical vision of American society can be presented. At the same time, this must be understood as the product of textual and symbolic procedures, not as an essential international reality. The same image, unfortunately, is used as a reason for resenting the imaginary collective, "the Japanese."

In conclusion, the international media echo is caught up in a larger system of seeing and talking about nations as if they were essential unities; as such it is a useful resource for the staging of international relations, but it also contributes to the maintenance of this way of speaking. Therefore, in speaking about the international echo, it is important to be aware that the collectivities both represented and doing the representing are surely political and legal, but also symbolic entities.

If "true" interpublic relations are impossible, always needing some form of textual or symbolic mediation whether through news text or public opinion polls, this does not necessarily mean that the whole idea should be rejected, just understood as such. The next step is to discover more or less productive ways of utilizing the media echo. This chapter has hinted at a beginning to such a process, contrasting "dialogic" stories, which are keyed to understanding matters from the Other's perspective, against "ethnocentric" stories, which are keyed to making the home audience look good, at the expense of a seemingly incomprehensible or immoral Other. While we might ultimately accept the collectives thus represented as contingent or just "part of the story," in the realm of practical international politics, these are the kind of symbolic communicative moves that drive the stories journalists tell about nations in relationships.

NOTE

[1] All translations, unless otherwise noted, were done by the author.

REFERENCES

Anderson, B. (1991). *Imagined communities: Reflections on the origin and spread of nationalism.* New York: Verso. (Original work published 1983)

Ando, H. (1991). *Nichibei joho masatsu* [Japan–U.S. news friction]. Tokyo: Iwanami Shinsho.

Arno, A. (1984). Communication, conflict, and storylines: The news media as actors in a cultural context. In A. Arno & W. Dissanayake (Eds.), *The news media in national and international conflict* (pp. 1–15). Boulder, CO: Westview Press.

Asano, M., Okabe, R., & Miyamoto, N. (Eds.), *Nichibei joho masatsu* [U.S.–Japan news friction]. Tokyo: Nihon jijieigo bunkai.

Bloom, W. (1990). *Personal identity, national identity, and international relations.* Cambridge, England: Cambridge University Press.

Boulding, K. E. (1959). National images and international systems. *Journal of Conflict Resolution, 3*, 120–131.

Buchanan, W., & Cantril, H. (1953). *How nations see each other: A study in public opinion.* Urbana, IL: University of Illinois Press.

Carey, J. W. (1989). *Communication as culture: Essays on media and society.* Boston: Unwin Hyman.

Der Derian, J., & Shapiro, M. J. (Eds.). (1989). *International/intertextual relations: Postmodern readings of world politics.* Lexington, MA: Lexington Books.

Eagleton, T. (1990). *Nationalism, colonialism, and literature.* Minneapolis, MN: University of Minnesota Press.

Egan, J. (1989, October 9). Sony's big-picture strategy. *U.S. News and World Report,* 35–37.

Frederick, H. A. (1993). *Global communication and international relations.* Belmont, CA: Wadsworth Publishing.

Gamson, W. A., & Modigliani, A. (1989). Media discourse and public opinion on nuclear power: A constructionist approach. *American Journal of Sociology, 95,* 1–37.

Glasser, T. L., & Salmon, C. T. (Eds.). (1995). *Public opinion and the communication of consent.* New York : Guilford Press.

Hallin, D. C., & Mancini, P. (1989). *Friendly enemies: The Reagan-Gorbachev summits on U.S., Italian and Soviet television.* Perugia, Italy: Provincia di Perugia.

Hartley, J. (1992). *The politics of pictures: The creation of the public in the age of popular media.* New York: Routledge.

Herbst, S. (1992). *Numbered voices: How opinion polls shape American politics.* Chicago: University of Chicago Press.

Japan-is-different thinking in America [Bei de "Nippon ishitsuron"]. (1989b, October 9). *Asahi Shinbun,* 2.

Krauss, E. S. (1996). Media coverage of U.S.–Japan relations. In S. J. Pharr & E. S. Krauss (Eds.), *Media and politics in Japan.* Honolulu, HI: University of Hawaii Press.

Ladd, E. C., & Bowman, K. H. (1996). *Public opinion in American and Japan: How we see each other and ourselves.* Washington, DC: AEI Press.

McBride, S. (1980). *Many voices, one world.* New York: Unipub.

Morita, A., & Ishihara, S. (1989). *"No" to ieru Nihon* [A Japan that can say No]. Tokyo: Kobunsha.

Neff, R., Magnusson, P., & Holstein, W. J. (1989, August 7). Rethinking Japan. *Business Week,* 44–52.

Nishizawa. (1989, October 6). Kyoretsu! Bei no hanpatsu. *Yomiuri Shinbun,* 13.

Oehlkers, P. W. (1996). *Relating nations: A speech act approach to news mediated international relations.* Unpublished doctoral dissertation, Northwestern University, Evanston, IL.

Okamoto. (1989, November 1). Bei-masukomi no Nihon hihan gekika [The intensification of criticism of Japan in American media]. *Yomiuri Shinbun,* 7.

Okonogi. (1989, October 4). "Bei no tamashii kau" to beishi ["American soul bought" says American magazine]. *Asahi Shinbun,* 13.

Peters. J. (1995). Historical tensions in the concept of public opinion. In T. L. Glasser & C. T. Salmon (Eds.), *Public opinion and the communication of consent* (pp. 3–32). New York: Guilford Press.

Powell, B., Martin, B., Thomas, R., & Barry, J. (1989, October 9). Five ways to fight back. *Newsweek,* 68–72.

Reeves, J. (1994). *Cracked coverage: TV news, the anti-cocaine crusade and the Reagan legacy.* Durham, NC: Duke University Press.

Rowen, H. (1989a, October 1). Japanophobia: An easy cop-out. *The Washington Post,* p. H1.

Rowen, H. (1989b, October 9). Bei no kyousouryoku koujou ni yuueki [Will improve America's competitive position]. *Yomiuri Shinbun,* p. 7.

Sawada, H. (1990). "Nyuuzuuiku nihonhan" no yonen [Four years of the Japanese edition of *Newsweek*]. *Sogo Janarizumu Kenkyu, 132,* 98–102.

Schudson, M. (1995). *The power of news.* Cambridge, MA: Harvard University Press.

Schwartz, J., & Hammer, J. (1989, October 9). Japan goes Hollywood. *Newsweek,* 62–67.

Shapiro, M. J. (1988). *The politics of representation: Writing practices in biography, photography, and policy analysis*. Madison, WI: University of Wisconsin Press.

Shapiro, M. J. (1989). Representing world politics: The sport/war intertext. In J. Der Derian & M. J. Shapiro (Eds.) *International/intertextual relations: Postmodern readings of world politics* (pp. 69–96). Lexington, MA: Lexington Books.

Sneider, D. (1989, October 24). Inside the Japanese "invasion." *Christian Science Monitor*, p. 1.

Sonii shokku [Sony shock]. (1989, October 9). *Ashahi Shinbun*, p. 9.

Sony misread America's heart [Beikoku no kokoro o yomiayamatta Sonii]. (1989a, October 5). *Asahi Shinbun*, 5.

Suzuki, K. (1992). *Nichibei "kiki" to hodo*. [U.S.–Japan "crisis" and communication]. Tokyo: Iwanami Shoten.

White, L., & Leigh, R. D. (1972). *Peoples speaking to peoples*. New York: Arno Press. (Original work published 1946)

Wight, M. (1972). International legitimacy. *International Relations*, 1–29.

Yates, R. (1989, October 8). Sony: Columbia a landing, not invasion. *Chicago Tribune*, Section 7, p. 3.

II

Comparative Perspectives

4

Ideological Manipulation via Newspaper Accounts of Political Conflict: A Cross-National News Analysis of the 1991 Moscow Coup

Li-Ning Huang
Central Connecticut State University

Katherine C. McAdams
University of Maryland

From its inception, communication research has studied the structural and behavioral factors affecting the content of news. Some of the seminal research includes the newsroom and gatekeeper studies of Warren Breed (1955), Edward Epstein (1973), Herbert Gans (1979), Leon Sigal (1973), Gaye Tuchman (1978), and David White (1950). More recently, the development of critical/cultural studies has emphasized examining news content within the broader conception of "hegemony," which suggests that media messages are framed as a form of ideological mobilization for public support in maintaining the values or policies of the status quo.

From such a perspective, ideological mobilization takes place when the news frame through which events are presented gives one dominant or primary meaning rather than another (Parenti, 1986). Similarly, Hall (1982) has argued that particular news accounts may be ideological, "not because of the manifest bias or distortions of their surface contents, but because they were transformations based on a limited ideological matrix" (p. 72).

The bias in international news coverage within the United States has been studied extensively (see, for example, Ahern, 1984; Chang, 1988; Galtung & Ruge, 1965; Gans, 1979; Graber, 1989; Hopple, 1982; Lent, 1977; Mazharul Haque, 1983; McNelly & Izcarey, 1986; Peterson, 1981; Sreberny-Mohammadi & Grant, 1985; Stevenson & Cole, 1984; Van Dijk, 1984, 1988). These studies share the common finding that media coverage of foreign issues is often biased and negative, with a strong Western orientation. However, most of these studies are limited in two ways: First, their findings are limited to the United States and do not examine the dynamics of news bias cross-culturally, and second, they only deal with surface bias in foreign news content, leaving unexplained the deep structure that generates the patterns of the coverage.

Thus, this study, in an attempt to go beyond the description of international news and to place it in the broader theoretical framework of hegemony, examines how the United States', Taiwan's, and China's newspapers covered a political event, namely the Moscow coup of August 1991. In this event, Vice President Yanayev and other Communist members who opposed Gorbachev's economic and political reforms replaced President Gorbachev and took over the government. The nature of this event allows us to examine the ideological linkage between the media and the status quo in these three different political contexts. By comparing the news coverage of the Moscow coup, this study attempts to demonstrate how this foreign event was treated and defined, and in what context it was explained by the media in these three countries.

RELEVANT LITERATURE: OBJECTIVITY VERSUS HEGEMONY

News Objectivity

Although journalists claim to exclude personal values in reporting, Gans (1979) proposes that they cannot proceed without values. He argues that some "enduring values" are "unconsciously" built into news judgment (p. 182). These enduring values include ethnocentrism, altruistic democracy, responsible capitalism, small-town pastoralism, individualism, moderatism, social order, and national leadership, which are rarely explicit and can be found in many different types of news stories over a long period of time.

Similarly, McQuail (1977) suggests several possible appearances of bias, including explicit argument and compilation of evidence favoring one point of view; a tendentious use of facts and comments without any explicit statement of preference; the use of language, which colors an otherwise factual report and conveys an implicit but clear value judgment; and the omission of points favoring one side, in an otherwise straight news report.

Numerous content analyses have sought to evaluate the objectivity of news coverage and have challenged the claims of media objectivity. Several studies (Altheide & Snow, 1979; Epstein, 1973; Tuchman, 1978) have argued that the news media structure their representation of social and political events in ways that are not manifest in the events themselves. They conclude that, far from being a detached observer, the media actively help to construct the world. As the MacBride Report, a U.S. wire service, points out, "the act of selecting certain news items for publication, while rejecting others, produces in the minds of the audience a picture of the world that may well be incomplete or distorted" (qtd. in Weaver & Wilhoit, 1983, p. 134).

The process of news encoding includes selecting codes that assign meanings to events as well as placing events in a referential context. This process of coding becomes especially problematic when one is dealing with an event that disrupts the normative consensus or challenges the status quo. Hall (1977) argues that the codes describing these problematic events are selected to create consensus.

The process of creating consensus comes about through what Carey (1989) would call the ritual mode of communication, which considers newspaper reading less as sending or gaining information and more as a portrayal and reinforcement of a particular view of the world. Carey emphasizes that "what is arrayed before the reader is not pure information but a portrayal of the contending forces in the world" (p. 20). Newspapers, says Carey, "do not operate as a source of effects or functions but as dramatically satisfying, which is not to say pleasing, presentations of what the world at root is" (p. 20).

For example, the cold war news frame once organized virtually all foreign affairs coverage into a coherent ideological picture supportive of American world hegemony. Hallin (1987, p. 17) points out that the cold war ideology is produced through a primarily "unconscious" process, employed by journalists not so much to make a political point as to "package" the presentation of news in terms they assume the audience will find interesting and easy to understand.

Hegemony and the News Media

The hegemony theory predicts that media content is influenced by the elite intentions and functions to create consent within the population. The powerful groups control the messages of the media in search of an enduring basis for legitimate authority (Gitlin, 1980; Gramsci, 1971; McQuail, 1987; Shoemaker, 1987). Gitlin suggests that "hegemony is a ruling class's domination of subordinate classes through the elaboration and penetration of ideology into their common sense and everyday practice" (p. 253). In other words, worldviews, belief systems, and social values are accepted not by coercion, but rather by creating consent, which legitimatizes the existing distribution of power.

In liberal capitalist societies, the dominant class does not produce and disseminate the ideology alone. Hegemony is accomplished through the agencies of religion, family, politics, art, law, education, and the mass media (Hall, 1977; Gitlin, 1980), which Gitlin called "ideology-shaping institutions" (p. 254) and Althusser (1971) called "ideological state apparatuses" (pp. 135–149).

According to Hallin (1987), the concept of hegemony plays a double role in the study of the media. First, it is used to "conceptualize the political function of the media" (p. 4). The media play the role of maintaining the dominant political ideology: they propagate it, glorify it, explain the world in its terms, and, at times, modify it to adapt to the demands of legitimation in a changing world.

At the same time, the concept of hegemony is employed to "explain the behavior of the media, the process of news production itself" (Hallin, 1987, p. 4). Hallin observes that the media themselves are subject to the hegemonic process. The dominant ideology shapes the production of news and entertainment. That is why the media can be expected to function as agents of legitimation, despite the fact that they are independent of direct political control.

Shoemaker (1987) points out that this hegemonic approach suggests that U.S. media owners have a vested interest in seeing the status quo continue, because they are part of the U.S. power structure, defined by Dreier (1983) as "the top positions in the institutional structure of the society" (p. 441). The members of this powerful structure, Dreier says, may hold different opinions on some topics, but maintain consensus after all.

Hegemony theory thus suggests that, although the media will criticize the status quo, establishing their own legitimacy as news organizations, the criticism will never be structural—that is, something that seriously threatens or changes it (Gitlin, 1980). Hallin (1987) argues that even in periods when the media do not support the foreign policy elite, they tend to at least equally not support any attempts to challenge the establishment.

In the context of foreign affairs coverage, to say the media play a "hegemonic" role is to say that they contribute to the maintenance of consent for a national system of power. This national system of power varies across countries. In the Western world, it refers to the capitalist system dominated both politically and economically by the United States, while in China, it refers to Communism or socialism.

Foreign News Coverage

Following the work of Galtung and Ruge (1965), a body of research that makes a strong argument for the bias in foreign news reporting was developed. Buzek, Robison, and colleagues (cited in Nnaemeka & Richstad, 1981), for example, provide various studies of the role of ideology in the process of news selection. The conclusion these studies make is that ideology represents a strong force in shaping both the kind of foreign news that the press in socialist systems project to their readers and the editorial decisions they make regarding the amount of Western-produced international news and information disseminated in the Communist world.

Another influential study has been Gerbner's (1961) comparative study of *Nepszabadsag*, the socialist Hungarian daily, and *The New York Times*, the capitalist American daily, as well as other works (see also Gerbner, 1964; Gerbner & Marvanyi, 1977; Schramm, 1959; Siebert, Peterson, & Schramm, 1956). Gerbner's analysis of the reporting pattern of the two dailies revealed that the *Times* was consistent with the market-oriented ideology of a capitalist system in which conflict, tension, arousal, and sensationalism constitute the news. Several other international communication analyses, such as Galtung and Ruge (1965), Hester (1971, 1973), Shilter (1974, 1976), and Smith (1969) reach similar conclusions.

Several other scholars (Chang, Shoemaker, & Brendlinger, 1987; McNelly & Izcarey, 1986; Stevenson & Cole, 1984; Viswanath, 1988; Weaver & Wilhoit, 1981, 1983) have criticized American news coverage of foreign countries—especially of less developed countries—as biased, largely because it is characterized by the violent, the bizarre, and the conflictual. Chu (1985) observes that the mass media, in reporting political or military crises in a foreign country, usually depict one side—for example, the government—as a villain and portray the opposition as the hero.

Similarly, Weaver and Wilhoit's (1981, 1983) analysis of foreign news coverage in AP and UPI wire services suggested that the bulk of the wire service coverage focused on political and military activity and crime. Along the same lines, Agbese and Ogbondah's (1988) analyses of the *New York Times*, *Washington Post*, and *Wall Street Journal's* coverage of coups in Nigeria revealed that if a government supportive of American interests was overthrown, the political change was greeted with hostility by the U.S. press.

Each of these studies echoes the influential work of Chomsky and Herman (1979), who have long contended that the Western media are part of an ideological apparatus that falsifies, obscures, and reinterprets the facts in the interest of those who dominate the economy and political system. Herman and Chomsky (1988) and Parenti (1986) have provided numerous examples when they argue that the major role of the U.S. press is to continually recreate a view of reality supportive of existing social and economic class power. The analysis that follows examines the coverage of the 1991 Moscow coup across three countries to investigate how each country's press constructed the reality of this foreign event.

BACKGROUND OF THE MOSCOW COUP

On August 19, 1991, TASS (the Soviet Union's official news agency) announced that Soviet Vice President Gennady Yanayev replaced Mikhail Gorbachev as president because Gorbachev was ill and unable to perform his duties. The new president declared that a "state of emergency" was established in order to save the Soviet Union from "the profound and comprehensive crisis, political, ethnic and civil strife, chaos and anarchy that threaten the lives and security of the Soviet Union's citizens and its sovereignty, territorial integrity, freedom and independence" (Dobbs, 1991, p. A1).

The media reported that Vice President Yanayev was assuming presidential powers under a new entity called the State Committee for the State of Emergency. At that time, Gorbachev was vacationing on the Black Sea coast, and there was no word of his whereabouts. The statement made by the Emergency Committee said that the Soviet Union's new leaders wanted to live in friendship with the rest of the world and would observe all international agreements.

Western newspapers reported that the officials who seized power were conservative Communist members and opposed to the reforms of President Gorbachev. After the establishment of the Emergency Committee, columns of tanks and armored cars entered several parts of Moscow as well as key sites of the Baltic republics and surrounded several sensitive communications facilities.

Within hours of learning that Soviet President Gorbachev had been replaced, thousands of Muscovites gathered around the capital to argue and plead with the army troops and tank crews. The largest and most organized demonstrations against the takeover were led by Boris Yeltsin, who urged Soviet people to resist the government takeover by Communist hardliners.

On August 20, the resistance appeared to be growing around the Soviet Union, with leaders in the Ukraine and Kazakhstan denouncing the takeover and thousands of people attending protest demonstrations. On August 22, the self-proclaimed eight-man State of Emergency Committee collapsed. President Mikhail Gorbachev returned to Moscow and the members of the Committee were arrested. As news of the collapse of the Committee spread throughout the country, tanks and trucks began to leave Moscow and the Baltic republics. On August 23, Gorbachev demanded the resignation of his entire government, and Communist Party organizations were shut down throughout the republic.

STUDY HYPOTHESES

Since this event "overthrew" Gorbachev—a symbol of economic and political reforms—it was assumed that the nature of this event conflicted with countries that had a democratic political ideology, but was compatible with Communist societies' political ideology. Based on this assumption, we expected to find similar news coverage patterns of this event across the two democratic capitalist countries—the United States and Taiwan—and substantially different news treatments between these two democratic countries and China. The following hypotheses were formulated:

1. The news coverage in China would tend to favor the Emergency Committee by more frequently using the committee as a news source, whereas coverage in the U.S. and Taiwan would favor the "reformists"—Gorbachev, Yeltsin, and the demonstrators—by using them more frequently as news sources.
2. The Chinese government would support this event, whereas the American and Taiwanese governments would oppose this event.
3. Chinese newspapers would use favorable terms while reporting this event, whereas American and Taiwanese newspapers would present it with the use of negative terms.

METHODOLOGY

A quantitative content analysis was conducted to compare how the Moscow coup was reported by the press in three countries—the United States, Taiwan and China—during the first three-day period (August 19–21, 1991). Two prominent newspapers from each of the three countries were selected for the study: *People's Daily* (*Renmin Ribao*) and *Enlightment Daily* (*Guangming Ribao*) of China, *United Daily* and *China Times* of Taiwan, and *The Washington Post* and *The New York Times* of the United States.

The Moscow coup occurred on August 19, 1991. Because of the 12-hour difference between the East and the West, the time frame for the content analysis was from August 19 to 21 for American newspapers and August 20 to 22 for Taiwanese and Chinese newspapers.

The sample for this study included hard news about the Soviet coup and the ensuing anti-coup demonstrations, excluding editorials, feature stories, news analyses, profiles, and commentaries. Moreover, since this study attempts to test the assumption that the dominant political ideology in each country affects its Moscow coup news coverage, reportage about the reaction of one country toward this event appearing in that country's newspapers was coded.

The unit of analysis was each news story. The factors that may influence the direction of news coverage, such as news sources, terminologies used to describe this event, event leaders, and its legitimate status as well as the nation's reaction toward this event, were coded.

Concerning the intercorder reliability, two Mandarin-speaking graduate students, one from Taiwan and the other from mainland China, coded all selected Chinese news stories and both of them and one American graduate student coded all selected American news stories. Holsti's formula (1969) was used to determine the intercorder reliability coefficients. For the Chinese newspapers coded by the two Mandarin-speaking students, the intercorder reliability coefficient was .91 for *People's Daily* and .92 for *Guangming Daily*.

For the *Washington Post*, the reliability coefficient was .82 between the American and Chinese students, .92 between the American and Taiwanese students, and .85 between the Taiwanese and Chinese students. The overall reliability coefficient among the three students was .81.

For the *New York Times*, the reliability coefficient was .85 between the American and Chinese students, .93 between the American and Taiwanese students, and .89 between Taiwanese and Chinese students. The overall reliability coefficient among the three coders was .83.

Categorization

News sources. This variable is used to assess the media's hegemonic function as legitimating the political authorities and government's policy by using sources that clearly articulate ideological positions supportive of each country.

Terminology. Each article was also coded for the language used to describe this event, event leaders, and its legitimate status. Terms used to describe this event ranged from negative words such as *putsch*, *overthrow*, and *crime* to neutral terms such as "internal change" and "Kremlin power change." In addition, terminology used to describe the main figures also ranged from negative words such as *putschists*, *plotters*, *hoodlums*, and *hardliners* to neutral terms such as "new rules" and "new government."

The descriptive terminology about the legitimate status of this event fell into three subcategories: approval, opposition, or no description used. The approval language included words such as *legitimate* and *constitutional*. The opposition language included words such as *unconstitutional, illegitimate*, and *misguided*.

The use of these specific lexical and syntactic choices was seen as crucial. Bennett (1980) argues that the simple act of labeling something can affect human behavior toward that thing and even "transform" the nature of the thing itself. For example, calling the event an "internal change" implies a stepping down of Gorbachev because of health problems, while a "military coup" that "overthrows" Gorbachev clearly implies a violent takeover.

Government's reaction toward this event. Only articles relevant to the reaction of one country toward this event appearing in that country's newspapers were coded. After reviewing all the news items during the three-day time frame, the authors found three stories concerning the Chinese government's reaction: two *People's Daily* stories and one *Guangming Daily* story; 12 news items about the U.S. government's reaction: six *Washington Post* stories and six *New York Times* stories; and eight articles concerning the Taiwan government's reaction: six *United Daily* stories and two *China Times* stories. Subcategories for these variables included negative, positive, indifferent, and hesitant to make any comment.

FINDINGS AND DISCUSSION

News Sources

Important differences were observed in the three press systems' use of news sources. As shown in Table 4.1, 35 percent of American stories used U.S. government sources. Most of the stories using U.S. official sources were negative toward the coup, suggesting measures such as condemnation and suspension of economic aid. The claim that the American media opposed the coup and supported the demonstrations is supported by the finding that 21 percent of news items used or quoted Yeltsin's or the democratic side's opinion. Although 14 percent of American news sources were Soviet Acting President Yanayev or the Emergency Committee, the percentage is low, compared to the one shown in the Chinese press (25 percent). Similar to the American press, the percentage of Emergency Committee as a news source is also low in the Taiwanese press (11 percent).

Furthermore, China's press system relied heavily on TASS, the official Russian news agency. Over half (65 percent) of the news came from TASS, compared to 26 percent of Taiwanese stories. The American press seemed to have discredited the TASS source generally. While both Taiwan and China relied on TASS for further information about the coup, only 9 percent of American news was supplied by TASS.

TABLE 4.1.
News Sources

	U.S.		Taiwan		China	
	n	%	n	%	n	%
U.S. government	15	34.9				
China government					2	10.0
Taiwan government			8	11.1		
U.S.S.R. acting president/committee	6	14.0	8	11.1	5	25.0
Yeltsin/Gorbachev/their aides	9	20.9	12	16.7		
TASS	4	9.3	19	26.4	13	65.0
Other countries	2	4.7				
Others	6	14.0	15	20.8		
Unidentifiable	1	2.3	10	13.9		

Government Reaction

Regarding the three countries' governmental reactions toward this event, as can be seen in Table 4.2, of the 43 American hard news stories covered during the sample period, there were 12 stories concerning the U.S. government's reaction. All 12 stories "condemned" the coup and denied its legitimacy. The Bush administration went so far as to ask other Western countries to suspend economic aid.

Even though the American and Taiwanese press both condemned this event, the intensity of their reactions was different. The Taiwan government's reaction was not as strong and emotional as that of the U.S. government's. There was a total of eight stories in Taiwanese newspapers dealing with the Taiwanese government's reaction. Although this event was a Communist coup, there were only two (25 percent) stories stating the Taiwanese government's condemnation. The other six stories (75 percent) reported the Taiwanese government's hesitation to make any comment or political decision because there was no official political relationship between Taiwan and the Soviet Union. Most of the news articles during the sample period concerning the impact of this event on Taiwan focused on the economic effects rather than on the political effects.

While the democratic countries were "stunned" by this event, China's government proclaimed that it would not interfere in other countries' internal affairs. There was only one story concerning the Chinese government's reaction in each of the selected Chinese newspapers during the three-day period. The two stories expressed the view that the Chinese government would respect the Soviet people's choice. No condemnation or accusation appeared in any Chinese news.

TABLE 4.2.
Reaction Terminology on the Event Used by Three Countries' Newspapers

	U.S. (N=12)		Taiwan (N=8)		China (N=2)	
	n	%	n	%	n	%
Negative: "Condemn/denounce" "Avoid legitimacy" "Suspend aid"	12	100.0	2	25.0		
Positive: "Welcome it"	0		0		0	
Indifferent: "Not interfere the internal affairs of Soviet Union"					2	100.0
Hesitated to make any comment for the present moment			6	75.0		

The reason the Chinese government did not support this event and claimed to be an outsider could have been that no one could predict whether this coup would succeed or not, especially when the American government strongly condemned this act and planned to suspend economic aid. If the Chinese government had made their position clearly by supporting the coup, the foreign relationship between China and the Soviet Union would have been at risk if the coup failed in the end.

Terminology to Name This Event

There was evidence of differential use of terminology across the three countries. No negative terms were used by the Communist/socialist press in reference to the Kremlin leadership change, whereas some negative language was used by the press from the capitalist countries, providing support for the hypothesis. The dichotomy found in the news treatment of this event can be seen as reflective of the different dominant political ideologies.

As Table 4.3 on page 68 illustrates, the American press used the strongest and most emotional words while reporting this event. Ten different words were used by American newspapers to label this event. The most frequently used words were "coup" (31 stories), "overthrow" (11 stories), "ouster" (10 stories), and "takeover" (10 stories). Other words with negative implications were "putsch" (6 stories), "crime" (3 stories), and "grab of power" (2 stories). The word "putsch," which perhaps has the most negative connotation, was used only by American newspapers.

The terminologies used by American and Taiwanese newspapers were similar, but the relative frequency of use was slightly different. For Taiwanese papers, like the American press, the most frequently used word was "coup" (37 stories). The Taiwanese press also used negative words such as "overthrow" (10 stories), "ouster" (26 stories), "grab of power" (11 stories), "rightist coup" (3 stories), and "crime" (2 stories). However, while the strongly negative word "putsch" was used only by American newspapers, the comparatively neutral word "stepdown" was used only by the Taiwanese press (15 stories).

In addition, some neutral terms such as "Kremlin power shift" and "political change" were also used by the American and Taiwanese press. "Kremlin power shift" was used in five stories and nine stories, respectively, in American and Taiwanese newspapers. However, only these kinds of neutral terms were used by Chinese newspapers. The Chinese press regarded the event as merely "political change." Although "coup" was mentioned by the Chinese press, that was because that story was explaining from the viewpoint of the State Emergency Committee that the act was not a "coup." Other negative terms such as "rightist coup," "crime," "overthrow," or "ouster" were never found in the Chinese coverage of this event. In doing so, Chinese newspapers suggested legitimacy of the Emergency Committee's power takeover.

TABLE 4.3.
Terminology to Name the Event

	U.S.	Taiwan	China
Coup	31	37	2
Rightist coup/Reactionary coup	4	3	
Takeover	10	8	
Putsch	6		
Crime	3	2	
Internal change/	2		2
Political change			
Kremlin power shift	5	9	
Ouster/Being ousted	10	26	
Overthrow/Being overthrown	11	10	
Stepdown	15		
Grab of power	2	11	

Descriptive Terminology About the Event's Legitimate Status

The analysis of the descriptive terminology used to describe this event's legitimate status also revealed pronounced differences among the three countries, as Table 4.4 illustrates. Again, the result provides evidence that political ideology influenced media use of adjectives when describing this event.

Chinese newspapers did not use as many adjectives as did American and Taiwanese papers, failing to support the hypothesis that the Chinese media would use positive adjectives to describe this event. Some 85 percent of Chinese stories

TABLE 4.4.
Descriptive Terminology of the Event

	U.S. (N = 43)		Taiwan (N = 72)		China (N = 20)	
	n	%	n	%	n	%
Against: "Unconstitutional" "Illegitimate" "Misguided"	23	53.5	17	23.6	1	5.0
Pro: "Legitimate" "Constitutional"	1	2.3	1	1.4	2	10.0
No descriptive Terminology found	19	44.2	54	75.0	17	85.0

described this event as neither legitimate nor unconstitutional. In other words, most of the Chinese stories remained more "impartial" than American and Taiwanese newspapers. Only one story (5 percent of coverage) in Chinese newspapers reported that Yeltsin denounced the Emergency Committee as an "unconstitutional" organization, and only two stories (19 percent of coverage) quoted Yanayev's emphasis that the Committee was "constitutional."

The Taiwanese press was neither as "impartial" as the Chinese media, nor as "strongly resistant" as the American media toward this event. Table 4.4 shows that 75 percent of stories remained impartial, whereas 24 percent of stories described this event as "unconstitutional." Only one story (1 percent) mentioned that this event was legal.

Like Taiwanese newspapers, only one American story (2 percent) mentioned that this act was legal. However, over 50 percent of American stories described it as "unconstitutional," "illegitimate," or "misguided." The word *misguided* was used only by the American press. Moreover, 19 stories (44 percent) remained impartial, the lowest percentage among the three countries.

Terminology to Name the Event Leaders

The analysis of the terminology used by newspapers to identify the event leaders shows some interesting similarities between American and Taiwanese newspapers, as well as important differences between the two democratic countries and China.

As Table 4.5 illustrates, while both American and Taiwanese newspapers used some negative words such as "hardliners" and "putschists" to label the leaders, the Chinese press used only one term, "State Emergency Committee," to name the

TABLE 4.5.
Terminology to Name the Event Leaders

	U.S.	Taiwan	China
Hardliners	16	27	
Putschists	5	1	
New Rulers	10	17	
Adventurists	4	1	
Coup plotters	17	14	
Hoods/hoodlums	1		
Renegades	1		
New Kremlin group/ New government	5	15	
Junta	6		
Emergency Committee	16	35	12
Conservatives	11		

leaders. This result supports the claim that the Chinese press did not oppose the act made by the eight committee members.

Coincidentally, the most frequently used negative terms in both American and Taiwanese stories were "hardliners" (16 and 27 stories, respectively) and "coup plotters/leaders" (17 and 14 stories). Other words with negative implications used by both presses were "putschists" (5 and 1) and "adventurists" (4 and 1). Although both American and Taiwanese newspapers sometimes used neutral terms such as "new rulers" (10 and 17 stories), "new Kremlin group/new government" (5 and 15), and "Emergency Committee" (16 and 35), American newspapers used more negative terms such as "hoods/hoodlums" (one story), "renegades" (one story), and "junta" (6 stories) to name the leaders. These negative terms were not used either by the Taiwanese or by the Chinese press. Moreover, the term "conservatives" was used only by the Taiwanese press in contrast with "reformists."

CONCLUSION

This study examined the characteristics of news coverage of the Moscow coup in three countries to detect the ideological bias in news selection and presentation. By quantitatively analyzing news sources, terminologies to name this event and event leaders, and descriptive terminology about its legitimate status, this study found that, first, political ideology corresponded to the direction of news coverage in all three countries. In other words, newspapers in democratic countries tended to portray the event of the Moscow coup in a negative frame, whereas newspapers in the Communist country portrayed this event in a less negative way. In addition, American and Taiwanese newspapers appeared to report this event from the perspective of the demonstrators (the Soviet public) or Gorbachev, whereas Chinese newspapers appeared to report this event from the perspective of the Emergency Committee (called "coup plotter" by American newspapers).

Second, the American government's reaction, which was strongly negative, corresponded to its "negative" direction of news coverage of the Moscow event, whereas Taiwan and China government reactions were less extensively covered in their newspapers. The U.S. government opposed this event and American papers heavily quoted the U.S. president's and officials' condemnation of the coup. While the American government's reaction of condemnation was emphasized in the American news coverage, the other two countries' reactions were less negative and less emotional and were not manifested in their newspaper coverage. Third, the American and Taiwanese coverage of the Moscow event were similar to each other in terms of news direction and news emphases. Both were substantially different from the Chinese coverage.

China's and Taiwan's "stand-by" foreign policy did not appear to lead to a balanced or impartial news coverage. Although the Chinese press used relatively neutral terms while reporting this event, their news presentation and emphases were biased to favor the Emergency Committee members with no coverage given to the anti-coup demonstrations. The coverage in Taiwan was also biased by emphasizing the anti-coup demonstrations and using negative terms to describe this event.

Taken together, the present research found that each country's news coverage of the Moscow coup was framed from an ideologically acceptable perspective to maintain the existing political system. The above major findings support the assumption of hegemony theory that the news content is framed within the ideology of the powerful to mobilize public opinion. It appears that, in covering the Moscow coup, journalists encoded the news event with a "dominant or preferred meaning," constructing the social and political realities and helping maintain the dominant political-economic system.

Within the existing ideological consensus, there does exist a certain range of view points on domestic and foreign policy issues. However, as Parenti (1986) points out, we cannot interpret that phenomenon as a plurality of ideas and ideologies, because those views do not challenge a country's fundamental establishment. Herman (1985) argues that the diversity of news, which has been widely investigated in gatekeeper studies, is only meaningful in terms of individual incidents, rather than in a frame of ideological patterns.

The media are powerful in shaping public perception and opinion of foreign issues. Most people do not have direct experience with foreign countries and have to rely on the mass media for information and for interpretation of foreign issues. The media thus play an essential role in manipulating public support for government interests. The news media generally accept official definitions of those who are America's friends and enemies and describe them accordingly. From this perspective, the mass media influence not only *what* we think, but also *how* we think about foreign issues in order to maintain social and political order.

REFERENCES

Agbese, P. O., & Ogbondah, C. W. (1988). The U.S. press and political changes in the Third World: The coverage of military coups. *Political Communication and Persuasion, 5*, 33–48.

Ahern, T. J., Jr. (1984). Determinants of foreign news coverage in U.S. newspapers. In R. L. Stevenson & D. L. Shaw (Eds.), *Foreign news and the new world information order* (pp. 98–113). Ames, IA: Iowa State University Press.

Altheide, D. L., & Snow, R. P. (1979). *Media logic.* Beverly Hills, CA: Sage.

Althusser, L. (1971). *Lenin and philosophy and other essays.* New York: Monthly Review Press.

Bennett, W. L. (1980). *Public opinion in American politics.* New York: Harcourt Brace Jovanovich.

Breed, W. (1955). Social control in the newsroom: A functional analysis. *Social Forces, 33*, 326–335.

Carey, J. W. (1989). *Communication as culture.* Boston: Unwin Hyman.

Chang, T. K. (1988). The news and U.S.–China policy: Symbols in newspapers and documents. *Journalism Quarterly, 65*, 320–327.

Chang, T. K., Shoemaker, P. J., & Brendlinger, N. (1987). Determinants of international news coverage in the U.S. media. *Communication Research, 14*, 396–414.

Chomsky, N., & Herman, N. (1979). *After the cataclysm*. Boston: Southend Press.

Chu, L. L. (1985). An organizational perspective on international news flow: Some generalizations, hypotheses, and questions for research. *Gazette, 35*, 3–18.

Dobbs, M. (1991, August 19). Close aides oust Gorbachev. *The Washington Post*, p. A1.

Dreier, P. (1983). The position of the press in the U.S. power structure. In E. Wartelle, D. C. Whitney, & S. Windahl (Eds.), *Mass communication review yearbook* (Vol. 4, pp. 439–451). Beverly Hills, CA: Sage.

Epstein, E. (1973). *News from nowhere: Television and the news*. New York: Random House.

Galtung, J., & Ruge, M. H. (1965). The structure of foreign news. *Journal of Peace Research, 2*, 64–91.

Gans, H. (1979). *Deciding what's news: A case study of* CBS Evening News, NBC Nightly News, Newsweek *and* Time. New York: Pantheon.

Gerbner, G. (1961). Press perspectives in world communication. *Journalism Quarterly, 38*, 313–322.

Gerbner, G. (1964). Ideology perspectives and political tendencies in news reporting. *Journalism Quarterly, 4*, 495–508.

Gerbner, G., & Marvanyi, G. (1977). The many worlds of the world's press. *Journalism of Communication, 27*, 52–66

Gitlin, T. (1980). *The whole world is watching: Mass media in the making and unmaking of the new left*. Berkeley, CA: University of California Press.

Graber, D. A. (1989). *Mass media and American politics*. Washington, DC: Congressional Quarterly.

Gramsci, A. (1971). *Selections from the prison notebook* (Q. Hoare & G. N. Smith, Eds. & Trans.). New York: International Publishers.

Hall, S. (1977). Culture, the media and the "ideological effect." In J. Curran, M. Gurevitch, & J. Wallacott (Eds.), *Mass communication and society* (pp. 315–348). London: The Open University Press.

Hall, S. (1982). The rediscovery of "ideology": Return of the repressed in media studies. In M. Gurevitch, T. Bennett, J. Curran, & J. Wollacott (Eds.), *Culture, society and the media* (pp. 56–90). London: Methuen.

Hallin, D. C. (1987). Hegemony: The American news media from Vietnam to El Salvador, a study of ideological change and its limits. In D. L. Paletz (Ed.), *Political communication research* (pp. 3–25). Norwood, NJ: Ablex.

Herman, E. S. (1985). Diversity of news: Marginalizing the opposition. *Journal of Communication, 35*, 135–146.

Herman, E. S., & Chomsky, N. (1988). *Manufacturing consent*. New York: Pantheon.

Hester, A. (1971). An analysis of news from developed and developing nations. *Gazette, 17*, 29–43.

Hester, A. (1973). Theoretical considerations in predicting volume and direction of international information flow. *Gazette, 19*, 238–247.

Holsti, O. R. (1969). *Content analysis for the social sciences and humanities*. Reading, MA: Addison-Wesley.

Hopple, G. W. (1982). International news coverage in two elite newspapers. *Journal of Communication, 32*, 61–74.

Lent, J. A. (1977). Foreign news in American media. *Journal of Communication, 27*, 46–50.

Mazharul Haque, S. M. (1983). Is U.S. coverage of news in Third World imbalanced? *Journalism Quarterly, 60*, 521–524.

McNelly, J. T., & Izcarey, F. (1986). International news exposure and images of nations. *Journalism Quarterly, 63*, 546–553.

McQuail, D. (1977). *The analysis of newspaper content.* London: Her Majesty's Stationery Office.

McQuail, D. (1987). *Mass communication theory.* Beverly Hills, CA: Sage.

Nnaemeka, T., & Richstad, J. (1981). Internal controls and foreign news coverage: Pacific press systems. *Communication Research, 8*, 97–135.

Parenti, M. (1986). *Inventing reality: The politics of the mass media.* New York: St. Martin's Press.

Peterson, S. (1981). International news selection by the elite press: a case study. *Public Opinion Quarterly, 45*, 143–163.

Schramm, W. (Ed.). (1959). *One day in the world's press: Fourteen great newspapers on a day of crisis.* Stanford, CA: Stanford University Press.

Shilter, H. I. (1974). Freedom from the "free flow." *Journal of Communication, 24*, 110–117.

Shilter, H. I. (1976). *Communication and cultural domination.* White Plains, NY: International Arts and Sciences Press.

Shoemaker, P. J. (1987, June). Building a theory of new content. *Journalism Monographs, 103.*

Siebert, F., Peterson, T., & Schramm, W. (1956). *Four theories of the press.* Urbana, IL: University of Illinois Press.

Sigal, L. V. (1973). *Reporters and officials: The organizational and politics of newsmaking.* Lexington, MA: D. C. Heath.

Smith, R. F. (1969). On the structure of foreign news: A comparison of the *New York Times* and the Indian white papers. *Journal of Peace Research, 6*, 24–25.

Sreberny-Mohammadi, A., & Grant, N. (Eds.). (1985). *Foreign news in media: International reporting in 29 countries* (Report No. 93). Paris: UNESCO.

Stevenson, R. L., & Cole, R. R. (1984). Patterns of foreign news. In R. L. Stevenson & D. L. Shaw (Eds.), *Foreign news and the new world information order* (pp. 37–62). Ames, IA: Iowa State University Press.

Tuchman, G. (1978). *Making news.* New York: The Free Press.

Van Dijk, T. A. (1984). *Structures of international news: A case study of the world's press.* Amsterdam: University of Amsterdam, Department of General Literary Studies.

Van Dijk, T. A. (1988). *A news analysis: Case studies of international and national news in the press.* Hillsdale, NJ: Lawrence Erlbaum.

Viswanath, K. (1988). International news in U.S. media: Perceptions of foreign students. *Journalism Quarterly, 65*, 952–959.

Weaver, D. H., & Wilhoit, G. C. (1981). Foreign news coverage in two U.S. wire services. *Journal of Communication, 31*, 55–63.

Weaver, D. H., & Wilhoit, G. C. (1983). Foreign news values in two U.S. wire services: An update. *Journal of Communication, 33*, 132–148.

White, D. M. (1950). The "gatekeeper": A case study in the selection of news. *Journalism Quarterly, 27*, 383–390.

5

International News in the Latin American Press

Jose-Carlos Lozano
Edgar Gomez
Tecnologico de Monterrey, Mexico

Alejandra Matiasich
Alfredo Alfonso
Universidad Nacional de La Plata, Argentina

Martin Becerra
Universidad Nacional de Quilmes, Argentina

Ada Cristina Machado Silveira
Universidad Federal de Santa Maria Rio Grande do Sul, Brazil

Magdalena Elizondo
Jorge Marroquin
Tecnologico de Monterrey, Mexico

Luciane Delgado Aquino
Francisco-Javier Martinez
Universidad Autonoma de Barcelona, Spain

This chapter reports the findings of a content analysis of one chronological and one composite week of some of the leading daily newspapers in Latin America and Spain. This study answers questions posed by cultural imperialism and newsmaking approaches about the degree of dependence of Latin American newspapers on the transnational news agencies, the regions of the world covered the most, the amount and quality of news articles about other Latin American countries, and the topics most frequently included. While attention paid to the local geographic region was higher than other regions, including industrialized ones, topics were more negative in the news about developing countries (including Latin American ones), and dependence on the transnational news agencies was high. The chapter concludes with a discussion of the implications of the findings for the goals of regional integration and a more balanced international agenda.

In a recent article, Vincent (1997) suggests that international news flow is still limited and biased, despite some improvements in the last 20 years:

> A major concern continues to be that newspaper content often appears to have a U.S. and/or Western bias. U.S. news agencies are said to manage 80 percent of the international news in Latin America, for example, and in many countries a significant percentage of both national and regional news is thus controlled (Beltran & de Cardona, 1979, p. 39; Masmoudi, 1979, p. 172). (p. 178)

In his proposals for a meaningful debate on the future of the New World Information and Communication Order (NWICO), Vincent suggests achieving a more balanced flow of news through a fairer distribution of wealth, resources, and power. He also argues for "adequate communication flow monitoring" by both academics and communicators (p. 1997, 181). According to Vincent, studies about international news flow have been dominated by American scholars: "This literature still lacks solid theoretical insights and tends to be methodologically crude, with little hypothesis testing" (p. 188). Vincent adds that more research on news flow must be carried out, both at the level of individual countries and at the macro level of regional comparisons. Our study seeks to redress this situation by focusing on the Latin American media.

STUDIES ABOUT INTERNATIONAL NEWS IN THE LATIN AMERICAN PRESS

Latin America and the Caribbean (with a population of approximately 462 million people) are underdeveloped regions with many economic and social problems. These regions, however, play a dynamic role in the communication field. Most of the countries within these regions have strong media systems. Some of them, like Mexico, Brazil, Venezuela, and Argentina, are important exporters of television programs to many parts of the region and even to other parts of the world (that is, Asia, Europe, and Russia).

Salwen, Garrison and Buchman (1991) point out that the Latin American case has a number of

> regionally and even internationally prestigious newspapers.... Most of the best news-papers are published in the largest nations, including Mexico, Brazil, and Argentina. A number of them have earned reputations for defiantly challenging autocratic governments. But by and large, most of them are driven by market demand and are interested in providing their readers with both news and entertainment and earning profits, just as in any other industry. (p. 273)

Many newspapers in the most important countries of Latin America fulfill most or all of Salwen's criteria for prestigious newspapers. They are complete in international coverage, are concerned with interpretation, are graphically dignified, serious, lacking sensationalism, impartial, and imaginative (Merrill, cited in Salwen, Garrison, & Buchman, 1991).

Several studies have documented the coverage of Latin America or particular countries of the region in the U.S. press (compare Clement & Sonntag, 1989; Gozenbach, Arant, & Stevenson, 1992; Larson, McAnany, & Storey, 1986; Lozano, 1989a, 1989b; McAnany, 1983; Wallis & Baran, 1990). Larson, McAnany, and Storey's conclusions about the coverage of Latin America on U.S. network televi-sion are illustrative of the findings obtained by most of the studies:

> It is no exaggeration to say that any Latin American would be appalled to find how narrowly focused was the view through U.S. television news of his or her country. It is as if Mexico, for example, were only a land of oil wells, immigrants about to slip over the U.S. border, or erupting volcanoes and earthquakes. The sense of caricature presented by a view of Latin America derived solely from television news is disturb-ing, especially if we make two assumptions: first, that Latin America is an area of significant policy interest to the U.S. and second, that an informed public is an important element in the policy-making process toward the region.

Studies about international news in the Latin American press, in contrast, are scarce. A pioneering study was made by the Centro Internacional de Estudios Superiores de Periodismo para America Latina (CIESPAL; International Center for Higher Education Studies in Journalism for Latin America) in 1962. The CIESPAL project did a content analysis of two weeks of 28 different daily newspapers in 19 Latin American countries. It also studied the same two weeks of the *New York Times*, *Le Monde*, *The Times*, and *Izvestia* to make comparisons with the Western and the socialist press (CIESPAL, 1967).

The findings of this descriptive study showed some trends in the Latin American press that are still relevant today:

- weak coverage in each particular Latin American newspaper of other Latin American countries, despite the interdependence among these countries and their common problems;
- almost total dependence of all dailies on three transnational news agencies for international news: UPI and AP (79.3 percent of all foreign news) and AFP (13.4 percent); and
- a tendency of stressing trivial and nonimportant events when covering other Latin American countries.

From the year 1962 to the present, there have been no studies similar in magnitude about international news flow in the Latin American press. The closest to this kind of study is the one carried out in 1979 by UNESCO and the International Association for Media and Communication Research (IAMCR), which included three Latin American countries: Argentina, Brazil, and Mexico.

In this UNESCO/IAMCR study, Stevenson and Cole (1984) found that criticisms for not taking into account the local region were not warranted in any newspaper included in their analysis:

> The Mexican media give more attention to Latin America than to anywhere else; the Zambian media give more time and space to Africa.... On the average, about half of the foreign news in Third World media originates in the local geographic region. (p. 37)

News of the local region was most emphasized; news from Western industrialized countries received the second most attention; and news in Third World newspapers about other developing regions was largely invisible (Stevenson & Cole, 1984; see also Sreberny-Mohammadi, 1990). According to Stevenson and Cole's findings, it was the Third World, not the First World, that dominated the news of the Third World, including Argentina and Brazil. News in the Mexican press, on the other hand, was about even between the Third and the First worlds.

With respect to "bad news," Stevenson and Cole (1984) found that in general most international news was about politics, regardless of geographical origin. The coverage of accidents and disasters was similar in news about the First World and about the Third World. Sreberny-Mohammadi (1990) reaches a somewhat different conclusion. According to her, "news everywhere appears to be defined as the 'exceptional event,' with coups and catastrophes being newsworthy wherever they occur" (p. 13). Not all international communication scholars agree with the critical standpoint of NWICO advocates who reject the "coups and earthquakes" mentality of foreign news about the Third World. Wallis and Baran (1990), while supporting NWICO's plea for more news about developing countries, seemed to embrace the traditional view of focusing on "bad news" when covering Latin America:

Few foreign news editors would deny that coverage of South and Central America is less than satisfactory. It's a part of the world where military dictators have come and gone (though some have stayed on), where nations have staggering foreign debts (but one of them, Brazil, is becoming a major supplier of arms to Third World nations), where armed confrontation has been a constant feature of the 80s (Falklands/Malvinas, Grenada, Nicaragua, Panama, and so on), a part of the world which supplies drugs to the U.S. and Western Europe. No one could claim such areas were not of interest, that they do not warrant the general attention of those wanting to know about the world. (p. 184)

Regarding the dependence of Latin American countries on the Western news agencies, Sreberny-Mohammadi (1990) argues that "the methodology proved rather crude for distinguishing the source of a new item" (p. 13). Many of the international news items did not specify the originating source. Consequently, the news attributed to the "Big Four" was underestimated, and the degree of dependence on them was not reliable.

Finally, both Stevenson and Cole (1984) and Sreberny-Mohammadi (1990) point out the narrow range of topics emphasized by the press all over the world: hard news topics and actors such as politics, war, economics, and sports. Accidents and disasters were not big news in any part of the world.

In a content analysis of several of the leading Latin American TV news programs, Garcia Nunez de Caceres (1997) found that the United States received the greatest amount of time in their international coverage. News about the U.S. in the main TV news programs of Colombia, Brazil, Venezuela, Bolivia, Argentina, Peru, and Chile was more prominent and more balanced than news about other Latin American countries, which received the most coverage after the United States. Sports, politics, natural disasters, and accidents were the four topics receiving the most attention in the news programs.

Confirming the findings of newsmaking and media sociology studies about the predominance of official or political actors in the news, UNESCO/IAMCR found that between 25 and 60 percent of all actors in international news were political figures (Sreberny-Mohammadi, 1990). In a parallel analysis of the coverage of wire services to eight different regions of the world, Weaver and Wilhoit (1984) found that politicians were the most frequently mentioned actors in the news: "These parallel findings once again suggest that what is emphasized in Western news agencies is also, to some extent, what is emphasized in the press systems of many countries" (p. 176). Garcia Nunez de Caceres (1997) confirmed this in his study of the seven Latin American TV news programs: 74 percent of all actors in international news were politicians.

The remaining studies of international news in the Latin American press tend to be micro studies about particular newspapers in individual countries. In 1982, Rota and Rota (1987) carried out a content analysis of international news published by the leading newspapers in Mexico City. They found that only four categories accounted for 73 percent of all international news. These were the same four categories detected by the UNESCO/IAMCR study: sports, foreign governments and politics, economy, finance and labor relations, and war and defense. In addition, 90 percent of all international news items were supplied by news organizations based in the United States and Western Europe: "Such an extremely high percentage of information coming from American and Western European news sources clearly indicates a high level of dependency of the Mexican press on few and arguably homogeneous sources of information" (p. 171). Rota and Rota also determined that coverage of the United States and Western Europe in the leading Mexico City newspapers accounted for 55 percent of all the international information. News about Latin America represented 30 percent of all international news, showing a much more unbalanced situation than the one detected three years earlier by the UNESCO/IAMCR study for this country.

After this review of the literature, we can conclude that international news in the Latin American press has been scarcely studied. The findings of the few regional studies that exist show that Vincent's (1997) concern for the continuing need for a balanced flow of news through a fair distribution of wealth, resources, and power is still valid in the case of Latin American news media.

Our research questions in this study are closely related with the arguments, concerns, and findings discussed above:

How much attention do the selected Latin American newspapers pay to international news?

Is there a tendency to focus more attention on international news about the local region (other Latin American countries) or about the United States and Western Europe?

What topics receive more coverage in international news? Are topics different between news about the United States/Western Europe and Latin America or other developing regions?

How dependent are contemporary Latin American dailies on Western news agencies, particularly the "big four" (AP, UPI, AFP, and Reuters)? Are news sources more diversified than in the early 1960s and early 1980s?

METHOD

Sample of Daily Newspapers

This study was based on a content analysis of the leading daily newspapers in each of the following Latin American countries: Argentina, Brazil, Chile, Dominican Republic, Mexico, and Nicaragua. In addition, the sample included two Spanish newspapers in order to compare the amount and type of international news coverage in Latin American dailies with the press in an industrialized country with cultural and historic proximity to the region (see Table 5.1).

The dailies were selected because they were the elite papers with large circulation and prestige in their respective countries. Table 5.1 shows the name of each daily, the country of origin, and its declared circulation.

Time Sample

Following the tradition of content analysis of the world's press such as the one carried out by UNESCO/IAMCR in 1979 (see Sreberny-Mohammadi, 1990), this study was based on one chronological week and one composite week. The chronological week was selected in order to analyze the international coverage in an actual week of the Latin American press and to detect general emphasis and tendencies. The composite week was included to compensate for a possible break of the normal pattern of international news coverage by extraordinary events. The chronological week was from May 12 to May 18, 1997. The composite week spanned the end of May through the beginning of July (May 19 and 27; June 4, 12, 20, and 28; July 6).

Research Teams

This project was conducted on a regional basis with the support of the Asociacion Latinoamericana de Investigadores de la Comunicacion (Latin American Associa-

TABLE 5.1.
Names, Countries of Origin, and Circulation of Daily Newspapers
Included in the Study

Newspapers	City	Country	Declared circulation
Clarin	Buenos Aires	Argentina	800,000 (weekdays) 1,500,000 (Sundays) (Declared)
La Nueva Provincia	Bahia Blanca	Argentina	37,500 (Declared)
Zero Hora	Porto Alegre	Brazil	141,000 (weekdays) 260,000 (Sundays) (Certified)
El Mercurio	Santiago	Chile	Unavailable
Listin Diario	Santo Domingo	Dominican Republic	Unavailable
Excelsior	Mexico City	Mexico	200,000 (Declared)
El Norte	Monterrey	Mexico	138,878 (weekdays/Certified) 154,451 (Sundays/Certified)
La Tribuna	Managua	Nicaragua	Unavailable
El Pais	Madrid	Spain	532,887 (Certified)
Vanguardia	Barcelona	Spain	239,462 (Certified)

tion of Communication Researchers) and the Graduate Program in Communication of the Instituto Tecnologico y de Estudios Superiores de Monterrey. There were two research teams: one in Monterrey, Mexico, and one in Barcelona, Spain.

Each research team received a set of general instructions describing the method of sampling and the categories of analysis, and each was responsible for collecting the data from the newspapers assigned to them. The project was coordinated in Monterrey, Mexico.

Unit of Analysis and Main Categories

The international news item was the unit of analysis. News briefs, news stories, feature stories, op-ed pieces, and columns dealing with events outside of the home country were included in the definition of an international news item. Letters from readers, obituaries, paid information, political cartoons, and international news items in sections of the paper dealing with sports, entertainment, culture, and tourism were not included. Situations or events in other countries dealing explicitly with national actors or policies were coded as "Home news abroad," and not as international news. All individuals or institutions quoted explicitly in the international news item were included in the definition of "actors in the international news item."

There was no sampling of units of analysis. All international news items and actors included in each of the 14 editions of each daily were coded. Each item was coded on the following variables: origin of the news item, country the news item focused on, length of the item, source, topic, and genre of the international news item.

Field Work

Two pretests were carried out in order to design a coding schema that would be useful and reliable in accounting for all the differences and kinds of emphases, topics, and tendencies in the sample of newspapers. In addition, three reliability checks were done to ensure that the coding book was clear and that each coder followed the same criteria for coding each item. The reliability checks for all variables reported values of at least .80.

The research teams in Barcelona coded their newspapers and entered the data in spreadsheet files. The Monterrey team was in charge of receiving all data files, merging them in a single database and processing the statistical analysis of the data.

RESULTS

The attention paid by the sample of Latin American and Spanish dailies to international news was not homogeneous. On average, each paper printed about 20 international news stories per day, but the figures ranged from only eight stories in the Argentinian daily *Nueva Provincia,* to 36 in the Mexican newspaper *El Norte* (see Table 5.2). It is interesting to note that some local newspapers published in the provinces, such as *El Norte* in Monterrey, Mexico, and *Vanguardia* in Barcelona, Spain, printed more international news stories than did the national dailies published in the capitals of countries such as Argentina, Nicaragua, and Chile. Foreign coverage was higher in Mexican and Spanish newspapers and lower in the local dailies of Brazil and Argentina and the national newspaper of Chile. Surprisingly, *Listin Diario,* from the Dominican Republic, devoted more space to foreign news than newspapers from bigger countries like Mexico, Argentina, and Chile. Compared to 1979 data (Sreberny-Mohammadi, 1990), *El Clarin* and *Excelsior* decreased the number of international news stories per day from 20 and 39, to 13 and 32, respectively.

Table 5.3 shows that all dailies, except *Zero Hora* from Brazil and *El Norte* from Mexico, paid more attention to other Latin American countries than to the United States. In *El Clarin* of Argentina, 37 percent of the international news was devoted to other Latin American countries in contrast to only 11 percent devoted to the United States. The Chilean *El Mercurio*, illustrates different results. The percentages were 25 percent to Latin America and 8 percent to the U.S. As to *Listin Diario* of the Dominican Republic, the percentages were 37 percent to Latin America and 17 percent to the U.S., and in the Nicaraguan *La Tribuna*, the percentages were 49 percent to Latin America and 15 percent to the U.S. The Mexican newspapers, despite their country's proximity to the United States and the existing commercial

TABLE 5.2.
Total Number of International News Stories in Latin American and
Spanish Daily Newspapers

Newspaper	News stories	Total square centimeters	# stories per day	Total square centimeters per day	Mean
El Clarín (Argentina)	185	56389	13.21	4028	304.8
Nueva Provincia (Argentina)	107	19244	7.64	1375	179.9
ZeroHora (Brazil)	138	41954	9.85	2997	302.6
El Mercurio (Chile)	258	40403[a]	19.84	3108	156.6
Listín Diario (Dominican Republic)	344	87661[a]	26.46	6743	254.8
EL Norte (Mexico)	505	146460	36.07	10461	290
Excelsior (Mexico)	449	79205	32.07	5658	176.4
La Tribuna (Nicaragua)	198	44174[b]	16.5	3681	290.9
El País (Spain)	273	92159	19.5	6583	267.9
Vanguardia (Spain)	269	73412	19.21	5244	342.6

a= Of 13 editions instead of 14.
b= Of 12 editions instead of 14.

TABLE 5.3.
Origin of International News in Latin American and Spanish Daily Newspapers: May-July 1997

Region	El Clarín Argentina	Nueva Provincia Argentina	ZeroHora Brazil	El Mercurio Chile	Listín Diario Dominican Republic	El Norte Mexico	Excelsior Mexico	La Tibuna Nicaragua	El País Spain	Vanguardia Spain
Latin America	37%	25%	6%	25%	37%	24%	30	49	10	5
Europe	32	39	31	38	23	24	22	16	51	59
Africa	6	12	6	6	6	6	5	8	11	12
Asia	13	9	25	21	14	18	18	10	19	18
Oceanía			1	1	0	0	0			
United States	11	13	32	8	17	27	22	15	7	3
Canada	1	1	1	0	1	0	1	1		
N=	(185)	(107)	(68)	(258)	(344)	(505)	(449)	(198)	(273)	(269)

Note: Columns may not total 100% because of rounding.

agreement between the two nations (the North American Free Trade Agreement), were about even in their coverage of both regions. Mexico City's daily *Excelsior* devoted more attention to other Latin American countries than to the United States; *El Norte*, published in a northern Mexican nation with close economic ties to the U.S., dedicated 27 percent of its international news to the U.S. versus 24 percent to other Latin American countries—a very small difference indeed. *Zero Hora*, of Brazil, was the only newspaper that provided more coverage to the U.S. than to other Latin American countries. Only 6 percent of their international news was devoted to other countries in the region. These findings suggest that CIESPAL's conclusions in 1962 about weak coverage of the region in each particular Latin American newspaper were not warranted according to the sample of 1997 newspapers. Our data coincides with Stevenson and Cole's (1984) findings regarding the importance of foreign news originating in the local geographic region in Third World media. According to them, coverage in 1979 of the local region dominated the news of the Third World, including Argentina and Brazil. News in the Mexican press was about even between the Third and the First worlds. Eighteen years later, the situation seems to be very similar. Coverage of other Third World regions, as in the UNESCO 1979 study, was very low. In all 10 dailies, news about Europe was higher than news about Asia or Africa. All dailies, with the exception of the two Mexican newspapers, devoted equal or more attention to Europe than to the U.S., despite the strategic importance of the latter in the region.

In general, most international news in all of the dailies was about national politics and crisis news (violent conflicts, uprisings, guerrilla activities, drug trafficking). Table 5.4 shows that other crisis news, such as internal political crisis, corruption in political life, and so on, was also prominent in most of the papers. While the first topic (national politics) coincides with UNESCO's findings for 1979, the second and the third topics show a tendency to highlight crisis news, validating NWICO's concerns.

Table 5.5 shows that developing countries, unfortunately, received more negative coverage than industrialized countries. Sixty-six percent of the news about Africa was negative, 54 percent of Asia, and 51 percent of Latin America. In contrast, only 14 percent of Canada's, 25 percent of Europe's, and 36 percent of the U.S.'s coverage was negative. These findings confirm NWICO's claims of qualitative imbalance in international news that favors industrialized nations.

In 1962, the study of CIESPAL found a heavy dependence of all Latin American dailies on three transnational news agencies for international news: UPI and AP (79.3 percent) and AFP (13.4 percent). In the late 1970s, Beltran and Fox (cited in Vincent, 1997, p. 178) concluded that U.S. news agencies managed 80 percent of the international news in Latin America. In contrast, our study found a diversified situation, with no clear predominance of any of the "Big Four" agencies. *El Clarin* (Argentina), *El Mercurio* (Chile), *Listin Diario* (Dominican Republic), and *El Norte* and *Excelsior* (Mexico) attributed their foreign news to a variety of agencies, including their own correspondents or envoys in the case of *El Clarin*, *El Mercurio*,

TABLE 5.4.
Topics in international news in Latin American and Spanish daily newspapers: May-July 1997

Topic	El Clarin Argentina	Nueva Provincia Argentina	ZeroHora Brazil	El Mercurio Chile	Listin Diario Dominican Republic	El Norte Mexico	Excelsior Mexico	La Tribuna Nicaragua	El Pais Spain	Vanguardia Spain
Diplomatic and political activities between countries	10%	6%	1%	8%	6%	6%	12%	12%	13%	16%
Diplomatic and political conflicts between countries	5	5	3	3	3	3	6	5	4	2
National politics	22	16	19	31	19	12	18	13	21	35
Conflicts, internal crisis, corruption in political life	17	10	3	5	4	9	8	5	13	12
Violent conflicts, uprisings, guerrilla, drug trafficking	11	12	12	11	9	13	9	16	14	11
Peace treaties or initiatives, negotiations with guerrilla groups, positive results in the war versus drugs	3	3	5	6	6	4	4	5	5	6
Economic affairs	9	1	2	6	4	4	4	2	4	2
Commercial agreements, economic integration between Latin American countries		1	1	3						
Economic problems, unemployment, poverty, corruption, strikes and protests		1	2	1	1	1	4	1		
International aid for disasters, poverty, or hunger							1			

	(185)	(107)	(138)	(258)	(344)	(505)	(446)	(198)	(273)	(266)
Economic aid for industrial development, education, family planning, and so on				4	1	1	1		1	1
Social problems in general, health, housing, illiteracy		1	1							
Education, health and family planning campaigns, social security, and services	2	1	1	2	1					
Crime	2	12	1	2	2	6	8	2		
Political violence, torture, disturbs	4	5	3	3	3	8	7	8	7	5
Accidents and natural disasters	1	9	2	1	6	2	3	1	1	
Religion	1	3	2							
Science, technology, medicine	3	5	3	1	2	2	3	1		
Sports	7	3	2	3	6					
Show business, people, movies, radio, TV		4	4	1	2	1				
Tourism, travel	2	3	4	3	3	1	1			
Ecology, environment, conservationism, pollution problems, or solutions	1						5			
Human interest, odd happenings, animals, society	1	5	1	1	1	1				
Illegal immigration			1	2	2					
Other topics	14	22	4	11	20	16	12	5	16	6
N=	(185)	(107)	(138)	(258)	(344)	(505)	(446)	(198)	(273)	(266)

Note: Columns may not total 100% because of rounding.

TABLE 5.5.
Topic of International News by Region of Origin in Latin American and Spanish Daily Newspapers: May–July 1997

Topic (global)	Latin Am	Europe	Africa	Asia	Oceania	USA	Canada
Positive or neutral	48%	72%	33%	43%	80%	53%	86%
Negative	51	25	66	54	36	14	
Other (not defined)	1	3	1	3	20	11	
Topic							
Diplomatic and political activities between countries	5	15	1	9	10		
Diplomatic and political conflicts between countries	5	2	2	6	4	7	
National politics	21	30	11	16	7	79	
Conflicts, internal crisis, corruption in political life	12	9	16	7	6		
Violent conflicts, uprisings, guerrilla, drug trafficking	9	5	36	20	8	7	
Peace treaties or initiatives, negotiations with guerrilla groups, positive results in the war versus drugs	5	3	13	6	4		
Economic affairs	4	8	1	1	3		
Commercial agreements, economic integration between Latin American countries	3	1	1		3	7	

	(577)	(797)	(178)	(413)	(5)	(381)	(6)
Economic problems, unemployment, poverty, corruption, strikes and protests	4	2	1	1	1		
Social problems in general, health, housing, illiteracy	1		1	1			
Education, health and family planning campaigns, social security and services	1	1			2		
Crime	5	3	3	2	9		
Political violence, torture, disturbs	9	4	8	7	4		
Accidents and natural disasters	2	1	1	5	2		
Religion	1	2	1	3	1		
Science, technology, medicine	1	2	1	20	8		
Show business, people, movies, radio, TV	1	4	2	2	3		
Ecology, environment, conservationism, pollution problems, or solutions				20	3		
Human interest, odd happenings, animals, society	5	4	3	5	40	9	
Other topics	3	2	1	4	20	9	
N=	(577)	(797)	(178)	(413)	(5)	(381)	(6)

Note: Columns may not total 100% because of rounding.

TABLE 5.6.
Percentage of International News Stories Attributed to Each News Agency by the Latin American and Spanish Daily Newspapers: May–July 1997

Agency	El Clarin Argentina	Nueva Provincia Argentina	Zero Hora Brazil	El Mercurio Chile	Listin Diario Dominican Republic	El Norte Mexico	Excelsior Mexico	La Tribuna Nicaragua	El Pais Spain	Vanguardia Spain
Correspondent or envoy	45%	3%	6%	12%	2%	10%	14%		72%	62%
AP	1		19	23	7	8	1		1	1
UPI				3	1	5				
AFP	4			20	33	7	12	30	5	11
Reuter	4	10	1	13	5	4	6	5	5	
EFE	4	34	12	14	7	9	53	7		
Unspecified agencies			5	2	1	5	3			
Correspondent and agencies						1	6			
Other USA agencies or services	3		1	10	4	1				
Other European agencies or services			7	17	7		1			
Two or more international agencies	21	33	7	1	31	33	1	7		
National agency	8	19			7	5				
Unidentified	9	2	92	3	6	13	3	3	4	
N=	(185)	(107)	(146)	(258)	(344)	(505)	(449)	(198)	(273)	

Note: Columns may not total 100% because of rounding.

Excelsior, and *El Norte* (Table 5.6). However, compared with the Spanish dailies (over 60 percent of their international news was gathered by their own correspondents or envoys), the Latin American newspapers were more dependent on international agencies. *La Tribuna* (Nicaragua) and *Zero Hora* (Brazil) were less diversified in their sources. The Argentinian and Mexican newspapers had the largest number of news stories attributed to more than one agency, showing a positive tendency to combine different sources in single stories. However, the "Big Four," plus the Spanish international agency EFE, accounted for 85 percent of international news in *La Tribuna*, 59 percent in *Listin Diario*, and 52 percent in *El Mercurio*. Only one Latin American newspaper, *El Clarin* of Argentina, gathered a sizable percentage of its international news from its own correspondents or envoys. Consequently, although Latin American dailies showed some improvement in their use and diversification of news sources, they still relied heavily on the "Big Five."

DISCUSSION

The present findings suggest that the eight Latin American and two Spanish dailies pay considerable attention to foreign news, an average of 20 news stories per day. Most of the Latin American dailies devoted more coverage to other countries in their local region than to the United States, although three dailies paid more attention to Europe than to their own region. These findings suggest that NWICO's and cultural imperialists' concerns regarding a predominance of news about the metropolitan center of the region and a neglect of other Latin American countries is not warranted in most of the papers. In fact, our findings are similar to those obtained from the 1979 UNESCO study by Stevenson and Cole (1984): Foreign news originating from the local geographic region is more common than foreign news originating in industrialized countries. The neglected regions, however, were other Third World regions such as Africa and Asia, a finding similar to Stevenson and Cole's, which makes NWICO's plea for a balanced flow of information still somewhat relevant.

International news in Latin American and Spanish newspapers is primarily about national politics and crisis news. While the former may provide a more neutral image of the countries involved, the latter may promote the undesirable images that NWICO and many international scholars have fought. Our findings support the claims of NWICO in that international news about Third World countries has a tendency to be negative. Only 24 percent of all news about Europe and 36 percent of all news about the U.S. was negative. In contrast, 66 percent of all news about Africa and 51 percent of all news about Latin America was negative. These findings show a tendency in the Latin American dailies to present industrialized countries in a better light than developing countries. The international coverage of other Latin American countries does not seem to be adequate in regard to the goals of economic and political integration of the region. Only a meager 3 percent of the news was about commercial agreements and economic integration between Latin American countries. The space devoted to diplomatic and political activities between countries was higher for Europe and the United States than for Latin America.

In general, Latin American newspapers seemed to have diversified their sources of international information in comparison to the 1960s and 1970s, but they still seem to depend on a few transnational agencies like AFP, EFE, and AP. They are a long way from reaching the percentage of foreign coverage gathered by their own correspondents in papers published in industrialized countries such as Spain or the United States.

The role of Latin American newspapers in the movement toward globalization in the region, and the formation of decision-making processes and a public opinion related to the international context is still waiting to be fully accounted for. But, for the time being, the evidence from content analyses like this suggests that Latin American newspapers continue to be major players in the dissemination of news about their own region and about the world. Unfortunately, their role may not be as positive as the region may need.

REFERENCES

CIESPAL. (1967). *Dos semanas en la prensa de America Latina* [Two weeks in the Latin American press]. Quito, Ecuador: Author.

Clement, N. C., & Sonntag, I. L. (1989). U.S. periodical reporting on Mexico. *Frontera Norte, 1*, 91–104.

Garcia Nunez de Caceres, J. F. (1997). *Informacion internacional en siete noticieros latinoamericanos de television* [International news in seven Latin American television news programs]. Unpublished master's thesis, Tecnologico de Monterrey, Monterrey, Mexico.

Gozenbach, W. J., Arant, M. D., & Stevenson, R. L. (1992). The world of U.S. network television news: Eighteen years of international and foreign news coverage. *Gazette, 50*, 53–72.

Larson, J. F., McAnany, E. G., & Storey, J. D. (1986). News of Latin America on network television, 1972–1981: A Northern perspective on the Southern Hemisphere. *Critical Studies in Mass Communication, 3*, 169–183.

Lozano, J. C. (1989a). Imagenes de Mexico en la prensa norteamericana: Analisis comparativo de la cobertura de Mexico en Time y Newsweek de 1980 a 1986 [Images of Mexico un the U.S. press: A comparative analysis of Mexican coverage in *Time* and *Newsweek*, 1980–1986]. *Comunicacion y Sociedad, 7*, 77–102.

Lozano, J. C. (1989b). Issues and sources in Spanish-language TV: A comparison of *Noticiero Univision* and *NBC Evening News. Frontera Norte, 1*, 151–174.

McAnany, E. (1983). Television and crisis: Ten years of network news coverage of Central America, 1972–1981. *Media, Culture & Society, 5*, 199–212.

Rota, J., & Rota, G. S. (1987). A content analysis of international news published by the leading newspapers in Mexico City. *Studies in Latin American Popular Culture, 6,* 165–182.

Salwen, M. B., Garrison, B., & Buchman, R. T. (1991). Latin America and the Caribbean. In J. C. Merrill (Ed.), *Global journalism: Survey of international communication* (2nd ed., pp. 267–310). New York: Longman.

Sreberny-Mohammadi, A. (1990). The "world of the news." In L. J. Martin & R. E. Hiebert (Eds.), *Current issues in international communication* (pp. 8–17). New York: Longman.

Stevenson, R. L., & Cole, R. (1984). Patterns of foreign news. In R. L. Stevenson & D. L. Shaw (Eds.), *Foreign news and the New World Information Order* (pp. 37–62). Ames, IA: Iowa State University Press.

Vincent, R. (1997). The future of the debate: Setting and agenda for a New World Information and Communication Order. In P. Golding & P. Harris (Eds.), *Beyond cultural imperialism: Globalization, communication & the new international order.* Thousand Oaks, CA: Sage.

Wallis, R., & Baran, S. J. (1990). *The known world of broadcast news: International news and the electronic media.* London: Routledge.

Weaver, D. H., & Wilhoit, G. C. (1984). Foreign news in the Western agencies. In R. L. Stevenson & D. L. Shaw (Eds.), *Foreign news and the New World Information Order* (pp. 153–185). Ames, IA: Iowa State University Press.

6

A War by Any Other Name: A Textual Analysis of Falklands/Malvinas War Coverage in U.S. and Latin American Newspapers

Carolina Acosta-Alzuru
Elizabeth P. Lester Roushanzamir
University of Georgia

On April 2, 1982, Argentina invaded the Falkland/Malvinas Islands. This action created an international controversy that soon escalated into a full-fledged war with Great Britain. The invasion was received in Argentina with ecstatic jubilation. In contrast, reactions in Great Britain ranged from shock to wounded pride (Beck, 1988). The end of the crisis came 10 weeks later, with Argentina's surrender on June 14. "It was a textbook example of a limited war—limited in time, in location, in objectives and in means" (Freedman, 1982, p. 196).

Ostensibly, the conflict appeared straightforward: The two sides were clearly defined and the conflict had a definite beginning and an unambiguous end. However, the dispute that was at its root, the question of sovereignty over the archipelago, remains unresolved.

The Falklands/Malvinas War became a major news story and was followed with interest all around the world. People's knowledge and perceptions of the conflict were heavily dependent on media accounts of the events. The media construct and define the events for their audience, assigning to these events different degrees of importance. In a very important sense, news stories are versions of reality. They are narratives that "acquire layers of meanings in the course of their use in everyday life; some are authentic, others are contrived and all are constructed" (Aulich, 1992, p. 3). Furthermore, media coverage of war is a significant topic since the media almost always play a meaningful role in the conflict. There are tensions between the need for secrecy of the military, on the one hand, and the need for publicity of the media and the citizens right to know and be informed on the other.

In the tradition of cultural studies, this chapter explores how the Falklands/Malvinas War was constructed by four major newspapers: *The New York Times* (United States), *El Mercurio* (Chile), *Excelsior* (Mexico), and *El Universal* (Venezuela). The media aspects of this conflict have been explored from the British side (Adams, 1986; Greenberg, 1983; Harris, 1983; Hooper, 1982; Kennedy, 1993), and from the Argentine side (Caistor, 1992; Fox, 1984). But how was this war covered in other countries? Is there a relationship between foreign policy and international news coverage?

This study addresses the relationships between: a) news coverage and foreign policy; b) news coverage and the construction of events; and c) news coverage and the "available stock of meanings" (Hall, 1975, p. 12) that the newspapers assumed and used in their construction of the Falklands/Malvinas War.

CONTEXT

The Falklands/Malvinas War

The Falkland/Malvinas Islands are located in the South Atlantic Ocean, 300 miles east of the Argentine coast, 340 miles northeast of Cape Horn (Rasor, 1992). The population in 1982 was about 1,800, most of them living in the capital of Port Stanley/Puerto Argentino. The "kelpers," as the inhabitants are called, in reference to the seaweed that is copious in the waters around the islands (Rasor, 1992), are almost totally British, and "almost totally separated, by both language and politics, from the continent" (Strebeigh, 1981, p. 86).

The confrontation that riveted the world from April to mid-June of 1982 was the escalation of a 150-year old dispute between Argentina and the United Kingdom over the Falkland/Malvinas Islands. The roots of the dispute lie on the differences between the Argentine and British versions of the history of these islands.[1] Both sides claim discovery and in consequence ownership of the archipelago.

In 1965, the United Nations called on Argentina and Great Britain to negotiate over their respective claims to the islands. Another UN resolution urging a settlement of the dispute was called in 1974. Peter Beck (1991) noted that in the beginning of 1982, the Falklands/Malvinas question occupied number 242 on the list of priorities of the British foreign office. Meanwhile, the issue had become the number one priority for the Argentine government since December 1981 (Cardoso, Kirschenbaum, & Van der Kooy, 1983).

On Thursday, April 1, 1982, British intelligence reports indicated a likely Argentine invasion of the Falkland/Malvinas Islands (Adams, 1986). Great Britain took several diplomatic steps, including requesting the United States to convince the Argentine government against invading (Haig, 1984). However, Argentina attacked and by April 2, it had seized the capital of Port Stanley. The next day, the United Nations Security Council passed Resolution 502, demanding Argentina's withdrawal.[2] Meanwhile, Argentine forces captured the South Georgia Islands and Britain announced the formation of a task force.

Latin American countries supported Argentina's claims over the islands. However, they were divided in their judgment of the invasion. One side, represented by Brazil, Chile, Colombia, and Mexico, insisted that the procedure was unacceptable to the international community. The other position, exemplified by Peru and Venezuela, argued that by avoiding negotiations for 150 years, Great Britain had left the Argentines with no other recourse than the use of force.

On April 8, U.S. Secretary of State Alexander Haig began his "shuttle diplomacy" efforts (Haig, 1984). His mediation attempts failed and on April 30, the U.S. openly sided with Great Britain, provoking feelings of betrayal in most Latin American nations (Chang-Rodríguez, 1991). The next day, Britain started the naval bombardment of East Falkland/Isla Soledad's airstrips. The Falklands/Malvinas crisis had escalated into a full-fledged war. At this point, Latin American nations rallied around Argentina in support of its cause and classified Great Britain as the "real aggressor" in the crisis (Kirkpatrick, 1989–1990). Only Colombia and Chile remained neutral.

On the second day of fighting, the Argentine cruiser *General Belgrano* was sunk by British torpedoes while outside the exclusion zone. Two days later, Britain lost the ship *HMS Sheffield* to Exocet missiles.

British forces landed on Port San Carlos on May 21, establishing a beach head from which to advance toward Port Stanley/Puerto Argentino. On May 29, Britain captured Goose Green and Port Darwin, taking 1,500 prisoners (Rasor, 1992). British advances were reflected in a hardening of its diplomatic position. On June 4, it vetoed Argentina's call for a cease fire in the United Nations (Adams, 1986).

June 12 marked the beginning of the battle for Port Stanley/Puerto Argentino, which ended with Argentina's surrender on June 14 and the reoccupation of the islands by Great Britain. But the war's end did not bring a solution to the sovereignty dispute. The islands are still claimed by Argentina, based on what they define as their "historical rights." The British base their claims on the principle of self-determination of the islanders. The matter remains unresolved.

Mexico and *Excelsior*

In 1929 different Mexican revolutionary factions came together and formed the Partido Revolucionario Institucional (PRI; Institutional Revolutionary Party). Since then, the PRI has dominated Mexican politics in particular, and Mexican life in general. It is the longest governing party in the world (Heuvel & Dennis, 1995).

Alisky (1981) classified Mexico under the category "nations with media guidance" (p. 27). Mainstream media rally around the power elite, the established leadership, the PRI. Historically, the Mexican government has given precedence to the Revolution's goals: land reform, development, industrialization, and the nurturing of Mexican nationalism. Press freedom and other political freedoms were not among these goals.

In the 1980s, a third of the Mexican adult population was unable to read. Less than 20 percent of the population read newspapers. Moreover, 60 percent of the total daily newspaper circulation was concentrated in the three large urban centers: Mexico City, Guadalajara, and Monterrey (Alisky, 1981).

After a slight loss in circulation, *Excelsior* remained the leading daily in Mexico at the beginning of the 1980s[3] (Alisky, 1981). Its layout is old-fashioned, characterized by dense writing and few photos; it is not reader-friendly. Front pages usually carry a banner headline and at least 15 stories, all of which have small deck headlines (subheads set in a smaller type size) and jump to the inside of the paper, where they can still jump from one page to another. International news usually come from AP, UPI, or AFP and, occasionally, special correspondents file stories.

During the year of the Falklands/Malvinas War, Mexico was suffering the rigors of a grave economic crisis. President Miguel de la Madrid was forced to devaluate the peso, nationalize the banks, and establish monetary exchange controls (Chang-Rodríguez, 1991). However, during the 10 weeks of the war, media attention was focused on the conflict. At one point, *Excelsior* had two special correspondents stationed in Buenos Aires and one in London.

Chile and *El Mercurio*

Argentina and Chile have many things in common: a population with a strong European inheritance, a very high literacy rate (90 percent), and a border. Chile and Argentina have a territorial dispute regarding the Beagle Channel that dates back to 1843 (Embassy of the Argentine Republic, 1978). At times, both countries have called each other "expansionists" and in 1978 they were on the brink of war (Bruno, 1981).

It was widely believed in Chile that Argentina could have invaded the Beagle Channel islands instead of the Falkland/Malvinas Islands (Sanfuentes, 1992).

Although Chile condemned the invasion as an act of unwarranted aggression from Argentina, it later declared and maintained a neutral position throughout the conflict. In August 1973, General Augusto Pinochet toppled President Salvador Allende, assumed power, and enforced repressive anti-Communist policies in every avenue of Chilean life, including the freedoms of expression and press. The country was (and is still) basically run by a small group of families who are decision-makers in the government, the military, the business sector, and the media. These elites were closely associated to the Pinochet government.

El Mercurio, which was considered one of the best newspapers in Latin America (Merrill, 1968), has now a somewhat tarnished image because of its association with the Pinochet government. The paper is owned by the Edwards, a leading Anglo-Chilean family. *El Mercurio* follows a conservative, pro-establishment line. During the Pinochet era, only those newspapers owned by the Edwards and Picó families were allowed to be published (Heuvel & Dennis, 1995).

El Mercurio features three pages of news and editorials in its first section, followed by an extensive section of society pages, whose presence is an indication of the importance of the elites in the country's life. International news typically appear at the end of the first section and are largely drawn from wire services, especially AP, UPI, AFP, ANSA of Italy, and EFE of Spain.

Venezuela and *El Universal*

Alisky (1981) classified Venezuela and Costa Rica as the only Latin American nations "with media freedom" (p. 122). In 1982, Venezuela was still considered Latin America's wealthiest nation in terms of annual income. Oil rich and with a democratic tradition dating back to 1958, Venezuela boasted the freest press in Latin America.

With an 88 percent literacy rate and a 75 percent urban population (Alisky, 1981), it is no surprise that the two most influential dailies are based in Venezuala's capital, Caracas: *El Universal* and *El Nacional*. *El Universal* does not have an explicit editorial line, but prints a variety of views on its op-ed pages (Heuvel & Dennis, 1995). However, it is perceived as a conservative paper in contrast with the more liberal *El Nacional*.

El Universal's front page typically features at least 15 stories. Most of them consist of only the headline and deck headlines; the text is found in the inside pages. Headline size indicates the story's relative importance to the reader. "Kicker" lines are consistently used to clarify or qualify the headlines. International news stories are featured on the first section of the newspaper. These stories are exclusively from news services, especially from AP, UPI, AFP, Reuters, ANSA, EFE, DPA, and TASS of the Soviet Union.

Venezuela shares borders with Colombia, Brazil, and Guyana. In the past 150 years, border disputes have been a factor in Venezuela's history. However, the most important one is the ongoing polemic with eastern neighbor Guyana, a former British colony. In 1970, 12 years before the Falklands/Malvinas War, Guyana and Venezuela signed the Port of Spain Protocol, by which the controversy entered a dormant stage (Singh, 1982). In March 1982, before Argentina invaded the Falkland/Malvinas Islands, the Venezuelan government announced that it would not renew the protocol (Braveboy-Wagner, 1984; Fenty, 1982).

Although Venezuela has never resorted to warfare in any of its territorial disputes, from time to time some voices rise to favor a military solution, especially to the Guyana problem. Militaristic talk increased during the Falklands/Malvinas War. Venezuela took a definite pro-Argentina stance during the conflict. More importantly, coverage of this war was immersed in and deeply influenced by the controversy with Guyana.

The United States and *The New York Times*

The United States were immediately drawn into the Falklands dispute. Initial responses showed a lot of ambivalence from the U.S. government. A neutral stance was chosen at the beginning and attempts at mediation were held by Secretary of State Alexander Haig (Rasor, 1992).

Although the U.S. government never took a stance regarding what it defined as "the substance of the dispute," which is the sovereignty issue,[4] eventually the United States supported Great Britain in the conflict. This support was translated into sanctions against Argentina and British access to American weapons, logistics, intelligence, communications, and base facilities (Weinberger, 1992).

In 1980, *The New York Times* was ranked as "the best or near-best paper in the United States" (Merrill, 1980, p. 220). Of all American newspapers, it is the closest to being a newspaper of record. A definite agenda-setter, many of its readers are very influential in American life. It also boasts an international readership, which makes it a member of the world's elite press (Merrill, 1980). One of its strengths is its international news coverage, which is considered unrivalled. Thoroughness characterizes *The New York Times*. Its coverage of the Falklands/Malvinas controversy was no exception. Special correspondents in London, Buenos Aires, and Washington provided eyewitness accounts from these places.

The New York Times's front page presents five to seven stories that usually jump to the inside pages. Differences in type and placement assign degrees of importance to the news. The lead story is always placed at the top right-hand side. Banner headlines are unusual; therefore, when one of them is present, the story is automatically emphasized. Although by 1980 the *Times* had editorially supported eight democrats and four republicans for president, Merrill (1980) described its editorial line as "independent."

FOREIGN NEWS AND FOREIGN POLICY

Many researchers have dedicated their scholarship to finding explanations for foreign news coverage patterns. Some of them believe that ideology is a strong influence

(Gerbner, 1964; Graber, 1989; Hallin, 1987). National interest has also been stressed as an influential factor (Chomsky, 1987; Herman & Chomsky, 1988; Skurnik, 1981) as well as cultural and geographical proximity (Galtung & Ruge, 1965; Graber, 1989).

Wang (1992) compared the media coverage from six different countries of the 1989 Chinese students demonstration. Her results indicated that political ideology and diplomatic sensitivity or government interest influenced the overall direction of the coverage and its actual content and themes. These findings seem consistent with Vilanilam's (1983), who studied and compared the influence of foreign policy in the U.S. and India's press systems. Vilanilam concluded that geographic proximity of the reported country was not as important as foreign policy significance to the reporting country's press system. These findings direct us to study the delicate relationship between foreign news and foreign policy.

Bullion (1983) analyzed press roles in foreign policy reporting and concluded that "the more authoritarian the society, the more compatible or complementary are press and diplomacy, and the more the press serves as a policy instrument" (p. 187). The implication is that in the United States, a libertarian society, the press seldom serves as a policy instrument.

However, both Welch (1972) and Malek (1988/89) found a noticeable similarity between the U.S. foreign policy toward Indochina and Iran and *The New York Times*'s editorial stance. Moreover, Shoemaker, Danielian and Brendlinger (1991) found that events that occur in nations politically and/or economically significant to the U.S. are more likely to be considered newsworthy. If this is true, then the Administration definitely sets the agenda for foreign news.

Herman and Chomsky (1988) believe that the U.S. media do not perform the normative watchdog role for foreign policy that people assume the media play. They described a propaganda model, or set of "filters" through which the premises of discourse and interpretation are fixed. For Herman and Chomsky, the media actually contribute to the preservation of the status quo by forming a seamless alliance between corporate and government interests. Rachlin (1988) also stresses the existence of a hegemonic culture that fixes, postulates, and establishes frames of reference for the perception and interpretation of reality. In 1993, Herman analyzed paired case studies regarding foreign policy performance, human rights violation, plane shoot-downs, and Third World elections and how these were reported in the media. He concluded that "the mainstream media tend to follow a state agenda in reporting on foreign policy" (p. 45). Lester (1994) has also done work supporting these contentions.

CULTURAL STUDIES: UNITED KINGDOM, UNITED STATES, AND LATIN AMERICA

British cultural studies shifts communication research from a behavioral to an ideological perspective (Hall, 1982); thus, the research framework focuses on the ideological role of the media, which are viewed as a crucial cultural and ideological force. Further, the reconstitution of the ideas and behaviors shared by the people who produce and consume the cultural texts of a particular society is achieved by analyzing these texts and consequently the society's culture.

British cultural scholars stress that there is no way to know reality directly; it is the effects of reality that we study. Reality is defined, and its definition cannot be divorced from ideology. It cannot be divorced from power either. Who defines reality? How are events signified in a particular way? Who decides what code will be used for this signification/definition? There is a power structure that determines the representation/definition of reality. This representation/definition is in tune with a dominant ideology. Alternative representations/definitions are treated from the dominant ideology's perspective and tend to be silenced, distorted, or presented as deviant from the "norm."

Budd, Entman, and Steinman (1990) argue that American cultural studies are not as critical as their British counterpart. American cultural scholars avoid Marxist analysis and assign more power to the audience. They also shy away from political-economic approaches, which minimize the commodification of audiences. Ideology is not at the center of the analysis: "...a form of cultural studies that does not perforce reduce culture to ideology, social conflict to class conflict, consent to compliance, action to reproduction, or communication to coercion" (Carey, 1989, p. 109).

After World War II, Latin American communication research followed North American theoretical and methodological models. Content analysis and audience and effect studies followed the positivist tradition. UNESCO sponsored works that complied with imported models of research.

However, by the 1970s, dissatisfaction with these lines of research lead to the development of different, distinctive approaches to communication research. Eliseo Verón, an Argentinean scholar, headed a strong semiotic current. Armand Mattelart, then in Chile, and Héctor Schmucler, from Argentina, dedicated themselves to Marxist political-economic analysis.

"The cultural studies that has emerged from Latin America during the last decade is theoretically sophisticated and subtle. But it seems to lack the explicit Marxism and feminism of the researchers and activists who emerged in the 1970s" (O'Connor, 1991, p. 60). The work focuses on the effects of the culture industries and the media in transforming Latin American everyday life.

Guillermo Sunkel (1985), a member of the Centre for Contemporary Cultural Studies at the University of Birmingham, has looked into the emergence of the popular press in Chile after 1930. Carlos Monsiváis (1976, 1978, 1979) has written about the emergence of an urban popular culture in Mexico during the period 1930–1950. Monsiváis believes there is no popular culture of resistance to the Mexican culture created by the country's culture industry.

Marxism has also influenced Latin American cultural studies. The Peruvian José Carlos Mariátegui, who lived in Italy from 1919 to 1923, was influenced by Italian Marxists like Gramsci. His *Seven Interpretative Essays on Peruvian Reality* (1971), originally published in Spanish in 1928, has influenced a generation of Latin Americans. Of his many contributions to Latin American thinking, it is his sense of how the economy and culture are intertwined that has most definitely shaped Latin American cultural scholars.

One of the most important figures in Latin American cultural studies is the Argentinean Néstor García Canclini. Exiled in Mexico because of the authoritarian regimes of the 1970s and 1980s in Argentina, his early work was in the sociology of art (1977, 1979). Later, he turned his attention to the study of popular culture as it relates to notions of hegemony and resistance.

García Canclini (1992) argues that a "global restructuring of society and politics" (p. 31) has substituted traditional Latin American dependency theory. For him, culture in Latin America has become a site for "negotiation" and "hybridization" across the multiple spheres of Latin American societies, it is no longer a fixed entity.

Jesús Martín-Barbero (1988) is also an essential figure in Latin American cultural studies. For him, the "people" means more than the proletariat, and culture is more than ideology (see O'Connor, 1991). Interestingly, Martín-Barbero mirrors Richard Johnson (1986/1987) in arguing for a study of culture that does not separate production, reception, and cultural form. One of his most important contributions is the definition of a Latin American "popular" that is unique: "compared to what might happen in the United States or in Europe—where to talk of the popular is to refer solely to 'massness' or to the folklore museum—in Latin America, the popular still denominates a space of profound conflict and an unavoidable cultural dynamic" (Martín-Barbero, 1988, p. 464).

In Latin America, there is a brand of cultural studies that is "more rooted in the life of the everyday than anything that passes for cultural studies in the USA" (Davies, 1995, p. 164). Its research is directed toward topics of identity, popular, imperial, and political culture. It is underpinned by the particular elements of Latin America's stark contrasts and uneven modernity.

> The systems by which meanings are circulated in a society resemble a maelstrom rather than an engineering diagram. It is a system of conflicting currents in which the slope of the ground always favors one set, but whose flow can be disrupted and even diverted if the terrain is rocky enough. (Fiske, 1994, p. 198)

Latin American cultural studies tackle the region's own maelstrom. By analyzing a text—newspaper coverage of the Falklands/Malvinas War—we attempt to study the conflicting currents and the slope of the U.S., Mexican, Chilean, and Venezuelan grounds during the South Atlantic conflict.

METHOD

Textual analysis in the tradition of Stuart Hall's Introduction to *Paper Voices* (1975) was the chosen methodology for this study. Textual analysis recognizes that texts are polysemic. That is, they do not have "a" meaning. Textual analysis practitioners argue that meaning is a social production and that language "is the means by which the role of the media is changed from that of conveyors of reality to that of constructors of meaning" (Curtin, 1995, p. 3).

The first task was the selection of the newspapers/countries to be analyzed. This selection was made using the following criteria: 1) the countries should represent a North–South contrast, since the actual Falklands/Malvinas War became a North–South conflict; 2) the Latin American countries chosen should exhibit diversity among their domestic situations and among their positions regarding the South Atlantic War; 3) the newspapers should be considered papers "of record" in their respective countries; and 4) the U.S. newspaper should have a strong international news coverage tradition.

The first stage of the analysis involved a "long preliminary soak" (Hall, 1975, p. 15) in the text. Every story related to the conflict, that was printed during that time period (74 days) in those four newspapers, was read. Focusing on the particular stories while preserving "the big picture" and choosing an exemplar (sample) for closer analysis were the immediate results of this first stage.

The sample was selected on the basis of specific dates that were crucial in the conflict. The selected dates were: 1) April 3 to April 8, the first week of coverage; 2) April 30 to May 5, when the United States openly sided with Great Britain, the war started, the British sunk the *General Belgrano*, and Argentina sunk the *HMS Sheffield*; 3) May 28 to May 30, the Battle of Darwin and Goose Green; and 4) June 13 to June 15, the last three days of coverage. Eighteen days of coverage were selected for the next stage.

The second stage involved the close reading of the chosen text and preliminary identification of present discursive strategies. This reading was done on a date by date basis and the findings were noted on an "analysis sheet" that was placed with the four newspapers of the day. Placement, size, and headlines were noted along with the narrative structure, tone, stylistic intensification, the use of metaphors, and the omissions detected. Contradictions, similarities, and contrasts between the different newspapers were also noted.

The interpretation of the findings within the larger framework of the study constituted the third stage of the procedure. The "analysis sheets" were analyzed as pointers to the text. Recurrent patterns were noted, and the dominant reading was identified. The analysis yielded a wealth of findings—only one of which is presented here—namely, the different forms of "cultural consensus" regarding the Falklands/Malvinas War that were constructed in the four newspapers, which were then contrasted with the foreign policy stance of each country.

ANALYSIS

April 3: The Conflict Begins

On April 3, 1982, newspapers of the world heralded the news that Argentina had occupied the Falkland/Malvinas Islands. The four newspapers of this study were no exception. The wording of their front-page headlines defined the Argentinean action and provided a framework for the ensuing conflict's coverage.

The New York Times's "Argentina seizes Falkland Islands; British ships move" ("Argentina Seizes," 1982) establishes that Argentina has grabbed the islands named "Falkland." With its choice of the verb "seize," *The New York Times* framed the action as Argentina virtually snatching the islands, implying that these islands do not belong to the seizing country. By calling the islands "Falkland," *The New York Times* takes a position regarding their ownership. All the related headlines of the day call the islands "Falkland" (see "Falkland Islands at a Glance," 1982, p. A6; Middleton, 1982, p. A6). The only mention of the name "Malvinas" is buried in an inside story: "the islands, which the Argentines call Islas Malvinas" (Gwertzman, 1982, p. 6). In this statement, the Argentines are isolated as the only users of the term "Malvinas," ignoring other Spanish-speaking and Portuguese-speaking countries who also use this term. The statement also establishes an Us:Other ratio (Lester-Massman, 1991), in which the "other," the "different" is Argentina. The reader is lead to believe that the norm, the "real" name of the islands is "Falklands," not "Malvinas." This definition of the conflict in which the norm, the legitimate, the way things should be is the British way, and the deviant, the illegitimate, and the exception is the Argentinean way, will describe most of *The New York Times* coverage of the 10-week conflict.

"Ocupa Argentina las Malvinas; GB rompe relaciones" ["Argentina occupies the Malvinas; GB breaks ties"] (Herrero, 1982) was the front-page banner headline with which *Excelsior* announced the invasion of the islands. The choice of the verb "occupy" suggests a less aggressive Argentina than the *New York Times*'s choice of "seize." The islands were called "Malvinas" in the headline as well as throughout the day's coverage of the events. In the main story, datelined in Buenos Aires, we find: "las Malvinas—que los británicos denominan Falkland Islands" ["the Malvinas—which the British denominate Falkland Islands"] (Herrero, 1982, p. 1A). In this case, an Us:Other ratio is established in which the "other" is Great Britain. As explained before, the creation of this ratio implies the definition of a norm and a deviation (from the norm). In this case, *Excelsior* establishes the term "Malvinas" as the norm, and the term "Falklands" as the deviation. As was the case with *The New York Times*, the reporter singles out "the British" as users of the term "Falklands," bypassing the fact that the term "Falklands" is dominant in a large sector of the world.

In its editorial "Precipitación Argentina" ["Argentinean hastiness"], *Excelsior* stresses that the islands belonged to Argentina "hasta el momento en que la expansión británica lo hizo objeto de su conquista" ["until the moment in which the British expansion made it an object of its conquests"] ("Precipitación Argentina,

1982, p. A6). However, the same editorial underscores the recklessness of the Argentinean action and places it outside the realm of what is considered acceptable behavior among nations. "El procedimiento seguido no encaja, por su cariz unilateral y violento, en el marco de sistemas que deben proseguir los países civilizados" ["the procedure doesn't fit, for its unilateral and violent overtones, in the framework of the systems that should be followed by civilized countries"] (p. A6). This is the main characteristic of *Excelsior*'s coverage: The cultural ties between Argentina and Mexico and the Argentinean right to the islands are never denied; but the invasion is not condoned. The conflict, then, is defined as an "occupation" by force of the islands.

"Invasión argentina sin resistencia" ["Argentinean invasion without resistance"] proclaimed *El Mercurio*'s front page on April 3, 1982, giving Argentina the role of invader and trespasser. An invasion is a form of aggression and that is exactly the depiction of the conflict by *El Mercurio*. The kicker line, "Archipiélago de las Malvinas" ["Malvinas Archipelago"] (1982, p. A1), takes second place behind "Argentina." The message is clear: Argentina invaded, there was no resistance, and it happened to take place in the "Malvinas." The islands are not important at this point. *El Mercurio* gives preeminence to the subject and perpetrator Argentina and defines the conflict as an invasion, an infringement. Argentina is the aggressor.

El Universal's main headline is very similar to the one in *Excelsior*. It describes Argentina's action as an "occupation." "Argentina ocupó las Malvinas en operación naval y aérea" ["Argentina occupied the Malvinas in a naval and air operation"] ("Argentina ocupó," 1982, p. 1-1). Moreover, the third deck headline of the story voices Argentina's own interpretation/justification of the actions taken: "El mandatario argentino anunció al país que no se trata de una invasión sino de una recuperación de ese territorio en poder de los ingleses desde 1833" ["The Argentinean head of government announced to the country that this is not an invasion but the recuperation of the territory that has been under British power since 1833"] (p. 1-1). The conflict then is defined as the "recovery" of territory originally possessed by Argentina. "No se trata de una invasión sino de una contrainvasión" ["It is not an invasion, but a counterinvasion"] (Rechani Agrait, 1982, p. 1-2), the "original" invasion being Great Britain's takeover of the islands more than 100 years ago. This justification/legitimization of Argentina's actions will characterize most of *El Universal*'s coverage throughout the conflict. The Venezuelan newspaper defines the conflict as a recovery by Argentina of what is rightfully theirs. The invasion is presented as the way to regain the "normal" condition of the islands, that is, the Falklands/Malvinas are Argentinean.

April 4: United Nations Resolution 502

On this date, *The New York Times*'s front page presents six different stories/issues to its readers, among them the Falklands/Malvinas conflict. The main headline for this particular story announced: "London ordering 35-ship task force to the Falklands." Two deck headlines announcing reports datelined in the United Nations and

London are placed under the main headline. "U.N. asks pullout" is the deck headline for a story from the United Nations, reporting that "[t]he Security Council demanded today that Argentine forces withdraw immediately from the Falkland Islands which they seized from Britain Friday" (Nossiter, 1982, p. 1A). Both in the headline and in this sentence, the U.N./Security Council is the subject of the statement, the one that performs the action, "demanding" Argentina's withdrawal from the "Falkland Islands."

In contrast, *Excelsior*'s front page displays a banner headline in which Great Britain is the subject. "Logra Inglaterra una condena contra Argentina en la ONU" ["England achieves U.N. condemnation of Argentina"] ("Logra Inglaterra," 1982, p. 1A). Attention here is centered around "England" and its "achievement." The UN is placed in a secondary position with respect to Britain. Under the banner headline, in a smaller font, a deck headline declares: "Exige que se retire del archipiélago" ["Demands that it withdraws from the archipelago"] (p. 1A). By being placed under "England achieves..." the subject of the deck headline then becomes "England." The reader's impression is that "England demands" Argentina's retreat, instead of being a UN exigency.

Like in *The New York Times*, the UN Security Council is the subject in *El Mercurio*'s front-page headline. And, like in the *Times*, the story is second in importance to the reports about the British task force being sent to the islands. "Demandan inmediato retiro de Argentina" ["Demands Argentina's immediate withdrawal"] is the headline of the story that interests us. It is preceded by the kicker line, "Consejo de Seguridad de la ONU" [UN Security Council] ("Demandan inmediato," 1982, p. A1). The kicker presents the subject, the Security Council.

El Universal's main headline refers to Venezuela expressing its solidarity to Argentina. A secondary headline mentions that England is sending a "portaviones" ["carrier"] ("Inglaterra envía," 1982, p. 1-1) to the islands, not a task force, just a carrier. Third in importance, the headline: "La ONU exige retiro de Argentina" ["The UN demands Argentina's withdrawal"] ("La ONU," 1982, p. 1-1) tops a three-line story from AP's wire service, which very succinctly describes the Security Council vote and the content of its resolution. By placing it as third in importance, *El Universal* leads its readers to also consider the *story* as being third in importance. The fact that the story is only three lines long contributes also to its diminished importance to Venezuelan readers.

On this date, *El Universal*'s emphasis on Venezuela's and Venezuelans' solidarity with Argentina is patent. While the main headlines of *The New York Times*, *Excelsior*, and *El Mercurio* were dedicated to the United Nations resolution that Argentina should pull out from the islands, *El Universal*'s front-page headline read: "Gobierno venezolano expresó solidaridad con Argentina" ["Venezuelan government expressed solidarity with Argentina"] ("Gobierno venezolano," 1982, p. 1-1). In the same issue, there are five stories about different Venezuelan sectors expressing their solidarity with the Argentinean action. The reader is lead to believe that there is a consensus among Venezuelans regarding this conflict. No alternative views are presented. This amazing uniformity is displayed in *El Universal* throughout the conflict.

May 2: First Attacks

The conflict has become the most important story in *The New York Times*. A big banner headline indicates the importance given to the story. "Air and sea battles erupt off Falklands as Argentina counters attacks by British" (1982, p. A1). Under this headline, two stories datelined in Buenos Aires and London share equal importance. The story from Buenos Aires is headlined "Ships reported hit, Buenos Aires also claims 2 planes shot down, 2 others damaged" (Schumacher, 1982b, p.A1). The headline for the London story is "Bases are shelled" (Apple, 1982a, p. A1). There are evident differences between these headlines. The choice of verbs is critical to the reporting of these actions. Buenos Aires "claims," which means that Buenos Aires asserts in the face of possible contradiction, that two British planes were shot down. Ships are "reported" hit by Buenos Aires, while reports from London assert that bases "are" shelled, which implies that the mentioned shelling "is" a fact. The headlines of both stories do not imply that the reports have the same degree of truth in them.

El Mercurio's main headline highlights the British attack: "Fuerzas británicas atacaron las Malvinas por aire y mar" ["British forces attacked the Malvinas by air and sea"] ("Fuerzas británicas, 1982, p. A1). The story is accompanied by a photograph of a British plane in action. The emphasis is placed on the British side and no Argentine counterattack is mentioned on the front page. Only a deck headline asserts that "ambos bandos proclamaron perjuicios y bajas en el enemigo" ["both sides proclaimed losses and casualties in the enemy"] (p. A1).

In contrast, *Excelsior* focuses on Argentina. The banner headline voices General Galtieri's words: "Se combate en las Malvinas; costará vidas" ["Fighting in the Malvinas; it will cost lives"]. A large deck headline asserts "Pérdidas británicas; falló un desembarco" ["British losses; failed landing"] ("Se combate," 1982, p. 1A). Moreover, the front page displays two stories from Buenos Aires and no stories from London. In consequence, the day's events are construed as negative to the British side.

Argentina is also the protagonist in *El Universal*'s front page: "Argentina derribó aviones y dañó barcos británicos" ["Argentina downs planes and damages British ships"]. British actions are mentioned only in the kicker line, which is a third of the size of the headline: "Tras el bombardeo en el aeropuerto de las Malvinas" ["After the bombardment of the Malvinas airport"] ("Argentina derribó," 1982, p. 1-1). It is important to point out that there is no mention of the fact that it was Great Britain who bombarded the airport. A casual reader may not realize this fact, and perhaps may even believe that the bombardment was executed by Argentina. Furthermore, due to the relative sizes of the kicker line and the headline, *El Universal* readers will assume that Argentina's actions, shooting down two planes and damaging ships, are more important than the British attack to the islands' airport. *El Universal*'s front page depicts the day's events as a definite "win" for Argentina.

May 3: Sinking of the *Belgrano*

While *The New York Times* and *El Mercurio* displayed front-page headlines about this incident, *Excelsior* and *El Universal* had no headlines about it. For *The New York Times*, this is the day's most important story. A headline announcing "Argentine cruiser damaged in British submarine attack outside Falkland war zone" is accompanied by a photograph of the cruiser (1982, p. A1), and by two stories datelined in Buenos Aires and London. The Buenos Aires story reports that Argentina has acknowledged that the *Belgrano* has been torpedoed (Schumacher, 1982a). The London story explains Britain's reasons for hitting the cruiser "on the edge" of the war zone (Borders, 1982b, p. A1). None of the stories mention whether the *Belgrano* has been definitely lost, or if there were any casualties.

The top third of *El Mercurio*'s front page boasts a photograph of the ill-fated cruiser. Under the picture, the headline announces: "Torpedeado crucero 'Belgrano'" ["Torpedoed cruiser 'Belgrano'"] ("Torpedeado," 1982, p. A1). The story is from UPI's wire service. Deck headlines report that Argentina acknowledges that the cruiser "fue alcanzado y sufrió averías" ["was hit and damaged"] (p. A1), and that the British Ministry of Defense expressed that the cruiser represented a menace to the task force.

Excelsior, on the other hand, does not mention the incident in its front page, which was dedicated to report on Latin American feelings toward the U.S.–Great Britain alliance ("Repudio," 1982). It is in a story headlined "Se repliega la flota a 150 Kms. de la isla" ["The task force retreats to 150 Kms from the island"] (Riva Palacio, 1982, p. 1A) that we find an allusion to the *Belgrano*. The story's main theme is the Argentine successes in the incipient war. Buried in page 12A, we find the *Belgrano*. The cruiser is reported "hit" by a British torpedo suffering damages in the attack (Riva Palacio, 1982). The placement and size of the reference is in stark contrast to those in *The New York Times* and *El Mercurio*.

El Universal's front-page main headline is dedicated to the diplomatic efforts to stop the war. The other headline on this page refers to the fact that both sides claim victories ("Ambas partes," 1982). Under this headline, there is a collection of three stories from AP's wire service. The third story datelined in London reports the *Belgrano* being hit and damaged.

This date is especially important for the analysis, since it highlights how headlines determine the significance of a story. All newspapers had the information about the incident. Two decided to print front-page headlines underscoring the event and assigning to it a high degree of significance. Two decided to report the story succinctly and unobtrusively while focusing on other aspects of the war. By the following day, May 4, all four newspapers had the *Belgrano* as the day's most important story. By then it was known that the *Belgrano* had sunk carrying most of its 1,042 sailors.

May 29: Capture of Darwin and Goose Green

On this date, half of *The New York Times* front page was dedicated to the Falklands/Malvinas conflict. The main headline declared: "Britain announces capture of 2 Falkland settlements in push toward capital." Immediately under it, a deck headline states: "Claim is contested" (Borders, 1982a, p. A1). *The New York Times* is cautious in the treatment of this story. The headline is not stating a fact; it is merely reporting that Britain "announced" the capture. Moreover, the paper immediately warns the reader that such an "announcement" is being contested. The author is also very careful about reporting the action, even when analyzing its consequences for Argentina. "The Argentine forces at Darwin and Goose Green were well dug in, and their defeat, if the British reports are correct, could be psychologically important to both sides" (Borders, 1982a, p. A1). The reader will understand that this is only Great Britain's version ("if the British reports are correct") of the events.

El Mercurio, on the other hand, announces the story as a fact. "Victoria británica en Darwin y Goose Green" ["British victory in Darwin and Goose Green"] ("Victoria," 1982, p. A1). The story, datelined in London, is from UPI. In it there is no reference to Argentina's version of the incidents. An infographic placed on page A12 depicts British offensive in the islands. A text box explains: "Gran Bretaña anuncia captura de Puerto Darwin y Goose Green" ["Great Britain announces capture of Port Darwin and Goose Green. Argentina denies it"]. But placement is crucial, especially to the average newspaper reader who relies on the front page for an understanding of what is happening. Therefore, readers of *El Mercurio*'s front page will understand the capture of Darwin and Goose Green as a "done deal," a fact, since this is the way the newspaper is presenting the events.

The Pope's visit to Great Britain occupies the banner headline on *Excelsior*'s front page. Under this headline and its accompanying story and photograph, two smaller, parallel headlines announce stories from Buenos Aires and London. To the left, the Buenos Aires headline states: "Repelen en Puerto Darwin a las tropas británicas" ["British troops repelled in Port Darwin"] (Riva Palacio & Uribe Navarrete, 1982, p. 1A). To the right, the London headline: "Anuncia GB la captura de dos enclaves en las islas" ["Great Britain announces the capture of two island settlements"] ("Anuncia GB," 1982, p. 1A). By being placed under the main story and to the left, the headline from Buenos Aires is probably read immediately before the one from London.[5] The reader will "know" about British troops being "repelled" in Port Darwin before reading Britain's announcement of the capture of two (unnamed in the headline) settlements.

Once again, the choice of verbs in the two stories is crucial to their understanding. From Buenos Aires, we learn that the British troops have been repelled by Argentine troops, "confirmó esta noche el Estado Mayor Conjunto de las fuerzas armadas" ["confirmed tonight the joints chief of staff of the armed forces"] (Riva Palacio & Uribe Navarrete, 1982, p. 1A). While we read from London that the British Minister of Defense "informó" ["informed"] that British troops had captured two settlements ("Anuncia GB," 1982, p. 1A). "Confirm" implies verification, validation, and authentication. It is a stronger verb than the simple "inform" of the London story. With the placement of these stories and their choice of verbs, the *Excelsior* reader is induced to assign more importance and more truthfulness to Buenos Aires' version of the events than to London's.

"Argentina resiste avance inglés hacia Darwin y Goose Green" ["Argentina resists English advance toward Darwin and Goose Green"] is *El Universal*'s front-page main headline. Furthermore, the kicker line states that a British frigate and two British helicopters have been damaged ("Argentina resiste," 1982, p. 1-1). Although the first deck headline asserts that a London communique announces the capture of the two "key positions," this statement is totally overshadowed by the larger headline in bold print. In consequence, the reader is lead to believe that in this war, Argentina is more successful than Britain. *El Universal*'s headline is in stark contrast with *El Mercurio*'s. The Venezuelan newspaper depicts the events as successful "resistance" by Argentina, while the Chilean newspaper defines them as a clear "win" for Great Britain.

June 15: The War Ends

Although *The New York Times* front page is dedicated mostly to the Lebanon-Israel conflict, a banner headline proclaims: "Britain announces Argentine surrender to end the 10-week war in the Falklands" (1982, p. A1). The authority to define the events is assigned to Great Britain, the source of the "announcement." The story under this headline is datelined in London and has a photograph of a smiling Margaret Thatcher. "Argentine forces in the Falkland Islands have surrendered, halting the war in the South Atlantic," "there was no confirmation of the surrender from Buenos Aires...but the Argentine high command announced...an unofficial cease-fire" (Apple, 1982b, p. A1). Although *The New York Times* is once again cautious with the wording, for the reader the bottom line is that Argentina has surrendered and the war is over.

This is also the gist of *El Mercurio*'s front page. "Se rindieron fuerzas argentinas" ["Argentine forces have surrendered"] ("Se rindieron," 1982, p. A1). A large picture of Margaret Thatcher smiling and waving reinforces the idea that Argentina has lost. For *The New York Times* and *El Mercurio* readers, Argentina's surrender is a fact. The conflict is over. Not so for *Excelsior*. The Mexican newspaper's banner headline asserts: "Cesan el fuego y se discute la rendición de Argentina" ["Cease fire and Argentina's surrender is being discussed"] ("Cesan," 1982, p. 1A). The inference is that Argentina is merely considering surrender. The conflict is *not* over.

Like *The New York Times*, *El Universal*'s main headline states that Argentina's surrender has been "announced by Great Britain" ("Rendición," 1982, p. 1-1), which does not mean that it has actually happened, but is stronger than *Excelsior*'s assertion that the surrender is "being discussed." However, a lenghty inside story contains an enormous headline trumpeting: "Se rindió Argentina" ["Argentina surrenders"] ("Se rindió," 1982, p. 1-6). This headline is as strong in its assertion as the front-page headline in *El Mercurio*. The difference lies in its placement as an inside story. Nevertheless, for *El Universal*, the conflict is over.

The most interesting aspect of *El Universal*'s front page is that the only other Falklands/Malvinas headline on this page announces that the Venezuelan president "ratifica" ["ratifies"] Venezuela's solidarity with Argentina ("Solidaridad," 1982, p. 1-1). The "solidarity" theme is once again played in *El Universal*, even after the war is over.

The analysis of this date, the last day of the war, highlights once again the power of wording and placement in defining events. Just like on the first day of coverage analyzed, the choice of words defines the events in different ways: "Argentina has surrendered," "Argentina's surrender being discussed." The former implies that the war is over, the latter does not.

"FALKLANDS" OR "MALVINAS"

"Falklands" for *The New York Times*; "Malvinas" first, and then "Falklands" for *El Mercurio*; "Malvinas" for *Excelsior* and *El Universal*. What is in a name? In the case of this particular conflict, the choice of names reflected the choice of point of view regarding the territorial dispute and the war. The use of "Falklands" or "Malvinas" became a discursive strategy. "Discourse is about the production of knowledge through language" (Hall & Gieben, 1992, p. 291). This fact was well-known to Argentines, whose textbooks and maps depict the islands in the same color as the Argentine territory and with the name "Malvinas." Meanwhile, most world atlases presented the islands as "Falklands."

The choice of names for these islands reflects different positions regarding their ownership. Like the maps, the names become symbolic emblems of the territorial claims of both sides. When countries other than the ones directly involved in the dispute select a name for these islands, they are in fact selecting a political stance, and more importantly, they are producing a certain brand of knowledge. Thus, the Falklands/Malvinas War was waged not only in the South Atlantic, but also in the arena of language. A parallel war was fought over the name of these islands. The "Falklands" or "Malvinas" War represents the substance of the dispute: the war over sovereignty rights. And although the military war is over, the "Falklands" or "Malvinas" War is not.

"Bestowing a name confers and confirms legitimacy" (Caistor, 1992, p. 54). These definitions, these constructions are then pervasively ingrained in culture. Now, Americans still call the islands "Falklands." So do Chileans, while Mexicans and Venezuelans still call them "Malvinas." Their "knowledge" and cultural and political stances have not changed.

FALKLANDS/MALVINAS WAR COVERAGE
AND FOREIGN POLICY

The New York Times took a frank pro-Great Britain position before the Reagan government decided to side with the British. Actually, the *Times* editorial position bluntly requested the government to do away with any neutral positions, and to acknowledge that the long-term U.S.–Great Britain relationship could not be compared or put in a balance with the U.S.–Argentina relationship. Although the American government never pronounced itself on the matter of sovereignty of the islands, the *Times*, with its use of the name "Falklands," expressed what its position was in regard to the islands' ownership.

Chile declared its neutrality over the conflict. This neutrality, however, was considered by other Latin American countries as a "cold shoulder" attitude toward Argentina. Neutrality in reference to that close a neighbor was interpreted by the Latin American community as a position against Argentina. Meanwhile, the Chilean media presented a pro-Great Britain stance on the conflict, which reflected the country's looming territorial dispute with Argentina over the Beagle Channel.

El Mercurio's coverage of the Falklands/Malvinas War was so extensive, it could be defined as obsessive. From the day of the Argentine invasion until the day before the Argentine surrender, it was the only issue (international or even national) covered in the front-page headlines. There were few exceptions, mainly when the soccer World Cup was played in Spain, some games would get front-page headlines. There are three possible explanations to this obsessive coverage. The first one may be that it reflects Chile's long-standing love–hate relationship with its neighbor, Argentina. The second explanation may be that it reflected the government's fears that Argentina might also challenge Chile for disputed territory. Still a third explanation may be that in a time when Chile was governed by Pinochet, when human-rights abuses were rampant, and when *El Mercurio* had a close relationship with the government, the Falklands/ Malvinas story was the perfect distraction from Chile's tough reality.

At the onset of the conflict, *Excelsior* reflected the Mexican government's ambivalent position toward the conflict. The "Malvinas" belong to Argentina, but the invasion is not an acceptable procedure to recover them. Interestingly enough, the more the conflict escalated, the more *Excelsior*'s coverage became pro-Argentine. Especially after the United States sided with the British, both *Excelsior* and the Mexican government stopped mentioning the inadequacy of Argentina's method of recovering the islands. The conflation of Great Britain and the United States as a menacing, imperialist bloc is one of *Excelsior*'s recurring themes. It reflects Mexico's uneasiness toward its northern neighbor, the United States.

El Universal and the Venezuelan government were never ambivalent toward the conflict. Their solidarity with Argentina was explicit and very consistent from the beginning of the crisis. The conflict was constructed as an "us versus them" dispute, in which a consensus was built around the idea that Argentina was right on every action. Moreover, Venezuelans, like Argentineans, were lead to believe in Argentina's triumph up until the very end of the conflict. In a country that prides itself on being one of Latin America's most stable democracies and whose freedom of expression and media independence are widely recognized, it is ironic that no alternative views were printed. Space and print were allotted to any person or entity who wanted to voice yet another solidarity-with-Argentina statement. Different opinions simply cannot be found. Furthermore, the headlines' wording was such that *El Universal*'s version of the war was radically different from that of *The New York Times*, but no different at all from the government's official position.

Finally, in all four countries, the newspapers analyzed presented a version of the events that was compatible with the country's already committed diplomatic position. It was the same for authoritarian Chile, one-party Mexico, and even for two of the most liberal societies, the United States and Venezuela. In all of them, and no matter what model of the press is adhered to, the press took a stance that explicitly mirrored the government's position.

Through textual analysis, the cultural works performed by the texts are perceived and the connection between the actual war and its four versions are described. However, the analysts' identities must be acknowledged, since they become part of the interpretive process. "The starting point of critical elaboration is the consciousness of what one really is" (Gramsci, 1971, p. 324). The interaction between two authors—a Venezuelan who "lived" the Falklands/Malvinas War in the United States, and an American scholar interested in the representation of Others from the position of American cultural hegemony—certainly conditions the choice of topic and our interpretations.

The study of texts (that is, the news stories) as an everyday indicator of the systems of meanings present in each of the countries analyzed, shows the different versions of this particular war. A set of events are constructed in four different ways yielding four different "knowledges," four different "realities" that are not divorced from each country's context. Our findings, along with other research, show that what passes for political consensus within nations may be attributable to hegemonic ideological work within culture industries. The tie between the culture industries and both national and global political-economy suggests the position that media occupy in promoting and solidifying the status quo. Our study here, including as it does four nations/newspapers, uncovers the relationship between press and official policy regardless of normative press functions.

NOTES

[1] Peter Beck (1988) describes the two versions in pages 29–83 of his book *The Falkland Islands As an International Problem*.

[2] The vote was 10 for (Great Britain, Uganda, Zaire, Guyana, Togo, Jordan, Ireland, Japan, France, and the United States), four against (Spain, Panama, China, and Poland), and one abstention (the Soviet Union).

[3] Today, *Excelsior* is the second newspaper in Mexico. Conservative daily *El Universal* is the circulation leader (Heuvel & Dennis, 1995).

[4] It must be pointed out, however, that in their respective memoirs, both Alexander Haig and then-Minister of Defense Caspar Weinberger stress that they considered the islands as being British (Haig, 1984; Weinberger, 1990).

[5] The relationship between placement and significance of a story is discussed by Stuart Hall (1975) on pages 19–20 of his Introduction.

REFERENCES

Adams, V. (1986). *The media and the Falklands campaign.* New York: St. Martin's Press.

Air and sea battles erupt off Falklands as Argentina counters attacks by British. (1982, May 2). *The New York Times*, p. A1.

Alisky, M. (1981). *Latin American media: Guidance and censorship.* Ames, IA: Iowa State University Press.

Ambas partes se atribuyen victorias [Both sides claim victories]. (1982, May 3). *El Universal*, p. 1-1.

Anuncia GB la captura de dos enclaves en las islas [GB announces capture of two island settlements]. (1982, May 29). *Excelsior*, pp. 1A, 11A, 21A.

Apple, Jr., R.W. (1982a, May 2). Bases are shelled. *The New York Times*, pp. A1, A12.

Apple, Jr., R.W. (1982b, June 15). Triumph by London. *The New York Times*, pp. A1, A15.

Argentina derribó aviones y dañó barcos británicos [Argentina downs British airplanes and damages British ships]. (1982, May 2). *El Universal*, pp. 1-1, 1-5, 1-7.

Argentina ocupó las Malvinas en operación naval y aérea [Argentina occuppies the Malvinas in sea and air operation]. (1982, April 3). *El Universal*, p. 1-1.

Argentina resiste avance inglés hacia Darwin y Goose Green [Argentina resists English advances towards Darwin and Goose Green]. (1982, May 29). *El Universal*, p. 1-1.

Argentina seizes Falkland Islands; British ships move. (1982, April 3). *The New York Times*, p. 1-1.

Argentine cruiser damaged in British submarine attack outside Falkland war zone. (1982, May 3). *The New York Times*, p. A1.

Aulich, J. (Ed.). (1992). *Framing the Falklands War: Nationhood, culture and identity.* Philadephia: Open University Press.

Beck, P. (1988). *The Falkland Islands as an international problem.* London: Routledge.

Beck, P. (1991). The conflict potential of the "dots on the map." *International History Review, 13*, 124–133.

Borders, W. (1982a, May 29). Britain announces capture of 2 Falkland settlements in push toward the capital. *The New York Times*, pp. A1, A4.

Borders, W. (1982b, May 3). London cites peril. *The New York Times*, pp. A1, A12.

Braveboy-Wagner, J. A. (1984). *The Venezuela-Guyana border dispute: Britain's colonial legacy in Latin America.* Boulder, CO: Westview.

Britain announces Argentine surrender to end the 10-week war in the Falklands. (1982, June 15). *The New York Times*, p. A1.

Bruno, J. L. (1981). *Mediaciones papales en la historia* [Papal mediations in history]. Montevideo, Uruguay: Ministerio de Relaciones Exteriores.

Budd, M., Entman, R. M., & Steinman, C. (1990). The affirmative character of U.S. cultural studies. *Critical Studies in Mass Communication, 7*(2), 169–184.

Bullion, S. J. (1983). Press roles in foreign policy reporting. *Gazette, 32,* 179–188.

Caistor, N. (1992). Whose war is it anyway? The Argentine press during the South Atlantic conflict. In J. Aulich (Ed.), *Framing the Falklands war: Nationhood, culture and identity* (pp. 50–57). Philadephia: Open University Press.

Cardoso, O. R., Kirschbaum, R., & Van der Kooy, E. (1983). *Malvinas: La trama secreta.* [Falklands: The secret plot]. Buenos Aires: Sudamericana.

Carey, J. W. (1989). *Communication as culture.* Boston: Unwin Hyman.

Cesan el fuego y se discute la rendición de Argentina [Cease fire and Argentina's surrender being discussed]. (1982, June 15). *Excelsior,* p. 1A.

Chang-Rodríguez, E. (1991). *Latinoamérica, su civilización y su cultura* [Latin America, its civilization and culture]. Boston: Heinle & Heinle.

Chomsky, N. (1987). *On power and ideology: The Managua lectures.* Boston: South End Press.

Curtin, P. A. (1995, August). *Textual analysis in mass communication studies: Theory and methodology.* Paper presented to the Qualitative Studies Division at the AEJMC National Convention, Washington, DC.

Davies, I. (1995). *Cultural studies and beyond: Fragments of empire.* London: Routledge.

Demandan inmediato retiro de Argentina [Immediate Argentinian withdrawal being demanded]. (1982, April 4). *El Mercurio,* pp. A1, A12.

Embassy of the Argentine Republic (1978). *Argentina Chile: Present situation on the border controversy in the southern region.* Washington, DC: Embassy of Argentina.

Falkland Islands at a glance. (1982, April 3). *The New York Times,* p. A6.

Fenty, A. A. (1982). *Never this land: An account of Venezuela's greedy expansionist claim to Guyana's territory.* Georgetown, Guyana: Guyana Ministry of Information.

Fiske, J. (1994). Audiencing: Cultural practice and cultural studies. In N. K. Denzin & Y. S. Lincoln (Eds.), *Handbook of qualitative research* (pp. 189–198). Thousand Oaks, CA: Sage.

Fox, E. (1984). Mass communications in the Falklands/Malvinas war. *Media, Culture and Society,6,* 45–51.

Freedman, L. (1982). The war of the Falkland islands, 1982. *Foreign Affairs, 61*(1), 196–210.

Fuerzas británicas atacaron las Malvinas por aire y mar [British forces attack Malvinas by air and sea]. (1982, May 2). *El Mercurio,* pp. A1, A16.

Galtung, J., & Ruge, M. H. (1965). The structure of foreign news. *Journal of Peace Research, 2*(1), 64–90.

García Canclini, N. (1977). *Arte popular y sociedad en América Latina* [Popular art and society in Latin America]. Mexico City: Grijalbo.

García Canclini, N. (1979). Artesanías e identidad cultural [Handcrafts and cultural identity]. *Culturas, 7*(2), 1–14. Paris: UNESCO.

García Canclini, N. (1992). Cultural reconversions. In G. Yúdice, J. Franco, & J. Flores (Eds.), *On edge: The crisis of contemporary Latin American culture* (pp. 29–43). Minneapolis, MN: University of Minnesota Press.

Gerbner, G. (1964). Ideological perspectives and political tendencies in news reporting. *Journalism Quarterly, 41*(3), 495–508, 516.

Gobierno venezolano expresó solidaridad con Argentina [Venezuelan government expressed solidarity with Argentina]. (1982, April 4). *El Universal*, p. 1-1.

Graber, D. (1989). *Mass media and American politics*. Washington, DC: Congressional Quarterly.

Gramsci, A. (1971). *The prison notebooks: Selections*. New York: International Publishers.

Greenberg, S. (1983). *Rejoice!: Media freedom and the Falklands*. London: Campaign for Press and Broadcasting Freedom.

Gwertzman, B. (1982, April 3). Reagan in a phone call, tried to deter invasion. *The New York Times*, p. 1-6.

Haig, A. M. (1984). *Caveat: Realism, Reagan, and foreign policy*. London: Weidenfeld & Nicholson.

Hall, S. (1975). Introduction. In A. C. H. Smith (Ed.), *Paper voices: The popular press and social change, 1935–1965* (pp. 11–24). London: Chatto & Windus.

Hall, S. (1982). The rediscovery of "ideology": Return of the repressed in media studies. In M. Gurevitch, T. Bennet, J. Curran, & J. Woollacott (Eds.) *Culture, society and the media*. (pp. 56–90). London: Methuen.

Hall, S., & Gieben, B. (Eds.). (1992). *Formations of modernity*. Milton Keynes, UK: Polity Press.

Hallin, D. C. (1987). Hegemony: The American news media from Vietnam to El Salvador, a study of ideological change and its limits. In D. L. Paletz (Ed.), *Political communication research: Approaches, studies, assessments* (pp. 3–25). Norwood, NJ: Ablex.

Harris, R. (1983). *Gotcha!: The media, the government, and the Falklands crisis*. Boston: Faber & Faber.

Herman, E. S. (1993). The media's role in U.S. foreign policy. *Journal of International Affairs, 47*(1), 23–45.

Herman, E. S., & Chomsky, N. (1988). *Manufacturing consent: The political economy of the mass media*. New York: Pantheon.

Herrero, R. (1982, April 3). Argentina ocupa las Malvinas; G.B. rompe relaciones [Argentina occupies Malvinas; GB breaks relations]. *Excelsior*, pp. 1A, 31A.

Heuvel, J. V., & Dennis, E. E. (1995). *Changing patterns: Latin America's vital media*. New York: Columbia University Press.

Hooper, A. (1982). *The military and the media*. Aldershot, England: Gower.

Inglaterra envía portaviones a la reconquista [England sends cruises to reconquer]. (1982, April 4). *El Universal*, pp. 1-1, 1-6.

Invasión argentina sin resistencia [Argentinean invasion without resistance]. (1982, April 3). *El Mercurio*, p. A1.

Johnson, R. (1986/1987). What is cultural studies anyway? *Social Text, 16*, 38–80.

Kennedy, W. V. (1993). *The military and the media: Why the press cannot be trusted to cover a war*. Westport, CT: Praeger.

Kirkpatrick, J. J. (1989–1990). My Falklands War and theirs. *The National Interest, 18*, 11–20.

La ONU exige retiro de Argentina [The UN demands Argentina's withdrawal]. (1982, April 4). *El Universal*, p. 1-1.

Lester, E. (1994). The "I" of the storm: A textual analysis of U.S. reporting on Democratic Kampuchea. *Journal of Communication Inquiry, 18*(1), 5–26,

Lester-Massman, E. (1991). The dark side of comparative research. *Journal of Communication Inquiry, 15*(2), 92–106.

Logra Inglaterra una condena contra Argentina en la ONU [England achieves UN condemnation of Argentina]. (1982, April 4). *Excelsior*, pp. 1A, 12A.

Malek, A. (1988/89). *New York Times'* editorial position and the U.S. foreign policy: The case of Iran. *Gazette, 42*(2), 105–119.

Mariátegui, J. C. (1971). *Seven interpretative essays on Peruvian reality* (M. Urquidi, Trans.). Austin, TX: The University of Texas at Austin Press.

Martín-Barbero, J. (1988). Communication from culture: The crisis of the national and the emergence of the popular. *Media, Culture and Society, 10*, 447–465.

Merrill, J. C. (1968). *The elite press: Great newspapers of the world*. New York: Pitman.

Merrill, J. C. (1980). *The world's great dailies: Profiles of fifty newspapers*. New York: Hastings.

Middleton, D. (1982, April 3). Falkland conflict may test the new Royal Navy. *The New York Times*, p. A6.

Monsiváis, C. (1976). Notas sobre la cultura mexicana en el siglo XX [Notes on Mexican culture in the XX c.]. In *Historia general de México* [General history of Mexico] (Vol. 4, pp. 303–476). Mexico City: El colegio de México.

Monsiváis, C. (1978). Notas sobre cultura popular en México [Notes on Mexican popular culture]. *Latin American Perspectives, 5*(1), 98–118.

Monsiváis, C. (1979). Cultura urbana y creación intelectual [Urban culture and intellectual creation]. *Casa de las Américas, 116*, 81–93.

Nossiter, B. D. (1982, April 4). U.N. asks pullout. *The New York Times*, pp. 1A, 18A.

O'Connor, A. (1991). The emergence of cultural studies in Latin America. *Critical Studies in Mass Communication, 8*, 60–73.

Precipitación argentina [Argentine hastiness]. (1982, April 3). *Excelsior*, p. A6.

Rachlin, A. (1988). *News as hegemonic reality: American political culture and the framing of news accounts*. New York: Praeger.

Rasor, E. L. (1992). *The Falklands/Malvinas campaign: A bibliography*. New York: Greenwood Press.

Rechani Agrait, L. (1982, May 2). ¿Y la solidaridad hispánica? [And the Hispanic solidarity?]. *El Universal*, p. 1-2.

Rendición argentina anunció Gran Bretaña [Great Britain announced Argentinean surrender]. (1982, June 15). *El Universal*, pp. 1-1, 1-6.

Repudio latinoamericano a la alianza Gran Bretaña-EU [Latin American disgust toward Great Britain–U.S. alliance]. (1982, May 3). *Excelsior*, pp. 1A, 10A, 34A.

Riva Palacio, R. (1982, May 3). Se repliega la flota a 150 Kms. de la isla [Sea forces stop at 150 Kms. from island]. *Excelsior*, pp. 1A, 12A.

Riva Palacio, R., & Uribe Navarrete, J. (1982, May 29). Repelen en Puerto Darwin a las tropas británicas [British troops repelled in Port Darwin]. *Excelsior*, pp. 1A, 8A.

Sanfuentes, F. (1992). The Chilean Falklands factor. In A. Danchev (Ed.) *International perspectives on the Falklands conflict: A matter of life and death* (pp. 67–84). New York: St. Martin's Press.

Schumacher, E. (1982a, May 3). Buenos Aires confirming attack, calls it "a new act of aggression." *The New York Times*, pp. A1, A12.

Schumacher, E. (1982b, may 2). Ships reported hit. *The New York Times*, pp. A1, A12.

Se combate en las Malvinas; costará vidas: L. Galtieri [L. Galtieri: combatting in the Malvinas; it will cost lives]. (1982, May 2). *Excelsior*, p. 1A.

Se rindieron fuerzas argentinas [Argentinean forces surrender]. (1982, June 15). *El Mercurio*, pp. A1, A10.

Shoemaker, P. J., Danielian, L. H., & Brendlinger, N. (1991). Deviant acts, risky business and U.S. interests: The newsworthiness of world events. *Journalism Quarterly, 68*(4), 781–795.

Singh, J. N. (1982). *Diplomacy or war: The Guyana-Venezuela border controversy.* Georgetown, Guyana: Cedar Press.

Skurnik, W. A. E. (1981). Foreign news coverage in six African newspapers: The potency of national interests. *Gazette, 28,* 117–130.

Solidaridad con Argentina ratificó el Presidente Herrera [Solidarity with Argentina ratified by president Herrera]. (1982, June 15). *El Universal*, pp. 1-1, 2-1.

Strebeigh, F. (1981). A lonely but free life at the southern edge of the world. *Smithsonian, 12*(6), 84–93.

Sunkel, G. (1985). *Razón y pasión en la prensa popular: un estudio sobre cultura popular, cultura de masas, y cultura política* [Reason and passion in the popular press: A study about popular culture, mass culture and political culture]. Santiago, Chile: ILET.

Torpedeado crucero "Belgrano" [Torpedoed cruiser "Belgrano"]. (1982, May 3). *El Mercurio*, pp. A1, A12.

Victoria británica en Darwin y Goose Green [British victory in Darwin and Goose Green]. (1982, May 29). *El Mercurio*, pp. A1, A12.

Vilanilam, J. V. (1983). Foreign policy as a dominant factor in foreign news selection and presentation. *Gazette, 32,* 73–85.

Wang, S. (1992). Factors influencing cross-national news treatment of a critical national event. *Gazette, 49,* 193–214.

Weinberger, C. W. (1990). *Fighting for peace: Seven critical years in the Pentagon.* New York: Warner.

Welch, S. (1972). The American press and Indochina, 1950–56. In R. L. Merritt (Ed.), *Communication in international politics* (pp. 207–231). Urbana, IL: University of Illinois Press.

III

National Perspectives

7

Hegemonic Frames and International News Reporting: A Comparative Study of the New York Times Coverage of the 1996 Indian and Israeli Elections

Ritu K. Jayakar
Indiana University

Krishna P. Jayakar
Penn State University

In 1996, two democracies, India and Israel held elections to choose a new parliament. The polls were regarded as crucial turning points in both countries. In Israel, the future of the Israel-Palestinian negotiations and the Middle East peace process was perceived to depend on the outcome of the elections. In India too, the fortunes of the historic Congress Party and the continuation of the economic liberalization program initiated by the Rao government hinged on the election results. It was therefore natural that the elections in these two countries attracted a lot of international media attention. In the United States, major national newspapers such as the *New York Times*, the *Los Angeles Times*, the *Washington Post*, and the *Chicago Tribune* gave the two elections considerable coverage.

Some differences in the extent and quality of coverage can be expected between events in two countries as different in their geographical location, population, economic development, and sociocultural background as India and Israel. However, it has been argued that the differences in news coverage do not arise only from incidental factors such as the above, but from structural motivations such as the political preferences and strategic perceptions of the United States. This argument has been called the "journalism of deference," by which the news media tend to view international events through the eyes of official Washington, in contrast to the objective, impartial perspective emphasized in journalistic training (Dorman & Farhang, 1987). This study attempts to examine this argument through an analysis of the quantitative and qualitative differences between the *New York Times* coverage of the 1996 elections in India and Israel.

The choice of the *New York Times* to furnish the research text for this analysis is based on precedent, with several scholarly studies of international coverage in the U.S. print media focusing on this "prestige newspaper" (Chang, Shoemaker, & Brendlinger, 1987; Dorman & Farhang, 1987; El Zein & Cooper, 1992; Malek, 1997; Riffe, 1996). The *New York Times* has attracted much research attention in part because it was found to be far ahead of other metropolitan newspapers in the U.S. in the scope and quality of its international coverage. Semmel (1976), for example, found that the *New York Times* printed almost 25 percent more international stories than the *Los Angeles Times*, 40 percent more than the *Miami Herald*, and twice as many stories as the *Chicago Tribune*. Also, in terms of column inches, the *New York Times* was similarly ahead. The newspaper has also devoted a larger proportion of its news space to international coverage; for example, international stories represented 44 percent of all stories on the front page (Haque, 1983).

To study the differences in election coverage on the quantitative level, measures such as the duration of coverage, the total number of articles, total column length of all published stories, and placement of articles are employed. While the quantitative measures indicate the relative importance placed by the *New York Times* on the coverage of the two elections, it is the qualitative analysis that most effectively supports the central thesis of this study. Framing theory is employed to analyze the qualitative aspects of the coverage. The study identifies the major themes and motifs of the coverage of the two elections, and arranges them within a narrative framework that communicates not only factual information, but also a set of attitudes and evaluatory approaches toward the two events.

To set the context for this analysis, this chapter discusses some important studies dealing with the coverage international events receive in the U.S print media. It introduces the main ideas of framing theory, on the basis of which the qualitative differences in the coverage of the two elections can be analyzed. It discusses methodological issues as well as quantitative and qualitative results. This chapter ends with a summarization of the discussion and presents the major conclusions of the study.

DETERMINANTS OF INTERNATIONAL NEWS COVERAGE IN U.S. PRINT MEDIA

It is a truism in journalism research that not all events receive similar coverage. Events and individuals have to compete for limited space in the media, and the events that do get covered are filtered through editorial gatekeepers. International news coverage is no different. Several studies have tried to determine the characteristics of international media events covered in the U.S. press.

Historically, international news has received relatively less importance in the U.S. print media (Hess, 1996). A study of 60 newspapers in nine different Western countries showed that U.S. newspapers ranked last in the coverage of international news and current affairs (Gerbner & Marvanyi, 1977). There have been periodic changes in the attitude of U.S. print media toward international news. Until World War II, the U.S. print media did not give much attention to the coverage of international news. Once the U.S. became a world power after the war, the U.S. media came to view the world through a cold-war prism. International news developments were depicted as episodes in an ongoing East–West struggle. Countries as small as Cuba and Nicaragua got prominent coverage in the U.S. media because of their perceived association with the Soviet Union. After the disintegration of the USSR in 1989, the focus shifted to issue-based stories and emerging economic competition (Dennis, 1993).

Chang, Shoemaker, and Brendlinger (1987) mentioned seven determinants of newsworthiness for international news:

- normative deviance of the event (defined as oddity or uniqueness of the event, which would break the norm had it occurred in the U.S.)
- relevance to the U.S.;
- potential for social change;
- geographical distance (with closer countries preferred in news coverage);
- language affinity;
- level of press freedom; and
- similarity in economic systems.

Hester (1973) found that news coverage of a foreign country is dependent upon its geographical size, population, economic development, and the duration of its status as a sovereign nation. According to these measures, Hester arranged the countries of the world on a hierarchy. In addition, he argues that cultural affinity and economic association between nations are important determinants of news coverage. Culture affinity here includes the social-historical connections between the two countries, such as a common language, travel, migration of population, and mother country-colony status. Economic association includes trade, investment, and financial aid between countries.

However, the single major determinant of the coverage a foreign country gets is the involvement of the U.S. itself in the affairs of that country (Chang, Shoemaker, & Brendlinger, 1987; Gerbner & Marvanyi, 1977). It is also shaped by the foreign policy priorities of the U.S. and its economic interests. For example, Chang and colleagues studied the coverage of international news and current affairs on network television and in the *New York Times* and concluded that relevance to the United States and the normative deviance of the event were equally important as determinants of coverage. Events with greater potential for social change got more attention from the *New York Times*, whereas geographical nearness drew the attention of television news. Any event in which the U.S. was involved diplomatically or was otherwise related got much better coverage than an event of comparable importance that did *not* involve the U.S.

Many studies have also been done on the coverage accorded to Third World events in the U.S. press. These studies concluded that there was an imbalance in the volume, direction, and content in the global flow of news and information (Masmoudi, 1979; Smith, 1980). Not all countries from the five continents get proportionate coverage in the U.S. (Gerbner & Marvanyi, 1977). These authors observe that Third World countries do not receive as much coverage in the media of the developed world as the developed countries do in the media of the Third World. They also point out the excessive emphasis on "bad news" from the Third World, focusing on crisis-oriented news, such as famine, civil war, political and economic instability, and disease (Riffe & Shaw, 1982). Smith (1980) says that a reason for this imbalance might be that the ownership of communication resources, like news agencies, audiovisual production companies, telecommunications companies and so on, is concentrated in the West.

Quantitative differences between the news coverage of events in India and Israel can be expected, because the two countries differ on many of the criteria identified by the studies discussed above. Historically, Israel has enjoyed a close relationship with the U.S.; the creation of Israel itself in 1948 owed a lot to U.S. influence. The U.S. protected the new nation diplomatically, exercising its veto power in the United Nations Security Council numerous times on behalf of Israel. For its part, Israel has been a key ally of the U.S. in the Middle East, whose rich oil deposits make the region economically and strategically important for the United States. America today has multiple foreign policy stakes and economic commitments in Israel.

India on the other hand, has not been historically allied with the political or economic agenda of the United States. As a nonaligned state, India has championed the cause of the developing nations in world fora, which often placed it in the opposite camp from the United States. There was also a widespread impression among policymakers in the U.S. that India leaned towards the former Soviet Union, in spite of its nonaligned ideology. Also, India's socialist industrial and economic policies proved to be a barrier to U.S. investment and trade with that country. In India too, there was disappointment and anger with U.S. arms sales and support for a succession of military dictatorships in neighboring Pakistan.

Relations between the world's *largest* democracy and its most *powerful* democracy were never cordial, but recent years have witnessed a transition. In 1991, India initiated an ambitious liberalization program that welcomed foreign investments into vital technology sectors, and removed many of the restrictions on trade and manufacturing put in place by years of socialism. American investors and businessmen have responded enthusiastically to the liberalization. The U.S. foreign policy establishment too has begun to take greater notice of India.

To summarize, important factors that influence the coverage that an event in a foreign country receives in the U.S. media are characteristics of the news story itself, as well as the economic, political, and diplomatic relevance of the country for the U.S. The historically close ties that Israel has enjoyed with the U.S. and the on-again-off-again nature of the Indo–U.S. relationship suggest that the elections in Israel would receive more extensive coverage than the Indian elections.

HEGEMONIC FRAMES

Many of the studies discussed above focus on the amount of coverage an international news event receives in the U.S. print media. At the same time, the qualitative aspects of the coverage are also important: In addition to its reporting function, the media also takes upon itself an interpretive function, especially if the subject of the news story is relatively far removed from the domain of experience of the reader. In international news reporting, the interpretive function of the media therefore becomes more important. It permits the media not just to selectively communicate information, but to transmit a particular narrative framework for it. As this section argues, these master narratives about international events are influenced by the ideological preferences of the state and makes the print media a crucial element in perpetuating the structure of power and influence that keeps the modern world system in place. In the words of Edward Said:

> [The] twining of power and legitimacy, one force obtaining in the world of direct domination, and the other in the cultural sphere, is a characteristic of classical imperial hegemony. Where it differs in the American century is the quantum leap in the reach of cultural authority, thanks in large measure to the unprecedented growth in the apparatus for the diffusion and control of information. (1993, p. 291)

An entire body of theoretical and empirical analysis has come up aimed at identifying the dominant narrative frameworks in news reporting. The fundamental concept in this literature is the idea of frames, which Gamson (1989) defined as the "central organizing idea or story-line that provides meaning to events related to an issue" (p. 157). Entman (1991, 1993) highlighted two different aspects of frames: they constitute both the sense-making processes and textual attributes of the news story. They arise in the normal process of news writing as both a linguistic and sense-making device that enables communication from journalist to reader. According to Entman, the cold war provided a frame to make sense of international events in the post-war years, just as the horse race provided a popular frame for electoral campaigns. Gitlin (1980), in his analysis of the students' movement of the 1960s, explained framing as the "persistent selection, emphasis and exclusion" of events and issues by media. Through the suppression of unnecessary detail, and the elaboration of elements that can communicate ideas to the reading public in terms of their own culture, the journalist constructs news as a narrative within the frame. "The media frame is largely unspoken and unacknowledged, organizes the world both for journalists who report it, and in some important degree, for us who rely on their reports" (p. 7).

Once internalized by the journalist and reader, frames are so effectively camouflaged in our thought processes that they become difficult to uncover without rigorous analysis. "(F)rames are difficult to detect fully and reliably, because many of the framing devices can appear as 'natural,' unremarkable choice of words or images" (Entman, 1991, p. 6). These effects are not achieved through the one-time usage of a metaphor or visual image. They are created, sustained, and reinforced through repeated usage, until the way of thinking advocated by the frame has been effectively internalized. "Through repetition, placement, and reinforcing association with each other, the words and images that comprise the frame render the one basic interpretation more readily discernable, comprehensible, and memorable than others" (p. 7).

Several scholars have speculated on the institutional origins of the news frames within which international events are reported. They found that the dominant interpretive frameworks for international news are closely tied to the strategic perceptions of the home country. In other words, journalists come to accept the frames provided by national foreign policy establishments as the appropriate lenses through which to view developments in a foreign country. Dorman and Farhang (1987) have labeled this the "journalism of deference," by which "the American news media...have projected foreign politics and conflict through the ideological lens ground by official Washington, which has given a distorted view of the world to the American public" (p. 204). Through an analysis of the U.S. print media coverage of Iran over nearly three decades, Dorman and Farhang demonstrate that the predominant news frame followed the perceptions of the foreign policy establishment about the ruling regime in that country.

As Malek and Weigand (1997) take care to point out, it would be too simplistic and wrong to suppose that the foreign policy establishment "controls" the mass media or vice versa. The congruence between the worldviews of officials and the press arises from a variety of organizational, economic, and ideological reasons. For example, editors often cross-check facts and interpretations from reporters in the field against copy from other news sources, which makes it difficult for a report that conflicts with the general interpretation of the news event to get into print. Economic considerations require reporters in the field to cover huge territories, especially in international reporting. They seldom have the time to develop expertise in the affairs of any one country, or to cultivate credible local sources. Reporters thus come to depend excessively on the "digested wisdom" of the national foreign policy establishment or the local diplomat from the home country. Budget constraints also encourage news agencies to rely on local stringers, who may have a self-interest in filing only those despatches the home office wants to hear about (Berry, 1990; Dorman & Farhang, 1987). Some scholars have also put forward ideological explanations. Journalists unconsciously absorb and internalize the hegemonic assumptions, which provide the frames for the selection and presentation of news by the media (Gitlin, 1980; Rachlin, 1988). The result is that the media "do not let the 'counter-hegemonic' realities penetrate the press" (Rachlin, 1988). The narrative tone of the news remains tied to a country's ideology (Rachlin, 1988).

When dominant news frames are colored by the foreign policy perceptions of the ruling establishment, the resulting international coverage takes on hegemonic implications. By creating and sustaining a particular worldview among readers in the home country, such "hegemonic frames" mobilize support for foreign policy actions. For example, the enormous expenditure on nuclear deterrence and its domestic consequences, such as higher taxes and lower expenditure on social programs, was supported partially by the media projection of the cold war frame. Similarly, domestic support for a U.S. role in the 1991 Gulf War was sustained by the media's projection of America's special responsibility as the world's sole surviving superpower. However, particular images in the media may challenge the established hegemonic frame, and circumscribe foreign policy actions too. For example, the My Lai story during the Vietnam War raised deep and disturbing questions about the U.S. role in Indochina. The evocative image of the lone protestor stopping a column of tanks in Tiananmen Square has come back to haunt successive U.S. administrations keen on normalizing relations with China in the name of strategic dialogue and trade. However, as Dorman and Farhang (1987) point out, these instances of "revelatory journalism" are the exceptions rather than the norm. "They often depended more on the enterprise of individual reporters than on routine journalistic practice, and usually gained currency despite the press system—not because of it" (p. 208). These news reports that challenge the established order are more likely to occur when there are deep divisions within the foreign policy establishment.

METHODOLOGICAL ISSUES

A complete list of the stories from the *New York Times* about the 1996 elections in India and Israel was prepared by searching two online databases—the Expanded

Academic Index and the National Newspaper Index—and the hard copy version of the *New York Times* Index. The study excluded the post-election coverage because the immediate aftermath of elections saw a series of dramatic developments in both countries. These included a short-lived minority government in India and the revival of Arab-Jewish tensions in Israel.[1] These developments contributed to increased coverage beyond normal post-election levels. Stories not related to the elections but published during the pre-election period have also been excluded.

The articles were analyzed on a number of quantitative variables:

- the *duration of coverage* (defined as the total elapsed period from the appearance of the first pre-election article to the last, which in both cases was the day of the election);
- the total *number of articles* and *total column length* of all the stories published;
- *placement* of the article (on the front page, back page, editorial page, international section, letter to the editor, special supplement, or other) and whether a related story highlighting the facts discussed in the main story is placed alongside;
- *size of the headline in columns* (like placement and length of article, the size of the headline measured in number of columns is also an indicator of the importance the editor gives to the news item);
- *source of coverage* (whether the article has a correspondent byline, or is an agency report); and
- the presence of *illustrations* (such as accompanying photos, maps, text boxes, and charts and graphs).

Taken together, these elements highlighted an association of word-image-narratives in the stories.

For a comparative analysis of the intensity of election coverage, the five-month period preceding the declaration of results was divided into five 30-day measurement intervals. For Israel, election results were not declared until May 31, so the 30-day measurement intervals were counted backward from May 30. The Indian election results came on May 9, therefore the 30-day measurement intervals for it started backward from May 8. This way, five 30-day measurement intervals were identified for both cases, and the number of news stories that appeared in each interval was measured.

Scholars have used a variety of methodological approaches for the identification of frames in news stories, including quantitative, qualitative, textual, comparative, and discursive (Baker, 1997). For the qualitative analysis in this study, a comparative approach is adopted. Entman (1991) suggested that frames could be revealed through a comparison of the coverage for news events that could have been covered similarly. By juxtaposing contrasting textual choices, the similarities and differences in the news frames are revealed and the frame is exposed as an artifact of our sense-making processes. "Comparison reveals that such choices are not inevitable or unproblematic, but rather are central to the way the news frame helps establish the literally 'common-sense' (i.e., widespread) interpretation of events" (Entman, 1991, p. 6). This chapter follows Entman's suggestion in comparing the *New York Times* coverage of the Israeli and Indian elections of 1996.

A recent proposal for frame analysis dealt with techniques that seek to isolate "framing sites," such as headlines, subheads, photographs and their captions, quotes, and so forth within the text, which are then analyzed for an argumentative structure: a specific claim about the event, supporting data, and justification for the credibility of the data (Baker, 1997). A more holistic approach is adopted for this study because frames are "an inherently qualitative construct...[based on]...the internal relations within texts, which are damaged if collapsed into reductive measures" (Reese, 1997, p. 1). However, particular attention was given to the "framing sites" within the text where ideological frames are more likely to be revealed, following Baker's suggestion.

QUANTITATIVE FINDINGS

The Israeli elections had 37 stories with a total column length of 729 inches, giving an average length per story of 19.1 inches. The total length of headlines in columns was 104 (average length of headline, 2.7 columns) and 13 stories had accompanying illustrations (35 percent of the total number of stories). The first story appeared on January 19, 1996, thereby indicating a duration of coverage of 131 days. (A list of all stories on Israel is provided in Table 7.1 in the Appendix). The Indian election, in comparison, had a considerably fewer number of stories. There were a total of 20 stories with a total column length of 458 inches. The average length per story was 22.9 inches, about 20 percent more than for Israel. The total length of headlines in columns was 56 (average length of headline, 2.8 columns) and 13 stories had illustrations (65 percent of the total number of stories). The first story appeared on February 25, 1996, indicating a duration of coverage of 72 days. (See Table 7.2 in the Appendix for a complete list of all India stories.)

Stories about the Israeli election started appearing in the *New York Times* five months before the election, whereas the Indian elections began to receive coverage only about three months before the election. The intensity of the India and Israel coverage are compared in Figure 7.1. The y-axis shows the number of stories that appeared in each of the five 30-day measurement periods preceding the elections. The initial coverage of the Indian election was delayed, with the first story appearing only in the third month. The most prominent difference in the number of the stories came in the election month itself. Against 26 stories on the Israeli elections, only 17 stories on the Indian election appeared in the month immediately preceding the elections in the two countries.

The use of photographs, illustrations, and maps was the same for both India and Israel, but since India had fewer stories, the use of graphic elements was more

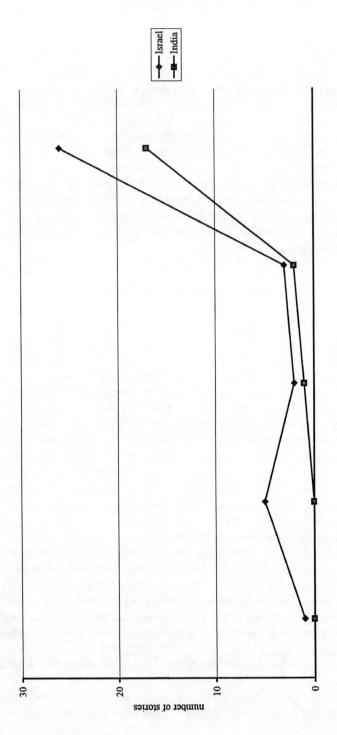

FIGURE 7.1. Number of stories per month in the 5-month period preceding elections.

132

intensive, when measured as the number of stories with accompanying illustrations. In terms of the source of coverage, Israel had only one agency report and the rest were correspondent bylines. For India, there were three agency news items in the world news section, as well as two op-ed pieces and one editorial. The same correspondent, John F. Burns, covered all the stories. Apart from the number of stories, it is the placement that shows how much importance the editor attaches to a news event. There were six front-page stories for Israel, 16 percent of all stories on the Israeli elections. In contrast, only two stories on the Indian election appeared on the front page (10 percent of total stories). The average length of a story on Indian elections (22.9 column inches) was more than that for Israel (19.7 column inches). This is partly because a larger proportion of Indian news stories had accompanying illustrations, which typically occupied more space.

QUALITATIVE FINDINGS

As we have seen, news frames are a form of communicative short-hand employed by journalists to communicate simplified and easily understood versions of complex events. They are especially useful in international news reporting because most newspaper readers do not have experience or contextual information about foreign countries to aid in the sense-making process. Also, frames are most effective when they are in conformity with the readers' existing belief structures and prior knowledge. Frames that contradict the little snippets of information readers have about foreign countries are thus studiously avoided in international news reporting. This is most clearly revealed in the *New York Times* reports on the Indian elections.

India's purported exoticism and "otherness" is manifest not only in Rudyard Kipling's famous words "West is west, and East is east, And Never the Twain Shall Meet," but is present even within India's discourse about itself—especially evident in its tourism promotion literature. Witness the famous Indian "Maharaja," the mascot of the Indian state-run airline. Such stereotypes are also recalled in the *New York Times* coverage of the Indian elections. Four central themes informed the news frame employed for the Indian election coverage: royalty, caste, religion and superstition, and corruption. All these themes work together in a news frame to confirm and reinforce India's exoticism and Third World status. This news frame presents few surprises to the average newspaper reader in the U.S.

Royalty. An example of this theme is a report on a prominent Indian politician, who also happened to belong to a former royal family. The *New York Times* (1996, April 25)[2] headlined the article "Maharaja on Hustings in India's Elections," in spite of the fact that India abolished royal privileges a half century ago, almost at the time the politician was born. The lead talks about the politician's grandfather (who happened to share the same first name) to reconstruct the splendor of the bygone era of kingship in India. It reads: "Among Indian maharajahs, Madhavrao Scindia's name is legendary. Seventy-five years ago, he led the Prince of Wales, later King Edward VIII, on a tiger hunt so elaborate that it entered Indian folklore. At a banquet, liquors and cigars were served from a solid silver electric train that circled the table, pausing by each guest" (1996, April 25, p. A3). The ambience evoked by this article and the associations it seeks to establish have little contact with contemporary Indian politics. But in terms of news frames, this coverage is indeed appropriate because of its seamless continuity with the mythic image of India as an exotic country of maharajahs, tiger hunts, and royal excesses. The article goes on to list all candidates in the election with ties to former royal families, some of them candidates of minor political parties or eccentrics with no chance of winning at the hustings.

Caste. With its connotations of a rigidly hierarchized, ritually bound, and deeply divided society, India's traditional caste system appears to be very different from the modern ideal of the egalitarian, secular, and unified civil society.[3] It has also proved to be eternally fascinating to Western observers. Several articles in the *New York Times* during the run-up to the 1996 Indian elections referred to caste: "Caste Loyalties, Democratic Promises" (1996, April 7), "Lower Castes Hold the Key As India Gets Ready to Vote" (1996, April 10), and "India's 'Avenging Angel': Candidate of Low Caste" (1996, May 6).

Unfortunately, caste is perhaps one of the least understood sociological terms. One statement in the *New York Times* coverage is particularly revelatory of prevailing misconceptions and worthy of detailed analysis: "The key to the politics of...a hamlet of mud-faced homes about 50 miles from the capital city of Uttar Pradesh state, is that all 25 families who live there, clustered about a single well, share the surname Yadav...a cow-herding clan" (1996, April 10, p. A1). First of all, there is confusion in vocabulary, which arises when caste is sought to be explained in terms of western concepts. The Yadavs, a many million strong caste spread over a huge area in the northern plains of India, are not a 'clan' in the conventional anthropological sense of the term, which denotes a group of families claiming descent from a common ancestor.

Second, the definition of the Yadavs as a "cow-herding clan" conveys the impression of a static society in which professions and socioeconomic status are determined hereditarily. Though certain occupations have been associated with particular castes in the traditional system, this is fast changing in contemporary India. As the renowned sociologist André Béteille points out, "Today it is possible to achieve a variety of economic and political positions in spite of one's birth in a particular caste, although the latter is still very important in setting limits within which choice in the former is possible" (1996, p. 45). In fact, the increasing importance of the Yadavs in the politics of northern India arises from the educational progress and economic power the community has achieved in recent years.

Third, political preferences do not flow automatically from caste affiliations, as Indian political parties have discovered to their cost in successive elections. By stating that "the key to the politics" of the village is the common surname, the coverage implies that the Indian voter is somehow susceptible to the "herd mentality" and incapable of individual judgment. This perception is reinforced by a caricature accompanying another story (1996, April 7), which showed a shabbily dressed, evidently poor man being led by the hand by a portly, prosperous-looking man dressed in traditional attire toward a carpeted polling booth.

In general, the coverage neglects the profound transformation in the concept of caste taking place in Indian society today. The socioeconomic ferment in modern India has accelerated the breakdown of traditional caste hierarchy, with upwardly mobile caste groupings increasingly demanding a more equitable share of the political and economic pie. Though caste identities are still very important in contemporary India, the gradual disappearance of their hierarchical ordering has made them more akin to ethnic groups (Fuller, 1996). Like racial and ethnic groups in the U.S., castes in Indian politics are becoming the nodes for political mobilization on issues such as affirmative action and civil rights. By perpetuating traditional notions of caste, the *New York Times* coverage failed to take into account these transformations in Indian society and politics.

Religion and superstition. The third element of the news frame on the Indian election coverage was religion and superstition. The rise of the "Hindu nationalist" opposition as a challenger to the ruling Congress Party received some coverage. For example, on headline proclaimed "Hindu Party's Rising Election Hopes Trouble Many Traditionalists" (1996, May 5). The coverage stressed the threat that the rise of this Party posed to India's minority Muslim community, and the fears that the future of India's secularism might be threatened. These ideas reflect the Western media's widespread disbelief that Hindu-majority India could be secular, in spite of a half-century of inclusive governance.

The theme of religiosity tied in with superstition as well. One news story mentioned that India's prime minister was turning to prayer as the votes were being counted, "seeking divine intervention for a favorable result" (1996, May 8, p. A8). The same article went on to state that the prime minister had "travelled across India consulting Hindu astrologers on a propitious date [for the election]." Another article was on a religious leader who had been indicted on fraud charges, whose alleged connections to the prime minister had appeared in some Indian newspapers in the run-up to the elections (1996, May 4, p. 4). The article also had a photograph of the holy man, with long, flowing beard and hair. The caption read: "The Hindu holy-man Chandraswamy, a confidant of Prime Minister P.V. Narasimha Rao, was held yesterday on fraud charges."

Corruption. The last news item mentioned above segues neatly into the next dominant theme of the news frame: corruption and criminalization of politics. A number of articles dealt with corruption at the highest levels of Indian government, or with criminals running for electoral office. One article (1996, May 6) focused exclusively on Phoolan Devi, a reformed criminal who was running for parliament. It pointed out that Phoolan Devi was an example of the ever-growing number of politicians with criminal records. Another set of articles referred to a corruption scandal that had led to the resignation of several ministers from the Rao government just months before elections were announced. Not only politicians of the ruling party, but also key opposition leaders were implicated in the scandal. Reeling from these revelations, the mood of the election was portrayed as one of general despondency and exhaustion, the incumbent government described as "bracing for setback," and the opposition parties in "disarray" (1996, April 5, p. 3).

It was mentioned in the quantitative results that a larger proportion of Indian news stories had an accompanying graphic, typically a photograph, though other graphic elements such as locator maps, portraits of politicians, and cartoons were also used. Of these, locator maps help the reader to process the information in the text, and do not present much scope for semantic manipulation. Curiously, there were two photographs of Prime Minister Rao's cut-outs. *Cut-outs* are huge portraits of national leaders fashioned out of canvas and bamboo scaffolding, which are erected on street corners during elections in India. One front page photograph in the *New York Times* (1996, April 26) showed a cut-out of Prime Minister Rao being carried to an election rally at New Delhi. The caption read that "the promise Mahatma Gandhi held out to millions of poor is a distant dream and the capital city is 'rife with slums'" (p. 1). The story makes a semantic association between the poverty of the people, the "larger-than-life" leaders who hold sway over them, and the failure of the state to deliver on promises made decades ago. A more devastating critique of India's efforts to maintain its democratic traditions cannot possibly be found.

Prime Minister Rao and his election campaigns and statements received tepid coverage. He was referred to as an "unimpressive campaigner" and compared unfavorably to charismatic predecessors like Rajiv Gandhi and Indira Gandhi (1996, April 5): "Apologetically, Rao tells voters that his name is not Gandhi." In the same story: "Aged 74, with a rambling monotone, a countenance that seems frozen in a frown and a stature that leaves him virtually hidden behind banks of microphones at election rallies, Mr Rao has become a cartoonist's dream." The entire election, involving more than 500 million voters, was variously described as "boring," "desultory," "dull," and strangest of all "sanitized" (1996, May 7).

Framing works not only through the presentation of information, but through the suppression of contradictory ideas and images. For example, there was very little mention of the economic liberalization program initiated in 1991, which had helped avert a grave foreign exchange crisis and boosted growth rates from barely 2 percent in 1991 to 7 percent in 1996. When the reform process was mentioned, it was critical in its tone: an early report (1996, April 5) said that economic reforms could "accrue benefit only to 150 million middle class city dwellers bypassing 600 million mostly poor villagers." Another example is from an editorial (1996, April 30): "Like others around the post-cold-war world, Indians are not yet convinced that capitalism and the creation of wealth will do more than socialism to ease economic disparities and violent ethnic and religious conflicts." The reforms are portrayed not as a general opening-up of the economy, but as last-ditch efforts to avoid the effects of "creaky socialism" (1996, May 8).

The reporting had other omissions as well. Most of the coverage was on the politics of northern India, with the south and the economically powerful west being almost totally neglected. International coverage is often based on idiosyncratic criteria like the home-base of foreign correspondents. In the case of India, most foreign correspondents prefer to stay on in the capital of New Delhi (which is in the north). Key issues like employment, economic growth, and the historic elections in the terrorism-affected northern province of Kashmir received practically no coverage.

None of the *New York Times* stories were factually incorrect. But in the absence of stories on other aspects of the elections, like the use of a sophisticated satellite-based computer network to keep track of electoral results, or the economic issues confronting the electorate, this coverage perpetuated images of India as a tradition-bound, backward, and superstition-ridden country.

By contrast, the coverage of the Israeli elections was framed almost exclusively in terms of the Israel-Palestinian peace talks. Two major themes can be perceived. At the most abstract level, the news frame projected the theme "Peace in Palestine," by stressing the importance of the election for securing stable peace in the Middle East. The second theme was what can be called the "Horse Race" metaphor for electoral competition. The *New York Times* constructed a personal conflict between the main candidates based upon their perceived personality traits and political attitudes. The dichotomous construction of the two candidates as "hero–villain" and "good–bad" was based upon their well-known positions, but refined and unified through selection and suppression of all conflicting information. The *New York Times* was consistently supportive of the reelection of Prime Minister Shimon Peres, who was projected as crucial to the Israel-Palestinian peace talks. It was observed that there was a close congruence between the U.S. foreign policy establishment and the *New York Times* in their assessment of the importance of the 1996 elections in Israel, and in their perception of the need for a Peres win to further the peace process. This linkage, which Dorman and Farhang (1987) called the "journalism of deference," dominated the coverage of the Israeli elections.

Peace in Palestine. Many articles in the *New York Times* stressed the importance of the Israeli election outcome not only for peace in the Middle East, but for the whole world. For example, one headline reads: "As Israelis Prepare to Vote, the World Watches Closely" (1996, May 28). "Israelis can choose peace or paralysis" was the subheading for another article (1996, May 12). The coverage also stressed the historic nature of the elections: an editorial was titled "A Vote on Israel's Future" (1996, February 14). There was a ready context for the dominance of this theme: the peace process had received a setback with the assassination of Prime Minister Yitzak Rabin in November 1995. Most observers considered the 1996 elections to be crucial for the peace process, because it would choose Israel's principal peace negotiator.

The Horse Race. The second theme in the *New York Times* news frame was the personality clash between the two principal candidates. The coverage consistently stressed Peres's experience and wisdom and the unfitness of Netanyahu for office. "Mr. Netanyahu's image as a smooth operator and slick talker made him unworthy compared with Mr. Rabin's old-fashioned decorum and soldierly reserve," read one front-page story (1996, March 30, p. 1). Another front-page headline declared that "Peres is winning the heart of non-voting students" (1996, May 23, p. 1). Peres was portrayed as a man of experience, decorum, and vision, "a more serious candidate with real background" and Netanyahu as the one who is "young, and energetic but driven by fear" (1996, May 27, p. 7). In the report on a television debate that Netanyahu clearly won, the *New York Times* interviewed a typical Israeli family. The woman of the household was quoted as dismissing the 30-minute debate format as inadequate for articulating something as complicated as a vision for peace (1996, May 27).

On the other hand, all Peres decisions were justified by the U.S. government and in their coverage by the *New York Times*. One example was Peres's decision to submit the final pact with the Palestinians to a referendum in Israel (1996, March 2). The announcement was criticized by the Palestinian Authority as yet another obstacle for peace and dismissed by Netanyahu as an election gimmick. But the *New York Times* gave it unconditional editorial endorsement: "A referendum is good policy as well as good politics" (1996, March 3, p. A14).

From an American perspective, Steven Erlanger wrote the Israeli elections were "a democratic exercise of vital importance—not only for Israelis in the first place, but also for the rest of the Middle East and thus for American foreign policy" (1996, May 26, p. 3). Early in the electoral process, the U.S. foreign policy establishment determined that the peace process would be best served by a reelection of Shimon Peres in the 1996 elections. Peres was a known quantity for the U.S. and he had already made his commitment to peace clear. On the other hand, Benjamin Netanyahu was untested, and his support base included political parties bitterly opposed to the surrender of land in return for peace. The U.S. decided to extend as much help as it could to enable Peres to win reelection. This interest of the U.S. government was clear when President Clinton himself campaigned for Peres.

A close parallel existed between the objectives of the Clinton administration and the editorial line of the *New York Times*. The last three years of Labor party rule in Israel were described as a "lifetime of change" in which the economy boomed and peace was made with Jordan and the Palestine Liberation Organization (editorial, 1996, May 26). A column by Thomas L. Freidman (1996, May 12) talked of Israel's economic prosperity under Rabin and Peres. Peres himself was portrayed as the best bet for peace. One subheading proclaimed: "Peres and Peace on Many Tongues" (1996, May 28), and "Give Shimon Peres and Peace a Chance." Throughout the closely contested run-up to the election, Peres was repeatedly reported to be in a slim but consistent lead. One headline said "Peres Maintains a Slim Lead in Israeli Polls as Election Nears" (1996, May 24). Columnist Anthony Lewis (1996) wrote a column entitled "Why Peres Still Looks Like a Winner in Israel." On the other hand, the opposition Likud party was generally portrayed negatively. One article said that it had not come up with a "realistic platform that takes the account of the new reality" (1996, May 29, p. A19).

It is evident that reports of Israel's economic growth under the Rabin-Peres governments were largely a media creation. Freidman's article (1996, May 12) on Israel's economic growth under Rabin and Peres was contradicted by a letter to the editor a few days later (1996, May 19), which pointed out that there had actually been a decline in Israel's economic growth rate and that the country had been running up an import-surplus repeatedly. Israel's average national growth rate for 1990–1993 was 6.4 percent and this rate came down marginally to 5.7 percent in 1993–1995. The inflation rate had declined from 12 percent in 1992 to 10 percent in 1995. The import-surplus had mounted from $3.5 billion in 1989 to $11.1 billion just before elections. This is a mixed bag of economic results, and requires some selective interpretation before a clear case for economic growth during the Labor government can be made. The *New York Times* coverage seemed to substantiate Berry's (1990) and Dorman and Farhang's (1987) research that reporters are often driven by national foreign policy objectives instead of providing objective coverage.

In contrast to the Indian election coverage, which stressed caste, regional, and religious differences, the Israeli election coverage only infrequently referred to the multicultural population of Israel (1996, May 19; 1996, May 22). Though the coverage aired the apprehensions of the minority Arab group, it concluded that though the Arabs had ample reasons to be displeased with the Peres government, they would favor it in the elections so that a Likud victory would not slow down the peace process. Another headline stated "Israeli Candidates vie for 'Ethnic Vote'" (1996, May 19). The point of the article was the crucial role that minority groups and orthodox religious groups play in the electoral outcome.

SUMMARY AND CONCLUSIONS

As indicated by studies on the determinants of international news coverage in the U.S. press, the Israeli elections were found to have received substantially more coverage in the *New York Times* than the Indian elections. The pre-election coverage of Israel began at an earlier period, included a larger number of articles, and were consistently better placed in the newspaper than stories on the Indian elections were. Nevertheless, coverage of the Indian elections was more comprehensive than expected. In the month immediately preceding the election, fully 17 stories on the Indian elections appeared in the *New York Times*, a frequency of better than once every two days. Reasons for this might be the increased U.S. business interest after India's economic liberalization program was initiated in 1991, and the diplomatic rapprochement between the two countries in the post-cold war period.

Both the Israeli and the Indian coverage displayed evidence of news frames, further substantiating the importance of such interpretive frameworks in international news reporting. In Israel, the predominant news frame was the Middle East peace process. The elections were contextualized as the process by which the Israeli people will choose their principal negotiator for peace. In addition, the electoral conflict was framed in terms of the personalities of the two major contenders with one candidate portrayed more favorably than the other. Peres symbolized peace, the stability of experience and the reliability of the old soldier, while Netanyahu represented the threat of instability, the uncertainty of youth, and smooth-talking guile. In the Indian case, the news frame was clearly ethnocentric. It tended to portray India as the "exotic East," with the persistent coverage of issues such as poverty, religion and superstition, and caste. Indian voters were portrayed as controlled by strange, atavistic urges and age-old socioreligious practices, rather than the rational, rule-governed behavior of Western electorates. The *New York Times* coverage emphasized the difference between India and Western society, and confirmed its continuing status as the "other" in Western discourse.

How "otherness" was projected can be seen by comparing the ways in which sociocultural divides were portrayed in the Indian and Israeli cases. In the Indian case, the rise of caste-based politics was framed in terms of ferment in India's traditional caste system, with an unbroken chain of cause-and-effect from ancient oppression to present-day rebellion. This framing failed to take into account distinctly modern aspects of India's caste politics, such as democratic mobilization for affirmative action and civil rights. On the other hand, the Arab-Israeli conflict was framed in terms of clearly contemporary concerns such as national security and popular self-determination, though religious and ethnic animosities in the Middle East have an equally impressive historical pedigree that reaches back to biblical times. In other words, Western readers can relate to the Arab-Israeli conflict using terms from the popular political lexicon, while the caste issue in India is an incomprehensible controversy in an alien social system, the "other."

Though news frames were evident in the coverage of both elections, the choice of news frames was revelatory of the differences in the strategic perceptions of the U.S. with regard to the two countries. In the Israeli case, there was close correspondence between the *New York Times*'s editorial line and the foreign policy objectives of the United States. In stressing the decisive nature of the elections for securing a durable peace in the region, and the importance of a Peres victory for the peace process, the *New York Times* was clearly echoing the perceptions of the U.S. foreign policy establishment. This lends further support to the "journalism of deference" argument put forward by Dorman and Farhang (1987).

In sharp contrast to the Israeli coverage, the "journalism of deference" was conspicuous by its absence in the coverage of the Indian elections with little evidence for an editorial line advocating any particular outcome. There was perfunctory endorsement for the incumbent prime minister Rao as a better bet to preserve secularism and economic liberalization, but no parallel to the unequivocal support of the Peres campaign in the Israeli coverage. The dominant news frame depicted India as an exotic land, full of superstition, feudal royalty, impoverished masses and god-men. Clearly, no U.S. foreign policy objective was advanced by this interpretive framework. We argue that this ambivalence in the Indian election coverage was because there was no well-articulated U.S. foreign policy preference hinging on the outcome of the 1996 elections in India. Though India has risen in U.S. strategic perceptions after the initiation of its economic liberalization program in 1991, its role in U.S. global policy is still not clear. In the absence of foreign policy guidelines, the *New York Times* fell back on ethnocentric patterns of discourse, which tried to describe and evaluate an alien "other" in terms of prevailing Western norms.

While the lack of a clear connection between the editorial line of the *New York Times* and U.S. policy interests in the Indian case seems to challenge the "journalism of deference" argument, it actually demonstrates an interesting exception to the rule. Where the foreign policy establishment makes a coherent statement about its political or strategic interests in a country, the media will reflect these perceptions in its interpretive framework. On the other hand, when the foreign policy interests of the U.S. in another country are unclear or equivocal, this study suggests that newspaper coverage will fall back on ethnocentric patterns of discourse, which stress the "otherness" of the foreign country. Ironically, this consistent emphasis on "otherness" validates foreign policy disinterest and perpetuates a pattern of low or minimal engagement with the foreign country.

APPENDIX

TABLE 7.1.
Coverage of Israeli Election in the *New York Times*

S. No.	Date	Story Length (inches)	Illustrations	Headline length	Byline/agency (column)	Placement
1	19-Jan	16	—	4	Steven Erlanger	International
2	5-Feb	12	—	4	Serge Schemann	International
3	8-Feb	2	—	1	Reuters	World Brief/intl
4	12-Feb	24	—	3	Serge Schemann	International
5	14-Feb	11	—	2	Editorial	Editorial
6	22-Feb	12	—	4	Serge Schemann	International
7	14-Mar	17	—	2	William Safire	Op-Ed
8	30-Mar	60	two photos	2	Serge Schemann	Front/Intl
9	2-Apr	20	—	2	Joel Greenberg	Front/Intl
10	3-Apr	11	—	2	Editorial	Editorial
11	3-May	16	—	1	Anthony Lewis	Op-Ed
12	9-May	25	—	6	Serge Schemann	International
13	12-May	18	—	4	Thomas Freidman	Op-Ed
14	16-May	23	—	4	Serge Schemann	International
15	17-May	16	—	2	Anthony Lewis	Op-Ed
16	18-May	17	—	3	Serge Schemann	International

TABLE 7.1.
Continued

S. No	Date	Story Length (inches)	Illustrations	Headline length	Byline/agency (column)	Placement
17	19-May	16	—	3	Serge Schemann	International
18	19-May	32	—	letters	Editorial/letter	
19	21 -May	30	photo	4	Serge Schemann	International
20	22-May	19	photo	3	Joel Greenberg	International
21	23-May	25	photo	4	Serge Schemann	International
22	24-May	13	—	5	Serge Schemann	International
23	25-May	28	photo	4	Serge Schemann	International
24	26-May	17	photo	4	Joel Greenberg	International
25	26-May	17	—	2	Joseph Berger	International
26	26-May	11	—	1	Editorial	Editorial
27	26-May	33	photo	2	Steven Erlanger	other
28	27-May	30	photo	3	Serge Schemann	Front/Intl
29	27-May	17	—	3	Joseph Berger	International
30	28-May	20	photo & map	1	Joel Greenberg	International
31	28-May	28	—	2	Serge Schemann	International
32	28-May	19	—	2	Thomas Freidman	Op-Ed
33	29-May	19	photo	2	Joseph Berger	Front/Intl
34	29-May	30	infograph	4	International	
35	29-May	8	—	2	Serge Schemann	International
36	30-May	28	photo	4	Serge Schemann	Front/Intl
37	30-May	18	—	2	Joseph Berger	International

TABLE 7.2.
Coverage of Indian Election in the *New York Times*

S. No.	Date	Story length (inches)	Illustrations	Headline length (column)	Byline/agency	Placement
1	25-Feb	24	photo	3	John F. Burns	International
2	20-Mar	2	—	1	Reuters	World Brief/intl
3	5-Apr	32	photo	4	John F. Burns	International
4	10-Apr	40	photo & map	4	John F. Burns	International
5	26-Apr	20	photo & map	4	John F. Burns	International
6	26-Apr	48	photo & map	2	John F. Burns	International
7	26-Apr	6	photo	2	—	Front
8	28-Apr	58	photo & map	4	John F. Burns	International
9	30-Apr	6	text-box	2	—	International
10	30-Apr	11	—	2	Editorial	Editorial
11	1-May	2	—	1	Reuters	World Brief/intl
12	2-May	2	—	2	Reuters	World Brief/intl

TABLE 7.2.
Continued

S. No.	Date	Story length (inches)	Illustrations	Headline length (column)	Byline/agency	Placement
13	2-May	17	2	—	William Safire	Op-Ed
14	3-May	26	—	4	John F. Burns	Front
15	4-May	20	photos	2	John F. Burns	International
16	5-May	46	photo & map	2	John F. Burns	International
17	6-May	18	photo & map	4	John F. Burns	International
18	7-May	20	caricature	4	Amitav Ghosh	Op-Ed
19	7-May	20	—	1	John F. Burns	International
20	8-May	40	photo	6	John F. Burns	International

NOTES

[1] In India, neither the Congress nor the opposition alliances could get a majority in parliament. The rightist Bharatiya Janata Party and its allies were invited to form the government, but could not establish a parliamentary majority. After two weeks of uncertainty, the leftist United Front came to power backed from the outside by the Congress. In Israel too, the ruling party lost to the Likud Party. Benjamin Netanyahu, the new prime minister, soon began to adopt a hard-line stance toward the peace process, resulting in heightened tension in the entire region.

[2] All references to *New York Times* articles are available in Tables 7.1 and 7.2. To save space and spare the reader periodic interruptions, the articles are referred to in the text only by the date on which they appeared in the newspaper.

[3] Caste has been defined as "a small and named group of persons characterized by endogamy, hereditary membership, and a specific style of life which sometimes includes the pursuit by tradition of a particular occupation and is usually associated with a more or less distinct ritual status in a hierarchical system" (Béteille, 1996, p. 46).

REFERENCES

Baker, S. (1997, October). *Frames in claims clothing: A qualitative method for the identification of frames in newspaper texts.* Paper presented at the Inaugural Conference for the Center for Mass Communication Research, University of South Carolina, Columbia.

Berry, N. O. (1990). *Foreign policy and the press: An analysis of the New York Times' coverage of U.S. foreign policy.* New York: Greenwood Press.

Béteille, A. (1996). *Class, caste and power: Changing patterns of stratification in a Tanjore village.* Delhi, India: Oxford University Press.

Chang, T. K., Shoemaker, P. J., & Brendlinger, N. (1987). Determinants of international news coverage in the U.S. Media. *Communication Research, 14,* 396–414.

Dennis, E. E. (1993). Life without the "evil empire": New ways to make sense of the world. In *Media and foreign policy in the post-cold war world* (pp. 5–12). New York: Freedom Forum Media Studies Center.

Dorman, W. A., & Farhang, M. (1987). *The U.S. press and Iran: Foreign policy and the journalism of deference.* Berkeley, CA: University of California Press.

El Zein, H., & Cooper, A. (1992). New York Times coverage of Africa, 1976–1990. In B. Hawk (Ed.), *Africa's media image* (pp. 133–146). New York: Praeger.

Entman, R. (1991). Framing U.S. Coverage of international news: Contrasts in narratives of the KAL and Iran Air incidents. *Journal of Communication, 41*(4), 6–27.

Entman, R. (1993). Framing: Toward clarification of a fractured paradigm. *Journal of Communication, 43* (4), 51–58.

Erlanger, S. (1996, May 26). Just whose elections are they, anyway? *New York Times*, p. 3.

Friedman, T. L. (1996, May 12). Waiting for the wild card. *New York Times*, p. 13.

Fuller, C. J. (1996). Introduction: Caste today. In C. J. Fuller (Ed.), *Caste Today* (pp. 1–31). Delhi, India: Oxford University Press.

Gamson, W. A. (1989) News as framing: Comments on Graber. *American Behavioral Scientist, 33* (2), 157–161.

Gerbner, G., & Marvanyi, G. (1977). The many worlds of the world's press. *Journal of Communication, 27*, 52–66.

Gitlin, T. (1980). *The whole world is watching: Mass media in the making and unmaking of the New Left.* Berkeley, CA: University of California Press.

Haque, S. M. M. (1983). Is U.S. coverage of news in the Third World imbalanced? *Journalism Quarterly, 60*, 521–524.

Hess, S. (1996, March). Media mavens. *Society, 32*, 70–79.

Hester, A. (1973). Theoretical considerations in predicting volume and direction of international news flow. *Gazette, 19*, 238–247.

Lewis, A. (1996, May 3). Bombs and politics. *New York Times*, p. 31.

Malek, A. (1997). *New York Times'* editorial position and U.S. foreign policy: The case of Iran revisited. In A. Malek (Ed.), *News media and foreign relations: A multifaceted perspective* (pp. 225–246). Norwood, NJ: Ablex.

Malek, A., & Weigand, K. E. (1997). News media and foreign policy: An integrated review. In A. Malek (Ed.), *News media and foreign relations: A multifaceted perspective* (pp. 3–27). Norwood, NJ: Ablex.

Masmoudi, M. (1979). The new world information order. *Journal of Communication, 29*, 172–185.

Rachlin, A. (1988). *News as hegemonic reality: American political culture and the framing of news accounts.* New York: Praeger.

Reese, S. D. (1997, October). *Framing public life: A bridging model for media study.* Paper presented at the Inaugural Conference for the Center for Mass Communication Research, University of South Carolina, Columbia.

Riffe, D. (1996). Linking international news to U.S. interests: A content analysis. *International Communication Bulletin, 31*(3–4), 14–18.

Riffe, D., & Shaw, E. (1982). Conflict and consonance: Coverage of the Third World in two U.S. newspapers. *Journalism Quarterly, 59*, 617–626.

Said, E. W. (1993). *Culture and imperialism.* New York: Knopf.

Semmel, A. K. (1979). Foreign news in four U.S. elite dailies. *Journalism Quarterly, 53*, 732–736.

Smith, A. (1980). *The geopolitics of information: How Western culture dominates the world.* New York: Oxford University Press.

8

Medusa's Gaze: North American Press Coverage of the Peruvian Hostage Crisis*

Gina Bailey

Simon Fraser University

> International crises are moments of truth, not only for governments and other
> political actors, but for the mass media as vehicles of political communication.
>
> Hackett (1991)

Contrary to the popular cold war sentiment, "If you want peace, you must prepare for war," Elise Boulding, founding member of the International Peace Research Association and Professor Emerita at Dartmouth College, has repeatedly stressed since the late 1970s: "If you want peace, you must prepare for peace" (qtd. in Buckmaster, 1980, p. 16). Given that the majority of North American citizens rely on print and broadcast news as their primary sources for information about international conflicts *and* that media coverage of foreign affairs has been found to influence not only public opinion, but high-level foreign policy deliberations as well (Dorman & Farhang, 1987), it behooves us as media researchers to ask several

---

*I am grateful to Simplicio Paragas for his help in formulating this chapter.

questions about the media's current level of performance in reporting on international affairs.

First, do North American media reports on foreign events, conflicts, and relations, overall, help prepare for or hinder peace oriented processes and negotiations? Johan Galtung, professor of peace studies, has developed several proposals to help guide both domestic and foreign reporters toward peace-oriented story construction. The first two and perhaps the most pertinent for this study are: 1) whenever there is a conflict, give voice to *all* parties involved in the conflict; and 2) the media should try to make explicit some theories, intellectual frames of reference, and the "discourse" or "paradigm" within which a conflict is to be understood. In other words, news workers need to attempt to render the implicit, explicit (Galtung & Vincent, 1992). As measured by these indices, how well are North American news organizations performing?

Second, are there specific and identifiable "blindspots" or consistent patterns of omissions in North American foreign news coverage, as many researchers have suggested (Galtung & Vincent, 2000; Hackett, 1996; Herman & Chomsky, 1988; Parenti, 1993), that wittingly or unwittingly undermine peace-oriented processes? And third, *within* North America, is there a difference in foreign news coverage resulting from varied ideological news frames *between* Canada and the United States?

In relation to the latter question, earlier research (Gitlin, 1980) has offered evidence to support the hypothesis that, in the past, there existed differences in news frames within which Canadian and American reporters constructed their stories and discourses. "Frames," as generally defined, refer to persistent patterns of cognition, interpretation, and presentation, of selection, emphasis, and exclusion by which symbol-handlers routinely organize discourse (Gitlin, 1980). According to Gitlin, the dominant frames or "main outlines" in U.S. media are: 1) privilege of private property relations that honor the prerogatives of capital; 2) priority of the national security state; and 3) emphasis upon individual success within corporate and bureaucratic institutions.

In comparison, Hackett (1991) found that Canadian news frames include the following: 1) provides greater space for welfare paternalism and regional and cultural fragmentation; 2) places less emphasis on national security; and 3) Provides greater space for contesting cultural ideologies and therefore employs less *explicit* binary frames, that is, Us/Them, either/or. However, since the onset of the post-cold war era and these results, there have been enormous geopolitical shifts, including increased transnational concentration of media holdings and the signing of the North American Free Trade Agreement (NAFTA). These political realignments, treaties, and trends may have had an impact upon the nature of foreign news output. As Bagdikian and many others argue: "The greater the dominance of a few giant firms, the more uniformity in what each of them produces" (1992, p. 245). This study was designed to explore these possible shifts and specifically address the following questions: Does current North American foreign news discourse support peace-oriented processes as defined by Galtung's proposals? Are there consistent and identifiable patterns of omission? Do continuing differences exist between Canadian and U.S. news frames in reporting international conflict?

If, since the end of the cold war, "irrational anti-Western terrorism and fanaticism" (Hackett, 1991, p. 103) have replaced the "evil empire"/Communism as the primary threat to North American national security, and "terrorist acts" (and those involved) are currently portrayed as the ultimate deviant "Other," as has been proposed by many media scholars (Chomsky, 1993; Ericson, Baranek, & Chan, 1991; Hackett, 1991; Hallin, 1986; Picard, 1993), then an international act labeled "terrorism," such as the Peruvian hostage crisis, should most effectively reveal the dominant frames of news reporting in both the U.S. and Canada. This study will therefore focus specifically upon the Peruvian hostage crisis as a case study to explore current frames of foreign news coverage in North American media and to trace any framing shifts that may have occurred since Gitlin's research. The Peruvian hostage crisis is particularly salient for this type of research because neither country was *directly* involved (each, however, had citizens taken as hostages). The event itself did not take place on either one's "home turf." Interest and self-esteem were not *directly* challenged. It did not *overtly* revolve around U.S. foreign intervention and it was not a case of Canadian journalists covering specifically American events, or vice versa. Therefore, any differences and/or similarities that emerge in coverage can be more confidently attributed to "overall" frames as opposed to "situational."

TEXT IN CONTEXT

Although the North American press often pairs the term "democracy" with Peru and has exhibited enthusiastic support for President Fujimori's "tough on terrorist" posture, Peru, more accurately, has been governed by a civilian-military regime rather than by democratic principles. Evidence of this misnomer is pervasive. From 1980 until the present, it has been estimated that 30,000 Peruvians have been murdered or have "disappeared" (Lavender, 1997, p. 2). Amnesty International attributes approximately 53 percent of these killings to the Peruvian military and approximately 45 percent to the anti-government "rebel" group known as the Shining Path. The MRTA, the group that held the hostages in Lima, are said to be responsible for approximately 1 percent (Amnesty International, 1997).

Over the first five and a half years of Fujimori's administration, 820 cases of "disappearances" at the hands of members of the Peruvian security forces have been documented. Of those not found dead, 560 remain unaccounted for (Human Rights Watch, 1997). Reports also document that 228 (known) people have been extrajudicially executed. Those detained in military bases often suffer systematic beatings, near drownings, electric shocks, hanging by the arms for prolonged periods, rapes, and threats of mutilation or death. Those who are not released or killed, are charged and brought to trial, to face Fujimori's infamous hooded jurors, or "faceless courts," as they are sometimes called. These courts have a 97 percent conviction rate, and they have sentenced over 5,000 people to prison since 1992 (Washington Office on Latin America, 1997). Those jailed on terrorism charges and awaiting "trial" are often housed in the notorious prison of Yanamayo, 15,000 feet in the mountains of Puno.

Economically, Peruvian citizens have not fared much better. Since Fujimori's radical and rapid implementation of neo-liberal economic policies in the early 1990s, which resulted in Peru becoming the fastest growing economy on the planet in 1994, the number of people who fall into the category of "very poor" in Peru has almost doubled from 7 million to 13 million (Lavender, 1997). The majority of Peruvian profits are corporate (especially in the mining industry) and tend to quickly flow out of Peru's national boundaries. The little that remains is most often filtered to a small percentage of the population (that is, the urban elite) (Chatterjee, 1997). Seventy thousand children die yearly of malnutrition and preventable diseases (CSRP, 1996). Unemployment figures are reported to be modest, but underemployment is pervasive at 80 percent, forcing 60 percent of the population into poverty and another 20 percent into destitution, (that is, not adequately nourished and/or starving) (Lavender, 1997). The remaining 20 percent of the population lives in what the *New York Times* and the *Wall Street Journal* have, in recent years, called "...an economic miracle."

METHODS AND MEASURES

Content and textual analysis were conducted upon all 76 "A" section articles published in *The Globe and Mail, The Toronto Star, The New York Times*, and *The Washington Post* during the first 10 days of the hostage crisis (December 19-31, 1996; exact days differ due to differing publication schedules in Canada and the U.S.). Previous research on the coverage of what was reported by the press as "acts of terrorism" suggests that the "frames of reporting" are well established within the first week (Picard, 1993, p. 86). Contrary to popular belief, a prolonged international crisis is not positively correlated to an increase in background and contextual information. The Canadian samples consisted of 38 articles—19 from *The Globe and Mail* and 19 from *The Toronto Star*. The U.S. samples also, coincidentally, consisted of 38 articles—22 from *The New York Times* and 16 from *The Washington Post*. These specific papers were chosen as samples due to their perceived prestige in their respective countries and therefore their influence upon public opinion, policy debate, and smaller presses.

Sixteen overarching categories were constructed. Six quantitative categories were designed to measure general content. These categories are:

1. *Sources* - determines hierarchy of "voices"; who is legitimized and who is marginalized;
2. *Gender of Source*;
3. *Gender of Journalist*;
4. *Reference to National Security* - determines potential shifts in emphasis since Gitlin's (1980) research and measures place emphasis upon law/order frames;
5. *Attribution of Problem* - determines perceived "threat"; and
6. *Emphasis/Focus* - determines patterns of emphasis, exclusion, and range and depth of discourse.

Frequency was calculated for all variables and cross-tabulations were calculated for *between* country comparisons. Traditional intracoder reliability measures were applied.

The textual analysis was guided by the construction of 10 categories. Eight consisted of the presence or absence and the contextualization of the terms "democracy," "terrorist," "Communist," "free market/capitalist," "Maoist," "Marxist," socialist," and "human rights." The presence or absence of an explicit definition of each term was also noted. These categories were designed to measure the "space" allowed for contesting ideological discourses. Frequency and cross-tabulations were also calculated for these catagories. For the purpose of this study, ideology is conceptualized as:

> ...an integrated set of meanings, values and beliefs that governs the way we perceive the world and ourselves; it controls what we see as "natural" or "obvious" and often serves to establish and sustain relations of power that are systematically asymmetrical. (Becker, 1982, p. 69)

Ideological bias often manifests itself as "the partial presented as the whole" (Ericson, Baranek, & Chan, 1987). In other words, certain forms of knowledge are privileged and certain discourses are favored.

The remaining two textual categories were comprised of "interpretive news frames and themes" (includes adjectives and terms used to describe people, groups, and actions, that is, state-sponsored terrorism is often described as "counter-insurgency") and "misinformation." Sources and publications utilized as benchmarks (in the service of contextualization and the identification of possible misinformation) include: Amnesty International, Latin American Connexion, Human Rights Watch, Committee to Support Revolution in Peru, Carleton University's School of International Affairs, Washington Office on Latin America, Nicaragua Solidarity Network of Greater New York, Workers World News Service, Covert Action Quarterly, the United States' Department of State Human Rights Reports, and the MRTA website, on which members regularly post information, ideas, analysis, and communiqués.

QUANTITATIVE RESULTS: FREQUENCY

All categories were tabulated by presence/absence, and therefore they do not total 100 percent, except for "Gender of Journalist" category. Articles often had more than one source and more than one theme.

Very few potentially politically descriptive terms were defined. The Canadian paper, the *Globe and Mail*, used the phrase "free market reform" but did not make reference to the specific features of the reform. The same paper also used the term "democracy," but only in reference to a quote by Nestor Cerpa, the leader of the MRTA, who was quoted as saying: "Peru is a dictatorship dressed as a democracy." On the other hand, the *Washington Post* did list several features of a capitalist market in one of its articles. The context was to illustrate Peru's recent progress toward "market reforms" evidenced by the increase in Peru's GDP. The *Toronto Star* reviewed two Peruvian situations, one relating to deplorable prison conditions and the other to the lack of a right to a fair trial, in the context of human rights. The

TABLE 8.1.
Hierarchy of Sources Utilized, by Country, in Coverage of the Peruvian Hostage Crisis

% of all articles			
Canada	%	United States	%
1. Peruvian Government[1]	34	Peruvian Government	38
2. Canadian Government	21	'Expert' Other Than Government	32
3. Japanese Government	17	U.S. Government	23
4. Hostages (released)	16	Other[2]	22
5. Red Cross	15	Red Cross	22
6. MRTA[3]	9	MRTA	17
7. Government-Other[4]	8	Japanese Government	14
8. Expert Other Than Gov't.	8	Government-Other	12
9. U.S. Government	7	Hostages (released)	13
10. Other	8	Human Rights Organization(s)	8
11. Human Rights Organization(s)	4	Canadian Government	8
12. Peruvian People	4	United Nations	3
13. United Nations	3	Peruvian People	3

1. "Government" includes military, police, diplomats, and civil service.
2. "Other" includes journalists, business spokesperson, family of hostages, and unknown.
3. Tupac Amaru Revolutionary Movement
4. "Government-Other" comprises Cuba, Guatemala, Uruguay, Russia, and the G-7.

TABLE 8.2.
Gender of Sources

	% of all articles	
	Canada	United States
Female	18	23
Male	81	92
Unknown	47	57

TABLE 8.3.
Gender of Journalist

	Canada	United States
Female	10	0
Male	10	38
Unknown	18	0
Total Articles	38	38

TABLE 8.4.
Reference (Implicitly or Explicitly) to National Security

	% of all articles		
Canada	13%	United States	26%

TABLE 8.5.
Attribution of Problem (Perceived Threat)

	% of all articles		
Canada	%	United States	%
1. MRTA	40	MRTA	51
2. Terrorism in General	18	Terrorism in General	26
3. President Fujimori	8	Other	9
4. Peru's Economic Policies	3	Peru's Economic Policies	5
5. Other[1]	3	President Fujimori	3
6. Prime Minister Hashimoto	1	Prime Minister Hashimoto	0

1. Other includes resentment of Japanese wealth and Peru's Justice System.

TABLE 8.6.
Hierarchy of Themes

% of all articles

Canada	%	United States	%
1. Crisis[1]	29	Political Policy Issues[2]	24
2. Political Policy Issues	22	Hostages[3]	24
3. MRTA Demands	20	MRTA Demands	24
4. Hostages	18	Crisis	20
5. Personality[4]	17	Personality	18
6. Peru's Relation To Japan	12	Peruvian Rebel 'terrorism' past/present	15
7. Canada As 'Peace' Negoti ator	8	Peru's Relation To Japan	15
8. Humanization of MRTA	8	Prison Conditions	11
9. Peruvian Rebel 'terrorism' past/present	7	Economic issues as a consequence of crisis	8
10. Suspension of Constitution	7	History of Peruvian Government	8
11. State of Emergency/Martial Law	5	Human Rights Issues	7
12. Economic History of Peru	5	Economic History of Peru	5
13. Econ. issues as a consequence of crisis	3	Peru's Relation to U.S.	4
14. History of Peruvian People	3	Other[5]	4
15. Peruvian Human Rights Issues	3	Humanization of MRTA	4
16. Human consequence to current economic policy	3	Trial Procedure	3
17. Peru's Relation To U.S.	3	State of Emergency/Martial Law	3

#	Item	
18.	Peru's Relation To Canada	3
19.	Peru's Relation To Foreign Entities[6]	3
20.	Prison Conditions	3
21.	Trial Procedures	3
22.	History of Peruvian Government	1
23.	Peruvian State 'Terrorism'	0
24.	War On Drugs	1
25.	Peru's Relation To CIA	0
26.	U.S. Military Training of Peruvian Military	0
27.	Religion	0
28.	Other	0

Item	
Suspension of Constitution	3
Peru's Relation To Foreign Entities	3
Human consequence to current economic policy	1
History of Peruvian People	1
Peruvian State 'Terrorism'	0
Peru's Relation To Canada	0
Peru's Relation To CIA	0
U.S. Military Training of Peruvian Military	0
War On Drugs	0
Religion	0
Canada As 'Peace' Negotiator	0

1. "Crisis" includes who, what, where, when, etc....
2. "Political Policy" issues includes strategy for the release of hostages as opposed to ideological issues.
3. "Hostages" include safety, conditions, and releases.
4. "Personality" includes the personalization of those involved—personal successes and/or failures as opposed to structural.
5. "Other" includes Lori Berenson and Fujimori's relation to his military regime.
6. "Peru's Relation to Foreign Entities" includes Cuba, G-7, Russia, Guatemala, and Uruguay.

TABLE 8.7
Politically Descriptive Terms

	% of all articles		
Terms	Canada %	Terms	United States %
1. Terrorist	20	Terrorist	34
2. Marxist-Leninist	12	Marxist-Leninist	35
3. Free Market/Capitalism	5	Free Market/Capitalism	9
4. Human Rights	4	Human Rights	8
5. Maoist	3	Maoist	9
6. Democracy	3	Democracy	3
7. Communist	0	Communist	4
8. Socialism	1	Socialism	0

Globe and Mail used the term "socialism" once to illustrate its global failure as a political strategy. "Communism" was employed twice by the *New York Times* but lacked explicit connection to anything other than the two words that preceded it: "Cuban-style Communism."

QUANTITATIVE RESULTS: CROSS-TABULATIONS

Cross-tabulations were executed for all variables, *comparing* Canadian and American dailies. Significant results, at the .05 level, were found between the following: 1) Canada and the use of the Canadian government as a source; 2) the U.S. and the use of the U.S. government as a source; 3) the U.S. and the use of "Expert other than government" as a source; 4) the U.S. and the use of "Other" as a source; 5) the United States and male reporters; 6) the U.S. and "Reference to National Security"; 7) the U.S. and "Attribution of Crisis as MRTA"; 8) the U.S. and "History of the Peruvian Government" as the focus of the article and prison conditions; 9) Canada and "Canada as Peace Negotiator" as the focus of the article; and 10) the U.S. and the use of the terms "terrorist" and "Marxist."

In other words, the results of this study indicate that in reporting on international crises, Canada, not surprisingly, is more likely to predominantly use the Canadian government, as opposed to relying on the U.S. government, as a source of information, and to portray itself as a "peace-negotiator." Similarly, the United States is more likely to use the U.S. government as a main source of information. More interestingly, however, is that the American press utilized both "experts" outside the government arena and "other" sources significantly more than did Canada. The range of sources was much wider for the U.S. than for Canada. The U.S. press was also more likely to employ male reporters and either implicitly or explicitly refer to "national security" issues. Furthermore, the terms "terrorist" and "Marxist" were more likely to be used by the U.S. The U.S. also focused upon prison conditions and the history of the Peruvian government and attributed the "cause" of the crisis primarily to the MRTA.

DISCUSSION OF QUANTITATIVE ANALYSIS

Sources

Whereas the *Washington Post, New York Times,* and *Toronto Star* had their own foreign correspondents stationed in Lima, the *Globe and Mail* did not. Instead, the *Globe and Mail* relied heavily upon Reuters, the Associated Press, the Canadian Press, the *New York Times,* and its own Ottawa Bureau for information on the developments in Peru. Although one might expect a greater range and constellation of "voices" to emerge from those papers with reporters near any given crisis due to increased access to interviewees, this was not the case in this study. The sources used between papers, as well as between countries, were strikingly similar. Governmental sources cumulatively comprise the largest category. Oppositely, human rights organizations, United Nations branches, and the Peruvian people themselves form the least utilized and most marginalized categories. The only significant differences between the U.S. and Canada (aside from using their own respective governments as primary sources) were in the U.S.'s reliance upon "experts" outside the government arena and "other" sources. Yet, the textual analysis revealed that while the U.S.'s range of sources was more varied, the sources tended to either repeat what other "elite" sources had already stated or supported the views of government officials. Much like the promised 500-channel television universe, more commentary does not equal different and varied viewpoints nor depth of analysis.

There have been many structural and instrumental reasons offered as to why governmental officials and other "elites" are so often overused for sources in times of foreign crises. These reasons include the recent decimation of the foreign press corps given the increasing costs of supporting a foreign bureau in relation to the pressure of deadlines and government officials' accessibility and willingness to comment (Dorman & Farhang, 1987); the organizational culture of the press, which includes training, educational curriculum, implicit mores, and the hierarchical structure of the corps and their "disciplinary apparatuses" (Pedelty, 1995; Schudson, 1978); the underlying deep structure of Western narrative, which naturalizes certain dichotomies and social hierarchies (Galtung, 1987); the complicitous relationship between press owners and senior editors, nation states and commercial/corporate business interests (Herman & Chomsky, 1988; Winter, 1997); Western conceptualizations of "objectivity" and "professionalism" in relation to who is deemed adequate to possess such qualities (Bagdikian, 1992; Hackett & Zhao,

1997; Parenti, 1993); and what has been referred to as "pack journalism" (Crouse, 1973). Overseas "pack journalism" often results from journalists' overall lack of "...systematic knowledge of a country, its political and cultural history, even its language..." (Dorman & Farhang, 1987, p. 194). Media scholar Todd Gitlin explains:

> Reporters covering the same event find it convenient (and prudent) to borrow angles, issues, and questions from each other. Borrowed frames help them process a glut of facts—on deadline. Especially when reporters are in unfamiliar social territory, and when enough of them are clustered in that unfamiliar territory to constitute a social group, they are liable to become a *hermetic* group, looking around the circle of reporters, rather than outward to the event, for bearings. (1980, p. 96)

Regardless, however, of particular reasonings, the consequences of marginalizing the majority of voices remains the same—a highly undemocratic means of communication that serves as a self-referential and autistic "lap dog" rather than its mythic role of "watch dog." The results of this study show little difference between the U.S. and Canada in what group of voices are privileged and what groups are marginalized. Both countries illustrate well the current contradiction between the supposed function of the Fourth Estate to call into question "official positions," and its reliance upon those positions to construct the majority of articles.

Gender

The results also indicate little difference between the U.S. and Canada in the gender of sources used. However, the gender of the journalist was significant. One journalist, Linda Diebel, who reports for the *Toronto Star's* Latin American bureau, was the single contributor to this resulting difference. Although this particular quantitative category cannot yield any specific variations, the textual analysis of the "emphasis of article" did. Linda Diebel's articles contributed to the entire 8 percent of the "humanization of the MRTA" category. She was the only journalist to broach the subject of what the hostages had for Christmas dinner compared to what the majority of Peruvians were consuming. In effect, she was the only journalist to draw attention to the "double standards" so often prevalent in press coverage between what are considered "necessities" in the "First World" and luxuries in the so-called "Third World." Likewise, her articles often attempted to link the MRTA demands with the actual conditions within which they were made as evidenced by one article headlined, "Rebels With A Cause?". And, whereas both countries' papers were overall silent on human rights issues, she questioned Ottawa's seemingly narrow emphasis upon mining conglomerates and trade interests in Peru.

Although it is beyond the scope of this study to detail the results of the numerous research projects on the relationship of gender to journalistic practices (Bailey, 1995; Gallagher, 1985; Mills, 1988; Rakow, 1987), it is notable that this study supports the general hypothesis that gender, *if given the organizational opportunity,* does effect what is reported upon and how. Given that foreign policy, hostage negotiations, and war and war-related issues have been the sacred cows of the men involved and of male reporters, it is perhaps appropriate to rename these events to reflect the reality of the situation. As suggested by Galtung in *Communication and Culture in War and Peace* (1993), "...semantic inertia makes it so easy to talk about war glibly..." (p. xi). He suggests:

> Peace is the usual condition of Homosapiens, in spite of the bad record for violence in general and the collective violence of centrally organized groups, in particular wars. But why say Homosapiens when in reality almost all of this is done by males? How about changing the terminology, from war to male-war or something like that... (p. xi)

Reference to National Security

The data from both quantitative and textual analysis indicate that although the "enemy" has changed since Gitlin's (1980) research, the American press continues to frame international events and crises involving "Leftist" governments or movements as potential threats to national security more than Canada. There exists a plethora of evidence to support the claim that since the 19th century, the U.S. press has considered any deviation from "free enterprise" as being anti-American and therefore treated with persistent hostility (Parenti, 1993). The question, however, in this research was: "Has Canada followed suit?" Coverage of this particular incident would suggest not.

Attribution of Problem

The single significant difference between Canada and the U.S. in the category of "Attribution" was in that Canada was less likely than the U.S. to call the MRTA's activities as the *primary* cause of the crisis. This category, in conjunction with the textual analysis, was designed to measure the press' performance on presenting complex issues and the interrelatedness of social, political, and economic forces. This index, as well as the textual analysis, suggests both countries fail miserably. However, the amount of emphasis the U.S. placed upon the MRTA and "terrorism," at the exclusion of background and context, also suggests a sustained continuation of Us/Them, either/or binary framing. Additionally, a cursory review of editorials in all four papers revealed that the overwhelming majority of them focused upon themes of "law and order" (that is, "terrorist" versus law-abiding citizens).

Themes/Focus of Article

Again, in general, Canada and the U.S. reported upon events using similar patterns of emphasis/exclusion and range and depth of coverage. This may be due, in part, to the *Globe and Mail*'s heavy reliance upon foreign news services for information. The *slight* differences in hierarchy that did emerge can most often be attributed to the articles of Linda Diebel of the *Toronto Star* as previously explained.

Those categories actually yielding significant differences were the U.S. press and its emphasis upon the history of the Peruvian government and prison conditions and the Canadian press and its emphasis upon Canada as a peace-negotiator, due to Anthony Vincent's (a released hostage and Canadian ambassador) attempts to speak with both the MRTA and President Fujimori. The U.S.'s portrayal of the history of the Peruvian government was almost always favorable and prison conditions were most often linked with Lori Berenson, an American recently convicted in Peru of "terrorist" activity and sentenced to life in prison, rather than overall human rights issues within a so-called "democratic" state. Canada's focus upon itself as a peace-negotiator is understandable, given its cold war identity as world mediator and its dwindling role as such since the 1970s.

Perhaps the most revealing results of this index, in relation to similarities between countries, was not in what was emphasized, but rather in what was not covered. By reading the North American Press' background accounts, albeit limited, of Peru's relationship to other countries involved in the crisis, one gets the impression that although both Canada and the U.S. have investments in Peru, overall those taken hostage in both countries (along with everyone else *except* Japan) were simply victims of being in the wrong place at the wrong time. In other words, through omission, both countries are portrayed as having strictly a limited business relationship with Peru—a capitalist relationship with all its understated attendant ecological and human destruction to be sure—but nonetheless a "business as usual" partnership, in addition to the customary "humanitarian" foreign aid that flows from First World nation states to Third World (reader assumed) "democracies." With regard to the U.S. and its relation to Peru, nothing could be further from the truth.

From outside reports, it appears as if Fujimori's state-led "anti-terrorism terrorism," or as governments prefer to term it, "low-intensity warfare/counter insurgency." has been supported by the U.S. and its interests. The following assertions from nonpress sources, in combination, tend to support such claims:

- Since 1994, Peru has been the largest recipient of U.S. aid in Latin America, totaling $150 million in 1994 (Washington Office on Latin America, 1997). In 1997, *at least* 1.6 billion U.S. dollars were invested in Peru (Nikkei, 1997). The North American press did not report these figures, but did report Japan's contributions and investments *as if* Japan was the largest donor of monies to Peru.
- Peru's army officers are routinely trained at the controversial and infamous School of the Americas in Georgia, where the U.S. trains death squad police and military for Latin America (CSRP, 1996).
- In 1990, the U.S. opened a 100 acre firebase in Santa Lucia, the largest and most expensive U.S. military installation south of the Panama Canal. They have also

built several smaller "firebases" in the middle of revolutionary base areas (CSRP, 1996).

■ The CIA has long been alleged to support, train, and organize the Peruvian secret police/National Intelligence Service (SIN). "The CIA trains the SIN in everything from vetting witnesses to polygraph testing and has even donated jeeps" (*Newsweek*, May 10, 1993). Fujimori's former Vice President, San Roman, has stated, "... SIN directly oversees the drug trade and is equipped with the latest U.S. technology..." (Reuters, December 12, 1992). The CIA supports SIN mostly under the guise of the "war on drugs" as they have done several times as a cover for "... low-intensity military intervention in Latin America..." (CSRP, 1996).

■ Directly after a meeting between President Clinton and Fujimori in 1995 in New York, Clinton affirmed support for Fujimori as a "defender of democracy." Subsequently, Fujimori, not only escalated "anti-terrorist" activities, but announced: "We are going to have a little 'Vietnam' here" (*La Republica*, March 3, 1995).

■ Allegations of corruption implicate one of Fujimori's closest advisors, Vladimiro Montesinos. The most widely publicized allegations emerged in the civilian trial of Peruvian drug trafficker Demetrio Limonier Chavez, known as "El Vaticano," and 43 other military personnel implicated in drug trafficking. In August 1996, El Vaticano claimed that he paid Vladimiro Montesinos—de facto head of the Peruvian National Intelligence Service (SIN) and close advisor to President Fujimori—$50, 000 a month from July 1991 to August 1992. A Peruvian Drug Enforcement Agency (DEA) informant made similar allegations in testimony before an investigative committee of the Peruvian Congress in 1993 (Amnesty International, 1997).

In addition to these omissions, as previously mentioned, the MRTA made 12 demands for the release of the hostages. Several of these were related to extensive policy plans for the economic and social restructuring of Peru (MRTA Communiqués, 1997). These were not mentioned in any of the press reports.

DISCUSSION OF TEXTUAL ANALYSIS

Use of Politically Descriptive Terms

The category of "Politically Descriptive Terms and Their Definitions" was constructed to measure the "space" allowed for contesting ideological discourse. The underlying presupposition was: Given that the hostages were taken as a result of contesting political-economic views and in an attempt to draw attention to and correct widespread human rights abuses, coverage of those views could be measured by the terms used, the definitions offered, and their contextualization.

Not only was terrorism the most frequently employed term of those measured, by both countries, but it was also found to be one of the two signifiers used significantly more often by the U.S. press than by the Canadian press. Much research and many texts have been devoted to detailing its symbolic construction and the uses and abuses of choosing the term "terrorism" to describe the various activities of "anti-government," "anti-American," and "anti-people's movement" protests; especially in relation to media and social discourse (Alali & Eke, 1991; Dorman & Farhang, 1987; Nacos, 1994; Picard, 1993; Schmid & de Graaf, 1982; Schlesinger, Murdock, & Elliot, 1983). The consensus of this research has been that the term "terrorist" is far from connotatively innocent and static, but used differentially in the effective service of discrediting political violence directed against dominant institutional power (i.e., government, business, military). It has been absorbed into criminal and social discourses ranging from tragedies such as the bombing of Pan Am Flight 103 to the First Nation protesters at Gustafsen Lake in August 1995. And as Hackett has interestingly noted: "In 1978, the category terrorism was not yet in use; it took ideological labor to place it in the lexicon of everyday news" (1991, p. 192).

In *Understanding News* (1982), John Hartley asserts:

> ...the syntagm "terrorists liberated" although "grammatically correct" is unlikely. This is because, as Saussure puts it, "the arbitrary nature of the sign explains in turn why the social fact alone can create a linguistic system." The community is necessary if values that owe their existence solely to usage and general acceptance are to be set up. In other words, the sign "terrorist" and the sign "liberated" belong to two opposing discourses in social use. To the extent that there is a "general acceptance" of the value "terrorist," it precludes notion of approval. So, having selected "terrorist" from the paradigm of possible signs, you would find it easier to combine it with "captured," "over-ran," or "occupied" than with "liberated".... Likewise, "terrorist" as a complete sign differs from others which could be chosen, as, for instance "soldier," "freedom-fighter," "guerrilla," "volunteer," "gunman," etc. (p. 113)

The application of "terrorism" to describe the activities of the MRTA, aside from its obvious sensational appeal, is dubious at best. In this case, its contextual usage served to systematically and effectively close the interpretive space for thought and dialogue on the origins and consequences of Peru's social, economic, and political systems. It further served to lift the event out, as it were, of a sphere of legitimate controversy and resituate it into a sphere of deviance. According to Hallin (1986), this particular shifting of spheres, by the conscious and/or unconscious choice of terms and frames, is one of the ways in which the news media maintain ideological boundaries. These boundaries would have been less rigid and more open for controversy if, for example, in certain stories "hostages" had been called "prisoners of war," the imprisoned "terrorists" labeled as "social fighters" and Fujimori's taxation policies referred to as "burglaries," as is the case in the MRTA's communiqués.

"Marxism" also emerged as a significant sector when comparing U.S. and Canadian press releases. The U.S. employed the term to describe the MRTA more than twice as many times as Canada. "Maoist," "Marxist-Leninist," and "Communist" were also used more frequently by the American press. Neither country defined these distinct political systems and/or ideologies.

Although, again, many scholars have traced the double standards by which such labels are often conveniently applied to serve given interests (often capital's) at varying times—perhaps none, however, with the passion and accessibility of Parenti in *Inventing Reality*—few have taken note of the fact that to the majority of the North American public, these terms have no relational meanings, only pejoratively categorical meanings. Out of curiosity to see whether even the most "formally" educated could delineate the differences, I asked several of my undergraduate students (many from China), fellow Ph.D. candidates, and faculty members if they could articulate the difference between these systems. After a trip to the library to distinguish between them, I realized no one had correctly answered. The conclusion was that these terms are obviously not intended for description; hence the press' lack of clarification. But rather than describe politics, they were used to deny politics. They were used to reformulate the concept of resistance into deviance: Terrorist = Marxist = Leninist = Communist = Maoist = Different = Deviant = The denial of contesting views, politics and ideologies.

Dorman and Farhang (1987) reported similar results on their research of the U.S. press' treatment of Iran. They concluded:

> To deny the existence of politics in a given society is to refuse to raise the question of who gets what, when, and how as a result of the existing socio-economic order and therefore to remain blind to opposition to such a distribution of power and material wealth. (p. 231)

A further manifestation of this denial was the juxtaposition of many of the articles on Peru in *The New York Times*, with a Christmas reminder directly underneath it pleading: "Do Not Forget to Give to the Neediest."

Democracy and "free market/capitalism" were applied sparsely and, in general, equivalently by Canada and the U.S. Similarly, these terms were also not only not defined, but frequently conflated. The problem with this linguistic conflation is that the two systems are not inherently related, and in seeking the possibilities and/or limits to one system, the other is also necessarily and falsely heralded and/or implicated. Hence, consumer participation has become synonymous with citizens' participation. North American capitalism (domestic and exported) is premised on the optimistic faith that business people will refrain from unreasonable profits and that their growth will create increased prosperity for all. Although most market economy practices belie this premise, the belief nonetheless drives the discourse and is most often subsumed under the "ideals" of democracy.

If, perhaps, democracy is defined as the embodiment of popular will "where rulers are accountable to the ruled through a feedback process" (Galtung, 1996, p. 74) and as a balance of powers to guarantee justice, security, and equality, then Fujimori's Peru most certainly does not qualify as a democracy, nor will his economic "shock" reforms bring the country any closer to this "ideal" as alluded to in many of the articles referencing his economic policies. The conceptual fusion and coupling of democracy and capitalism necessarily creates systematic patterns of omissions in current news discourse, especially regarding the so-called "side-effects" or "externalities" of a market economy. Given the results of both the American and the Canadian coverage of the crisis in relation to the term "democracy," the words of a colleague resonate even more loudly: "Now that the connotation of democracy has been established, the arguments and sites of struggle are now over its denotation."

Disconcertingly, there existed a clear avoidance and minimization of human rights issues (source, emphasis, definition, and so on) by both countries. These results tend to support early assertions by Chomsky and Herman (1979). About U.S. news coverage of Latin America, they wrote:

...massive suppression, averting the eyes from the unpleasant facts concerning the extensive torture and killing, the diaspora, the major shift to authoritarian government and its systematic character, and the U.S. role in introducing and protecting the leadership of this client fascist empire. When the Latin American system of torture and exile is mentioned at all, it is done with brevity and "balance." (p. 12)

In other words, as explained by Hackett (1991):

Chomsky and Herman argue that American reportage of foreign regimes is characterized by a double standard rooted in U.S. relations with the regime under consideration. U.S. client states are treated as autonomous and receive relatively favorable press coverage, regardless of human rights records. By contrast, the media systematically emphasizes human rights abuses by regimes which the U.S. government regards as enemies. (p. 178)

Since 1979, multiple studies have been conducted in an effort to test Chomsky and Herman's "double standard" hypothesis and their U.S. press propaganda model (including Herman and Chomsky). Most notably were projects by Dorman and Farhang (1987), Hackett (1991), Picard (1993), Schmid and de Graaf (1982), Vilanilam (1985), and Whitaker (1987). The data overwhelmingly supports the "double standard" assertion. Likewise, the results of this study, conducted nearly 19 years after Chomsky and Herman's, signals the persistence of such systemic biases, omissions, and blindspots in foreign human rights reportage; only this time,

Canada is equally implicated. In the case of the Peruvian hostage crisis, these blatant omissions border on blatant misinformation.

INTERPRETIVE NEWS FRAMES AND THEMES

News Frames, Themes, and Characterizations

In addition to the tabulation of each story's "emphasis," "perceived threat," and use of "politically descriptive terms," characterizations were also noted. The following is a brief but representative list of each paper's overall characterization of those people and groups involved in the conflict.

The Globe and Mail
Peruvian people: "uneducated"; "witchdoctors who danced in the street"
President Fujimori: "strong-willed"; "crackdown on terrorism using bold strokes"; "A refrain throughout Latin America when countries faced gargantuan problems was: If only we had a Fujimori."
Japan: "lacks strong stance on terrorism" evidenced by "past mistakes."
Canada: negotiating for release of hostages was framed as "peace-keeping." No reference to peace-keeping in relation to overall social justice. Canadian firms operating in Peru were "trained to not flaunt wealth" as "preventative measures" against theft, kidnapping, and terrorism.

The Toronto Star (only female reporter and most contradictory descriptives)
MRTA: "masked"; "calm"; "dedicated"; "not highly educated but intelligent"; "well trained"; "well conducted"; "well disciplined"; "beautifully executed"; "washed up"; "daring", "violent"; "Pro Cuba"; "anti-American"; "marginalized"; "not educated"; "common working people."
Peruvian government/military: "hunters and capturers"; "embattled."
Hostages: "courageous"; "prominent"; "well-healed"; "agonized."
President Fujimori: "confrontational"; "hard-lined"; "intransigent."
Canada: "mediator."

The New York Times
MRTA: "hostile towards U.S." (most frequent use of terrorist and Marxist).
President Fujimori: "iron image"; "heroic efforts to attract investments"; "bold military measures."
Japan: "difference in Japanese and U.S. approach to terrorism."
Hostages: "living in squalor"; "a nightmare."

The Washington Post
MRTA: "defunked"; "delegitimized due to the collapse of communism."
President Fujimori: "neutralized terrorist activity"; "leader of democratic institutions."
United States: "supportive of Fujimori's tough on terrorism stance."

One does not have to employ Osgood's "Semantic Different Scale" to note that, except for the previously presented differences, both countries constructed similar frames and characterizations of those involved in the crisis. It has been argued that Western news workers (specifically American) have been conditioned to look for politics only in a liberal democratic context and tend to confuse this preference with the idea of politics itself (Dorman & Farhang, 1987). The consequence is to dismiss popular struggle elsewhere, especially in the "Third World," as not belonging to the realm of politics at all but rather to random (however organized the activity may be) acts of political protests and terrorism. The results of the thematic/characterization analysis, in combination with the quantitative data, reveal that such dynamics may be operative in this case. Structural determinants of Peru and its people are decontextualized and then recontextualized within a liberal discourse; history and culture thereby are eradicated. This recontextualization tends to serve as a domestication of "foreign" ideology or as some have conceptualized it "a rationalization and containment process" (Giroux, 1994).

Furthermore, as Dahlgren (1982) has argued, the dominant motifs of American coverage of the Third World are "social disorder, flawed development and primitivism." Dahlgren and others have proposed that these motifs:

> ... foster anti-historic mythic ways of seeing the Third World as "the Other," against which "we" define ourselves as the peaceful, ordered, stable, ethical, humanitarian, capitalistic, industrialized, and civilized West. The repeated representation of Third World political groups as terrorists and the West as victim is an effective way to reinforce the U.S/Other distinction...a distinction essential to both Cold War and the Fortress American frames. (Hackett, 1991, p. 196)

The representation of "Third World" peoples as "Other," when coupled with the recontextualization of nonliberal-oriented politics, very likely facilitates a form of "unconscious symbiotic collusion" between Western news workers and institutions of power wherein the necessary space for dialogue upon which contestation rests effectively collapses.

CONCLUSION

> Don't look for conspiracy; look for continuity—those structures
> that control in petty ways.
> Pedelty (1995)

Although the limitation of this study is clearly sample size, it nevertheless allows for some generalizations to be made regarding the initial questions posed.

Within North America is there a difference in foreign news coverage resulting from varied ideological news frames between Canada and the United States? According to the results of this study, using both Gitlin's 1980 and Hackett's

1991 research to provide the general criteria for differences, the previously noted gaps in news frames between Canada and the United States are closing. Whereas the American press continues to place more emphasis upon national security, Canada now appears to place an equal amount of emphasis upon private property relations and prerogatives of capital, as does the U.S. Similarly, the emphasis upon individual success within corporate and bureaucratic institutions is fairly equivalent. The previously reported spaces allowed for welfare paternalism and regional/cultural fragmentation within the Canadian press also seems to be shrinking, at least in the international arena. On the other hand, the data suggest that Canada continues to provide, albeit somewhat small, a greater opportunity for contesting ideologies as evidenced by the fact that they were significantly less likely to use the terms "terrorist" and "Marxist," two terms that have historically functioned as connotatively "deviant" signifiers within traditional North American news discourse.

Are there specific and identifiable "blindspots" or consistent patterns of omissions in North American foreign news coverage? Yes. When compared to and combined with other studies of this nature, many of these particular blindspots form consistent patterns of omission within North American foreign news coverage in general. The blindspots that emerged during this study are as follows:

Voices: MRTA, Peruvian people, Peruvian historians, human rights organizations, United Nations, women journalists, and women in general

Issues: Organized, state-sponsored murder/"terrorism," North American involvements in Latin America, North American military aid to Peru (including CIA and war on drugs funding), North American capital investments in Peru - consequences, North American humanitarian aid to Peru - disbursements and allotments, all human rights issues, liberal economic reforms - which ones - consequences

Terms: Definitions of politically descriptive terms

Do current North American foreign news framing and discourses support peace-oriented processes? When measured and guided by Galtung's first two proposals for a peace-oriented news media—whenever there is a conflict the media should give voice to both or *all* parties in the conflict, and try to make *explicit* some theories, the intellectual frames of reference, the "discourse" or "paradigm" within which a conflict is to be understood—there emerged little difference between Canada and the United States. Both countries effectively silenced those voices upon which the possibility of peace-oriented news rest, either by choice of sources, emphasis of articles, or ill-defined terminology.

Whether one argues an attribution for such shortcomings from the view that contemporary journalism is nothing more than another cog in the wheel of liberal capitalism, simply a for-profit business (peace may be good for humanity but bad for the press), or that the underlying tenets of journalistic practices are to blame, both culminate in situating the most "prestigious" dailies in North America as active agents of cultural violence. We live in an age where the link between power and narrative extends to the link between the erotics of seeing and the politics of power.

Like the myth of Medusa, power is currently tied to the control of vision both by the "pictures in our head" facilitated by the print-based media and/or the juxtaposition of images and narratives as represented by the visual media. The increasing role of the press as primary interpreter of international conflictual situations (i.e., as diagnosticians), positions them also as negotiators, despite the rejection of this role by the majority of reporters. Both responsibilities require multisited challenges to current conceptualizations of journalistic practices, at various levels of news organizations, which result in rendering invisible potential bridges to peace.

REFERENCES

Alali, D. A., & Eke, K. K. (1991). *Media coverage of terrorism*. London: Sage.

Amnesty International (1997, January 27). *Home page*. Available: http://www.Amnesty.org

Bagdikian, B. H. (1992). *The media monopoly*. Boston: Beacon Press.

Bailey, G. (1995). Body politics and missing themes of women in American news. *Media Development, XLII*, 31–34.

Becker, J. (1982). Communication and peace—the empirical and theoretical relation between two categories in social sciences. *Journal of Peace Research, 19*, 227–240.

Buckmaster, H. (1980, December). Interview with Elise Boulding. *Christian Science Monitor*, p. 16.

Chatterjee, P. (1997, Spring). Peru's new conquistadors. *Covert Action Quarterly, 60*, 11–17.

Chomsky, N. (1993). *What Uncle Sam really wants*. Berkeley, CA: Odonian Press.

Chomsky N., & Herman, E. S. (1979). *The political economy of human rights. Vol. 1: The Washington connection and Third World fascism*. Montreal: Black Rose Books.

Committee To Support Revolution in Peru (CSRP). (1996). *News From the People's War in Peru, 18*(14).

Crouse, T. (1973). *The boys on the bus*. New York: Random House.

Dahlgren, P., with Chakrapani, S. (1982). The Third World on TV news: Western ways of seeing "other." In W.C. Adams (Ed.), *Television coverage of international affairs* (pp. 45–63). Norwood, NJ: Ablex.

Dorman W. A., & Farhang, M. (1987). *The U.S. press and Iran: Foreign policy and the journalism of deference*. Berkeley, CA: University of California Press.

Ericson, R. V., Baranek, P. M., & Chan, J. B. L. (1987). *Visualizing deviance: A study of news organization*. Toronto: University of Toronto Press.

Gallagher, M. (1985, May). *Feminism, communications and the politics of knowledge*. Paper presented at the 35th Conference of the International Communications Association, Honolulu, HI.

Galtung, J. (1987). *United States foreign policy: As manifest theology*. La Jola, CA: Institute on Global Conflict and Cooperation, University of California at San Diego.

Galtung, J. (1993). Preface. In C. Roach (Ed.), *Communication and culture in war and peace* (p. xi). London: Sage.

Galtung, J. (1996). *Peace by peaceful means*. London: Sage.

Galtung, J, & Vincent, R. (1992). *Global glasnost*. Cresskill, NJ: Hampton Press.

Giroux, H. A. (1994). *Disturbing pleasures: Learning popular culture*. New York: Routledge.

Gitlin, T. (1980). *The whole world Is watching: Mass media in the making and unmaking of the new left*. Berkeley, CA: University of California Press.

Hackett, R. A. (1991). *News and dissent: The press and the politics of peace in Canada*. Norwood, NJ: Ablex.

Hackett, R. A. (1996). *Blindspots in The News? Project Censored Canada Yearbook*. Project Censored: Simon Fraser University.

Hackett, R. A., & Zhao, Y. (1994). Challenging a master narrative: Peace protest and opinion/editorial discourse in U.S. press during the Gulf War. *Discourse and Society*, 5, 509–541.

Hackett, R. A., & Zhao, Y. (1997). *Sustaining democracy? Journalism and the politics of objectivity*. Toronto: Garamond Press.

Hallin, D. C. (1986). We keep America on top of the world. In T. Gitlin (Ed.), *Watching television* (pp. 9–41). New York: Pantheon.

Hartley, J. (1982). *Understanding news*. London and New York: Methuen.

Herman, E., & Chomsky, N. (1988). *Manufacturing consent—the political economy of the mass media*. New York: Pantheon.

Human Rights Watch/Americas (1997, January 10). Home page. Available: hrwnyc@hru.org

Lavender, H. (1997, January/February). Hostage taking reveals other side of "miracle." *Latin America Connexions*, 2–4.

Mills, K. (1988). *A place in the news*. New York: Dodd, Mead and Company.

MRTA Communiqués. (1997, March 24). Home page. Available: http://www.Mex-web.com/mrta%20cost.htm

Nacos, B. L. (1994). *Terrorism and the media*. New York: Columbia University Press.

Nikkei. (1997, January 27). Companies in hostage crisis carry on. *The Nikkei Weekly*, 3.

Parenti, M. (1986). *Inventing reality: The politics of the mass media*. New York: St. Martin's Press.

Pedelty, M. (1995). *War stories: The culture of foreign correspondents*. London: Routledge.

Picard, R. (1993). *Media portrayals of terrorism: Functions and meanings of news coverage*. Ames, IA: Iowa State University Press.

Rakow, L. (1987). Looking to the future: Five questions for gender research. *Women's Studies in Communication, 10*, 79–86.

Schlesinger, P., Murdock, G., & Elliott, P. (1983). *Televising "terrorism": Political violence in popular culture*. London: Comedia.

Schmid, A. P., & de Graaf, J. (1982). *Violence as communication: Insurgent terrorism and the Western news media*. London: Sage.

Schudson, M. (1978). *Discovering the news*. New York: Basic Books.

Vilanilam, J. V. (1985). Foreign policy as a dominant factor in foreign news selection and presentation. *Gazette, 32*, 81–85.

Washington Office on Latin America (1997, January 9). Home page. Available: http://www.Amnesty.org

Whitaker, R. (1987). *Double standard: The secret history of Canadian immigration*. Toronto: Lester and Orpen Dennys.

Winter, J. (1997). *Democracy's oxygen: How corporations control the news*. Monteal: Black Rose Press.

9

In The Shadows of the Kremlin: Africa's Media Image from Communism to Post-Communism

Charles Quist-Adade
Wayne State University

Contemporary Russia is riddled with ethnic, racial, linguistic and territorial conflicts. While much is known about its ethnic and territorial cleavages, our knowledge of its racial attitudes is extremely limited. This chapter explores the extent to which the changes in the former Soviet Union (which led to the end of the cold war and the subsequent demise of communism) influenced Russian media coverage of African events during and after the rule of the architect of the changes, Mikhail Gorbachev.

The Western mass media has had largely adverse coverage of Africa that capitalized on its real and imagined weaknesses. During the colonial period, Western

---

*The author would like to thank professors Marlene Cuthbert and K. Ansu-Kyeremeh of the Department of Communication Studies, University of Windsor, for reading the original manuscript and making corrections and useful suggestions.

popular literature painted an image of a dark continent inhabited by rude savages and godless heathens (Melzer, 1988). Contemporary Western news media do not appear to have shifted far away from the colonial representations of Africa as a place where drought, disease, pestilence, and a host of other tragedies occur. Africa is now as it was in the colonial era a space of human suffering (Hawk, 1992).

What is perhaps less known is how the ex-Soviet media, established on the principles of "proletarian internationalism" and "solidarity with peoples fighting for their spiritual, political and economic liberation" (Yermoshkin, 1984, p. 8) covered Africa. This chapter attempts to fill this gap by first identifying the common themes in Soviet coverage during the Soviet pre-glasnost era and then examines coverage during the glasnost and post-glasnost eras.

PRE-GLASNOST COVERAGE OF AFRICA

Historically, the Soviet media have painted a rather simplistic, idealistic, and exotic picture of Africa. A well-known poster, popular among Soviets before *perestroika* summarizes it all: It depicts a muscular African man inside a map of Africa who has broken a hefty chain that had been tied around his hands and feet. ("Perestroika" is Russian for "restructuring." It was the economic plank in ex-Soviet leader Mikhail Gorbachev's two-pronged revolution to "give socialism a humane face." The other plank was "glasnost"—openness in the political/ideological sphere.) The inscription on the famous poster read: *"Svoboda Afrike"* ("Freedom to Africa"). Ostensibly, this was meant to solicit sympathy of the ordinary Soviet citizenry for the African freedom cause.

The Russian political bureaucracy, during the immediate pre-independence era in Africa in the late 1950s and early 1960s, preached that Africans would be better off by breaking the chains of colonial subjugation and Western dependence. Before glasnost, the mass media were instructed to educate the masses that racism or ethnic hatred had dissolved in the "new socialist consciousness"; that it was only in the *nespravdiliviy, dikiiy zapad* ("unjust, wild West") that black people were lynched (Davidson, Olderogge, & Solodinikov, 1966, pp. 46–70). To demonstrate the superiority of socialism over capitalism, Soviet television was saturated with images of homeless, unemployed blacks queuing for kitchen soup in London or Washington, D.C. Meanwhile, the numerous cases of racially motivated attacks and murders of African students in the ex-Soviet Union went unreported.

The tone of media reports about the plight of Africans on the continent and in the diaspora was that of sympathy and solidarity. Deliberate efforts were made to solicit the mercy, goodwill, and support of the Soviet citizenry for the "defenseless victims of capitalist injustice" and "neo-colonial plunder" (Fokeev, 1991, p. 34).

But even in the cold war years, the Soviet media were saturated with negative images of Africa. Pictures emanating from the continent were predominantly those that reflected the seamy side of African life. The blame for Africa's *otsalost* ("backwardness") was squarely put on Western imperialist and neo-colonialist plunder. Where something positive was shown, it was almost always to show the "positive" and modernizing effects of a Soviet "civilizing mission," such as the construction of Soviet-assisted projects in a "socialist-oriented" country.

In the pre-glasnost years, the Soviet media painted a picture of a continent in permanent crisis, in order to show the negative influence of Western presence in Africa. Africans were often shown as "innocent" victims of Western capitalist exploitation and imperialist "blackmail," who needed the "selfless" assistance of the "big-hearted" Soviet Union. The USSR, it was proclaimed, "has always been on the side of the oppressed nations, giving moral and material aid to the national liberation movements" (Davidson, Olderogge, & Solodinikov, 1966, p. 14).

During the cold war era, Soviet journalists, Davidson continues, described African leaders like Idi Amin of Uganda, Macias Nguema of Equatorial Guinea, and Jean Bokassa of the Central African Republic as "military men with patriotic feelings" (Davidson, Olderogge, & Solodinikov, 1966, p. 14), when in fact they butchered thousands of their own people. It is pertinent to mention here that in the 1970s, the Kremlin's Africa policy came to be swayed by a school of thought within the Soviet hierarchy that the USSR should devote its energies in Africa largely to military regimes—particularly those of radical character. The continent, it was noted, had a high percentage of governments under military rule or at least dominated by military elements. Moreover, a substantial number of these governments evinced a resolve to introduce major social transformations in their countries and a willingness to establish strong ties with the USSR (Albright, 1987).

POST-GLASNOST COVERAGE OF AFRICA

The extinction of Communism in Russia and Eastern Europe has led to the appearance of extreme right wing ideologies, nationalistic, anti-Semitic, and fascist ideas hitherto suppressed by the authoritarian system. Their influence in both society and the press is growing. In the former Soviet Union (FSU), the ideas of the national chauvinists and fascists have been aired in mass media and in parliament. In the main, they fault the FSU's policies in the Third World in general and in Africa in particular. In several articles in the mainstream press, politicians and journalists on the left–right political and ideological spectrum have found a scapegoat in the Kremlin's Africa policy. For example, a member of the Russian Parliament complained in the *Literator* newspaper that the former Communist leadership "wasted precious Soviet resources on peoples who have only began to call themselves a people, who have just descended from the palm trees, and have only managed to pronounce the word 'socialism'" (Travkin, 1990, p. 1).

In the mid-1980s, when Mikhail Gorbachev began his *perestroika*/glasnost reforms, the old time Marxist-Leninist state ideology gave way to "new thinking," which saw a new rapprochement with the Western "imperialists." The favorable press the ANC (and indeed many so-called progressive movements in the Third World) enjoyed in the pre-glasnost Soviet Union began to wane.

This was evident, for example, in Soviet media coverage of the release of Nelson Mandela. When Nelson Mandela was freed from 27 years incarceration by the apartheid regime in February 1990, Soviet television ran a mere 30 second report on the historic event at the very tail end of its major evening news program. The sports news of the day was considered more newsworthy than the release of the world's most famous prisoner.

Izvestiya, the government newspaper, did not carry any story on Mandela's release. Instead, it ran a story by its Southern African correspondent on threats from white South African nationalists to kill Mandela if he were freed. *Pravda,* the chief organ of the Communist Party of the Soviet Union (CPSU), did carry the story, but it was a dry, noncommittal, four-paragraph political profile buried under a commentary on the new Soviet–U.S. relationship on page 4.

The poor coverage given to Mandela's release mentioned earlier was not an isolated case. It is the trend in glasnost-style and post-cold war era journalism in the former Soviet Union, now the Commonwealth of Independent States (C.I.S.). *Perestroika* and glasnost in international news coverage went only as far as Europe, North America, and some parts of Asia. To Russian journalists, Africa lay in the darkness of the pre-glasnost, *zastoi* ("stagnation") years of the 1970s. That perhaps explains why hardly any report about Africa is complete without their favorite qualification *"cherny kontinent"* ("the dark continent"). The survey further revealed that contrary to popular belief, the ex-Soviet press, built on the principles of Marxist-Leninist proletarian internationalism and "natural solidarity with the oppressed peoples of the developing world" ("Mirnoe Sochustvovanoe," 1984, p. 1), falls far behind a number of Western publications in depth, frequency, and "objectivity," even given the latter's negative coverage of Africa.

For example, in November and December 1987, *Pravda* (Truth), *Izvestiya* (News), and January-March 1987 *Novoe Vremya* (New Times) published among them 107 journalistic pieces about 23 African countries, compared to 213 items about 22 African countries by the *Daily Telegraph, New York Times*, and *Newsweek* (January-March 1987). More than half (54.2 percent) were devoted to issues concerning the seamy side of African reality, that is about apartheid, civil wars, border clashes, famine, disease, and so on. Only 25.2 percent concerned positive occurrences in Africa, that is, stories that did not fall within the so-called "coup and famine syndrome," but covered topics such as the economy, agriculture, African cooperation, and unity.

Nearly half (45.8 percent) were news briefs of between 30 to 90 words, mostly culled from the main Western wire services—the Associated Press, Reuters, Agence France Press, and the United Press International. Apart from presenting an incomplete and superficial picture of Africa, the gatekeepers of the ex-Soviet publications ostensibly sought, by using Western sources, to absolve themselves from blame for the predominantly negative information. A graphic example of this blame-shifting approach was *Pravda*'s coverage of the origin of the AIDS disease debate. After its initial claim that the disease was artificially manufactured in a military laboratory in Fort Derricks, vehemently protested against by the American government with threats of suspending bilateral talks with the USSR, *Pravda* was compelled to revert to the "African (green monkey) origin of AIDS" version propagated in some Western publications. Thus, under the heading "It originated.... It's not a mutant" ("Proishodilos," 1987, p. 5), *Pravda* culled an article from *Newsweek* that claimed AIDS originated in Africa. But unlike *Newsweek*, who published a rejoinder from a Kenyan journalist to contest the "green monkey" theory, *Pravda* only published a 30-word summary of the *Newsweek* story. By publishing the article without any commentary and no follow-up, *Pravda* sought to tell its readers that the disease originated from Africa and used *Newsweek* to legitimize its claims.

African news only made it to the front page on one occassion. This was a telegram sent on board a plane by the former Ethiopian dictator, Mengistu Haile Mariam to Gorbachev that appeared on the front page of *Izvestiya* ("Of Maviama Gorbachevy," 1987). The stories that were published focused on famine, AIDS in Africa, "the debt trap," crocodiles in the Nile River, and Egyptian mummies. Some stories had racist undertones. For example, a prominent *Izvestiya* columnist, Alexander Bovin (now Russia's ambassador to Israel), wrote with "concern" that the continent could have a population explosion if efforts were made to check the effects of the AIDS disease. To him the disease appeared to be playing a positive role in Africa by keeping the population down!

Later surveys of the Soviet press showed that marginalization of Africa advanced with the pace of glasnost. The main stereotypes employed by Soviet journalists to describe issues involving Africans in the world context underwent drastic changes. In 1985, Africa's problems were attributed to factors such as "birthmarks of capitalism," "imperialist intrigues," and exploitation," "hostile bourgeois propaganda," "U.S. expansionist policies," "a plot against Africa," and many others. Terms like "solidarity," "disinterested aid," "proletarian internationalism," "socialist solidarity," and "socialist fraternity" (Popov, 1990, p. 36), still employed in 1987 to describe Soviet–African relations, disappeared in later years. In their place, new terms such as "universal human values," "global cooperation," and "de-ideologization of interstate relations," came to be used. At the same time, Africa began to be increasingly described as "dark continent."

To determine if there have been any significant changes in press coverage of Africa after the August 1991 aborted coup, which signaled the extinction of Soviet-style Communism and the disintegration of the Soviet Union, two ex-Soviet publications were examined—*Izvestiya* (March 1993) and *Novoe Vremya* (October-December 1991), for both value-loaded coverage and frequency.

For October-December 1991, *Novoe Vremya* carried 12 stories about Africa. Out of this total, as many as 9 were about South Africa. Two articles were positive; the first was a brief article under the rubric *"Lyudi"* ("People"), about the Kenyan environmentalist, Mangari Maathi. The second was on the political transition process in Zambia. Four articles were negative, reflecting the "coup-famine syndrome."

In one of the South African stories, President F.W. de Klerk was described as "reasonable," and the sole "initiator of the peace conference." It framed Mandela and Chief Buthelezi as responsible for deaths of civilians, including victims of "white attacks."

In 1987 (January-March), the tone of *Novoe Vremya*'s articles were generally sympathetic to the African cause, particularly the anti-apartheid struggle. Most of the articles were long (200–2,000 words). In 1991 (October-December), the opposite was the case. The articles were shorter (200–1,000 words). The ANC and its leaders were no longer praised for their "revolutionary resolve to overthrow the evil apartheid system." Instead, the ANC was seen as being part of the problem in South Africa. In 1987 (January-March), only 46 percent of the stories came from South Africa, but in 1991 (October-December), as much as 75 percent were devoted to South Africa alone. Only three other African countries—Kenya, Zambia, and Egypt—were covered.

A similar scenario emerged from the survey of *Izvestiya* for March 1993. The paper carried 21 stories during this period. Only one article was positive—covering oil export earnings for the Egyptian economy—and one was neutral—about Algeria severing diplomatic relations with Iran. Over 57 percent (12 stories) of the total number of stories presented negative coverage of Africa. Over 70 percent of the total number of articles emanated from South Africa and North Africa. No stories came from West Africa at all, while one was about the political turmoil in Zaire, in Central Africa.

Thus, it is clear from the above survey that the loss of interest in Africa by the Soviet/Russian press coincided with the period of the Kremlin's progressive disengagement from the continent. Not surprisingly, this was also the period of East–West rapprochement and the eventual ending of the cold war. The further the Soviet/Russian press trudged on the road to full-blown democracy, the less interest it showed in Africa. All this is logical, from the point of view of the reforms, which Gorbachev inaugurated in the spring of 1985 to "give socialism a human face," but which turned out to be an anti-Communist revolution. As the Soviet state ideology fell apart under the "new thinking," Soviet journalists, like the rest of the intelligentsia, appeared to be groping for a different vision of the world as a whole. Thus, the old image of Africans had to be recast to suit the new, "nonideological" Soviet vision.

Coverage of Africa now does no more than merely catalogue the familiar banes and woes of the continent—the world's highest infant mortality and adult morbidity rates, the lowest life expectancy, the threats of population explosion, AIDS, famine, and so on. While in the past such reports would surely have been spiced with accusations of "Western complicity" or "international finance capital pillage" (Gromyko,1985; see also Izvestiya, 1992), recent reports do not look for external culprits. Most articles now put the blame on Africans themselves. For instance, *Pravda*, in an article titled "We are Africans in a European home" (1991, p. 5), writes that Africans wasted the "solid" amounts of Western credits through bad management and corruption, and that tiny Belgium produces more goods than the whole of Africa taken together.

But the new marginalization also has something to do with the nature of the new eurocentrism engendered by Gorbachev's (1988) so-called "new thinking." The "new thinking" has turned out to be a form of rabid Euro-centrism and even racism. For journalists and politicians, "new thinking" and "universal human values" do not extend beyond the "common European home" and North America.

Excluded from this attitude is South Africa. It is now referred to as a land of eternal spring, an African El Dorado, "a corner in Heaven" (Chaplina, 1992), and "Heaven for whites" (Dubrovisky, 1991), and is reported on liberally and described in glowing terms. The press now traces Russia's historical links with the racist regime as dating back to the Anglo-Boer war, when Russian soldiers were said to have fought on the side of the Boers against the English. The ANC has been referred to as the "richest" liberation movement in the world and calls to cut aid to it have been made in the mainstream media, including *Pravda* and *Izvestiya*. The injustices of the apartheid system, the pet topic for Russian journalists during the cold war era, are hardly mentioned in recent reports.

CONCLUSION

This chapter explored the development of specific images of Africans in the Russian media before and after the demise of Communism by surveying the coverage of Africa by the ex-Soviet press and other media. The following conclusions were drawn:

First, the physics and the dynamics of superpower relations determined Soviet press interest in African events. Second, the Soviet press lost interest in Africa as soon as there was no longer ideological points to score against the West. Had Nelson Mandela been released even two years earlier, the Soviet press would have given entirely different coverage. His release would have been yet another victory for Communism.

Third, Africa got increasingly marginalized as the reforms advanced. Fourth, the paternalistic nature of ex-Soviet propaganda concerning USSR–African relations has led to an anti-African backlash that seeks to wrongly scapegoat Africans as "part of the problem." This frame now dictates news coverage on the continent, with the exception of South Africa.

Finally, with the Communist Party no longer setting the agenda for the press in the wake of the demise of communism, previously subdued anti-African prejudice has been given more transparency.

In conclusion, we can say that the stereotyped, one-sided, and simplified presentation of African problems distorts African reality and hence the perception of Russians about Africans, who see the continent as an embodiment of eternal chaos, political instability, primitive culture, civil disorder, corruption, and disease.

REFERENCES

Afrika, miyi sosushestvovanie. (1992, October 20). *Izvestiya*, p. 5.

Albright, D. E. (1987). *Soviet policy toward Africa revisited*. Washington, DC: Center for Strategic and International Studies.

Chaplina, N. (1992 , October 19). Zebra po imeni YuAR. *Chas pik*, p. 12.

Davidson, A. B., & Olderogge, D. A., & Solodinikov, V. G. (1966). *USSR and Africa*. Moscow: Nauka Publishing House.

Dubrovisky, A. (1991, July 18). Beliy rai? *Znamya yunosti*, p. 3.

Fokeev, G. (1991). Afrika v chem nash natsional'nyi interes? *Aziya i Afrika cegodniya, 5*, pp. 32, 34.

Gorbachev, M. S. (1988). *Perestroika i novoe myshlenie dlya nashei straniy i vsego mira*. Moscow: Progress Publishers.

Gromyko, A. A. (1985). *Aktualnie problemi otnosheniis strannami Afriki*. Moscow: Progress Publishers.

Hawk, B. G. (1992) *Africa's media image*. New York: Praeger.

Melzer, V. (1988). Africa through racist spectacles. *African Events, 2*, 54.

Mirnoe soshystvovanie. (1984, April 20). *Aziya i Afrika cegodniya, 1*.

Popov, Y. (1990). Sosialistecheskoe bratsvo. *Aziya i Afrika cegodniya, 4*, 36.

Proishodilos...ni mutant. (1987, December 29). *Pravda*, p. 5.

Telegrama ot Haili Mariama Gorbachevy. (1987, November 16). *Pravda*, p. 1.

Travkin, N. (1990, December 1). Nelziya tak zhit. *Literator*, p. 1.

We are Africans in a European home. (1991, October 12). *Pravda*, p. 5.

Yermoshkin, N. (1984). *Spiritual colonialism*. Moscow: Progress Publishers.

10

Covering the South Caucasus and Bosnian Conflicts: Or How the Jihad Model Appears and Disappears

Karim H. Karim
Carleton University

DOMINANT DISCOURSES AND COGNITIVE FRAMEWORKS

This study analyzes Canadian newspaper coverage of conflicts between Muslims and Christians in the South Caucasus and in Bosnia-Herzegovina. It discusses the mode of operation of foreign news reporting that reduces complex social and historical factors of war to the religious differences of combatants. In the North,[1] the nation-state is generally conceived as the most rational way to organize polities and as an entity that is not moved to action by what are often seen as irrational religious notions. Whereas journalists usually frame power struggles in the North as ideological or political, they tend to attribute most conflicts in the Southern parts of the world to ancient tribal, religious, or ethnic hatreds. Particular struggles which also have other complex social or economic causes are often reduced to Christian-

Muslim, Muslim-Jewish, Hindu-Muslim, and Sunni-Shia conflicts.[2] Such framing does not require much ideological labour either on the part of media workers or audiences in the North, given the historically constructed image of the Muslim as a primary Other (Hentsch, 1992; Said, 1981).

The following analysis does not function on the belief that there is centrally organized journalistic agenda-setting about Islam—the operation of the mass media in liberal political systems does not favor such overt orchestrations of information. Since human perceptions of everyday encounters are the products of social constructions of meanings rather than the results of objective observations, hegemonic meanings of events are developed through the engineering of societal consensus. Insofar as the bulk of a society subscribes in a particular historical period to a set of fundamental myths, one can speak of a dominant discourse that serves as a matrix for its members' discussions on various issues. The dominant discourses of a society are not manifestations of a monolithic or static set of ideological and cultural currents: their complexities, which reflect the ever-changing structures of power, are shaped by continually evolving and often contradictory combinations of the assumptions, hypotheses, and worldviews of socioeconomic and intellectual elites.

> We must remember that this is not a single, unitary, but a plurality of dominant discourses: that they are not deliberately selected by encoders to reproduce events within the horizon of the dominant ideology, but constitute the *field* of meanings within which they must choose. Precisely because they have become universalized and naturalized, they appear to be the only forms of intelligibility available; they have become sedimented as the only rational, universally valid ones...that these premises embody the dominant definitions of the situation, and represent or refract the existing structures of power, wealth and domination, hence that they *structure* every event they signify, and *accent* them in a manner which reproduces the given ideological structures—this process has become unconscious, even for the encoders. (Hall, 1979, pp. 343–344)

There is, therefore, not a deliberate plan by the mass media to portray specific issues in particular ways, but a hegemonic process through which they adhere to a common field of meaning.[3] It is pertinent, however, to study how certain types of media discourses manage to remain dominant, despite resistance from competing discourses (see Karim, 1993).

The international media, which are largely owned by elites in the U.S. and Western Europe (Bagdikian, 1997), are important channels of dissemination of the hegemonic communicative mode and usually function as instruments of global consensus-engineering. Dominant discourses continually reproduce themselves inter-textually in manners whereby the various communication channels that carry them constantly refer to each other. The mass media are indeed a marketplace of ideas, but the information that supports dominant cultural discourses usually appears in front pages of newspapers or beginnings of news broadcasts. By placing events into ideologically preferred frames, journalists continually highlight the factual evidence that buttresses the dominant discourses of society. Alternative discourses that attempt to offer different worldviews are generally recoded within the frameworks of dominant discourses.

Core images of the Muslim as constituting a danger to Europe seem to be drawn by the North-based global mass media from a collective cultural memory to inform contemporary interactions (Hentsch, 1992; Karim, 1997; Said, 1981). This process appears to have intensified in recent times with the emergence of a "threat vacuum" (Esposito, 1992) in the aftermath of the cold war and the popularity of the "clash of civilizations" (Huntington, 1996) approach to international relations, in which Muslims as a whole are presented as inimical to Western interests. The narratives of international reportage on Muslim societies, while not centrally determined, appear to borrow from these fields of meanings. This form of coverage by major news agencies is globally influential, even having an impact on countries with well-established media systems such as Canada. Although Canadian media institutions do operate a few foreign news bureaus, these are small and understaffed. A number of studies have concluded that Canadian newspapers tend to be heavily reliant on American, British, and French global news services for international content.[4] Soderland (1985, 1990) has demonstrated that while Canadian newspapers accorded less space to specific foreign events than American press, the coverage is qualitatively similar. The present inquiry shows how the dependence of Canadian newspapers on foreign news services, particularly Associated Press and Reuters, has made them adherent to their discourses on Muslims.

The fields of meanings within which journalists function are generally shared by other members of society; indeed, this is vital if media accounts are to be rendered coherent for audiences. Understanding is made possible when both the source and the recipient of communication subscribe to similar cognitive frameworks, which carry out the function of organizing fields of meanings. In his discussion of cognitive macrostructures, Tuen A. van Dijk defines a *script* as generally containing "all we know in our culture about a specific stereotypical type of episode" (1988, p. 18). The framework within which news media tend systematically to report confrontationary episodes as essentially caused by the religious beliefs of combatants can therefore be described as a religious strife script. A cognitive *model*, on the other hand, is that which bases the interpretation of the behavior of a particular group of actors on previous events involving actors with similar social backgrounds (van Dijk, 1988). The specific portrayal of Muslims in various settings as engaging in conflict as a consequence of Islamic beliefs could be termed a "jihad model." Although the Islamic term "jihad" connotes "a righteous struggle" and its import has been debated among Muslims for centuries as ranging in meaning from a personal spiritual struggle to war against non-Muslims[5] and other Muslims, it is usually depicted by the international media in a unidimensional manner as "Islamic holy war."

Dominant construction of conflicts between Christian and Muslim groups by the ostensibly secular Northern mass media has generally involved the portrayal of the Christian as the victim and the Muslim as the victimizer. In the cases where the facts clearly indicate that the reverse is true, that is when Muslims are victims and Christians are victimizers, the jihad model and the religious conflict script either completely disappear or are mitigated. Therefore, when Muslims were viewed as the primary victims in the war in Bosnia-Herzegovina, Serbs—not Christians— were the villains; on the other hand, when Lebanese Christians carried out the 1982 massacres in the Sabra and Shatila refugee camps in Beirut, Palestinians—not Muslims—were the victims. The religious strife script has also been dropped when larger ideological purposes appear to be at stake, as when covering the Central Asian involvement of Turkey, a country with a largely Muslim population, but which is also a member of NATO. It appears that particular scripts and models are dropped when they do not provide support for the prevailing fields of meanings.

MUSLIM AZERBAIJAN AND CHRISTIAN ARMENIA

An example of the use of the jihad model of journalism was the general coverage of the war in the mid-1980s and the early 1990s between Azerbaijan and Armenia, two former Soviet republics in the South Caucasus region. This conflict, which had broken out as the USSR was collapsing, was over Nagorno-Karabakh, a territory inside Azerbaijan with a majority of ethnic Armenians. In a study of the coverage by five American newspapers of this conflict from February through August 1988, Chorbajian (1990) found that:

> The religious strife model [sic] was the most commonly used framework for reader understanding. References to Christian Armenians and Moslem Azerbaijanis appeared in 20% of the articles (47 out of 230). Ethnic conflict and nationalism were nearly as common. References to democracy and self determination appeared only rarely.
>
> Couching events and issues in these terms...allowed the media to conceal the real conflict nexus which was Armenian-Turkish and not Armenian-Moslem. By doing so the media could conveniently avoid calling attention to NATO ally Turkey. Turkey and Turkic appeared in only 6% of the articles (14 out of 230). In most cases it was simply mentioned in passing that Azerbaijanis were a Turkic or Turkic speaking people. (pp. 6–7)

Most articles published in Canadian newspapers about the war between the Azeris and Armenians were filed from transnational news sources, particularly the U.S.- based Associated Press and the British-based Reuters, whose correspondents were reporting from Moscow. Their coverage generally seemed to be characterized by the tendencies outlined by Chorbajian, particularly the emphasis of religious backgrounds of actors over political, historical, territorial, or ethnic factors.

Stories reporting the conflict seemed almost mandatorily to identify the dominant religions of the two states. Typical of news stories about the conflict is the following first paragraph of a February 29, 1992 *Ottawa Citizen* article, attributed primarily to the *Washington Post* news service: "Troops of the former Soviet army were ordered Friday to withdraw from the war-torn enclave of Nagorno-Karabakh in a move that seems likely to lead to an escalation in the fighting between *Muslim Azerbaijan* and *Christian Armenia*" (emphasis added, p. A6). Such references to the religions of the Azeris and Armenians, without explaining how they related to the strife between them, seemed to imply that the war was a religious one involving a theological struggle and perhaps a battle for converts.[6] Readers inundated with reports about the militant march of Islamism would have been led to believe that this was yet another example of that phenomenon, even though there was little evidence to support such an assumption. However, the jihad model almost completely disappeared at the height of the coverage of a March 1992 massacre of Azeris by Armenians, and reappeared clearly only after the situation had peaked. The massacre occurred in Khojaly, an Azeri village in Nagorno-Karabakh. Figures for the number of deaths ran from as low as "dozens" up to a high of 1,000. This story seemed to upset the neat journalistic scheme in which the Christian Armenians of Nagorno-Karabakh were completely surrounded and oppressed by Muslim Armenians who occupied the rest of the country.

Specific methods of narration appear to have been adopted to mitigate the dissonant facts emerging from the coverage of the event in which Muslims were victims and Christians their victimizers. The reporting of the story in morning editions of *The Toronto Star* (the country's largest circulation daily), *The Globe and Mail* ("Canada's National Newspaper"), *The Montreal Gazette*, and *The Ottawa Citizen* between March 2 and 7, 1992, is analyzed below. Several trends can be identified in the coverage of the killings:

- the massacre itself was treated as a secondary issue, usually at the ends of articles;
- prominence was given to Armenian denials, and Azeri "allegations" were characterized as "gross exaggeration";
- difficulties were cited in verifying the exact number of deaths due to the inaccessibility of the area, despite the display of bodies on Azerbaijani television;
- the scale of deaths in the Khojaly massacre was downplayed by placing them within the general loss of life in the war at large;
- when the facts of an Armenian massacre of Azeri villagers became irrefutable, all indications of religious identity completely disappeared as did photographs of the bodies and mourners;
- even though the newspapers under study were using the same news wire material, the narrative in one daily began returning to systematic references about religion earlier than those in the others; and

■ there was a complete absence of comment on the massacre either in editorials or in opinion columns.

The following is a day-by-day tracking of the coverage of the Khojaly massacre in the four newspapers over six days.

The story first broke on Monday, March 2, 1992, in the *Montreal Gazette*, headlined "CIS moves to pull out troops: Azeri refugees accuse Armenians of killing hundreds" (p. B1). The main subject of the article by Reuters, datelined Agdam, Azerbaijan (a town close to Khojaly), was the troop pull-out by the Russian-led Commonwealth of Independent States; only three of the eight paragraphs (beginning with the fifth) dealt with claims of the massacre. An accompanying AFP (Agence France Presse) photograph showed an elderly Azeri man weeping "as a body of a child is brought into makeshift morgue in Agdam" (p. B1). In contrast to the usual reporting of the Azeri-Armenian war, there was no reference to the religious affiliation of the actors. None of the other three dailies mentioned the event that day.

On the following day, Tuesday, March 3, all four newspapers referred to "allegations" about the massacre. The piece that referred to the killings most clearly was a Reuters story and photo filed from Agdam published in the *Toronto Star* (p. A3). There was a sole, indirect allusion to religion in the caption of the picture: "An Azeri woman cries out for her dead father yesterday as his body lies in a mosque with those of other victims"; the religion of Armenians was not identified. The *Montreal Gazette* (p. A8) carried a write-up with a Moscow dateline by the *Los Angeles Times* news service, squeezed in between reports of troubles in other parts of the former Soviet Union. It had an AFP picture in which an "Azeri policeman removes the body of a girl near Khojaly, which Armenian militants attacked last week"; the surrounding field was strewn with bodies. No religion was mentioned. The *Globe and Mail*'s article (p. A8) on the event used Associated Press and Reuters stories, also filed from Moscow. Only 3 of the 14 paragraphs (beginning with the ninth) dealt with the killings; no photo was used. There were no indications of religious affiliations. The *Ottawa Citizen* (p. A6) was the only paper to carry a Canadian wire service article on the massacre, filed from Moscow by Southam News. Here too, the focus was on the Russian "troop exit rather than the killings." "Christian Armenians" were referred to in the context of a political settlement, not that of the deaths of Azeris—whose creed was not identified.

It is noteworthy that all four papers using four different sources (American, British, and Canadian) mentioned the reported numbers of casualties in the middle or end of the respective articles. The *Globe*'s (1992, March 3, p. A8) headline was, "CIS sends general to oversee pullout: Azerbaijani official says 50 killed as violence intensifies in enclave," with the figure of 1,000 deaths from Azeri sources not appearing until the tenth paragraph. *The Star*'s (p. A3) headline read, "Azeris mourn victims of alleged massacre"; the lead referred to dozens of bodies, but again, the figure of 1,000 was not mentioned until the ninth paragraph. Neither the *Montreal*

Gazette nor the *Ottawa Citizen's* headlines alluded to the massacre, with references to 1,000 not appearing until the middle of the articles.

In contrast to this tendency, figures of deaths were generally given prominence when Armenians were the victims as a result of the general conflict. A March 12, 1988, write-up in the *Ottawa Citizen* headlined "Armenian massacre reported" (p. A6) had placed the higher estimate of deaths in the lead paragraph and the lower one in the middle of the article. The first paragraph stated: "Witnesses to the violence in the Azerbaijani city of Sumgait spoke of a 'horrifying pogrom' and the killing of 'at least' 350 people, a man who visited the city Wednesday said here yesterday." And halfway down the report: "The [police] officer said that reports of Azerbaijanis storming the houses of Armenians were true and that about 300 people had been injured and 37 were dead." The religious strife angle was also emphasized here: "Shikov said that the violence in Sumgait was one-sided, with Azerbaijani Moslems killing Armenian Christians. 'This was no ethnic conflict,' he said. 'It was a genuine pogrom.'" The use of the word *pogrom*, which is most frequently used to describe attacks on Jews in late 19th- and early 20th-century Russia, thus linked a Muslim group in a former Soviet republic to a form of anti-Semitic violence.[7] The word was never used in the four dailies under study to describe the Armenian killings of Azeris in their coverage of the Khojaly massacre.

On Wednesday, March 4, evidence of large scale killings of Azeris in Khojaly grew but there were no photographs related to the story in any of the four Canadian publications. *The Montreal Gazette* (p. A8) had an article from the *Los Angeles Times* news service datelined Moscow and an editorial (p. B2) on the Azeri-Armenian conflict, although the latter dwelt only with the CIS pull-out. (During the entire week of the coverage of the massacre this was the only editorial on the war in the four journals.) *The Globe and Mail* (p. A9) printed a write-up filed from Agdam, with joint AP and Reuters credits. The *Toronto Star* (p. A13) used an AP article, also with an Agdam dateline, and the *Ottawa Citizen* (p. A6) had an AP story from Moscow. There was not a single mention of religion in any of the four papers. Thus, at the height of the ongoing discovery of the massacre, all references to the religious backgrounds of the victims or the villains had disappeared, as had pictures of the bodies or people mourning. However, all four newspapers prominently carried denials by Armenian officials about the large scale of Azeri deaths in their March 4th editions.

On Thursday, March 5, the *Citizen* did not have coverage of the Azeri-Armenian conflict. The *Star's* story (p. A13) from the *Los Angeles Times* news service, datelined Moscow, stated "Azeri TV shows piles of bodies." But again there was no accompanying picture and no mention of religion. However, the *Gazette* carried an AP article with an AP photo of an Azeri woman weeping at a gravesite, and *did* have three references to religious affiliations:

> Wails of mourning mixed with gunfire yesterday as fighting edged closer to this city bordering the disputed region of Nagorno-Karabakh and Azerbaijanis buried more

dead from last week's Armenian attack.

Azerbaijan's government called on the United Nations to send peacekeeping troops to patrol the mostly *Muslim* country's border with *Christian Armenia* and prevent further bloodshed in Nagorno-Karabakh.

The government condemned the assault on the town of Khojaly as deliberate genocide and accused former Soviet troops of complicity. A spokesman for the troops, now under the command of the Commonwealth of Independent States, flatly denied any involvement.

Presidents Boris Yeltsin of Russia and Nursultan Nazarbayev of Kazakhstan made urgent new appeals for a ceasefire in the bloodiest ethnic conflict in the former Soviet Union. Nazarbayev, a *Muslim*, said he was "especially stunned" by the storming of Khojaly. (emphasis added, 1992, March 5, p. A11)

The *Globe*'s front page had the same AP picture as the *Gazette*, with a write-up from AP and Reuters on an inside page. The initial paragraphs were largely similar to those in the Montreal paper; however, unlike the article in the *Gazette*, indications of religion were completely absent. Compare this paragraph in the *Globe*'s article with the one quoted above from the *Gazette*:

Wails of mourning mixed with gunfire yesterday as Azerbaijanis buried their dead and fighting edged closer to this city bordering on the disputed region of Nagorno-Karabakh.

Azerbaijan's government condemned last week's Armenian assault on the town of Khojaly as "deliberate genocide" and charged complicity by troops of the Commonwealth of Independent States. Commonwealth armed forces denied involvement.

Presidents Boris Yeltsin of Russia and Nursultan Nazarbayev of Kazakstan made urgent appeals for a ceasefire in the bloodiest ethnic conflict in the former Soviet Union. Nazarbayev said he was "especially stunned" by the storming of Khojaly. (1992, March 5, p. A8)

Without having access to the original wire copy from AP and Reuters, there is no way to know whether the *Globe*'s editor systematically edited out all references to religion or that the *Gazette*'s editor inserted them.

On Friday, March 6, the *Globe*'s article (p. A8) on the Azeri-Armenian war did make references to religion, albeit in the second to last paragraph: "Mr. Mutalibov accused Russia of being behind the recent upsurge of fighting and success by Christian Armenians in Nagorno-Karabakh, which is predominantly Armenian but lies within Muslim Azerbaijan." In the inverted triangle arrangement of the write-up, based on AP and Reuters stories from Baku (the capital of Azerbaijan), the most important facts seemed to be that two former Soviet republics, Azerbaijan and Moldova, were accusing Russia of escalating ethnic strife within their respective borders. It was only at the 11th paragraph that references to the Khojaly massacre began, with religious affiliations indicated in the 15th paragraph. The *Gazette* (p. A7) had a shorter version of the AP/Reuters story and an AP photo of family members weeping at the "coffin of Nagorno-Karabakh fighting" (not used by the *Globe*). The Montreal paper had only 11 paragraphs, which did not include the one referring to religion, since the bottom of the inverted triangle was omitted. Neither the *Star* nor the *Citizen* reported on the conflict in their March 6 editions.

On Saturday, March 7, the four dailies had articles about the resignation of the president of Azerbaijan. The *Gazette*'s report was by the Canadian Press (CP), with a Moscow dateline. The 10th paragraph made references to religion:

> Nagorno-Karabakh is a predominantly Christian Armenian enclave inside mostly Muslim Azerbaijan where more than 1,000 people have been killed in four years of ethnic violence. It's the longest-running and most violent of the many ethnic disputes in the former Soviet Union. (p. A10)

The write-up then went on to give brief accounts of recent casualties and of "Azerbaijani claims" of an Armenian "massacre" without giving any numbers. The story in the *Citizen* was credited primarily to Southam News with "files from CP and Washington Post" (p. A6). It is clear that the file from CP was the same as that used by the *Gazette*, since two paragraphs—including the one quoted above—were almost identical in both the articles. However, the references to religion made by the *Gazette* were absent in the Ottawa publication. It appears that either the *Gazette* editorially inserted religious affiliations or the *Citizen* removed them.

Interestingly, that day's issue of the *Citizen* had another article from CP on the same page as the Azeri-Armenian conflict, which did refer to religious loyalties but not to the Khojaly massacre. This was a story on Canadian medical aid, also filed from Moscow; it was placed next to the one on the resignation of the Azerbaijani president. The sixth paragraph read:

> Nagorno-Karabakh is a predominantly Christian Armenian enclave inside mostly Muslim Azerbaijan where more than 1,000 people have been killed in four years of ethnic violence. But a new level of fighting flared recently in the isolated mountainous region. (1992, March 7, p. A6)

Although the article mentioned "1,000" as being *all* the deaths during the previous four years, this was the same number of deaths attributed by Azeri sources to the Khojaly massacre. No direct allusions were made to recent reports of the Khojaly massacre, even though a spokesman for the International Committee of the Red Cross was quoted as saying that the Red Cross used part of the money to purchase 1,000 "body bags" to remove the bodies of recent fighting. While the urgent shipment of Canadian medical aid seemed to have been prompted by the recent massacre, the write-up did not clearly refer to the event. It appears that the paper was avoiding the identification of Armenians as Christians and Azeris as Muslims in stories where the former appeared to be the villains and the latter their victims.

The same seemed to be the case in that day's *Globe and Mail*, which also had two articles on the same page about the Azeri-Armenian situation. A Reuters piece from Baku reported on the stepping-down of the Azerbaijani president, stating that:

> The public outcry that led to Mr. Mutalibov's resignation was sparked by serious Azeri losses during Armenia's capture of the town of Khojaly last week.
> More than 100 bodies, many mutilated, were found in surrounding hills and Azeri officials said at least 1,000 people had been killed. (1992, March 7, p. A6)

No mention was made of religious backgrounds, which, however, did appear in the adjoining feature article (p. A6), written by the newspaper's Moscow bureau chief and datelined Yerevan (Armenia's capital). As in the CP file used that day by the *Citizen*, there was no reference to the massacre in the latter article that did describe Armenians as Christians and Azeris as Muslims. The *Star*'s piece on the Azerbaijani president's resignation, filed from Moscow by the *Washington Post* news service, related that "Azerbaijani militiamen have sworn to avenge an alleged massacre by Armenian forces last week in Khojaly, an Azerbaijani town in Karabakh" (p. A12). There were two Reuters photos related to the president's downfall but, again, no mention was made of the creeds of the Azeris or Armenians. However, immediately below this story was the continuation of a front-page feature story by the paper's Moscow bureau chief on the growth of "Islam's political appeal" in other former Soviet republics of Uzbekistan and Tajikistan (pp. A1, A12).

Therefore, from March 2 to March 7 the four newspapers' coverage of the massacre in Khojaly had consistently tended to downplay the event's significance. The claims of Azeris were described as "exaggerations" and the lower numbers of deaths were given prominence over the higher ones, even though in previous cases when Armenians had been killed the trend was reversed. There was no editorial comment condemning or even lamenting the loss of life in any of the four papers. Most remarkable of all was the almost complete disappearance of references to religion at the peak of the massacre's coverage. The newspapers seemed extremely reluctant to refer to the facts that the killers in this case happened to be Christians and their victims Muslims. Whereas religious affiliations tended gratuitously to be stated in the general reporting of the Azeri-Armenian war, the Khojaly massacre did not seem to fit the dominant model in which the Muslim Other was threatening Christendom.

In subsequent coverage of the conflict, the Khojaly massacre had become insignificant and the reportage went back to referring routinely to people according to their religious backgrounds within the jihad model. For example, a write-up in the March 11 issue of the *Globe*, credited to AP and Reuters and datelined Brussels (since it was written within the context of the Conference on Security and Co-operation in Europe's discussions), stated: "The mostly *Christian* Armenian enclave, with about 200,000 people, has been controlled by predominantly *Muslim* Azerbaijan since 1929" (emphasis added, p. A9). Compare this with the following, which had appeared in the *Toronto Star* (1992, March 4, p. A13) and *The Ottawa Citizen* (1992, March 4, p. A6) at the height of the reportage of the massacre, when both of these newspapers had used AP stories: "Nagorno-Karabakh's population of about 200,000 is mainly Armenian. But it is surrounded by Azerbaijan, which has administered the territory since 1929." At that time, it had apparently seemed inappropriate to refer to religions. Although the March 11 *Globe* story was accompanied by a picture of Azeri mourners at Agdam, it made no mention of the Khojaly massacre, but referred instead to the "ancient accusations" of Armenia and Azerbaijan against each other. Thus, ideological closure was effected over the event (which had resulted in the highest death toll of any single encounter in the war) by relegating it to the catalogue of "ancient accusations."

A March 14 feature article in *The Star* by a staff writer, who seemed to be working in the same manner, juxtaposed the Armenian "massacre" against "Azeri pogroms." He went on to broaden the jihad model to place the Azeri-Armenian struggle within "ancient rivalry" of "Islamic powers" such as Turkey, Iran, Iraq, and Egypt:

> But the South Caucasus situation is only part of a much wider conflict.
> Today, a struggle is going on for the leadership of the Islamic world.
> It is the same struggle that had been waged for centuries before the Western empires, with their overwhelming military technology, forced much of the Islamic world into a straitjacket.
> It is not a question of Sunni Muslims versus Shias, although that is part of it. Throughout history there have been East–West struggles in the region—between Greece and Persia, between Rome and Persia, between the Arabs and the Persians, between the Ottomans and the Persians.
> The increasing modernization of the Islamic world—and the fall of Communist Russia—has revived that struggle. (p. D5)

Through some remarkable contortions of logic, the writer attempted to show that the very modernization of the Muslim people was making them revert increasingly to their ancient ways. The implication was that if the Northern powers do not again force Muslim-majority countries into a neocolonial "straitjacket," the region would become a hotbed of religious militancy.

It is ironic that even when Muslims are massacred in large numbers by non-Muslims, the blame can be directed toward Islam. According to Jacques Ellul (1969), the integration propagandist can count on the inexhaustible capacity of the "current-events man" to forget the details of daily reporting:

> ... such a man is highly sensitive to the influence of present-day currents; lacking landmarks, he follows all currents. He is unstable because he runs after what happened today; he relates to the event, and therefore cannot resist any impulse coming from that event. Because he is immersed in current affairs, this man has a psychological weakness that puts him at the mercy of the propagandist. No confrontation ever occurs

between the event and the truth; no relationship ever exists between the event and the person. Real information never concerns such a person. (1969, p. 47)

Although such a complete divorce from the "truth" probably does not occur all the time, the continual output of the mass media overwhelms the person absorbed primarily with immediate happenings. A newspaper reader cannot be expected to refer to the details of previous reports to notice inconsistencies and contradictions; s/he merely retains an overall impression that conforms to the basic myths and cognitive models concerning the particular issue. In the coverage of the Azeri-Armenian conflict, the lasting impression is that of Islam destabilizing the global system of nation states.

GEORGIA, BOSNIA-HERZEGOVINA

Whereas the jihad model was only occasionally dropped as a frame for the Azeri-Armenian war, it has been almost completely avoided in the dominant reporting of conflicts where Muslims are normatively identified as victims. An AP feature article on former Central Asian Soviet republics in the June 15, 1992, issues of the *Ottawa Citizen* (p. A1) and the *Globe and Mail* (p. A6), which referred to the conflict between "Christian Armenians" and "Muslim Azeris," preferred to describe a conflict in "South Ossetia, a separatist region of Georgia" as "ethnic," even though the waring parties there also happened to be Christian and Muslim. The occasional backgrounder like that on the various "ethnic tensions" in the disintegrating Soviet Union published in the December 26, 1991, issue of the *Ottawa Citizen* from the *Chicago Tribune*, while citing the differing religious affiliations, expressly stated that the problem was "territorial." This write-up distinguished between the respective struggles of various peoples in Nagorno-Karabakh and Georgia:

Nagorno-Karabakh, a kind of Soviet version of Northern Ireland, is controlled by Shiite Muslims from Azerbaijan but populated mainly by Christian Armenians. It has witnessed hundreds of deaths as the Azeris asserted their control over the local Armenians.

An almost identical situation exists in the northern part of Georgia, where wealthier and better educated Georgians control an area known as southern Ossetia, which is populated by poorer Persian-descended people.

While there are religious elements involved—the Georgians are Christian, the Ossetians Muslim—the real distinction is over land and the desire of the Ossetians to be part of Russia, not Georgia.

Territorial disputes are also at the root of ethnic clashes between Muslim Abkhazians and Christian Georgians around the Black Sea coastal city Sukhumi. The area is the traditional homeland for Abkhazians, who reject the Georgians' domination. (p. A2)

According to this narrative, whereas the Armenians were the victims in Azerbaijan, the Ossetians and Abkhazians had this role in Georgia. Armenians in Nagorno-Karabakh were "controlled by Shiite Muslims from Azerbaijan" and there had been "hundreds of deaths as the Azeris asserted their control over the local Armenians." Whereas the "wealthier and better-educated Georgians control an area known as southern Ossetia, which is populated by poorer Persian-descended people" and that the Abkhazians "reject the Georgians' domination" over their "traditional homeland."

This conforms to what Ivie (1980) has identified as one of the classic ways of portraying victimage: "The usual strategy is to construct the image indirectly through contrasting references to the adversary's coercive, irrational, and aggressive attempts to subjugate a freedom-loving, rational, and pacific victim" (p. 284). "Control" and "domination" were ascribed to the Azeris and Georgians, whereas the victims (the Armenians, the "poorer" Ossetians, and the Abkhazians) strove to assert their own sovereignty over areas where they were in majority and that were their "traditional homelands" (*The Ottawa Citizen*, 1991, December 26, p. A2). It is also interesting to note the manners in which relationships with the "Islamic"[8] bogeyman Iran are constructed: while the Azeris were identified as Shiite[9] Muslims (the majority branch of Muslims in Iran), the Ossetians were described as "Persian-descended people." (Following the establishment of the Shi'ite *ulama*-led government in Tehran, the use of "Persia" and "Persians" has become a common discursive tactic for creating distance from Iran, which was historically also referred to as Persia).[10]

Thus, when the Christian was the victim, the conflict was constructed as being primarily religious; in the case where the Muslim had this role, it was constructed as being "territorial," even though territory was clearly the major problem in all these wars. No explanation was given for depicting the conflict in Nagorno-Karabakh as religious, except for implications arising from it being "a kind of Soviet version of Northern Ireland" and the Azeris being Shi'ite Muslims. And since "Shi'ite Iran" is generally viewed as wanting to export its revolution, the implication seemed to be that Shi'ite Azeris must also be working for the domination of Islam over Nagorno-Karabakh. One file photo used by the *Citizen* to illustrate the June 15, 1992, article showed an Azeri with a raised, clenched fist carrying a flag with a crescent and a star, considered to be an Islamic symbol.

The negative characterization of the Georgian government was especially evident in the dominant Northern discourses' depiction of the struggle between the supporters of the former president Zviad Gamsakhurdia (who was toppled from power in January 1992) and those Georgians who opposed his authoritarian rule. During that time, the Ossetians, who were being suppressed by Gamsakhurdia's government, emerged as victims in the coverage of this conflict by transnational news agencies' correspondents based in Moscow.

Georgia's image had also suffered in the reporting of its relations with Moscow, from which it was one of the earliest to secede. As specific "nationalities" within the Soviet Union began to agitate for autonomy or independence from Moscow in the late 1980s and early 1990s, the Gorbachev and Yeltsin governments were generally portrayed as holding on course the progressive programs of reform in the face of conservative communist reaction. There seemed to be apprehension among Western "experts" and Moscow-based journalists such as the *Los Angeles Times* correspondent who wrote in an article reprinted in the *Montreal Gazette*: "Such conflicts would provide conservatives with their most convincing argument—that democratization within the Soviet empire is impossible, and in fact suicidal" (1987, June 11, p. B3). Even though there were a number of divergences in the respective discourses of the West and the disintegrating Soviet Union, they seemed to converge on this issue. Since the conflict between the Georgians and the Ossetians—a tiny ethnic minority that has traditionally been loyal to Moscow—was placed within the larger one between the Georgian and the Soviet governments, Northern journalists did not seem to feel the need to couch the issue in religious terms.

However, the religious strife script *was* used by dominant Northern discourses in reporting an uprising in the mostly Muslim Chechnya, a small southern republic in the Russian federation bordering Georgia. One newsreader on the Newsworld channel of the Canadian Broadcasting Corporation stated that it was "the rebellious religion of Islam"[11] that was opposing Moscow. The Chechens had become part of the Muslim Other in the aftermath of the cold war. It is also worth noting that the dominant coverage of the conflict between Chechnya and the Moscow government stressed the "Islamic" zeal of Chechens in December 1994 and January 1995, when the latter were preparing for war.[12] However, subsequent to the brutal invasion of the republic by Russian troops and the clear emergence of Chechens as victims, references to religion almost completely vanished.

The religious conflict script was largely avoided in another war involving Christian and Muslim antagonists, which took place in Bosnia-Herzegovina in the early 1990s. Since 1968, Slavs of Muslim cultural backgrounds in the former Yugoslav region have been permitted to register officially as belonging to a "Muslim nationality," even if they were not practicing Muslims. Muslims in the former Yugoslavia are distinguished from "Serbs," "Croats," and other "nationalities," even though they share common ethnic origins with these groups. The "Serbs" emerged as the villains in their conflict with "Croatians" during 1991 and early 1992. When the focus moved to Bosnia-Herzegovina, the "Serbs," having been cast in the role of the victimizers, remained the villains and Bosnia's "Muslims" and "Croats" became the new victims. Following the large-scale atrocities by the "Serbs" against the "Muslims," the latter came to be identified as "the truest victims" (compare *The Ottawa Citizen*, 1992, July 31, p. A8). Since newspaper accounts covering the war did not explain that Bosnian "Muslims" were identified as such because that was their official designation as a "nationality" in the former Yugoslavia, the readership most likely saw this only as a religious identity rather than a religiocultural one. However, it seems remarkable that even though members of a religious group were named as primary victims, the dominant coverage of this conflict resisted framing it as a religious war. While there occasionally was coverage of "Croats" and "Serbs" going to church during cease fires and of Muslim burial ceremonies, the war was not described as "Christian-Muslim." The religious affiliations of the "Serbs" were either not identified within the context of the brutal conflict or their *Eastern Orthodox* beliefs were emphasized, harking back to the distinctions between the Western and the Eastern churches. Even in reports that indicated that both "Serb" and "Croat nationalists" were working together to take advantage of the Muslims' vulnerability to enlarge their respective territories, the conflict was not portrayed as a "Christian-Muslim" one. For example, the headline in the *Citizen*: "Croats, Serbs plot to isolate Muslims." (1993, May 15, p. A9)

The reluctance of Northern journalists in casting the Bosnian conflict as a religious one contrasted markedly with the manners in which other wars between peoples of Christian and Muslim backgrounds have been characterized as such. Statements by "Muslim fundamentalists" are usually taken at face value when they indicate that the reasons for their actions are "Islamic." But declarations by some "Serbs" that they were fighting for Christendom were largely treated with scepticism.[13] A Reuters article in the *Toronto Star* stated:

> Bosnia's Serbs, condemned internationally as the aggressors in a savage war, want to be seen as Christian crusaders saving Europe from Islam....
> "This is a religious war," said orthodox Bishop Vasil from the northeast Bosnian city of Tuzla. "The West does not understand."
> But skeptics say Orthodox churches in the area are poorly attended, and that the faith is being used as a cloak for purely political ends.
> "This is a war for land and money. Religion is an excuse," said a Catholic priest, one of the scared Croatian minority still living in Banja Luka.
> Muslim charity workers in the city agreed, saying relations with the orthodox Church were good before the war began. (1992, April 4, p. A14)

One rarely finds similar examples in the international media discussing how Islam may be used "as a cloak for purely political ends." The "religious" motives of "Muslim fundamentalists" seem beyond doubt because in dominant Northern scripts that is how Muslims are supposed to act (Said, 1981); true Christians, on the other hand, are not expected to engage in savage warfare.

Occasional television interviews of Bosnian "Muslims" depicted them making references to "Serb" snipers as "terrorists." But the journalists who reported that the "Serbs" were motivated in their attacks on "Muslims" by fears of perceived threats to the Eastern Orthodox Church in Bosnia-Herzegovina did not refer to the former as "Christian terrorists" or "Christian fundamentalists." And although the Bosnian Serbs were fighting against the internationally-recognized government of Bosnia-Herzegovina, they were rarely described as "rebels." In a letter to the *Globe and Mail*, Wilfred Cantwell Smith, a noted Orientalist, wrote:

The headline of your article Muslim Forces Threaten Canadians (June 21) is a flagrant illustration of a general anti-Islamic bias shared by most Westerners and fuelled by most Western media, especially in North America.

On the same page as the above article about threats, you speak in a longer article of "the beleaguered Bosnian government," Western "support of the Bosnian government," "the Bosnian government's dream of a pluralistic democracy," and so on, and never once mention that they are Muslim—for in that article they appear in a sympathetic light. Once there is a matter of their making an anti-UN move, however, this other article speaks of "the Muslim-led Bosnian government," and the headline refers only to their being Muslim.

I have not failed to notice that your reporting on the former Yugoslavia has throughout spoken of "the Serbs" and "the Croats." We never read, this past while, that the "christians" took all those UN hostages, including Canadians, although the Serbs are just as much Orthodox ..., and the Croats just as much Roman Catholic, as the Bosnian government and its supporters are Muslim. (1995, p. A12)

That this letter by a prominent Orientalist criticizing dominant discourses was published by the *Globe and Mail* (although his position as professor emeritus in the comparative history of religion at Harvard University may have had a lot to do with this) with the headline "Anti-Islamic bias shows," confirms that alternative discourses are not completely absent from "Canada's National Newspaper" nor from Orientalism. But such views only receive occasional exposure in the mainstream media.

Northern journalists have found the religious strife script a convenient narrative device to explain conflicts whose historical and sociological roots are complex. The jihad model has become a handy frame within which to report events relating to conflicts in which members of one of the warring groups happen to be Muslim. Northern media workers appear to be comfortable with this mode of news coverage since they share in a field of meaning that holds Islam to be a primary Other and a religion that promotes the use of violence. On the other hand, even though the Northern mass media ostensibly have no religious affiliations, they seem to be reluctant to identify Christians as villains, especially when they have victimized non-Christians. What appeared to be the almost mandatory attachment of the adjective "Christian" to Armenians in the coverage of the Azeri-Armenian war was dropped when the Armenian army massacred Azeri villagers. The jihad model and references to religion seem to disappear from Northern journalists' narratives in such cases. But they reappear when Muslims re-emerge as villains in the drama of political and territorial conflicts. While these may not be conscious tendencies on the part of media workers, they do appear do be remarkably consistent.

NOTES

[1] With the end of the cold war and the increasing coalescence of the interests of the West with those of Eastern Europe, it is pertinent here to use the geopolitical categories of North and South.

[2] For example, Western journalists had divided Beirut during the Lebanese civil war in the 1970s and the 1980s into "Christian East Beirut" and "Muslim West Beirut." The veteran British correspondent in the Middle East, G.H. Jansen, in discussing an incident in which the forces of a (Catholic) Maronite general were shelling parts of the city, indicates how the overlapping of religious communities within the various factions and geographical areas was distorted by this simplistic dichotomy: "The target for Aoun's gunners, many of whom are themselves Muslims, has been what is usually called 'predominantly Muslim West Beirut,' but at present there are almost as many Christians as Muslims in West Beirut" (1989, p. 57).

[3] See Malek (1997) for a range of discussions of political and ideological influence on foreign news reporting.

[4] Compare Maybee (1980); Robinson (1983); Soderland (1985, 1990); Soderland, Krause, and Price (1991); Soderland, Wagenberg, and Pemberton (1994); Surlin and Cuthbert (1986).

[5] Compare Arkoun, 1994; Maududi, 1976; Peters, 1977.

[6] Occasions in which Azerbaijanis had attacked Christian places of worship tended to be highlighted; for example, an article in the *Montreal Gazette*, about an aerial Azerbaijani bombing of Armenia, stated: "Yesterday morning, Sukhoi-25 jets raided residential areas of Stepanakert and dropped bombs near an Armenian church, Christ the Savior, in nearby Shusha at the precise moment the divine liturgy was being said" (1992, August 24, p. B1). It was as if the bombing by Azerbaijani planes was timed exactly to coincide with the sacred Christian ritual.

[7] Edward Said (1994) has noted that, despite the weight of historical evidence over the last 1,400 years that shows that relations between Muslims and Jews have for the large part been harmonious, certain Orientalists like Bernard Lewis have been laying the groundwork over the last few decades linking Islam to anti-Semitism (p. 317). The memories of several centuries of persecution of Jews by Christian Europeans has been partially eclipsed by the Arab-Israeli conflict, which began after World War II. Dominant discourses also occasionally relate Islam to Nazism. During the Gulf War, the demonization of Saddam Hussein was accomplished by endowing him with Islamic characteristics as well as by comparing him with Hitler. From time to time, the mass media carry casual remarks linking Islamism to Nazism, as in the Montreal newspaper *La Presse*'s review of a book on the veiling of Muslim women (1996, November 17, p. B6). The consequences of such discourses seem to be that the blame for all terrorist activities against Jews immediately falls upon Muslims, as in the 1994 bombing of a Jewish community center in Buenos Aires. It was not until one and a half years later, having failed to find any evidence of a Muslim link, that Argentinean authorities arrested neo-Nazis, including members of the country's army.

[8] Mohammed Arkoun remarks that "We can no longer use the word 'Islam' without quotation marks. It has been so misused and distorted by the media, Muslims themselves, and political scientists that we need a radical reworking of the concept" (1991, p. 50).

[9] The term "Shi'ite" has developed a negative connotation in Northern discourses since the Iranian revolution in 1979. A columnist for the *Atlanta Journal-Constitution* declared, "Where there are Shi'ites, there is trouble" (Said, 1981, p. 81). The word has also been decontextualized by some sources to refer to all forms of religious extremism; for example, an advertisement in the April 1988 issue of *Harper's* magazine referred to the Christian right in the U.S. as "Shi'ite Christianity."

[10] However, it is noteworthy that the use of "Iranian" had predominated during the reign of pro-Western Shah Mohammed Reza Pahlevi, who was overthrown in 1979. A pertinent example is this description of the Ossetians in a book on the peoples and customs of West Asia: "The Ossetians are an Islamic people who speak a language that is related to Iranian (Persian)" (Wouters, 1979, p. 43).

[11] Lorne Saxberg, 1:00 news bulletin, Newsworld channel, November 9, 1991.

[12] Compare Andrew Higgins, *The Independent*, "Fanaticism rooted in Stalin-era repression" (*The Ottawa Citizen*, 1994, p. B3); Reuters photo, captioned "Answering Call: Muslims from the village of Sernovodsk pray in a local mosque Friday after religious and political leaders called for a holy war against advancing Russian troops" (*The Ottawa Citizen*, 1994, p. G5); Michael Specter, *The New York Times*, "Religion and the defence of Chechnya" (*The Globe and Mail*, 1995, p. A17).

[13] Compare Lance Gay, Scripps Howard News Service, "The 500 Year War: The Balkans are still fighting battles that began in medieval times" (*The Ottawa Citizen*, 1992, p. B3); Kitty McKinsey, Southam News, "Serb leader pledges truce" (*The Ottawa Citizen*, 1992, p. H2); and John Burns, the *New York Times* news service, "Portrait of a Killer: A young Serb tells gruesome tale of death in the 'ethnic cleansing' of Bosnia" (*The Ottawa Citizen*, 1992, p. B1).

REFERENCES

Arkoun, M. (1991). Islamic cultures, developing societies, modern thought. In H. Salam (Ed.), *Expressions of Islam in buildings* (pp. 49–64). Geneva, Switzerland: Aga Khan Trust for Culture.

Arkoun, M. (1994). *Rethinking Islam: Common questions, uncommon answers* (R. D. Lee, Trans.). Boulder, CO: Westview Press.

Bagdikian, B. H. (1997). *The media monopoly*. Boston: Beacon Press.

Burns, J. (1992, November 28). Portrait of a killer: A young Serb tells gruesome tale of death in the "ethnic cleansing" of Bosnia. *The Ottawa Citizen*, p. B1.

Chorbajian, L. (1990, October). *Nagorno Karabakh: A study in mythmaking*. Paper presented at the Media and Crisis Conference, Laval University, Quebec City, Canada.

Ellul, J. (1969). *Propaganda: The formation of men's attitudes* (K. Kellen & J. Lerner, Trans.). New York: Alfred A. Knopf.

Esposito, J. L. (1992). *The Islamic threat: Myth or reality?* New York: Oxford University Press.

Gay, L. (1992, August 15). The 500 year war: The Balkans are still fighting battles that began in medieval times. *The Ottawa Citizen*, p. B3.

Hall, S. (1979). Culture, media and the "ideological effect." In J. Curran, M. Gurevitch, & J. Woollacott (Eds.), *Mass communication and society* (pp. 315–348). Beverly Hills, CA: Sage.

Hentsch, T. (1992). *Imagining the Middle East* (F. A. Reed, Trans.). Montreal, ON, Canada: Black Rose Books.

Higgins, A. (194, December 20). Fanaticism rooted in Stalin-era repression. *The Ottawa Citizen*, p. TK.

Huntington, S. P. (1996). *The cllash of civilizations and the remaking of world order*. New York: Simon & Schuster.

Ivie, R. L. (1980, November). Images of savagery in American justifications for war. *Communications Monographs, 47*, 279–291.

Jansen, G. H. (1989, September 8). The Papal attack on Syria: Unfounded and unwise. *Middle East International*, 57.

Karim, K. H. (1993). Reconstructing the multicultural community in Canada: Discursive strategies of inclusion and exclusion. *International Journal of Politics, Culture and Society*, 7(2), 189–207.

Karim, K. H. (1997). The historical resilience of primary stereotypes: Core images of the Muslim Other. In S. H. Riggins (Ed.), *The language and politics of exclusion: Others in discourse* (pp. 153–182). Thousand Oaks, CA: Sage.

Malek, A. (Ed.). (1997). *News media and foreign relations: A multifaceted perspective.* Norwood, NJ: Ablex.

Maududi, S. A. (1976). *Jihad in Islam.* Lahore, Pakistan: Islamic Publications.

Maybee, J. (1980, Winter). Reporting the Third World: The Canadian angle. *Carleton Journalism Review*, 6–9.

McKinsey, K. (1992, August 22). Serb leader pledges truce. *The Ottawa Citizen*, p. H2.

Peters, R. (1977). *Jihad in mediaeval and modern Islam.* Leiden, Netherlands: E.J. Brill.

Robinson, G. (1983). Foreign news values in the Quebec, English Canadian and US press: A comparison study. *Canadian Journal of Communication*, 9(3), 1–32.

Said, E. W. (1981). *Covering Islam: How the media and the experts determine how we see the rest of the world.* New York: Pantheon Books.

Said, E. W. (1994). *Orientalism.* New York: Pantheon Books.

Smith, W. C. (1995, July 5). Anti-Islamic bias shows [Letter to the editor]. *The Globe and Mail*, p. A12.

Soderland, W. C. (1985). Press reporting on El Salvador and Nicaragua in leading Canadian and American newspapers. *Canadian Journal of Communication*, 11(4), 353–368.

Soderland, W. C. (1990, March). A comparison of press coverage in Canada and the United States of the 1982 and 1984 Salvadoran elections. *Canadian Journal of Political Science*, 23(1), 59–72.

Soderland, W. C., Krause, R. M., & Price, R. G. (1991). Canadian daily newspaper editors' evaluation of international reporting. *Canadian Journal of Communication*, 16, 5–18.

Soderland, W. C., Wagenberg, R. H., & Pemberton, I. C. (1994, September). Cheerleader or critic? Television news coverage in Canada and the United States of the US invasion of Panama. *Canadian Journal of Political Science*, 27(3), 581–604.

Specter, M. (1995, January 17). Religion and the defence of Chechnya. *The Globe and Mail*, p. A17.

Surlin, S. H., & Cuthbert, M. (1986). Symbiotic news coverage of the Grenada crisis in Canada and the Caribbean. Canadian Journal of Communication, 12(3-4), 53–73.

van Dijk, T. A. (1988). *News analysis: Case studies of international and national news in the press.* Hillsdale, NJ: Lawrence Erlbaum.

Wouters, H. (1979). *Peoples and customs of the world: West Asia.* Geneva, Switzerland: Ferni.

11

Constructing International Spectacle on Television: CCTV News and China's Window on the World, 1992–1996

Tsan-Kuo Chang
University of Minnesota-Twin Cities

Yanru Chen
Nanyang Technological University, Singapore

As the last Communist stronghold since the demise of Communism in the former Soviet Union, and a rising superpower that holds the world's largest population, China represents an intriguing country of political, economic, social, and cultural intricacy and complexity. How it acts and reacts to the ebb and flow of world events or issues often defies conventional wisdom and common understanding in both academic and journalistic communities beyond its own geopolitical sphere. For the

*The authors wish to thank the School of Communication Studies at Nanyang Technological University for its administrative support.

first three decades after its founding in 1949, as an object of international communication research, China's mass communication structure and processes had been looked at within the propaganda and persuasion model against the backdrop of the cold war. The accepted knowledge is that, given the rigid, centralized command system, the Chinese mass media essentially served as the mouthpiece of the state in general and the Communist Party in particular. As such, they were structurally situated and ideologically required to promote a worldview and the state power dictated by the logic of class struggle and revolutionary imperative in a totalitarian system. This background belief in the literature left us with the idea that the structure of total control and mass indoctrination in China was made once and for all. The reality, however, is that it wasn't.

Using a social construction perspective of reality as a framework, the purpose of this chapter is threefold: First, to examine the form and content of China's window on the world in different settings (foreign news versus foreign policy news); second, to determine the changes, if any, of its reporting of international spectacle over time; and third, to identify the fundamental pattern of its worldview through an analysis of network of countries that have persistently attracted China's news attention and are presented accordingly.[1]

Since China adopted the late Deng Xiaoping's economic reform policy and opened its door to the West in the late 1970s, the country has increasingly redefined and repositioned itself vis-à-vis the world at large in political, social, economic, and cultural dimensions. Even after the 1989 Tiananmen Square incident in Beijing, in which a pro-democracy student movement was brutally crushed by force, China has continued on the established trajectory to both restructure its internal infrastructure, including the mass media industry, and pursue external relations through a variety of bold initiatives at high levels in recent years. Chinese President Jiang Zeming's summit meeting with President Clinton in the White House in November 1997 could be seen as a culmination of China's efforts to seek recognition and support of its domestic and foreign behaviors in the community of nations. The release and exile of Chinese dissident Wei Jingsheng to the United States about two weeks after the Jiang-Clinton meeting further underscored China's interactive strategy and communication skills in response to the international pressures on its human rights record.

The Chinese policy commitment and practices in the international arena suggest that a broader theoretical framework and a longitudinal methodological approach are needed to unravel the changing structure and processes of sociocultural and political-economic phenomenon in China—especially the shifting use of mass media from ideological necessity to market pragmatism over the past decade (see, for example, Lee, 1980; Wang & Chang, 1996). Earlier studies on Chinese mass communication from the 1950s through the 1970s had been informed by a structural and functional perspective—the mass propaganda and persuasion model—that had considered China's mass media as the quintessential part of the ideological state apparatus firmly controlled by the central authority (see, for example, Houn, 1961;

Liu, 1971; Schurmann, 1966; Yu, 1964). The identification of China as "Communist," a practice of condensational symbolism that was consistent with that in the news and official policy thinking before Sino-American normalization indicates a common thread underpinning their ideological focus on the country (see, for example, Chang, 1993).

Notwithstanding the symbolic undertone, for the first three decades since the People's Republic of China was founded, the accepted knowledge and background belief about the Chinese mass media often characterized them as "limited outlets, a centralized hierarchical organizational structure, a unified circulation system, and an invariable content" (Wang & Chang, 1996, p. 197). The persistent view appeared to imply that the form and content of Chinese mass media would remain unchanged and unchanging even if the world at large had witnessed rapid social changes. At a time when China was about to embark on its ambitious economic reform and open-door policy movement that has gradually picked up momentum ever since, such a strong background belief probably led Pye (1978) to argue that "any study of the spirit and practice of governance in China today must still take into account the fundamental findings" of earlier studies "on how the Chinese use the radio and the press to propagandize their goals and change the attitudes of their people" (p. 221).

This line of thinking, while consonant with the behavior of a militant and revolutionary China within the cold war framework, failed to leave room for the reality that has yet to come, particularly the emergence of China's "four modernizations" campaign in the late 1970s that set the economic reform in motion, leading eventually to a journalistic reform (see, for example, Polumbaum, 1990). Although skepticism abounds (for a discussion, see Huang, 1995), a growing body of empirical evidence in recent years has pointed out the changing structure and increasing potential in China's mass communication development. These changes included, but are not necessarily limited to, the following phenomena: professionalism in the Chinese journalism and mass communication education and staff training (see, for example, Greenberg & Lau, 1990; Hao & Xu, 1997); decentralization in organization control and production (see, for example, White, 1990; Yu, 1990); content variation in both print and broadcast media (see, for example, Chang, Chen, & Zhang, 1993; Wang & Chang, 1996); depoliticization of messages (see, for example, Lee, 1994); internationalization of media relations and cultural practices (see, for example, Chan, 1994; Hong, 1993, 1997); and market and audience orientation (see, for example, Chu & Ju, 1992; He, in press; Lull, 1991; Zhang, 1993).

In short, China's economic restructuring and policy reconfiguration have inevitably generated media reform in almost every aspect of the industry at a pace that was unthinkable during or before the Cultural Revolution (see, for example, Chu, 1994). To look at the changing phenomena in China today "through a narrow theoretical telescope designed years ago," as Chang and his associates indicated (1993, p. 192), "is to miss the opportunity for a better understanding of the larger picture or 'the widest range of opportunities for theory building.'" Echoing their call for broader conceptual and methodological approaches to the study of Chinese mass media, Huang (1995) argued that as far as China's prospects were concerned, "the current wide gap between conventional wisdom and hard evidence" required "a more balanced and level-headed view" (p. 68). This is not simply a matter of academic debate. In news reporting, the "old constructs" on China have also been deemed inadequate, in that the unpredictable society needs "a flexible and sophisticated journalistic perspective" (Tefft, 1993, p. 62). Such a narrow intellectual and professional range of vision of the Chinese society has long been considered to be "rooted not in China but in the United States" (Harding, 1984, p. 307). "The very first step" toward a better conceptualization, according to Huang (1995, p. 68), "should be to throw out much of our conventional wisdom." Epistemologically, a paradigm shift therefore is in order. It does not, however, imply condoning the state control over media ownership or the government's continuing effort to curtail press freedom in China.

This chapter is an attempt to go beyond the traditional, ideological perspective on the spirit and practices of China's mass media by examining its national television news through a longitudinal design within a sociological framework. The point of theoretical departure is the sociology of knowledge approach (see, for example, Berger & Luckmann, 1966), the essence of which—social construction of reality—has increasingly been applied in the field of mass communication research (see, for example, Adoni & Mane, 1984; Chang, Wang, & Chen, 1994; Cohen, Adoni, & Bantz, 1990; Gamson, Croteau, Hoynes, & Sasson, 1992; Neuman, Just, & Crigler, 1992). Although the evidence may still be sketchy, the studies of sociology of news and knowledge have provided challenging and penetrating insights into the interplay among social communication, public knowledge, and everyday life.

THE NEWS AND SOCIAL REALITY AS CONSTRUCTED SPECTACLE

The perspective of social construction of reality views news as essentially a form of knowledge that is necessary for any given society, whether democratic or authoritarian, to operate efficiently and effectively. The idea of news as a form of social knowledge has long been recognized by sociologists. Park (1955) argued convincingly that, because news is based on "fact that has been checked, tagged, regimented, and finally ranged in this and that perspective, according to the purpose and point of view of the investigator" (p. 74), its function "is to orient man and society in an actual world" (p. 86). More recently, Edelman (1992) suggested that "there can be no world of events distinct from the interpretations of observers" (p. 24). Consequently, "news reports divert attention from immediate experience and help focus it upon a constructed reality" (Edelman, 1988, p. 101).

If the immediate reality about the nation and society is largely delimited by a set of enduring values in the domestic news, as Gans (1979) has documented, it should be more so in foreign and international news when the setting is remote and undoubtedly beyond direct observation or experience for most people. In many situations, events or issues that occur outside a country's territorial boundaries often come to the public not as events or issues per se, but as news stories of those events or issues reported in the mass media, especially on television. From the event itself to the report of the event in the news (Rosengren, 1970), the process moves from the reality out there to the mediated reality in the mass media through a number of gatekeeping mechanisms, producing an end result that is mostly determined by the interaction between "objective" reality and a society's own pragmatic needs and social concerns (Cohen, Adoni, & Bantz, 1990).

Numerous studies have shown how various factors at both the micro and macro levels help contribute to the selection and presentation of news in the mass media. One common agreement is that news is culturally bound and socially constructed for public consumption and social integration (Shoemaker & Reese, 1991). It is culturally bound because news, like other forms of knowledge, tends to be organized by an ethnocentric system of values, such as relevance, familiarity, or psychological proximity (Bernstein, 1976). It is socially constructed because news, as a way of seeing and charting about the social world (see, for example, Gitlin, 1980), cannot be detached from the confines of the larger social structure in which the mass media locate themselves and practice their trade in accordance with the operational logic of their position (Ball-Rokeach & Cantor, 1986; Roshco, 1975). At the collective level, a society's fundamental worldview therefore is best captured and reproduced in the news or what Boulding (1956) called its "social transcript." For Edelman (1988), news reporting is a way of "world making" (p. 4). As such, "it is not what can be seen that shapes political action and support, but what must be supposed, assumed, or constructed" (p. 105). News can never be the way it is; it is chosen to be as stories or narratives.

Given its world-making capacity in the international arena, the mass media allow members of a society to understand their national position in relation to that of other countries and to act accordingly based on what and how the news constructs the reality beyond its immediate horizon in the first place. These pictures in our head, either individually or collectively, often represent a source of private perception and imagination and may evoke public identification and expectation about the object involved (Lippmann, 1922). To paraphrase Edelman (1988), it is not facts or observations, but the construction of international spectacle in the news, that are critical in defining and constituting the political world for the audiences. As a major stock of social knowledge in China (Chang, Wang, & Chen, 1994), there should be little doubt that the Chinese mass media would construct the world as international spectacles, providing internal interpretation to orient the people and society toward the external reality at large. How these snapshots of the world landscape are selected and presented in the news, especially on television, should help identify the dynamics of China's mass communication structure and processes at the international level.

TELEVISION AS CHINA'S WINDOW ON THE WORLD

Following rapid economic reform movement, the dramatic growth of television in China since the early 1980s has been considered to be "the single most important cultural and political development" after the end of the Cultural Revolution in 1976 (Lull, 1991, p. 59). The numbers of television, transmission, and relay stations as well as the population coverage rate are indeed impressive. In 1985, China had 202 television stations. By the end of 1995, the number had more than quadrupled, with 837 TV stations at national, provincial, municipal, and county levels. Television reached 45 percent of the Chinese population in 1978 and increased its coverage rate to nearly 85 percent 20 years later, with an audience of one billion. In 1995, all TV stations in China produced 2,739 news programs with a total of 80,799 hours, representing a tenfold increase from the 7,444 hours in 1985 (China Statistical Yearbook, 1996). The significance of news programs on Chinese television lies in the fact that the news hours far outnumbered those of educational programs (11,630 hours) by almost a 7 to 1 ratio in 1995.

The development of Chinese television is often characterized by the idea of "Three One Thousands"—1,000 TV stations over the air (more than 970 to be exact), 1,000 cable stations (more than 1,200), and 1,000 educational stations (Zhang, 1995). With its four channels, China Central Television (CCTV) stands as the national network, commanding a strong viewership around the country. The time slot immediately after the 7:00 evening news, for example, charges the highest advertising rate on Chinese television. In recent years, CCTV added several noon-hour news program and magazine type shows: "Focal Point," "Oriental Time and Space," and "News 30 Minutes." Because of their timeliness and investigative reports, these programs have enjoyed great success since their inception. Notwithstanding, the CCTV Network News remains the authoritative source of national and international news. The long-term plan of CCTV is "to develop conglomerate operations" and to become "a first class international TV station by 2,000" (Deng, 1997, p. 1). Its international effort can be best seen in the handover of Hong Kong from the British rule to the Chinese sovereignty on June 30, 1997. CCTV dispatched a total of 339 journalists (289 in Hong Kong and 50 in major international cities) to cover the ceremony live, the first time in CCTV's history a single event involved so many reporters, not to mention 500 to 600 more staff members in Beijing (Deng, 1997, p. 1).

The quantitative change in the distribution of Chinese television means more than a statistical count. It is clearly accompanied by a qualitative shift in its content production and presentation. One such indication is what Chan (1994) called "media internationalization" in China, a diffusion phenomenon that in recent years has witnessed Chinese television becoming more international in its programming format and geographical survey (Hong, 1993; Wang & Chang, 1996). For example, Wang and Chang (1996) have documented how China's TV programming and foreign imports evolved from a fixed program (movies) in a few select socialist countries (for example, former Soviet Union and North Korea) in the 1970s to various programs (for example, movies, documentaries, TV series, children's shows, informational programs, dramas, and sports) from a number of capitalist countries such as Japan, Taiwan, the United States, the United Kingdom, and West Germany in 1990.

What is more telling perhaps is that the trend of structural transformation in Chinese television programming did not seem to be affected by the 1989 Tiananmen Square crackdown. As far as Chinese television is concerned, "from the central station to the regional ones, overseas programs continued to be scheduled, with an increasing use of a wider variety of programming from non-Communist countries" (Wang & Chang, 1996, p. 206). While there may be some tensions in the process (Chan, 1994), the general conclusion reached in recent studies is that Chinese television will continue to serve as a window on the world, with the news standing at the forefront as a gateway to a remote reality that is far out of reach for most people in China (Hong, 1993; Li, 1991; Wang & Chang, 1996). This leads to two questions: First, what has been sketched about the world out there in the news? Second, how is it brought to the attention of Chinese television viewers?

If history is any guide, the only thing predictable about China's internal and external behaviors is its unpredictability. Given the volatility of the market in economic reform and the state's avowed political interest in news control (see, for example, Zhang, 1993), it is difficult to predict the form and content of Chinese national television news in the short run, let alone its long term property and prospect. It becomes more difficult to do so when China's TV news net is cast across foreign waters. For one thing, it represents an international effort to bring home spectacles for a domestic audience whose appetite may have been whetted by the gradual opening of the Chinese window on the outside world. Taking advantage of two sets of data collected over a 5-year span, the following research questions were addressed:

RQ1: What sector of the external reality (for example, countries) did China's national television news consider to be salient in its survey of the world's geopolitical landscape?

RQ2: How did the construction of international spectacles change over time?

RQ3: Did the worldview of TV news shift when China's position moved away from being an observer to that of a participant?

RQ4: What were the issues of general concerns in Chinese television news?

METHOD

Two sets of actual video content of the 7:00 evening National Network News on China Central Television (CCTV) were collected in 1992 and 1996. The 1992 data included daily newscasts from June 15 to July 15, with 5 days missing, while the 1996 data started on December 7. Although neither sample was randomly chosen, and the time frame was different, each study period was longer than that in any previous content analysis of Chinese television news. For a temporal comparison between "then and now," the roughly equivalent sample size (26 days in 1992 versus 25 days in 1996) was seen as providing a longitudinal indicator of the contemporary worldview of Chinese national television news. As will be discussed later, the time factor can be controlled to reveal the underlying pattern of how CCTV news constructed international spectacles with respect to the countries involved.

For the purpose of this chapter, two types of news stories were selected for content analysis: foreign news not involving China and foreign policy news concerning China and at least one other country. This conceptual classification is important because the former presents the world landscape as seen by China without its being part of the picture, whereas the latter projects China's position in the world in relation to others (Cohen, 1963; Davison, Shannon, & Yu, 1980; Trattner, 1982). "To assume that there is no difference in the views from 'here and there,'" as Chang, Chen, and Zhang (1993, p. 177) put it, "is to accept the conceptual implausibility that our perspectives of the world do not change according to where we may stand." Unless specified otherwise, the analysis throughout the chapter follows this distinction.

Each story was the coding unit, regardless of its length. All the stories were coded by coders who were fluent in the Chinese language and understood the format of Chinese television news. To facilitate comparison over time, the coding scheme was identical in both years. Based on Stevenson and Shaw (1984), the coding procedure recorded, among other things, the following elements: type of news, primary and secondary countries covered, geographical region, topic, and main theme. As part of a larger project in 1992, the reliability coefficients between two independent coders (Holsti, 1969) for the variables reported in this paper were: type of news, .98; primary country involved, .96; secondary country involved, .98; geographical region, .98; topic, .89; and main theme, .90. The reliability test of a 1996 sample showed similar high coefficients, demonstrating the stability and reproducibility of the coding scheme.

RESULTS

On CCTV, foreign policy news is a component of the domestic stories that occupy the front two-thirds of the newscast, while foreign news is slated at the bottom one-third. If domestic and foreign policy news stories appear longer or more frequently, they tend to cut into the time slot reserved for foreign news. During the 26-day study period in 1992, CCTV carried 247 foreign news stories and 107 foreign policy stories, with an average of about 14 such stories per newscast. In December 1996, the 25 days included 214 foreign news stories and 66 foreign policy stories, averaging 11 stories per lineup. The decrease in 1996 could be partly due to the increase in the number and length of domestic stories and some detailed coverage of Chinese foreign relations activities. In terms of average length, stories in 1992 were longer than those in 1996 in both foreign news (49.5 seconds versus 33.7 seconds) and foreign policy news (66.4 seconds versus 60.4 seconds). The number of countries covered was about the same in foreign news between 1992 (54) and 1996 (57), but differed significantly in foreign policy news (37 in 1992 versus 21 in 1996). Compared over time and across news categories, the world presented on CCTV was much larger in foreign news than in foreign policy news.

RQ1 sought to determine which countries in the world tended to be portrayed on China's news window. Table 11.1 provides the comparison of CCTV coverage of primary countries/entities between the two years within the two types of news. It is evident that CCTV's news spotlight often focused on a few prominent countries

TABLE 11.1.
Top Countries/Entities Covered on CCTV, 1992–1996[1]

Foreign news[2]				Foreign policy news[3]			
1992	%	1996	%	1992	%	1996	%
United States	13.3	United Nations	11.2	Tunisia	11.2	Russia	23.3
Yugoslavia	11.1	PLO	8.6	Hong Kong	9.2	Comoro Is.	8.3
Russia	8.0	United States	8.0	Ivory Coast	8.2	Hong Kong	8.3
United Nations	6.2	Russia	7.0	United States	8.2	United States	8.3
Great Britain	4.9	Hong Kong	5.9	Japan	6.1	Syria	6.7
South Africa	4.4	Israel	5.9	Armenia	5.1	United Nations	6.7
France	3.6	Japan	5.9	Taiwan	5.1	Great Britain	5.0
Germany	3.6	Iran	4.3	Cambodia	4.1	Hungary	5.0
Israel	3.6	Iraq	3.7	Morocco	4.1	Japan	5.0
Japan	3.1	Egypt	2.1	Great Britain	4.1	Azerbaijan	3.3
Australia	2.2					Togo	3.3
Czechoslovakia	2.2						
42 countries	33.8	47 countries	41.6	27 countries	34.6	10 countries	16.8
N =	225		187		98		60

[1]Entries include only primary countries that received more than 2 percent of total coverage in either foreign news or foreign policy news on CCTV.

[2]Foreign news refers to the activities of foreign individuals, groups, or other entities in any foreign country. It does not involve China.

[3]Foreign policy news refers to international relations and foreign policy activities between China and another country.

or entities (for example, the United States, the United Nations, Russia, Israel, and Japan) in foreign news when China stood as an observer, but changed its worldview when it became involved as a participant in foreign policy news. For example, Yugoslavia (11.1 percent) and Russia (8.0 percent) followed the United States (13.3 percent) in the 1992 sample as the top three countries in foreign news, but dropped out the top-10 lineup in foreign policy news in the same year. A feasible explanation is that shortly after the collapse of Communism, Russia—as the successor of the former Soviet Union—still represented a force in that region to be reckoned with. Diplomatically speaking, however, it was probably undesirable for China to engage Russia. The situation apparently was ripe for bilateral activity five years later. In 1996, Russia (23.3 percent) outnumbered all other countries in foreign policy news on CCTV when the two countries exchanged high-level official visits.

Because of the two samples' different time frames, the above findings can be reasonably attributed to "seasonable" or short-term factors (for example, China's external initiatives or a foreign country's temporary internal problems) that might have contributed to news coverage of a particular country on CCTV. In foreign policy news, for instance, the presence of Tunisia (11.2 percent), Ivory Coast (8.2 percent), and Morocco (4.1 percent) in 1992 and Comoro Islands (8.3 percent), Azerbaijan (3.3 percent), and Togo (3.3 percent) in 1996 certainly suggests the plausibility of such an explanation. To eliminate the time factor and country difference due to national idiosyncrasy, it should be illuminating to look at only those countries that had been reported on CCTV in both years, thus to some extent controlling for the temporal fluctuation. From a long-term point of view, this is tantamount to locating those countries to which CCTV's news antenna might be constantly turned. Table 11.2 reports the results.

If the data in Table 11.1 display the news picture of "world making" on CCTV according to the fleeting flashes or beeps of countries/entities on its news radar, the finding in Table 11.2 charts a regular and fixed pattern of countries/entities whose features might be counted more relevant in the Chinese environment, especially in the foreign policy arena. When common coverage in both years was taken into consideration, the number of countries was cut in half from that of either year in foreign news. The United States (10.9 percent) led the pack of 32 countries/entities, followed by the United Nations (8.5 percent), Russia (7.5 percent), Yugoslavia (6.6 percent), Israel (4.6 percent), the Palestine Liberation Organization (4.6 percent), Japan (4.4 percent), and Hong Kong (3.6 percent), with 34 other countries trailing off. From 1992 to 1996, the CCTV foreign news net clearly left out most of African, Southeast Asian, and Latin American countries. In foreign policy news, the CCTV net was even narrower, capturing only 11 countries/entities. Russia (9.5 percent) topped the two-year coverage that included Hong Kong, the United States, Japan, Great Britain, the United Nations, Bolivia, South Korea, the Philippines, Thailand, and Vietnam, in that order.

In contrast to the foreign news, the short list in foreign policy news on CCTV constructed an international spectacle in a way that reflected either the emerging

TABLE 11.2.
Countries/Entities Covered on CCTV from 1992 to 1996[1]

Foreign News[2]		Foreign Policy News[3]	
Country	Percent	Country	Percent
United States	10.9%	Russia	9.5%
United Nations	8.5	Hong Kong	8.9
Russia	7.5	United States	8.2
Yugoslavia	6.6	Japan	5.7
Israel	4.6	Britain	4.4
PLO	4.6	United Nations	3.8
Japan	4.4	Bolivia	1.9
Hong Kong	3.6	South Korea	1.9
Great Britain	2.9	Philippines	1.3
Germany	2.7	Thailand	1.3
South Africa	2.7	Vietnam	1.3
France	2.4		
Iran	2.2		
Iraq	1.9		
Australia	1.5		
Czechoslovakia	1.5		
India	1.5		
Italy	1.2		
Turkey	1.2		
Afghanistan	1.0		
Colombia	1.0		
Lebanon	1.0		
Philippines	1.0		
South Korea	1.0		
Tajkistan	1.0		
N=	412		158

[1]Entries include only primary countries that received coverage in both 1992 and 1996 in either foreign news or foreign policy news on CCTV, thus eliminating time factor and country difference. Percentage represents total coverage of the two years combined.

[2]Foreign news refers to the activities of foreign individuals, groups or other entities in any foreign country. It does not involve China. The following countries received less than 1 percent of total coverage: Canada, Netherlands, Norway, Spain, Sri Lanka, Syria, and Thailand.

[3]Foreign policy news refers to international relations and foreign policy activities between China and another country.

status of China as a world power or its concerns over matters closer to home. An obvious indication is that the worlds of foreign news and foreign policy news on the Chinese national television were not the same size or shape, depending mostly on where China might find itself in the scheme of things. The consistent coverage and relatively high visibility of several primary countries/entities (for example, the United States, Russia, Japan, and the United Nations) on CCTV over a period of five years apart cannot easily be dismissed as coincidence. An examination of secondary countries/entities in the same story further suggests that there exists some kind of "network" among the countries reported on CCTV.

As shown in Table 11.3, while some countries (for example, the United States, Russia, Yugoslavia, and Japan) often became news on CCTV all by themselves, several countries or entities such as the United Nations, Israel, the PLO, Iran, Cuba, or Moldavia probably would not be covered if they had not shared the spotlight with others. For example, the PLO and to some extent Israel tended to appear in a symbiotic relationship or flanked by other countries in the region. The source of connection between primary and secondary countries/entities could be rooted in international power balance (the United States versus Russia) and missions of the United Nations or regional conflicts (Israel versus the PLO). Such linkage seems to underscore an international, rather than parochial, outlook on Chinese national television news. The "network" structure emerges in Figure 11.1 on page 210 when countries that appeared with other countries in at least three stories either as the primary or secondary country on CCTV news in the two years combined were plotted. The cut-off threshold is arbitrarily chosen, but should minimize mere chance occurrence.

As far as foreign news on CCTV is concerned, the international spectacles centered around some key countries in North America, Western Europe, Middle East, and Eastern Europe, with the United States and United Nations dominating the attention and Russia, Germany, the PLO, and Iraq each serving as magnets in their respective region. The network pattern disappears, however, when primary and secondary countries/entities were examined in foreign policy news (Table 11.4 on page 211). The relationship between China and other countries in foreign policy news on CCTV was usually depicted on a one-to-one basis, with Russia taking the lead. In a few cases (Russia, Hong Kong, the United States, and Syria), foreign policy news could be functional in that Taiwan, whose Nationalist government lost to the Communists in the Chinese civil war and fled the mainland in 1949, was brought into the equation to reaffirm China's claim of its sovereignty over the island nation. Hong Kong is another case. The upcoming transfer of sovereignty between Britain and China put the colony high on the news agenda. Such evidence offers some support to the argument that social construction of political spectacle in the news is part of the process of definition of the world (Edelman, 1988). In foreign policy news on CCTV, both Taiwan and Hong Kong were largely defined from China's point of view.

TABLE 11.3.
Primary and Secondary Countries/Entities in Foreign News on CCTV, 1992–1996[*]

Primary	Secondary	Frequency	Other countries
United States (45)	–	29	Egypt, Germany, Iran, Iraq, Israel, Japan, Panama, Poland
	Russia	3	
	Yugoslavia	3	
	8 countries	10	
United Nations (35)	–	7	Cyprus, Iraq, Rwanda, Tanzania, United States, zaire, Azerbaijan, Kyrgyzstan, Moldavia, Bosnia-Herzegovina
	Yugoslavia	9	
	Ghana	5	
	10 countries	14	
Russia (31)	–	20	Germany, Iran, Kyrgyzstan, Moldavia, Ukraine, Uzbekistan
	6 countries	7	
Yugoslavia (27)	–	18	United States
	United Nations	7	
	1 country	2	
Israel (19)	–	2	Egypt, Jordan, Lebanon, Syria
	PLO	11	
	4 countries	6	
PLO (19)	Israel	15	Egypt, Lebanon, United States
	3 countries	4	
Japan (18)	–	13	South Korea, Russia
	United States	3	
	2 countries	2	
Iran (9)	–	2	Iraq, United States, Russia
	Turkey	3	
	3 countries	4	
Cuba (3)	United States	3	
Moldavia (3)	Russia	3	

[*]Foreign news refers to the activities of foreign individuals, groups, or other entities in any foreign country. It does not involve China. Entries include primary and secondary countries that appeared in at least three stories together in the two years combined. Absence of secondary countries means the country appeared alone in the news.

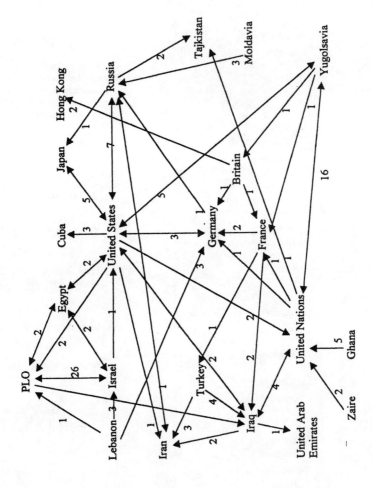

FIGURE 11.1. Network of foreign news coverage of countries/entities on CCTV, 1992–1996[*]

[*]The network of coverage includes countries that appeared with other countries in at least three stories either as the primary or secondary country on CCTV in the two years combined. Links to other countries that received fewer than two stories are excluded. The direction of the arrow indicates that the country was linked to the other country as primary country. Figures represent frequencies the two countries covered in the same story either as the primary of secondary country or both.

210

TABLE 11.4.
Primary and Secondary Countries/Entities in Foreign Policy News on CCTV,
1992-1996*

Primary	Secondary	Frequency	Other countries
Russia (15)	–	14	Taiwan
	1 country	1	
Hong Kong (14)	–	9	Britain, Russia, Taiwan
	3 countries	5	
United States (13)	–	10	North Korea, Taiwan, Yugoslavia
	3 countries	3	
Tunisia (11)	–	9	Saudi Arabia, PLO
	2 countries	2	
Japan (9)	–	9	
Ivory Coast (8)	–	7	Morocco
	1 country	1	
Britain (7)	–	3	Japan, Hong Kong
	2 countries/entities	4	
United Nations (6)	–	4	Brazil, Egypt
	2 countries	2	
Armenia (5)	–	5	
Comoro Island (5)	–	5	
Taiwan (5)	–	2	Philippines, Hong Kong
	2 countries/entities	3	
Cambodia (4)	–	3	Japan
	1 country	1	
Morocco (4)	–	2	Tunisia, United Arab Emirates
	2 countries	2	
Syria (4)	–	2	Taiwan
	1 country	2	

*Foreign policy news refers to international relations and foreign policy activities between China and another country. Entries include primary countries that appeared in at least four stories in the two years combined. Absence of secondary countries means the country appeared alone in the news.

The above findings indicate differential treatment of countries/entities between foreign news and foreign policy news on CCTV from 1992 to 1996, suggesting that in the process of news reporting, China's national television took certain aspects of the world reality to be relevant and others to be irrelevant to the domestic setting. The changing worldview seems to follow the logic of the range of vision based on the functional distance between China and other countries. Individually, countries in Africa and Central and South America did not fare well in foreign news.

Collectively, these regions remained obscure on CCTV. In foreign policy news, this is not necessarily the case, again showing the dual lens of Chinese television. Table 11.5 reports how various regions were configured on CCTV from 1992 to 1996.

In foreign news, although 10 countries in Africa were reported on CCTV during the two-year study period, their share of coverage was relatively small in each year as compared to that of countries in Eastern Europe/Russia, Middle East, North America, East Asia, or Western Europe. When China surveyed the world on its national television as an observer, Africa for the most part did not exist. So did Central and South America. Eastern Europe/Russia had the largest number of countries covered and enjoyed more coverage in both years. As a participant in international relations, China clearly had its news eyes focused on Africa and East

TABLE 11.5.
Geographical Regions Covered on CCTV, 1992–1996[1]

	Foreign news[2]			Foreign policy news[3]		
	1992	1996	Number of countries	1992	1996	Number of countries[4]
Africa	10.3%	5.6%	10	29.9%	21.4%	11
Australia/Oceania	3.0	2.1	3	3.4	–	2
Central America	–	–	1	–	2.4	1
East Asia	4.8	18.2	7	25.3	19.0	5
E. Europe/ Russia	32.7	11.9	17	9.2	35.7	5
Middle East	8.5	35.7	11	–	4.8	1
North America	12.7	7.0	2	6.9	9.5	1
South America	1.2	0.7	3	4.6	2.4	3
South Asia	7.9	10.5	11	10.3	4.8	8
Western Europe	18.8	8.4	12	10.3	–	9
N =	165	143	77	87	42	46

[1]Entries are based on primary countries covered in either foreign news or foreign policy news. Stories that involved United Nations, secondary countries, and countries from different regions were excluded. Because of rounding, percentage total does not add up to 100.

[2]Foreign news refers to the activities of foreign individuals, groups, or other entities in any foreign country. It does not involve China.

[3]Foreign policy news refers to international relations and foreign policy activities between China and another country.

[4]Figures represent primary countries covered at least once in either foreign news or foreign policy news of the two years combined.

Asia. In 1992, Africa (29.9 percent) and East Asia (25.3 percent) stood out among all regions on CCTV's window on the world. Five years later, they were outdistanced by Eastern Europe/Russia (35.7 percent), but still ranked among the top three regions. Like that of the individual countries, this phenomenon can be argued to be ephemeral, subject to the influence of time-bound factors delimited by the specific study period. To go beyond the short-term worldview, coverage of geographical region was reexamined based on primary countries reported in both years, thus eliminating time and country variation as contributing factors to the way of "making worlds" on China Central Television.

Related to the picture in Table 11.2, the data in Table 11.6 can be taken to delineate an extended worldview that identify the broader geopolitical areas deserving China's constant news watch. As is evident, in foreign news, Eastern Europe/Russia (22.3 percent), where China found many of its former Communist allies, and the Middle East (21.0 percent), where military confrontation and political tension could

TABLE 11.6
Coverage of Geographical Regions on CCTV in Both Years[1]

	Foreign News[2]		Foreign Policy News[3]	
	Number of countries	Percent	Number of Countries	Percent
Africa	1	3.6%	–	–%
Australia/Oceania	1	2.0	–	–
Central America	–	–	–	–
East Asia	3	12.1	3	34.2
E. Europe/Russia	4	22.3	1	19.7
Middle East	7	21.0	–	–
North America	2	15.7	1	17.1
South America	1	1.3	1	3.9
South Asia	5	6.6	3	7.9
Western Europe	7	14.8	1	9.2
N =	31	305	10	76

Entries are based on primary countries that were covered in both years, thus eliminating time and country variation as contributing factors in coverage of geographical regions. Stories that involved United Nations and secondary countries were excluded. Because of rounding, percentage total does not add up to 100.

[2]Foreign news refers to the activities of foreign individuals, groups or other entities in any foreign country. It does not involve China.

[3]Foreign policy news refers to international relations and foreign policy activities between China and another country.

be easily triggered across national borders, took a lion share of CCTV newscasts, with North America (15.7 percent), Western Europe (14.8 percent) and East Asia (12.1 percent) sharing a similar proportion. Africa, Australia/Oceania, South America, and South Asia carved up the rest. On a per country basis, however, the region that got the most coverage on CCTV was North America, followed by Eastern Europe/Russia and East Asia.

In the foreign policy arena, the priority of regions was reversed in that East Asia (34.2 percent) dominated the limited news window on China's international relations. Eastern Europe/Russia (19.7 percent) and North America (17.1 percent) were two other regions that saw considerably high Chinese diplomatic activities. What is more revealing is that, unlike the pattern in Table 11.5, Africa as a whole vanished from the overall presentation of foreign policy news. An important question to explore is, under what circumstances did these regions get covered on CCTV? Since diplomatic and governmental activities naturally constituted the thrust of foreign policy news, the analysis of foreign news should be demonstrative. Table 11.7 compares the news focus across seven regions that received at least 3 percent of the total coverage on CCTV in the two-year study period.

TABLE 11.7.
Regions and Foreign News Focus on CCTV, 1992–1996[*]

News Focus	Regions						
	Africa	East Asia	Eastern Europe	Middle East	North America	South Asia	Western Europe
Diplomacy/government	8.0%	6.5%	13.2%	37.1%	–	11.1%	14.3%
Military/defense	12.0	9.7	33.8	22.6	10.0	18.5	7.1
Economic/trade/business	–	6.5	11.8	9.7	16.7	3.7	7.1
Education/arts/culture	–	9.7	–	1.6	–	3.7	4.8
Technology/science	–	3.2	1.5	–	16.7	–	2.4
Transportation/tourism	–	–	–	1.6	3.3	–	2.4
Social unrest	40.0	–	5.9	9.7	6.7	–	7.1
Agriculture/forest	–	–	–	–	–	–	
Social service/health	–	3.2	2.9	–	6.7	3.7	4.8
Sports	4.0	6.5	1.5	3.2	3.3	–	11.9
Politics	28.0	48.4	25.0	12.9	6.7	44.4	11.9
Human interest/life style	–	–	1.5	–	3.3	–	4.8
Disasters/accidents	–	6.5	2.9	1.6	16.7	14.8	2.4
Crime/law	4.0	–	–	–	10.0	–	7.1
Ecology/environment	4.0	–	–	–	–	–	7.1
N =	25	31	68	62	30	27	42

[*]Entries include regions that received at least 3 percent of total coverage on CCTV in the two years combined, excluding Australia/New Zealand/Oceania and South America.

Within regions, except for North America and Western Europe, where no particular news focus was readily discernible, each of the other five regions had something more salient in their coverage on CCTV: social unrest (40 percent) in Africa, politics (48.4 percent) in East Asia, military/defense (33.8 percent) in Eastern Europe, diplomacy/government (37.1 percent) in the Middle East, and politics (44.4 percent) in South Asia. Among regions, this distinction generally holds true, portraying the state of political affairs or social practices in each region. A finding that is worth noting, and perhaps more telling about the construction of international spectacle on Chinese national television, is the fact that CCTV devoted more stories to disasters/accidents in North American than in any other region. In juxtaposition from region to region, this presentation of negative news in the region was accompanied by the highlight of technology/science. To paraphrase Edelman (1992), these remote spectacles do not necessarily promote accurate expectations

TABLE 11.8
Main Themes of News on CCTV, 1992–1996[1]

	Foreign Policy News[2]		Foreign News3	
	1992	1996	1992	1996
Nuclear arms proliferation	2.0%	2.3%	– %	– %
Racial issues	10.5	1.9	–	–
Religious/ethnic antagonism	18.2	0.9	2.8	–
Sovereignty	4.5	12.6	10.3	34.8
Economic reform	0.4	5.1	16.8	4.5
Relations with developing countries	0.4	0.5	20.6	13.6
Terrorism	2.8	2.3	0.9	–
Aggression/repression	5.3	5.1	–	–
East–West relations	0.8	1.4	–	6.1
Social justice	–	2.3	–	–
Democracy/democratic reform	2.4	3.3	0.9	–
National development	–	0.9	4.7	–
Regional cooperation	3.2	8.4	8.4	16.7
N =	247	214	107	66

[1]Based on multiple coding, the total percentage does not add up to 100. Entries are a percentage of total stories related to the theme in either foreign news or foreign policy news. Themes receiving fewer than four references in either foreign news or foreign policy news in the two years combined were excluded.

[2]Foreign news refers to the activities of foreign individuals, groups, or other entities in any foreign country. It does not involve China.

[3]Foreign policy news refers to international relations and foreign policy activities between China and another country.

or understanding, but rather evoke a drama that objectifies hopes and vulnerability there. In this regard, the themes on CCTV news deserve a closer look.

In this chapter, the themes referred to story angles, conceptual framework, and the like that were present in the news, but which might not emerge clearly from the classification of topics. They were conceived as aspects of news coverage that cut across the topics. Table 11.8 on page 215 shows the thematic analysis. It should be apparent that themes on CCTV differed from year to year and varied from foreign news to foreign policy news. In 1992, CCTV appeared to be more concerned about religious/ethnic antagonism (18.2 percent) and racial issues (10.5 percent) in its coverage of foreign news. By 1996, the themes shifted to sovereignty (12.6 percent) and regional cooperation (8.4 percent). In foreign policy news, the emphasis was on relations with developing countries (20.6 percent) and economic reform (16.8 percent) in 1992. Five years later, similar to foreign news, the themes of sovereignty (34.8 percent) and regional cooperation (16.7 percent) became prominent. The transformation of dominant themes from issues unrelated to the question of legitimacy in the early year to national integrity and area interdependence in recent years on CCTV news seems to underline China's determination to stay on its own course, even when the country was increasingly being integrated into the world's capitalist structure as a result of its economic reform and open door policy.

CONCLUSIONS AND DISCUSSION

With the possession of two data sets, each covering about a 4-week period on China Central Television news during the two years under study, this chapter is in a unique position to assess longitudinally how Chinese national television constructs international spectacles beyond its own national borders. Against the backdrop of social construction of reality, the point of theoretical departure is that China's ongoing economic march toward market reform and social reorientation to greater openness have led to a fundamental structural change that defies earlier mass persuasion and propaganda models. One key premise in this chapter is that as a form of social knowledge, news in China molds the external reality at large through a "world making" that helps define the size and shape of the remote geopolitical landscape for the Chinese audiences.

Although the two samples were not randomly selected and the time frame different, both years were relatively uneventful, unlike 1997, when Jiang visited the United States and the Communist Party held its 15th Congress. These events might have prompted many pseudo-events and skewed CCTV coverage. With an expanded study period in each year, the two points in time allow for a temporal comparative analysis between "now" and "then." By way of analytical control, the focus on Chinese Central Television permits better examination of the constructed reality in the news as short-term phenomenon and careful determination of a more permanent worldview projected by some underlying policy concerns and social practices in China. While content analysis is obviously inadequate in demonstrating the *process* of social construction of reality, it is capable of identifying the pattern of the mediated reality as a *product* of that process. If the consistency of form and content of the constructed spectacles can be reasonably established over time, the impact of social structure on the formation of news reality should become more plausible, albeit still lacking direct evidence. This is especially true in a more controlled society like China.

Notwithstanding its improvement of material well-being and relaxation of ideological rigidity since the early 1980s, China today still stands true to the idea of Communist superiority. As shown in its national television, China's worldview can be expected to be bound by its range of vision, which is largely determined by the logic of its views between here and there: "here" in the sense of China as a participant of what matters in foreign policy news and "there" in the sense of China as an observer of what happens in foreign news. Either way, the international spectacles reported in the news should say as much about the reality itself as those who construct or put a limit on it. Several conclusions can be drawn from the patterns exhibited in the data.

First, the world of foreign news differs from that of foreign policy news in both quantity and quality. In the former, the news net tends to be wider and is cast farther whereas in the latter, it is narrower and does not reach far. The short-term worldview in the news is often a response either to the tension and sentiment outside China's own immediate environment or to the current policy consideration and practices within its extended internal context. In the long run, the news configuration of the world appears to hinge on a system of functional relevance or systematic typification. As such, the general pattern of the external reality sketched on China's window on the world does not seem to deviate much from what has been documented in the literature: focus on some elite nations due to perhaps the default structure of international power balance and a few hot spots as a result of regional conflict and confrontation.

Second, the seemingly large spectacle on CCTV news features only a few major international actors. While the United States, Russia and, to a certain extent, the United Nations, clearly dominate both foreign news and foreign policy news on Chinese national television over time, it is probably their strategic location in the network structure that is more revealing. These three countries/entities not only represent strong news centers in their own right, but also become magnets linking, directly or indirectly, other countries from different regions in a news web. Although they do not show up alone in the CCTV newscast, many smaller and less powerful countries appear in the stories along with some "known" countries, either because of their challenge to the powers that be or owing to their close alliance with them. This "friend or foe" connection has been visible throughout the newscast. In a sense, the international outlook on Chinese national TV news adds certain subtle dimension to the dynamics of the world of foreign news in China. Economically, China's national door may be wide open to the outside world. Politically, for the vast majority of Chinese people who depend on television for a glimpse of the world, the "constructed window" on CCTV is surely limited in size and offers a much more particular view of what lies beyond the Chinese geopolitical horizon.

Third, the survey of the world's landscape on China's national television, while factual and timely, is highly selective, taking some constant snapshots from a few countries in areas closer to home and leaving out vast regions unfocused or totally ignored. To use a dated and somewhat problematic classification, as a Second World country, China's treatment of Third World nations is no better than that of the First World. Along with the total absence of development news about Third World countries, it is a reflection of the Chinese government's increasing pragmatism in its diplomacy. From a longitudinal viewpoint, Africa and Latin America simply do not exist on Chinese national television. The world that China's Central TV news brings to the attention of the Chinese people is one that largely lies within its sphere of influence: East and South Asia. Ethnocentrism in news reporting is thus the norm, not the exception, across national borders.

Fourth, although CCTV subscribes to news services such as Visnews for its foreign news spots, it does not identify the source in the stories. Basically, CCTV translates and edits the stories for its own broadcast. In major stories it would state this practice at the end. Consequently, as far as foreign news content is concerned in China, the mechanism of news classification and typification (see, for example, Tuchman, 1978) seems to be at work, offering definitions of the situation in a remote setting for the audience at home. For example, a regular viewer of CCTV would have no difficulty associating Africa with the phenomenon of social unrest or Eastern Europe/Russia and Middle East with issues of military and diplomatic nature. As to North America (essentially the United States), it seems to be more prone to natural disasters and accidents than any other region in the world.

Fifth, the news angles or conceptual framework that cut across various stories on China Central Television is limited in scope either by commission or omission. For instance, issues of human rights or social justice are rarely addressed on the TV news while the problem of sovereignty and regional cooperation is increasingly present in recent years. It means that China, as the last Communist superpower and an emerging economic power, is determined to orient the Chinese society and people to aspects of its main concerns or to steer them away from issues that may make the country look bad by comparison. It could also imply that the country is more assertive in its worldview regarding what it should perceive in the social reality and how it should construe it in the process of news production. The narrow range of international spectacles gives some support to the thesis that they are constructed to help evoke a sense of priority and expectation of either action or nonaction.

Finally, on a conceptual and methodological note, the two worlds of CCTV news—one in foreign news and the other in foreign policy news—point out the necessity of sound conceptualization and appropriate analytical approach in international communication research. Without such differentiation between the two concepts, the nuances in the differing worldviews, as exemplified by China's national television news, may be lost. Mixing the two, at best, will cancel out each other, obscuring the true, opposite phenomena. At worst, it may result in erroneous conclusions and unwarranted interpretations of a skewed relationship between variables. If the evidence from the longitudinal data in this chapter is any indication, the process of foreign news reporting and that of foreign policy news coverage in China do not necessarily originate from the same location; nor are they likely to follow the same trajectory. How each may end can be largely determined by where China wants it to be and what it may bring out along the way.

NOTE

[1] Part of the 1992 data is based on a larger research project sponsored by the U.S. Information Agency. The conclusions and interpretations presented in this chapter do not represent the views of USIA or of the U.S. Government.

REFERENCES

Adoni, H., & Mane, S. (1984). Media and social construction of reality. Toward an integration of theory and research. *Communication Research, 11*, 323–340.

Ball-Rokeach, S. J. & Cantor, M. G., (Eds.). (1986). *Media, audience, and social structure.* Newbury Park, CA: Sage.

Berger, P. L., & Luckmann, T. (1966). *The social construction of reality: A treatise in the sociology of knowledge.* New York: Anchor Books.

Bernstein, R. J., (1976). *The restructuring of social and political theory.* Philadelphia: University of Pennsylvania Press.

Boulding, K. E. (1956). *The image: Knowledge in life and sociology.* Ann Arbor, MI: University of Michigan Press.

Chan, J. M. (1994). Media internationalization in China: Processes and tensions. *Journal of Communication, 44*, 70–88.

Chang, T. K. (1993). *The news and China policy: The illusion of Sino-American relations, 1950–1984.* Norwood, NJ: Ablex.

Chang, T. K., Chen, C. H., & Zhang, G. Q. (1993). Rethinking the mass propaganda model: Evident from the Chinese regional press. *Gazette, 51*, 173–195.

Chang, T. K., Wang, J., & Chen, C. H. (1994). News as social knowledge in China: The changing worldview of Chinese national media. *Journal of Communication, 44*, 52–69.

China Statistical Yearbook. (1996). Beijing, China: China Statistical Publishing House.

Chu, G. C., & Ju, Y. A. (1992). *The Great Wall in ruins: Communication and cultural change in China.* Albany, NY: State University of New York Press.

Chu, L. L. (1994). Continuity and change in China's media reform. *Journal of Communication, 44*, 4–21.

Cohen, A. A., Adoni, H., & Bantz, C. R. (1990). *Social conflict and television news.* Newbury Park, CA: Sage.

Cohen, B. C. (1963). *The press and foreign policy*. Princeton, NJ: Princeton University Press.

Davison, W. P., Shannon, D. R., & Yu, F. T. C. (1980). *News from abroad and the foreign policy public*. New York: Foreign Policy Association.

Deng, Y. (1997, June 9). The big pinwheel garden at CCTV's Weihai Film and TV base opens. *CCTV TV Guide*, 1.

Edelman, M. (1988). *Constructing the political spectacle*. Chicago: University of Chicago Press.

Edelman, M. (1992). Constructing the political spectacle. *Kettering Review*, 24–29.

Gamson, W. A., Croteau, D., Hoynes, W., & Sasson. T. (1992). Media images and the social construction of reality. *Annual Review of Sociology, 18*, 373–393.

Gans, H. (1979). *Deciding what's news: A study of* CBS Evening News, NBC Nightly News, Newsweek *and* Time. New York: Vintage Books.

Gitlin, T. (1980). *The whole world is watching: Mass media in the making and unmaking of the new left*. Berkeley, CA: University of California Press.

Greenberg, B. S., & Lau, T. Y. (1990). The revolution in journalism and communication education in the People's Republic of China. *Gazette, 45*, 19–31.

Hao, X., & Xu, X. (1997). Exploring between two worlds: China's journalism education. *Journalism and Mass Communication Educator, 52*, 35–47.

Harding, H. (1984). The study of Chinese politics: Toward a third generation of scholarship. *World Politics, 35*, 284–307.

He, Z. (in press). Chinese Communist party press in a tug of war: A political-economic analysis of the Shenzhen Special Zone Daily. In C. C. Lee (Ed.), *Power, money, and the media: Communication patterns in greater China*.

Holsti, O. R. (1969). *Content analysis for the social sciences and humanities*. Reading, MA: Addison-Wesley.

Hong, J. (1993). China's TV program import 1958–1988: Towards the internationalization of television? *Gazette, 52*, 1–23.

Hong, J. (1997). Cultural relations between China and Taiwan. *Journal of Chinese Political Science, 3*, 1–25.

Houn, F. (1961). *To change a nation*. New York: Free Press.

Huang, Y. (1995). Why China will not collapse. *Foreign Policy, 99*, 54–68.

Lee, C. C. (1980). *Media imperialism reconsidered: The homogenizing of television culture*. Beverly Hills, CA: Sage.

Lee, C. C. (1994). Ambiguities and contradictions: Issues in China's changing political communication. In C. C. Lee (Ed.), *China's media, media's China* (pp. 3–20). Oxford, England: Westview Press.

Li, X. P. (1991). The Chinese television system and television news. *China Quarterly, 126*, 340–355.

Lippmann, W. (1922). *Public opinion*. New York: The Free Press.

Liu, A. P. L. (1971). *Communications and national integration in Communist China*. Berkeley, CA: University of California Press.

Lull, J. (1991). *China turned on: Television, reform, and resistance*. London: Routledge.

Neuman, W. R., Just, M. R., & Crigler, A. N. (1992). *Common knowledge: News and the construction of political meaning*. Chicago: University of Chicago Press.

Park, R. E. (1955). *Society: Collective behavior, news and opinion, sociology and modern society*. Glencoe, IL: The Free Press.

Polumbaum, J. (1990). The tribulations of China's journalists after a decade of reform. In C. C. Lee (Ed.), *Voices of China: The interplay of politics and journalism* (pp. 33–68). New York: The Guilford Press.

Pye, L. W. (1978). Communications and Chinese political culture. *Asian Survey, 28*, 221–246.

Rosengren, K. E. (1970). International news: Intra and extra media data. *Acta Sociologica, 13*, 96–109.

Roshco, B. (1975). *Newsmaking.* Chicago: University of Chicago Press.

Schurmann, F. (1966). *Ideology and organization in Communist China.* Berkeley, CA: University of California Press.

Shoemaker, P. J., & Reese, S. D. (1991). *Mediating the message: Theories of influences on mass media content.* New York: Longman.

Stevenson, R. L., & Shaw, D. L. (Eds.). (1984). *Foreign news and the new world information order.* Ames, IA: Iowa State University.

Tefft, S. (1993). In Beijing, Communism besieged. *Media Studies Journal, 7*, 59–64.

Trattner, J. H. (1982). Reporting foreign affairs. *Washington Quarterly, 5*, 103–111.

Tuchman, G. (1978). *Making news: A study in the construction of reality.* New York: The Free Press.

Wang, J., & Chang, T. K. (1996). From class ideologue to state manager: TV programming and foreign imports in China, 1970–1990. *Journal of Broadcasting and Electronic Media, 40*, 196–207.

White, L. T., III. (1990). All the news: Structure and politics in Shanghai's reform media. In C. C. Lee (Ed.), *Voices of China: The interplay of politics and journalism* (pp. 88–110). New York: The Guilford Press.

Yu, F. T. C. (1964). *Mass persuasion in Communist China.* New York: Praeger.

Yu, J. (1990). The structure and function of Chinese television, 1979–1989. In C. C. Lee (Ed.), *Voices of China: The interplay of politics and journalism* (pp. 69–87). New York: The Guilford Press.

Zhang, X. (1993). The market versus the state: The Chinese press since Tiananmen. *Journal of International Affairs, 47*, 195–221.

Zhang, X. (1995). Radio, television and video industry. In *Chinese Academy of Social Sciences Press, The state and trend of development in China, 1995–1996* (pp. 256–315). Beijing: Chinese Academy of Social Sciences Press.

12

Looking East, Heading West: Images of Former Friends and Foes in the Bulgarian Communist/Socialist Party Press, 1990

Anelia K. Dimitrova
University of Northern Iowa

In June 1990, for the first time in decades, three generations of Bulgarians went to the polls to freely exercise their political will. Several months had passed since November 10, 1989, when an internal party coup toppled the nearly 40-year-old Zhivkov regime. Lingering national frustration, personal anxiety, and above all, naive hope for a sudden democratic change, stirred, in part, by the emergence of homegrown opposition, appeared to forebode the end of Communist control. Many believed that given a choice, most Bulgarians would choose their freedom, and not their former oppressor.

But in June, in the first free multi-party elections in Bulgaria's recent history, the popular vote showed otherwise. United in the renamed Bulgarian Socialist Party

(BSP), the former Communists won 211 seats in the Grand National Assembly.[1] More important, their electoral victory revealed a truth that has since become abrasively literal for those who live it—the crumbling of the iron curtain did not mean the demise of the former regime. Rather, it signaled its post-Communist metamorphosis in the public arena.

When the ballots were counted, and the results announced, it became clear that the embryonic opposition was not the only loser. Branded by the trauma of totalitarianism, disenchanted veteran voters rationalized the BSP's electoral success with the dark humor of Bulgaria's oppressive past. For their part, Western observers and political analysts who had prophesied the eventual collapse of Communism in Eastern Europe ran out of compassion and advice.

But how could socialism—democratic socialism—and espoused by the same Communist hard-liners, unite and inspire the Bulgarian electorate at the very moment of the collapse of the Soviet Empire? Just as important, how could the renamed Communist party so successfully convince an embittered electorate and a distrustful international community of its new identity?

Crucial to the party's revamped image, and subsequently, to its electoral victory, was the question of Bulgaria's place in the international arena. Known to the world as the staunchest Soviet satellite, Bulgaria had little say in her own destiny. Bu the global transformations created, at least temporarily, the illusion that the injustices of the past could be remedied, and Bulgaria would forge more equitable relations with her former allies and with Western democracies.

To survive their own identity crisis, the party and its press championed this idea and made it one of the most important emphases in their public relations campaign. At its climatic point, during the Bulgarian Communist Party's 14th Extraordinary Congress, new- and old-style demagogues pledged they would reinvent themselves and the party. In addition, the BCP/BSP promised to provide the Bulgarian people with competent leadership in domestic and international affairs.

Hence, this chapter investigates the two different foreign policy agendas endorsed by the Communist/Socialist party during the critical months following Zhivkov's ouster on November 10, 1989, and before the multi-party elections in June 1990. The first agenda was outlined in the Manifesto for Democratic Socialism, and the BCP's election platform. Touted to the general public by a well-greased propaganda machine, this foreign policy directive was primarily targeted at the internal and external party opposition. Just as important, it documented the party's explicit intention to preserve the status quo through cosmetic maneuvers.

By contrast, the second foreign policy agenda was much less obtrusive and at the same time much more powerful. It transpired in the daily international coverage of the Communist Party's political tribune, *Delo/Duma*.[2] A virtual media monopolist, with unrivaled circulation, material resources, and correspondents stationed in the West, *Delo/Duma* was uniquely positioned to impact public opinion, and ultimately, to ensure the party's electoral success. As the party's organ, the newspaper framed its former patron, the Soviet Union, and her former adversary, the United States, in line with the party's foreign policy direction.

This chapter explores the tug of war between intentions, pledged by party documents, and direction, evidenced in the international coverage of the party press. It is argued here that *Delo/Duma*'s coverage of the superpowers provided the electorate with the language to think about the successful leadership of the Bulgarian Communist/Socialist Party. In those first months of uncertainty, hesitation, and confusion, when the failure of Communism glared in the global spotlight, *Delo/Duma*'s coverage of the superpowers anticipated the shift in Bulgaria's foreign policy. In particular, by deemphasizing certain aspects in the image of its former Big Brother and emphasizing others in the image of the United States, *Delo/Duma* built a new image of itself and the reformed party.

Manufactured by party ideologues for popular consumption, this image legitimized the transformation within the Communist Party and in Bulgarian society. It showcased a revitalized, knowledgeable party, fully capable of leadership in domestic and international politics, not an apologetic survivor of a discredited regime. On the other hand, careful selection of foreign news about the Soviet Union and the United States demonstrated the Communist Party's readiness to trade its ideological subservience to the Soviet Empire with an economic interest in the United States.

Delo/Duma's portrayal of former foes and friends during this eight-month period merits investigation because it illuminates the dynamics of foreign news in an ex-Soviet satellite in times of global and internal crisis. Unobscured by the pretense of objectivity, the newspaper's explicit connection with the party allows us to infer a direct relationship between international reportage and the BCP/BSP's foreign policy agenda. Furthermore, such exploration provides us with concrete evidence about the extent of the changes within the party ranks. Specifically, *Delo/Duma*'s international coverage highlights the discrepancy between professed loyalties, reflected in party documents, and foreign policy direction, charted by the editorial focus on world events. Last but not least, the subsequent analysis chronicles the specific challenges faced by Bulgaria's most powerful agenda-setting party newspaper in a formative period when ideological imperatives were being replaced by market demands.

To contextualize the relationship between international news and foreign policy in times of transition, the first part of this chapter reviews the transformation of the Bulgarian Communist Party. Next, to illustrate and explore the most significant step in the BCP's metamorphosis, the second part of this study examines *Delo*'s subsequent evolution into *Duma*. Special attention is paid to the newspaper's instrumental role in mobilizing popular consent and its efforts to stay afloat in a new competitive environment. During the examined period, economic pressures compelled the editorial staff to abandon the ideological prism of the past. To explore the market perspective through which the party press began to look at the world, the third part of this chapter reports on the content analysis of the images of

America, the Soviet Union, and Bulgaria. Finally, the conclusions note, among other things, that *Delo/Duma*'s coverage of the two superpowers can be construed as an indirect commentary on domestic events.

The primary sources used in this study ensure the cultural coherence of the interpretation offered below. Specifically, I have worked with original texts and party documents, as well as with articles published in *Bulgarian Journalist*, the professional publication of the mainstream Union of Bulgarian Journalists (UBJ). Moreover, I have conducted numerous interviews with Bulgarian media consumers and practitioners to include their perspectives in what seems to be a one-sided academic monologue about East European media in transition. In addition, to complement the insiders' perspective, I have researched American press coverage and academic works dealing with the period. For the content analysis, I have relied on micro-filmed *Delo* and *Duma* front-page international coverage.

In order to address this study's theoretical concern with the articulation (Noelle-Neumann, 1984) function of post-Communist media, this eight-month time frame was purposefully chosen to span the very inception of the transition period and the first elections. It is important to emphasize that during the examined period, even the shrewdest analysts were hesitant to forecast the extent to which the *aparatchik* structure would relinquish control. This ritualistic metamorphosis of the ideological paradigm, to paraphrase Gaye Tuchman (1978), however, was reflected clearly in *Delo/Duma*'s coverage of America and the Soviet Union.

News about the superpowers, just like international news in general, is negotiated in distant arenas. But for the Bulgarian Communist Party press, distance did not mean geography. Rather, it translated into ideological orientation. In a predictable formula, in its four-decade international coverage, *Delo* demonized the enemy and deified its friends, all in accordance with Politburo directives. In particular, the United States was portrayed negatively, while the Soviet Union was eulogized as a model country (Dimitrova, 1995).

But as researchers have argued, international news is oftentimes guided by ideological proximity, regardless of the social system in which a particular media operate. In civil societies, though, such manipulation is harder to sell because the press watches the government with the same intensity it monitors its competition. This means that in the area of foreign policy, the role of the media is to create "an atlas of policy possibilities, alternatives and choices" (Cohen, 1963, p. 13). By contrast, in totalitarian regimes, the explicit mission of the press is to shrink this atlas to the claustrophobic contours of the dictator's shadow.

Dictators aside, the culture of international news in Bulgaria has always had a different meaning than America's well-documented disinterest in foreign reportage. Even in totalitarian times, Bulgarians had more interest in the world than the world had in them. True, the carefully selected news diet did not allow common people to hear any good news about the West and deafened their ears with the "worldwide achievements of Communism."

Arguably, official propaganda in the form of international news had a cathartic effect on journalists and their readers. Party functionaries, posturing as foreign correspondents, vented their frustration on tabooed domestic topics by lashing out on the sins of the "rotten West." For their part, information- and experience-deprived audiences commiserated with the exploited working classes in the Third World and forgot about their own dismal present.

All of this came to an abrupt halt in 1989, when the spectacle of the Berlin Wall mesmerized the globe. Many voices and players, echoing the fluctuations of what sociologist Herbert Gans (1979) has called "meta-ideology" (p. 249), began to compete for inclusion in the symbolic arena created by the agenda-setting Communist Party newspaper. Together with party ideologues, market analysts and political strategists scrutinized every step of the superpowers. For obvious reasons, the action on the main stage hiked up the existing interest in international news in Bulgaria.

LITERATURE REVIEW

A predictable corollary of the televised fall of Communism was the resurgence of scholarly interest in the region. However, relatively few writers have attempted to thoroughly investigate how the collapse of the Soviet hegemony has redefined the relationship between the core and the periphery in terms of information power. Spurred by what Ralf Dahrendorf has called the "seemingly irremediable collapse of the center of authority" (1990, p. 112), most researchers from the West and the East hurried to chronicle the political and economic consequences of the Eastern European revolution (see, for example, Banac, 1992; Brown, 1991; Mason, 1996; Simons, 1993; Sugar, 1995). In Dahrendorf's analysis, this revolution resulted in the reunification of the First and the Second worlds into one entity, the world.

What, then, are the implications of this new unity for communication scholars, given the history of the NWICO research (see, for example, Frederick, 1993; Gatlung & Vincent, 1995; Stevenson, 1986; Stevenson & Shaw, 1984)? In terms of news flow, does this mean that post-Communist countries will continue to excite Western media professionals and scholars beyond their immediate focus on the revolution? Or does it mean that after a brief euphoria, both the ex-First and Second worlds will simply forget about one another and preoccupy themselves with their own local problems? And if the two have, as some have argued, begun to speak the same language, what has been lost in the translation (Dahrendorf, 1990)?

In his book, *Internationalizing Media Theory* (1996), John Downing ventures some answers. Focusing on Russia, Poland, and Hungary, the author argued that communication theory and cultural approaches have failed to adequately interpret the "planetary" changes in the post-Soviet nations (p. 229). Persuasive as Downing's argument may be, it raises another pertinent question: Is a new Second World emerging in political as well as in scholarly discourse? If guided by American media and academic interest in the region, one might conclude that, for the most part, the term "post-Soviet nations" excludes Bulgaria.

A 353-page collection of articles, which portrays the "momentous events" of the collapse of Communism as seen by *New York Times* correspondents, offers an insightful explanation. This book includes only one story on Bulgaria, which sketches the history of the Zhivkov regime on the occasion of its overthrow. At the end of this dispatch, the editors justify their minimal interest in Bulgaria with the following remark: "Dramatic as the Bulgarian changes were, they were less riveting than what was going on in the very heart of Europe, in Berlin" (Gwertzman & Kaufman, 1990, p. 187).

Not surprisingly, funding agencies have replicated this lukewarm attitude of editors and writers in the Bulgarian case. Marginal to the West just as it had been to Moscow, Bulgaria was left out of the first wave of U.S.-funded communication research projects (Dennis & Heuvel, 1990). More recently, researchers have discussed different aspects of Bulgaria's post-Communist media with varying degrees of precision and understanding of the cultural context (see, for example, Hester, Reybolds, & Conger, 1992; Hester & Reybolds, 1991; Splichal, 1994). Most notably, examining news reported in the West about the former Communist regimes, at least one researcher has concluded that by 1990, Bulgaria dramatically reduced its contacts with the Soviet Union, and with its former allies and the Third World (Zhong, 1994). Like their Western colleagues, Bulgarian media experts writing for Western (Deltcheva, 1996) as well as for domestic audiences have concentrated primarily on the emergence of the new media market (Iordanova, 1995; Karaivanova, Panayo, Petrov, & Konstantinova, 1995; Naidenov, 1995; Ognianova, 1997).

By contrast, this chapter is concerned with the metamorphosis of the Communist Party press in critical times (Dimitrova, 1998). Among other things, it contributes to the literature in the field by exploring the superpowers' international coverage in a satellite press in transition.

THE ATLAS OF POSSIBILITIES IN OFFICIAL PARTY DISCOURSE

Several important documents, approved at different times during the BCP's public metamorphosis, discussed the atlas of possibilities the party envisioned for itself and the nation. Two crucial questions were invariably posed, not always in the same order, about foreign policy. One was Bulgaria's future relationship with the Soviet Union and the socialist world. The other one was Bulgaria's relationship with the previously ignored Western democracies.

In a section significantly titled, "For a Common European Home—From the Atlantic to Ural," the BSP's election platform emphasized the party's intention to preserve its traditional ties with the Soviet Union and the Warsaw Pact. Reaffirming its goal to strengthen and further develop the political, economic, and spiritual closeness with the Soviet Union, the BSP argued that these connections were an "enormous national, cultural and economic capital, as well as a guarantee for national survival" ("Election Platform," 1990, p. 9).

In a similar language, another important text, the "Manifesto for Democratic Socialism," professed Bulgaria's loyalty to the Soviet Union, the other socialist countries, and the Third World. These foreign relations goals for the nation coincided almost verbatim with the party's own narrow interest, articulated earlier in the document. There, referring to themselves as "internationalists," party ideologues praised their centennial history and pledged they would capitalize on their long experience in international relations (1990, p. 2).

Such overlap between national and party agenda, especially in international relations, was not surprising given the history of totalitarianism. For four decades, a lifetime for millions, the Bulgarian Communist Party had been the nation.

But the "cardiac arrest," to borrow a phrase from Eva Hoffman (1993, p. 350), of the entire system compelled the BCP/BSP to recognize the need for another direction. Like many similar texts published in *Delo/ Duma*, the Manifesto noted that based on the national interest, Bulgaria should embrace Europe and the world. The world, of course, referred to the still unmentionable United States. Without this revised course, the party's political declaration further asserted, the construction of democratic socialism would be "unthinkable" ("Manifesto for Democratic Socialism," 1990, p. 2). In April 1990, the published BCP election platform reiterated the same motif:

> In order to build democratic socialism in this country [we need] to widely open Bulgaria to Europe. Bulgaria must take a deserving part in the creation of this European home. That means [we must take] the road to an integrated Europe, in which our country will not fence itself off in isolation, but rather, will draw on, and will contribute, modestly as it may be, to a common European culture; will integrate itself in contemporary economics, will embrace the politics of human rights, disarmament, understanding and peace. ("Election Platform," 1990, p. 9)

Such rhetoric framed Bulgaria's integration in Europe as a benchmark in the party's overarching goal to build democratic socialism, not as an inevitable corollary of the collapse of the system. In order to overcome the popular perception of system failure and solidify its leadership position in the face of changing global realities, the party became the messenger as well as the agent of renewal. Its main goal was to persuade the electorate that it was not a crippled, gilt-ridden sinner begging the public and the opposition for forgiveness and mercy. Rather, the BSP presented itself as a powerful agenda-setter, in charge of its own and the country's plight.

Always the caring "mother of the people," the party hastily darned the socks of Marxism-Leninism with threads of "democratic socialism." As the Manifesto explained, this hybrid of traditional Marxism and free enterprise was the party's timely response to the "contemporary processes and trends" in the world and at home (1990, p. 2). To preserve the socialist principle and at the same time to avoid any undesirable associations with their failed attempt to deliver the "bright future" with which they had previously lulled the masses, party ideologues sold democratic socialism to the Bulgarian public as "an alternative to the command-administrative apparatus" ("Our Choice," 1990, p. 4).

But *Delo/Duma* went even further than party documents in enhancing the BSP's chances for electoral success. In addition to its persuasive rhetoric, the newspaper remapped the world to reflect the party's foreign policy direction. Simply put, searching to reconcile its Stalinist past with its pretense for a "democratic present," the BCP/BSP looked East but gingerly moved West, and not just toward Europe, but more specifically toward the United States (see, for example, Engelbrekt, 1990; Lefebvre, 1994; Zhong, 1994).

Such discrepancy between verbal assurances and actions is always problematic in civil societies. But in those first months of Bulgaria's toddle to democracy, this strategy appeared to have a soothing and unifying effect on the people because it appealed to voters numbed by a common totalitarian past. On the one hand, to appease the hard-liners while it looked for ideological reorientation, the party paid lip service to its traditional ideological ties to the Soviet Union. On the other hand, the BCP/BSP's pledge for cooperation with Europe and the rest of the world was vague enough not to alienate the old guard, and yet, specific enough to secure the votes of two radically different groups.

Reformers in the party's own ranks, and undecided voters, who equally distrusted the old system and the emerging opposition, were a good target for such propaganda. To the extent to which they articulated it, the party press and documents framed the interaction with the West as a testament to the party's flexibility, not as a betrayal of its past.

GHOSTS OF THE PAST, PROMISES FOR THE FUTURE: THE BULGARIAN COMMUNIST PARTY MODERNIZES

Under Communism, the public sphere was guarded as zealously as the mausoleum of party guru Georgi Dimitrov in the heart of Sofia. In 1990, however, the reverential public silence enforced by the regime exploded in a frightening cacophony of noises and voices while the Red Star remained perched over Party headquarters (Dimitrova, 1992). At that time, Bulgarians were avid media consumers, divided, even within their own families, along party lines (Georgieva, 1991). Listening to the radio was not just an addictive national pastime. From the saleswomen in the department store, to the office workers in administration buildings, to the villagers tending their tomato patches, the radio became a way of life. Its omnipresence saturated the air with live political discussions, roundtable negotiations, and debates. Much to the surprise of foreign visitors, common Bulgarians breathed it all in.

The romance of the first demonstrations was infectious and inebriating. For years, public squares had only filled up when people obediently gathered to cheer the achievements of the Communist Party. But now it was different. The spirit of the street was empowering and feverishly liberating. Boundaries were tested and blurred. New spaces for (self) expression were created in the public sphere. Everything was political (Georgiev, Goranov, & Parchev, 1991).

With time, no doubt, the myths of the transition will multiply. Some will be swallowed by the memories of casual witnesses, others will be perpetuated by the avalanche of narratives that have since proliferated. Still others will be created as academics to explore the folklore of the period. But regardless of their viewpoint, all of these interpretations pale in comparison to the impact the collapse of the regime had on ordinary Bulgarians. Theirs was the drama of the disillusioned. While some of the older generation hearkened after the stability of the past, the middle generation found themselves at another crossroads. For them, it was impossible to be the same, yet, it was too late to start over and be someone else somewhere else.

However, the individual was not the only species forced to adapt to the new times. The corporate entity of the party was similarly compelled to rethink its existence. Metamorphosis became the main occupation of the *nomenklatura*. Factions such as the Alternative Socialist Organization (ASO), the Bulgarian Road to Europe, and the Democratic Forum emerged from university cafés and took their place in the public space. Furthermore, to present itself as a constructive actor in the political arena, the BCP promised free elections in 1990 and a new Constitution.[3] It also initiated the abolition of Article 1 of the old Constitution, which guaranteed its leadership role in Bulgarian society.[4] In March 1990, the party signed a four-part key political agreement with the opposition, which addressed the future of the political system, a national accord on the peaceful transition, and a commitment to a civil society. Other changes were imminent in the party's ideological orientation, in its relationship with society, and in the philosophy of its newspaper. Each will be reviewed briefly below.

IMAGE AS IDEOLOGY: THE 14TH EXTRAORDINARY CONGRESS

By far the party's most spectacular image quest took place during its 14th Extraordinary Congress. Convened on January 30, 1990, it was intended as a reconciliatory forum for the open discussion of the party's identity and future direction ("Manifesto for Democratic Socialism," 1990).

To etch this public relations stunt into the minds of millions, the party press dubbed it a Congress of "profound transformations" and "renewal." In an "electrifying" atmosphere, which won them even the applause of Western analysts, the delegates spoke their mind with unprecedented candor.

Among other issues, the delegates considered the divisive question of the party's name (Nikolaev, 1990). Reformers insisted that a new one was needed to "define not the final, but the immediate historical mission of the party" ("Manifesto for Democratic Socialism," 1990, p. 2). Appropriately, *Delo/Duma* covered the debates on the party's name change extensively and paid close attention to the subsequent membership referendum.[5] Finally, in April, the Bulgarian Communist Party christened itself the Bulgarian Socialist Party.

Eventually, the new name allowed the party not only to distance itself from the "crude deformations" in its own history, but to condemn them with the same vehemence with which the opposition did. Selective identification with the past became the party's survival strategy. Not surprisingly, the party press was just as horrified as the opposition media by the atrocities committed by the previous regime. In an ironic twist, the party took its new role so seriously that it offered to sponsor a documentary about the notorious labor camps that it had built ("The BCP Higher Council Decided, " 1990).

And while the opposition pressed the issue of the party's accountability for the ongoing moral and economic crisis, the new party's leadership dissipated the tonnage of its collective criminal record by picking a few scapegoats. Lustration was the road to survival (Bertschi, 1994).

But the cynicism with which the party championed its own crusade for justice served not only to displace the causes of the opposition. Equally important, it allowed the party to demonstrate its entrepreneurial spirit and transform its political power into economic fortitude. In essence, the new name legitimized the party's image. This blend of wisdom and innocence was as effective as dictate had been in the past. Its ultimate objective was not just to convince the electorate of the party's new identity, but to showcase its commitment to democracy.[6] Significantly, the party that had formerly identified itself with the working class now labeled itself the party of labor and intellect.

In this context, the two main goals highlighted by the Congress were the party's de-Stalinization and its transformation into a "modern Marxist party of a new type," which espoused the ideals of democratic socialism. It was only within the framework of democratic socialism, overnight party reformers maintained, that the transition in Bulgaria should take place. Defined vaguely as "a society of free working people, which guarantees equal rights to all citizens and equal opportunities for everyone's development," democratic socialism became the slogan for the transition period, just like the cliché of "developed socialist society" had been for the totalitarian years ("Manifesto for Democratic Socialism," 1990, p. 2).

Arguably, the glittering generalities in the above definition provided a relatively dignified transition from the dogmas of the past to the imperatives of the present. Specifically, they allowed the BCP to save face and appear vital and flexible, rather than opportunistic. Understandably, this mixture of socialism and free market initiatives appealed to a diverse electorate inside and outside the party, particularly because it appeared to herald a new era in Bulgaria's relationship with the world.

More important, flaunting the new chimera of democratic socialism, the BCP deflected the nation's attention from the far more serious question of its own responsibility for the current crisis. Party leaders embraced democratic socialism with the same ardor with which they had previously propagated Marxism-Leninism. This new social order, they now asserted, was not the utopia of Communism, but a realistic and unifying goal for the party and the people.

Such passionate sermons naturally puzzled the more critical public, who, in turn, wanted to know where these visionaries had slumbered during the past 40 years. And if they had existed, how come they were blind to the paradise of democratic socialism, which was so tangible, and so within reach. Brushing similar comments aside, party bureaucrats now pointed for confirmation of their words to the West. In fact, the achievements of the West European model were sold to the domestic public as a guarantee for success of a hypothetical Bulgarian version of democratic socialism. This was a safe ploy for the party in the absence of a culture of political opposition and electoral accountability.

Most important, such rhetoric allowed the party to neutralize the opposition's most powerful trump card—commitment to democratic reform and a market economy. In its coverage of the local scene, *Delo/Duma* flooded its pages with editorials that juxtaposed the "shock therapy" remedy proposed by the opposition to their vision of "gradual transition." Such reform was humane, these texts emphasized, because the party platform guaranteed the survival of the weakest members of society—the pensioners, the unemployed, and the children.[7]

One of the most significant documents approved by the Congress was the new party statute, which envisioned two conflicting missions for the party press. On the one hand, party publications were instructed to provide a forum for "all democratic social forces...journalists and citizens." At the same time, they were ordered to be on the alert and not to "allow propaganda and agitation which would benefit another party" ("Statute of the Bulgarian Communist Party," 1990, p. 3). Clearly, democratic discourse, as spelled out by this document, served the narrow objectives of the party, not the nation.

The statute went on to redefine the party's relationship to the national media. Walking a fine line between its former dictatorial role and its present democratic posture, the statute recognized the separation between party publications and the national press and boasted a policy of "democratic cooperation" with the still state-owned media. Furthermore, the document reaffirmed that censorship and secrecy, the modus operandi of the previous regime, gave way to the "principles of glasnost and publicity." Courtesy of Gorbachev, these principles were understood by the party machine as the extent to which the national media could be used to "popularize" its agenda.

Appropriately, the theme of party renewal and revitalization was successfully popularized during the election period. In numerous forums, publicized by the press, official voices continually dispelled the opposition's version that the overthrow of the Zhivkov regime was the party's last-minute attempt to avoid a fatal crash. Rather, as Alexander Tomov, member of the Movement for Democratic Socialism, told *Delo*, the party leadership took a proactive approach to the changes because of its "sound core" and its commitment to democracy. "It *created* November 10," Tomov insisted, "as a phenomenon by the democratic wing of the party, which is the carrier of the idea of democratic socialism" ("For Realistic," 1990, p. 4).

PARTY AND SOCIETY: SELLING COMPETENCE, NOT COMMUNISM

The BSP election platform further accentuated the party's leadership role in Bulgarian society. Critics charged that this program was nothing more than a "link in the chain" of irresponsible and meaningless promises (Velichkov, 1996). One of them, a campaign slogan above the masthead of *Duma*, assured the readers that successful election results would translate into "the well-being of every man" ("We Will Fight," 1990, p. 1).

Echoing many similar documents, the language of the BSP platform robbed the opposition of the initiative for reform and portrayed the party as the engine, not the victim of change:

> The change began with everything we did after November 10, 1989. We did away with censorship.... No constant "vigil" is kept on the thought of the people. The army and the militia are being depoliticized. The justice system and the prosecution are being elevated above party politics. The party is being divorced from the state. Education is breaking away from the ideological monopoly. We are untangling, slow as it may be, the knot of national ethnic enmity and hatred. The country is coming out of a heavy international isolation. The world is beginning to accept us.
>
> A motley press was born in Bulgaria. The many parties are already a reality. Religion is free.... Politicians discuss the national problems in front of everyone's eyes. There is a political opposition in the country. Bulgaria is on the way to a normal political life. All of us are learning the alphabet of democracy. ("Election Platform: A Change For All," 1990, p. 1)

Shunning the thorny question of its totalitarian illiteracy, the BSP positioned itself as a constructive player, learning to enunciate, together with many others, the syllables of democracy. In harmony with the dynamics of the times, the party portrayed itself as a "profoundly changed and changing" entity. Furthermore, to validate those transformations, the election platform endowed the Bulgarian people with something the party had previously denied them—the intelligence to choose leadership. In a move designed to appeal to an electorate, rather than to a party membership, the BSP tucked away ideology in the private sphere and declared that it opposed the "transformation of any ideology in an official ideology" ("Election Platform: A Change For All," 1990, p. 1).

Together with other palliative measures, the election platform diverted public attention from the fact that the BSP had been, was, and wanted to be in control. After all, regardless of external and internal pressures, the party was in charge because its leadership decided if and to what extent to relinquish power at a particular moment.

THE WORD (DUMA) AND THE WORLD

But in this oversaturated babble of statements, declarations, and documents, media credibility loomed as the most serious problem for the political forces in their ultimate goal to attain power. Pre-election performance of Bulgarian Radio and TV was placed under the supervision of the National Assembly in an effort to avoid biased coverage. In May, the BTA reported that in the four months since November 10, no one had been denied the registration of a new publication. The results were predictable—newspaper titles had mushroomed to 116 and magazines to 70 ("116 New Newspapers," 1990; Drost, 1991; Velinova, 1992).[8] As these numbers illustrated, the party's media monopoly was challenged, but a new problem was created: the political forces became the main publishers.

The Communist Party press, just like the party itself, was in search of a new direction. To showcase this quest for new names and faces, the Congress overwhelmingly elected Stefan Prodev, a dissident and talented publicist, editor in chief of *Rabotnichesko Delo (Workers' Cause)*. In his speech in front of the delegates, Prodev argued for reform because "if we miss this opportunity today, tomorrow, we will not be a party, but a political carcass" (Prodev, 1990a, p. 6). Much to the dislike of the conservatives, he praised the internal party opposition because they rejected the "old structures of ideological isolationism," and, above all, because they had an "unappeasable interest in the world" (p. 6). Adopting such a global outlook, Prodev insisted, would enable the party not only to survive, but to offer the electorate the only viable alternative to the external political opposition. In a discussion with his editorial staff, Prodev underscored *Delo*'s two important tasks—to assist the party in its reorganization and to become everyone's newspaper in Bulgaria ("A Newspaper," 1990).

In his first editorial in *Delo*, under a new rubric, significantly entitled "Word," Prodev pledged that the paper's guiding light "is and will remain the socialist idea" (1990a, p. 6). His programmatic statement deserves to be quoted at some length here because it accurately reflects the newspaper's new mission under new leadership in a new political environment:

The old words and the even older ideological clichés are irreversibly lost. No one can influence the public mind with them any more. And least of all, a daily, whose main duty is to assist the thought. In this sense, this newspaper comes out of one period and enters another. That's what mandates the change of ideas.... Its every line has to bring us together. It must foster trust.... From a newspaper of one great party, it must transform itself to become a newspaper of the nation. Of all of Bulgaria. From a voice of some—it must become the voice of all. Only then will its drum lead the people. Thousands of those who need faith. (Prodev, 1990a, p. 6)

But even those who needed faith, and those who gave it to them, had little use for the slogan, "Proletariat From All Countries Unite." Shortly after Prodev took over, it was removed from *Delo*'s masthead. Most significant, Prodev's professional ethics allowed the paper to disassociate itself with its old obsequious lapdog image. In fact, when the opposition press hurled accusations at him, Prodev managed to preserve the dignified tone of his powerful prose. Only the "professionally defended truth," he countered, "could empower the media to influence the spirit" (1990b, p. 5).

In search of this truth, *Delo* started, and *Duma* later continued, a series of investigative pieces about some "well-known pogroms in our history" ("Fear," 1990, p. 3). A small note in the upper left corner of the paper reassured the readers that the editors intended to continue with this series. More important, it revealed the real reason for printing the articles to follow. It was hoped, the note went on, that such reports will earn the "understanding and the pardon of the public" because *Delo* was a "forced" participant, not a willing partner in the dissemination and the endorsement of the former regime crimes.

Finally, the separation between the old and the new happened in print. On April 3, *Delo* ran a front-page historic picture—the removal of the sign "Workers' Cause" from the facade of the editorial building ("Farewell to *Delo*," 1990, p. 1). The visual analogy with the party's efforts to "dismantle" the past was subtle, but deliberate and understandable. The caption explained succinctly: "Farewell to *Delo*, A New Paper Is Being Born."

On the very next day, both the party and the newspaper showed the world their facelifts. The Bulgarian Communist Party renamed itself Socialist. The "most popular newspaper'" in the country, *Delo*, now called itself *Duma (Word)*.

But Prodev had more ambitious plans for *Duma* than just renaming it to evoke images of Bulgaria's heroic past.[9] He wanted it to be "the voice of times...to argue, and criticize," in short, to win diverse readership ("Farewell to *Delo*," 1990, p. 1. This was not a serious problem because the party still controlled the financial power, the printing facilities, the paper supply, and the distribution system.

Equally important, *Duma*'s layout and content also reflected the editors' objective to appeal to a wider audience. An entertainment page, called "Boulevard," attracted teenagers with stories about their overseas peers and the glamour of Hollywood. As he had vowed, Prodev opened the newspaper for comments and letters. Even though these voices rarely diverted from the path blazed by the Congress, they showed some variation of individual thought and opinion, not just a mindless recital of party directives.

Overall, for the examined period, *Delo/Duma* saw the world and Bulgaria in optimistic terms and turned a blind eye to visceral issues, such as the party's financial metamorphosis. Numerous articles exposed the "aggression" of the opposition, while others celebrated the vitality of the party and pointed to the BSP's "humane" solution of the crisis.[10]

But in the race for readers and voters, language was not the only vehicle for *Duma*'s hopeful message. In pictures as well as in words, politicians presented to the public a previously forbidden human side. Uncharacteristically good-spirited, they now smiled for the cameras, often in less formal situations.

Like their party leaders, common people beamed serenely for their portraits, and they professed their loyalty to the party's revised course. At a time when the stigma of the past made many members denounce their former affiliations, *Duma* published stories about the acceptance of new people in the party ranks.[11] On occasion, some letter writers' distrust for the opposition brewed into disgust, and their rowdy language reflected their feelings. But in its editorial tone, *Duma* rarely crossed the line of civilized debate. Rather, boasting its professionalism, *Duma* let the opposition portray itself with the language and color of the street.

By most accounts, *Duma* became the agent of change in the election debates with its opposition counterpart, *Demokratsia* (Naidenov, 1991). Opposition leaders agreed that while *Duma* was defending a rotten party, it was by far the most professional publication. When the BSP won the elections, the opposition quipped that the journalists at *Duma* were "warriors who knew they were fighting a lost battle, yet fighting it.... And they lost the battle of ideas and morals because they resorted to demagoguery and even untruths" (Neshkova, 1991, p. 17). Critics charged that despite its many foreign correspondents, *Duma* was giving readers "very scanty information" and its claim to professionalism was due to the fact that "the people who work there know better the corridors of power."[12]

FORMER FRIENDS AND FOES: BULGARIA, THE UNITED STATES, AND THE SOVIET UNION ON THE FRONT PAGES OF THE PARTY PRESS

As a testament of its professionalism and new outlook on the world, during the examined period *Delo/Duma* abandoned its black or white coverage of allies and enemies. In its international reportage on Bulgaria, the United States, and the Soviet Union, *Delo/Duma* tactfully articulated the BCP/BSP's vision for the direction of Bulgaria's foreign policy. Overall, a noticeable new spirit of cooperation with the West and the cautious move away from the Soviet Union characterize this period.

During the examined eight months, 366 international stories involved Bulgaria. In addition, 253 stories reported on the Soviet Union and 143 stories on the United States. A cursory glance at these findings appears to corroborate the foreign policy agenda of preserving the party's traditional ties with the Soviet Union. But a closer look at the structure and the content of the international news tells a different story.

THE SATELLITE IN BETWEEN: BULGARIA AS THE MEETING GROUND BETWEEN TWO SUPERPOWERS

During the first months of the transition, the role of the ruling party press was to convince the electorate of the world's, and particularly the West's, interest in and approval of the changes in Bulgaria. The result was an increased flow of international news in periods critical for Bulgarian society. Not surprisingly, *Delo/Duma*'s coverage of the world peaked prior to and during the elections. For instance, 67 stories, or 18 percent of the 366 articles involving Bulgaria and the world, ran in June, the election month. Sixty stories, or 16 percent, ran during the most heated weeks of the election campaign in May. Next, the newspaper's interest in the world increased again in April when the Bulgarian Communist Party changed its name to Socialist and *Delo* became *Duma*. Fifty-five stories, or 15 percent of all international news involving Bulgaria, appeared on the front page of the party newspaper during this period.

Naturally, the party press sought to validate its own transformation, as well as the party's revitalization and leadership, through the attention the world community paid to the processes in Bulgaria. However, the datelines of these stories reveal that the origin of the international news involving Bulgaria is primarily domestic. For example, 172 stories, or 85 percent of the 202 stories in which Bulgaria was the main actor, came from Bulgaria.

This finding supports previous research that the periphery has a limited potential to excite the world, and unless there is a major crisis in which the core is somehow involved, countries like Bulgaria rarely make international news. To compensate, at least partially, for this disempowerment by the core, the reflex of the periphery is to redistribute information about the world in such a way as to boost its own importance in the eyes of the domestic public. Interestingly, *Delo/Duma* reported more eagerly from the United States on stories involving Bulgaria than it did on stories about Bulgaria from the Soviet Union. For example, 21 stories originated from America and only 13 stories came from the Soviet Union.

Furthermore, the nature of Bulgaria's involvement with the world was adequately illustrated through the subjects of the 366 stories in which Bulgaria was either the first or the second actor. As might be expected, international politics was the most prominent category. Ninety-three stories, or 25 percent, revealed Bulgaria's interest in the political implications of the changes in the world as a whole.

The next most prominent issue of vital significance for Bulgaria's crisis, was the economy. Sixty-three stories, or 17 percent of the international news about Bulgaria, dealt with it. Subjects discussed in the newspaper ranged from the continuation of the existing economic agreements between Bulgaria and her former economic partners, to the attractiveness of the domestic market for foreign investors. "Foreign investors," of course, meant only one thing—Western.

Furthermore, reporting on the world interest in Bulgaria can be a powerful propaganda tool on the domestic front. For example, 51 stories, or 14 percent of all international news concerning Bulgaria, dealt with different aspects of world approval of the internal political and party changes in this country. Of these, 22 stories, or 43 percent, specifically addressed the approval of the international community of the changes within the Communist Party. Eighteen stories, or 35 percent, were about American and Western approval of the electoral victory of the BSP. By contrast, only 11 stories, or 22 percent, reported on the East European response to the political changes in Bulgaria. This means that *Delo/Duma* correspondents emphasized the approval of the West not only to validate the interparty changes, but also to convince the Bulgarian public that Western policymakers recognized the legitimate and peaceful electoral victory of the party.

These conclusions are further substantiated when examining the nature of Bulgaria's reported interactions with the United States and the Soviet Union. Thus, Bulgaria's most frequent partner on the international arena, measured by the second actor in the story, was America. For example, out of the 202 stories in which Bulgaria was the main actor, 33 stories, or 16 percent, were concerned with the contacts between Bulgaria and the United States. Without question, *Delo/Duma* trumpeted the loudest American interest in the election campaign, and, later, the U.S. official response to the BSP's electoral victory. Stories ranged from reports on official comments made by the State Department to analysis of commentaries published in the American press. Almost one-third of the stories, or 10 stories, about Bulgarian–American relations focused specifically on U.S. response to political transformations in Bulgaria.

Not surprisingly, *Delo/Duma*'s next most prominent issue in the relations between the two countries was economics. Eight stories, or 24 percent, covered economic initiatives. Next, six stories, or 18 percent of all news about Bulgarian–American relations, highlighted Bulgaria's interest in establishing and developing cultural connections with America. While American approval of the social and political transformations was the most emphatic way for the BCP to validate its political decisions, the party's interest in economic and cultural issues innocuously attested to its commitment to reform. Specifically, the party demonstrated its readiness to encourage foreign investors and cultural exchanges.

By contrast, out of the 202 stories in which Bulgaria is the main actor, only 13 stories, or 6 percent, portrayed Moscow as Bulgaria's second most prominent partner. In the Bulgarian–Soviet relationship, the newspaper emphasized issues such as international politics, international economics, and the brotherly approval of the transformations of the BCP/BSP. These categories meagerly yield seven, four, and two stories, respectively.

THE IMAGE OF THE UNITED STATES: INTEREST INSTEAD OF IDEOLOGY

During the examined period, *Delo/Duma* ran 143 stories about the United States on its front page. Again, interest in America peaked during the election month. For instance, 26 stories, or 18 percent of all stories about America, appeared in June. Predictably, the next period when *Duma* showed interest in America was when both the party and the newspaper changed their names. Thus, 24 stories, or 17 percent of all U.S.-related international stories, came out in April.

As might be expected, *Delo/Duma* reported extensively on news that originated in the United States. In fact, 73 stories, or 51 percent of all the stories involving America, came from the United States. Consistent with the previous findings, Bulgaria was the next most frequent dateline of news about the United States. Twenty-nine stories, or 20 percent of stories about America, originated in Bulgaria and reflected Bulgaria's domestic interest in the United States. By contrast, only 14 stories, or 10 percent of all stories about America, came from Moscow.

Most prominently, the U.S. was portrayed as a powerful actor on the international arena. Fifty-two stories, or 36 percent of all stories about the United States, dealt with international politics. Next, 19 stories, or 13 percent, addressed the political changes and elections in Bulgaria.

The next most significant subject category in the portrayal of the United States on the front page of the Communist/Socialist Party press reflects *Delo/Duma*'s emphasis on American economic power. Fifteen stories, or 10 percent, fell in this category. Finally, 11 stories, or 8 percent of all international news about the U.S., focused on culture.

Furthermore, America's most frequent partner on the international arena was the Soviet Union. For instance, in the 73 stories in which America was the main actor, the Soviet Union interacted with the United States in 18 stories, or 25 percent of the cases. The official nature of the interaction between the superpowers is revealed in the subjects of these stories. Predictably, the main subject of American–Soviet relations was international politics. Fourteen stories, or 78 percent, reported on subjects such as the meetings between Bush and Gorbachev and their negotiations about the future of Germany or the world.

Moreover, Bulgaria was America's second most frequent partner with 15 stories, or 21 percent. The subjects of those stories resembled the findings in the Bulgarian–American interactions reported earlier. For instance, nine stories dealt with U.S. response to the political changes in Bulgaria. Of these, American approval of the election results mattered the most. Five stories, or 33 percent, fell in this category.

THE IMAGE OF THE SOVIET UNION: CRUMBS OF GLORY FOR THE BIG BROTHER

During the examined period, 246 stories about the Soviet Union made the front page of *Delo/Duma*. Consistent with this newspaper's overall international coverage, these too peaked as tensions on the domestic front mounted. For instance, 44 stories, or 18 percent, ran in April, and 36 stories, or 15 percent, came out in June.

One hundred and sixty-two stories, or 66 percent of all the stories about the Soviet Union, came from Moscow. The United States was the next most frequent dateline on news about the Soviet Union. Twenty stories, or 8 percent, fell in this category. Finally, only 14 stories, or 6 percent, involving the Soviet Union came from Bulgaria. By comparison, 29 stories about America originated in Bulgaria for the same period.

Just as with the United States, the newspaper prominently covered the role of the Soviet Union in the international arena. One hundred and two stories, or 42 percent of all front-page stories about the USSR, fell in this category. Interesting, though not surprising, is the fact that the next most salient feature in the image of the Soviet Union is its relation to Communism. Topics such as the reorganization of the Communist Party of the Soviet Union (CPSU) and the decisions of its 23rd Extraordinary Congress closely mirrored the political transformation in the Bulgarian Communist Party and its 14th Extraordinary Congress. For example, 27 stories, or 11 percent of all stories involving the Soviet Union, dealt with changes in the Communist Party.

The next subject category reflects the beginning of the breakup of the Soviet Union. For example, 18 stories, or 7 percent, reported on the internal political transformations of the Soviet Union. Next, elections and parliamentary changes accounted for 17 stories, or 7 percent. The mounting tensions between Moscow and Lithuania, as well as the military conflict in the Soviet Republics, were downplayed. Only 14 stories, or 6 percent of all USSR-related stories, fell in this category.

The Soviet Union was the main actor in 164 stories. Of these, 75 stories, or 46 percent, were about the USSR alone. According to *Delo/Duma*, America was Moscow's most frequent second partner. Eighteen stories, or 11 percent of all stories in which the Soviet Union was the main actor, fell in this category. Almost exclusively, in 17 stories, or 95 percent of the cases, international politics and diplomacy made the news. Bulgaria, Moscow's second most frequent partner, was involved in only 16 stories, or 10 percent of all the stories in which the Soviet Union was the main actor. Their subjects shed light on the relationship between the two countries and the meaning of the Soviet–Bulgarian relations during the transition period. For example, international politics and diplomacy was the most prominent category with seven stories, or 44 percent. Only five stories, or 31 percent of Soviet–Bulgarian news, addressed Moscow's approval of changes in Bulgaria. Finally, *Delo/Duma* showed a minimal interest in the cultural aspects of the Soviet Union's image. Only two stories, or 13 percent, dealt with such issues.

CONCLUSION

This study examined the two foreign policy agendas publicized by the BCP/BSP during the first eight months of Bulgaria's transition. Specifically, it focused on the uneasy relationship between the party's clearly articulated goal to keep its traditional allegiances with its former allies, and its more obscure, yet pressing objective to replace its ideological gospel with the tenets of a free market. Official documents mapped out the party's immediate intentions to reposition itself as a constructive actor in the domestic and the international arena. At the same time, the dynamics of *Delo/Duma*'s coverage of the BCP's former friends and foes revealed a different foreign policy direction. The evidence presented in the chapter leads to the following conclusions.

First, this tug of war between intentions and direction was masterfully used by party propagandists to ensure the BSP's electoral success. While party hardliners were entertained with nostalgic visions of keeping the BSP's ties with Moscow and the countries of the Warsaw Pact alive, reformers within the party were pacified with the promise of democratic socialism.

Second, on the domestic front, the party confronted mounting pressure from within its ranks and the opposition. Rather than admitting defeat, the BCP/BSP took the initiative for reform into its own hands. It effectively countered the opposition's assaults with specific reform initiatives and reasserted itself as the agent of change. As a result, the BSP controlled the extent of its own metamorphosis and was able to get away with cosmetic changes.

Third, to convince a politically diverse electorate in its competence to lead, the BCP underwent some visible transformations. It abandoned its rule by dictate and attempted to present a moderate platform of reform. At its 14th Congress, the BCP advertised democratic socialism as its new vision for Bulgaria's future. This untried formula of democratic socialism was a relatively painless way for the party to repair its tarnished image in a political arena where it was no longer the only communicator.

Fourth, to showcase its commitment to reform and to distance itself from its criminal past, the Bulgarian Communist Party renamed itself Socialist. This maneuver preserved the socialist ideal and empowered the party to relate to the positive traditions in its centennial history. Subsequently, *Delo*, the BCP's "political organ," was transformed into *Duma*, the BSP's daily newspaper. With undisputed access to power and resources, and under new leadership, *Duma* became the most professional publication in a competitive media market.

Fifth, as *Delo/Duma*'s international coverage reveals, the party traded its former staunch ideological subservience to the Soviet Union with a growing economic interest in the United States. But news about and from America was used by party propagandists as a commentary on domestic events. *Duma*'s careful selection of news and emphases on specific parts of American news coverage validated the transformations in the party and in Bulgarian society. The Bulgarian Telegraph Agency's and *Duma*'s own foreign correspondents trumpeted America's response to the political processes in Bulgaria. The prominent editorial play of these dispatches falsely implied that the Bulgarian story was more important to the West than it actually was. In particular, *Duma* prided itself on the BSP's electoral success as much as it did on Washington's reluctant conclusion that the party had won a peaceful and legitimate victory. Ultimately, the U.S. approval of the changes in Bulgaria, reported by *Duma*, served to portray the BSP as a trusted partner in international relations.

Sixth, as for the Soviet Union, *Delo/Duma* continued its coverage of Big Brother along traditional party lines. For example, instead of focusing on the internal crisis of the Union, which would have revealed Moscow's despotic nature, *Delo/Duma* reported more extensively on Gorbachev's role in the international arena as a peacemaker.

Seventh, *Delo/Duma*'s continued coverage of the reorganization of other brotherly Communist parties, and above all the Soviet Union's, served two purposes. On the one hand, it legitimated and normalized the Bulgarian Communist/Socialist Party's own transformation. Just as important, such coverage presented the collapse of the Communist bloc not as the demise of the system, but as a new challenge for its survival.

In sum, in the first months of the transition in Bulgaria, the BCP/BSP hit on a winning formula—to look East while heading West. It paid lip service to the Soviet Union in an effort to appease the past. In the meantime, through *Duma/Delo*'s international coverage of the United States, the BCP/BSP persuaded a wider audience that it was the most competent, the most internationally recognized, and the most deserving party to become the democratic choice of a free, intelligent people.

And it worked.

NOTES

[1] Unless I specifically refer to the Bulgarian Communist Party (BCP) or the Bulgarian Socialist Party (BSP), I use BCP/BSP. This combined acronym captures the complexity of those first months. In addition, it alerts the reader of the continuity between the two entities.

[2] *Delo/Duma* is used for the stated reasons in footnote #1.

[3] The election date later became a contentious issue. The opposition wanted time to evolve as a political force with a unified campaign platform. Recognizing that its strength was rooted

in the organizational weakness of the opposition, the BCP insisted on speedy elections and blamed the opposition for wanting to delay the democratic transition.

[4] For example, the BCP allowed the Komsomol, its youth resource organization, and the trade unions, formerly servile puppets of the old regime, to work independently. Yet, the party showed reluctance to act when it came to disbanding the primary party organizations at work.

[5] According to Duma, by January 1990, the Bulgarian Communist Party had 983,899 members. Slightly over 81 percent took part in the referendum. Of those, 86.71 percent supported the name change. Only 12.66 disagreed ("Referendum Results," 1990, p. 1). Other names, which adequately capture the tension between the old and new trends within the party, were also considered. These were: Party for Democratic Socialism in Bulgaria, the Communist Party for Democratic Socialism, the Bulgarian Socialist Party, or the Renewed Bulgarian Communist Party. Interestingly, another party with the same name—the Bulgarian Socialist Party, a member of the opposition coalition—already existed. Claiming 10,000 members, it threatened legal action against the BCP. In its lead editorial, on April 11, 1990, Duma announced that the partys new name had been successfully registered in court the previous day ("Court Registers New Name," 1990, p. 1).

[6] The Central Committee was replaced by a Supreme Party Council, and the responsibilities of the former Central Control Revision Commission were split between the newly established Central Financial Audit Commission and the Commission on Party Ethics.

[7] In June 1989, researchers recorded Bulgarians attitudes to political terminology. Fifty-nine percent of the respondents reported a "positive attitude" toward democratic socialism, 49 percent to socialism, 43 percent to liberalism, 31 percent to Communism, and 32 percent to democratic capitalism. By contrast, only 18 percent responded positively to the term "capitalism." (The numbers have been rounded.) (Georgiev, Goranov, & Parchev, 1991).

[8] Observers predicted a swift demise of the new publications and some of the old ones due to the staggering economic conditions (see, for example, Drost, 1991). A useful chronological list of these publications can be found in Velinova, 1992.

[9] Christo Botev, Bulgarian national icon, fought for the liberation of Bulgaria from the Ottoman yoke. A poetic genius, Botev began publishing Duma of the Bulgarian Émigrés in June 1871 in Romania.

[10] A thoughtful analysis of the propaganda themes launched by the two major party dailies prior to the elections can be found in Raikov, 1990.

[11] For example, the 21-year-old mother of two smiles across four columns on Dumas front page, a place usually reserved for the dead-serious politicians of the past (1990, May 21, p. 1). Optimism, though, was not only reserved for the individual, but also for group portraits of BSP supporters, such as political rally-goers and Congress-style meetings. Appropriately, headlines reinforced positive thinking and feelings. For example: "Ten More Young People," 1990, p. 1; "A Smiling Pre-election Gathering," 1990, p. 1. Another lead article, "Awe-inspiring Meeting of the Socialists Rejects the New Totalitarianism" (1990), has the following caption, "We are Many! Do not count us per square meter" (p. 1).

[12] In an ongoing rubric, "When I Watch TV, Listen to the Radio, Read Newspapers," a Bulgarian journalist asked well-known intellectuals to comment on the processes in the domestic media (see Neshkova, 1991).

REFERENCES

A newspaper of the party's renewal. (1990, February 13). *Delo*, p. 6.

Banac, I. (Ed.), (1992). *Eastern Europe in revolution*. Ithaca, NY: Cornell University Press.

The BCP Higher Council decided. (1990, April 11). *Duma*, p. 1.

Bertschi, C. C. (1994). Lustration and the transition to democracy: The cases of Poland and Bulgaria. *East European Quarterly, 28*, 437.

Brown, J. F. (1991). *Surge to freedom: The end of Communist rule in Eastern Europe*. Durham: Duke University Press.

Cohen, B. (1963). *The press and foreign policy*. Princeton, NJ: Princeton University Press.

Court registers new name—Bulgarian Socialist Party. (1990, April 11). *Duma*, p. 1.

Dahrendorf, R. (1990). *Reflections on the revolution in Europe: In a letter intended to have been sent to a gentlemen in Warsaw*. New York: Random House.

Deltcheva, R. (1996). New tendencies in post-totalitarian Bulgaria: Mass culture and the media. *Europe-Asia Studies, 48*, 305–311.

Dennis, E., & Heuvel, J. V. (1990). *Emerging voices: Eastern European media in transition*. New York: Gannett Center for Media Studies.

Dimitrova, R. (1992). *Tribunal or forum*. Geneva: NAEF S.A.

Dimitrova, A. K. (1998). From proletariat to people: Public relations metamorphosis of the Bulgarian Communist Party and its political tribune before the first free multiparty elections in 1990. *East European Quarterly, XXXII (2)*, 167–195.

Dimitrova, A. K. (1995). *(De)constructing the enemy: America in the Bulgarian Communist party press, 1950–1990*. Paper presented at the AEJMC, Washington, DC.

Downing, J. (1996). *Internationalizing media theory—Transition, power, culture: Reflections on media in Russia, Poland and Hungary 1980–1995*. London: Sage.

Drost, H. (Ed.). (1991). *The world's news media*. London: Longman.

Election platform of the Bulgarian Socialist Party: A change for all. (1990, April 5). *Duma*, 1.

Election platform of the Bulgarian Socialist Party. (1990, April 16). *Duma*, p. 9.

Engelbrekt, K. (1990, April 13). Agreement with the USSR on step-by-step transition to hard-currency trade. *Report on Eastern Europe* (henceforth, *REE*), 1–3.

Farewell to Delo: A new newspaper is being born. (1990, April 3). *Delo*, p. 1.

Fear—the way to inspiration. (1990, February 27). *Delo*, p. 3.

For realistic and more humane transition to democratic socialism. (1990, January 18). *Delo*, p. 4.

Frederick, H. H. (1993). *Global communication and international relations*. Belmont, CA: Wadsworth.

Gans, H. (1979). *Deciding what's news*. New York: Pantheon.

Gatlung, J., & Vincent, R. C. (1995). *Global glasnost: Toward a new world information and communication order?* Cresskill, NJ: Hampton Press.

Georgiev, B., Goranov, G., & Parchev, I. (Eds.). (1991). *The road to the elections: The development of political public opinion in Bulgaria: Some new data*. Sofia, Bulgaria: Sofia University Press.

Georgieva, K. (1991). Television and radio in our newspaper boom. *Bulgarian Journalist 5*, 2–5.

Gwertzman, B., & Kaufman, M. (Eds.). (1990). *The collapse of Communism by the correspondents of the New York Times*. New York: New York Times.

Hester, A., & Reybolds, L. E. (Eds.). (1991). *Revolutions for freedom: The mass media in eastern and central Europe*. Athens, GA: University of Georgia Press.

Hester, A., Reybolds, L. E., & Conger, K. (Eds.). (1992). *The post Communist press in eastern and central Europe: New studies*. Athens, GA: University of Georgia Press.

Hoffman, E. (1993). *Exit into history: A journey through the new Eastern Europe*. New York: Penguin.

Iordanova, D. (1995). Media coverage of Bulgaria in the west and its domestic use. In F. L. Casmir (Ed.), *Communication in Eastern Europe: The role of history, culture, and media in contemporary conflicts*. Hillside, NJ: Lawrence Erlbaum.

Karaivanova, P., Panayotov, P., Petrov, M., & Konstantinova, Z. (Eds.). (1995). *Journalism in totalitarian and post-totalitarian society*. Sofia, Bulgaria: Sofia University Press.

Lefebvre, S. (Winter, 1994). Bulgarian's foreign relations in the post Communist era: A general overview and assessment. *East European Quarterly, 28*, 453–454.

The literary guillotine. (1990, April 4). *Duma*, p. 5.

Manifesto for democratic socialism in Bulgaria: A political declaration of the 14 extraordinary congress of the Bulgarian Communist Party. (1990, February 5). *Delo*, p. 2.

Mason, D. S. (1996). *Revolution and transition in East-Central Europe: Dilemmas in world politics*. Boulder, CO: Westview Press.

The most popular newspaper in this country changed its name. (1990, April 4). *Duma*, p. 1.

Naidenov, D. (1991). The big sheet. *Bulgarian Journalist, 3*, 3–4.

Naidenov, D. (1995). *Press journalism*. Sofia, Bulgaria: Sofia University Press.

Nikolaev, R. (1990, April 20). The Bulgarian Communist Party after its 'congress of renewal.' *REE*, 4–10.

Neshkova, M. (1991). Lea Cohen as...Lea Cohen. *Bulgarian Journalist*, 17.

Noelle-Neumann, E. (1984). *The spiral of silence: Public opinion, our social skin*. Chicago: Chicago University Press.

116 new newspapers and 70 new magazines registered. (1990, May 18). *Duma*, p. 2.

Ognianova, E. (1997). The transitional media system of post-Communist Bulgaria. *Journalism Monographs, 162*.

Our choice for the fatherland is democratic socialism. (1990, January 20). *Delo*, p. 4.

Prodev, S. (1990a, February 2). Word. *Delo*, p. 6.

Prodev, S. (1990b, May 7). Hatred Is Powerless to Defend the Truth. *Duma*, p. 5.

Prodev, S. (1993). *Carrying the cross: A three-year chronicle*. Sofia, Bulgaria: Christo Botev.

Raikov, Z. (1990). *Duma* and *Demokratsia* in the elections for the Grand National Assembly. *Contemporary Journalism, 4*, 60–73.

Referendum results. (1990, April 4). *Duma*, p. 1.

Simons, T. W., Jr. (1993). *Eastern Europe in the postwar world*. New York: St. Martin's Press.

Splichal, S. (1994). *Media beyond socialism: Theory and practice in East-Central Europe*. Boulder, CO: Westview Press.

Statute of the Bulgarian Communist Party, Approved by the 14th Extraordinary Congress of the BCP. (1990, February 6). *Delo*, p. 3.

Stevenson, R. L. (1986). *Communication, development, and the Third World: Global politics of information*. New York: Longman.

Stevenson, R. L., & Shaw, D. L. (Eds.). (1984). *Foreign news and the new world information order.* Ames, IA: Iowa State University Press.

Sugar, P. F. (Ed.). (1995). *Eastern European Nationalism in the 20th century.* Washington, DC: American University Press.

Tuchman, G. (1978). *News as construction of reality.* New York: Free Press.

Velichkov, G. (1996). *In the chaos of democracy.* Sofia, Bulgaria: Literaturen Forum.

Velinova, M. (1992). *One thousand newspapers.* Sofia, Bulgaria: Jusautor.

We will fight for the well-being of every man. (1990, April 11). *Duma*, p. 1.

Zhong, Y. (1994). The fallen wall and its aftermath: Impact of regime change upon foreign policy behavior in six east European countries. *East European Quarterly, 28,* 235–244.

13

New Mirror in a New South Africa? International News Flow and News Selection at the Afrikaans Daily, Beeld

Arnold S. de Beer
Institute for Media Studies in Southern Africa

For South African media and its audiences, as well as for mass communication researchers, the democratization developments in South Africa since April 1994 offered new opportunities in the field of news flow studies. Apart from its apartheid past, South Africa has been, as Giffard (1993) shows, an anomaly on the continent of Africa, as its media showed a very strong Western orientation and estrangement

---

*The author wishes to acknowledge and thank Elanie Steyn for her research and editorial participation with regard to the original research project that lead to this chapter and to a paper read on the same topic at the International Association for Mass Communication Research conference (De Beer & Steyn, 1996). At the time, Steyn was a researcher at the Institute for Communication Research at Potchefstroom University, South Africa.

This project was made possible by a research grant from the Faculty of Arts Research Committee, Potchefstroom University, and the Center for Research Development of the South African Human Sciences Research Council.

from its own continent. The result was that South African mass media images tended to be filtered through American- and European-based international news agencies.

For this chapter, a qualitative content analysis on international news flow at a single main-stream daily newspaper in South Africa was conducted within the framework of a broader international research project.[1] *Beeld* was chosen for this purpose because it is the biggest and most prominent Afrikaans daily in the country.

In this chapter, we explore whether an Afrikaans language newspaper such as *Beeld* still opens its "news window" in the post-apartheid era mainly toward Europe and America, and how such a newspaper would deal with an international hard news story such as that of the 1995 UN Women's Conference (UNWC) in Beijing, China.

It is suggested that a study on news flow (see Hjarvard, 1995) and "news mapping" (see, for example, Atwood, 1984; Sreberny-Mohammadi, 1995) within the South African media could not only lead to a better understanding of the way international news choices are made, but also of the way people in a changing society, and more specifically the readers of *Beeld*, get to know the world around them (see, for example, De Beer, in press).

In order to find answers to these and some other related questions, an international news research project was initiated at a meeting in Tampere, Finland, in 1994 under the chairpersonship of Kaarle Nordenstreng (1995) with Annabelle Sreberny-Mohammadi and Robert L. Stevenson as project leaders.[2] This chapter forms part of that project.

BACKGROUND

Different forms of media censorship affecting national and international news flow have existed in South Africa from the time the National Party came to power in 1948 until F. W. de Klerk became state president in 1989. In his policy speech to Parliament on February 2, 1990, De Klerk repealed some of the more severe restrictions (including the 1986 Emergency Rules) on the free flow of information. Even so, by the mid-1990s (at the time this chapter's research project was executed at *Beeld*), and even by mid-1998, when this chapter was written, a number of different laws dealing with the press were still in effect, though not strictly being enforced (Barker, 1998; Sanef, 1998).

The world generally regards the year 1994 as the beginning of a new era in South Africa. The April 27 general elections of that year officially put a stamp on the changes toward a new democratic dispensation in the country, with a consequent effect on the free flow of information. This chapter deals with news events at one South African newspaper in the aftermath of the elections, more specifically, September 1995.

The South African Media Scene

There are many facets that are unique to the South African newspaper scene. Apart from the pervasive influence of apartheid, the wide cultural variety of the country's peoples and the sheer vastness of the land have played an important role in the presentation and dissemination of information through newspapers. Its historical link with the Western world, together with Western news values, gave the South African newspaper its present form, with the British and American input being the most visible (see Diederichs & De Beer, 1998, for an overview).

The two historical elements of language and race have played an important role in the formation of the South African press. The development of the print media in South Africa is closely related to the development and impact of the former official languages of the country; at first English and Dutch, with the latter being officially replaced by Afrikaans in 1925.

In the first two decades of the 20th century, a political and cultural power struggle took place between the British imperial powers, their business interests and their press on the one hand, and the impoverished Afrikaner community, which struggled to survive as a group and to assert its own identity and language, on the other. This formed the basis for the historical division between the Afrikaans and English press. However, this division has been largely overtaken by apartheid and its pervasive influence on the media.

Relations between the English press in general and the government were strained ever since the National Party took office in 1948. Differences over political ideology and policies led to the English press being severely critical of the government. A situation developed where both parties distrusted and blamed each other for problems ranging from unrest to misrepresentation and treason. In contrast, the Afrikaans press was sometimes utilized to the full by the authorities and was often referred to by its opponents as the servile press (Diederichs & De Beer, 1998).

It was only in the early 1960s that the Afrikaans press started to change its function from "lapdog" to "watchdog." The Afrikaans press became more and more critical of the status quo, and since the 1970s and the 1980s, clashes between cabinet ministers, high-ranking political figures, prime ministers, and Afrikaans editors became the rule rather than the exception. New force was given to this movement by the establishment of *Beeld* (the object of study in this chapter) in 1974. For instance, in 1988 Willem Wepener, then editor of *Beeld*, crossed swords with the then state president, Pieter Willem Botha, by canvassing the release of ANC leader Nelson Mandela (1988, July 18) and by attacking aspects of the Group Areas Act concerning the forceful removal of blacks from white group areas. This was also the case in the early 1980s when Ton Vosloo, then editor of *Beeld* (1981, January 9) offered, amidst severe criticism of National Party structures, the possibility of talks between the ANC (banned at that stage) and the ruling National Party.

Influenced by apartheid, the press scene up to the 1980s displayed a mosaic of different categories of newspapers. These categories were identified by Tomaselli and Louw (1991), among others. While media scholars do not necessarily agree with this categorization, the broad framework it presents suffices for the purpose of this discussion:

- According to the Western model, the liberal press consisted of mainly anti-apartheid English language newspapers such as *The Rand Daily Mail*, *The Star*, and the *Sunday Times*.
- The Afrikaans press, on the other hand, was generally considered to be pro-segregation/apartheid, especially up to the late 1950s. Since the 1960s and especially with the establishment of *Beeld* in the 1970s, the Afrikaans press moved away from strict adherence to the policies of the National Party. Newspapers such as *Beeld* and the former Sunday *Die Beeld* gained an independent voice within the previous political-cultural hegemony of the Afrikaner people. By the late 1990s, only three Afrikaans dailies survived, *Beeld* (Johannesburg), *Die Burger* (Cape Town), and *Die Volksblad* (Bloemfontein), all published by Nasionale Pers (now called NasPers in order to deemphasize the Afrikaans "Nasionale").
- The conservative English-language press was confined to *The Citizen*, published by the Afrikaans press group Perskor, which supported the National Party on a number of issues, and which was born during the "information scandal" of the 1970s. (In an almost incredible turnabout, Perskor joined forces in the mid-1990s with the black empowerment group Kagiso to establish a new ownership structure of this once conservative mouthpiece.)
- The social-democrat anti-apartheid independent press, or the so-called *alternative* press. Under this category were *The Weekly Mail*, *Vrye Weekblad*, and *Indicator*. (Most of these newspapers, as well as those in the following three categories, faded or were closed in the post-1994 era, with the exception of *The Weekly Mail*, which joined forces with the United Kingdom's *Guardian* to become the weekly *Mail & Guardian*.)
- The progressive-alternative community press was also anti-apartheid and it included *Grassroots*, *Saamstaan*, and *Iliswe Lase Rini*. It was targeted at mainly the black and colored townships.
- The left-commercial anti-apartheid press, which put more emphasis on news than the above-mentioned newspapers did. Titles in this category included *South*, *New Nation*, and *New African*.
- The small neo-fascist, pro-apartheid, and right-alternative press, which included *Die Afrikaner* and *Sweepslag*.
- The press linked to the former Bantustan infrastructures, such as the pro-Inkatha *Ilanga*.
- The white-owned newspapers aimed at black readers included the *Sowetan*, *Imvo Zabantsundu*, *Post*, and *Extra* township editions or supplements in main newspapers like *The Star*, the *Sunday Times*, and *Rapport*. By the late 1990s, this situation had radically changed with the takeover by the United Kingdom's

independent group of the South African Argus Group to form Independent Newspapers South Africa, and with black empowerment groups such as New Africa Investments Limited (NAIL) getting a stake in the previously "white-owned" Times Media Limited (TML).

■ Other papers included regional newspapers, *free sheets* (newspapers distributed free of charge), student newspapers, in-house publications, industrial newspapers, religious newspapers, and foreign language titles.

This categorization is an indication of how the press situation in South Africa was like before the watershed years of the 1990s (see Louw, 1993). However, after 1994, the situation changed, with the white media monopoly being broken down and the press being democratized to accommodate a wider scope of voices and interests in the country (see De Beer, in press).

During the 1980s and up to the mid-1990s, chain ownership of publishing, especially newspaper publishing, was the rule rather than the exception. By the early 1990s, four press groups dominated the media scene: the English language Argus and Times Media groups, and the Afrikaans groups Nasionale Pers and Perskor. This ownership pattern emerged mainly in response to the cultural and political divisions prevalent in the apartheid society, but also through the challenge of the ever-increasing production costs and growing competition from other media, especially television.

By the mid-1990s, Nasionale Pers was the biggest traditionally Afrikaans press group, with a 1995 turnover of about 1.6 million and 6,000 employees. Founded in Cape Town in 1915, it grew from small beginnings into a giant conglomerate. Up to the 1950s, Nasionale Pers mainly restricted its newspaper activities to the Cape province and the Orange Free State, but the industrial development and urbanization of Afrikaners in the Transvaal led to the establishment of the Sunday paper *Die Beeld* in the 1960s and the daily *Beeld* in 1974. *Die Beeld* was later combined with *Dagbreek* to form the Johannesburg-based *Rapport*, in which Nasionale Pers had a 50 percent stake with Perskor.

Nasionale Pers' first daily newspaper was *Die Burger*, founded on July 26, 1915, under the editorship of Daniël Francois Malan. For the Afrikaner of those days, press and politics were closely related. (For a historical overview of Nasionale Pers, see Beukes, 1992; Muller, 1990.)

Nasionale Pers became a crusader publishing house for Afrikaner causes in the first half of this century. *Die Burger* was instrumental in cultivating the Afrikaner *volk*'s cultural consciousness (Muller, 1990). As such, it played an important role in the development of the Afrikaans language, the rise of the National Party in 1948, and the attainment of a South African Republic in 1961.

The political involvement of the Afrikaans press in South Africa thus lies deeply rooted in the struggle of Afrikaner nationalism, but also in the development of the policy of apartheid. Until the late 1970s, a close link was maintained between press and party, to the extent that party politicians and cabinet ministers were board members of Nasionale Pers and Perskor. When he became leader of the National Party in 1978, the former premier and state president Pieter Willem Botha formulated guidelines to effectively end the politicians' membership of these boards.

But Nasionale Pers's emphasis on Afrikanerdom and its ideals has changed over the years. Retired Nasionale Pers chairman, Professor Piet Cillié, stated in the company's 1990/1991 annual report: "We want to be more representative of the whole community in our undertakings. We see our destiny as that of a 'national press,' a country-wide, nationwide communication industry...."

By the 1990s, Nasionale Pers published newspapers, magazines and books countrywide and catered to the wide spectrum of South African readers. By the mid-1990s, Nasionale Pers published, apart from the three dailies mentioned earlier (*Die Burger, Die Volksblad*, and *Beeld*), the Sunday paper *City Press* (Johannesburg), aimed at the black market (this paper doubled its circulation between 1992 and 1996 to 271,220), as well as a large number of regional papers.

The advent of *Beeld* as a daily in September 1974 led to a bitter circulation war between the two Afrikaans press groups and more specifically between *Beeld* and *Die Transvaler*, the latter being established in 1937 as a mouthpiece for the National Party. The first editor was a sociology professor, Hendrik French Verwoerd, who later became prime minister and arch-architect of apartheid. By 1995, *Beeld* was the biggest Afrikaans daily with a circulation of over 110,000.

Like the 1980s and for the same reasons, chain ownership of newspapers remained the norm in the 1990s, and the four major publishing groups continued to control the publications with the highest circulation. However, by the mid-1990s, there was a new dynamic movement involving, inter alia, the birth of the black empowerment publishing group New Africa Investment Limited (NAIL) and Kagiso (discussed later). With the emergence of NAIL, press ownership was widened to five major groups, although there was some cross-ownership among the groups.

Besides the emergence of NAIL, there was also a notable rise of other black access and empowerment groups in the newspaper industry. Black empowerment in the press gained momentum in 1993 when the former Argus group (now called Independent Newspapers) decided to sell the *Sowetan* to NAIL. At the time, the *Sowetan* was the country's largest daily newspaper (ca. 210,000 copies per day in 1995). Independent Newspapers kept 42.5 percent of the stake to itself, gave NAIL a slight majority of 52.5 percent and 5 percent remained in the hands of the staff.

The other traditionally "white" groups also took part in the process of black media empowerment. Times Media sold a 30 percent share of its Eastern Cape operations to a consortium of local black businessmen and community organizations in April 1996. In one of the strangest media actions since 1994, Kagiso Trust Investment (KTI), a large black consortium with interests in book publishing, bought a 16.3 percent share in Persbel, the holding company of the conservative Afrikaans media group Perskor (Basson, 1998).

Following the drastic political rearrangement in South Africa, the traditional Afrikaans media group Nasionale Pers repositioned itself within the larger context of the country.

Nasionale Pers has broadened its shareholding by inviting members of its staff, but also the community in general to take up shares. All interest groups were represented in the body of 7,000 shareholders. As part of its black empowerment program, Nasionale Pers sold 51 percent of its shares in *City Press* to the Western Cape black business consortium, *Ukhozi Investments*, in which Nasionale Pers retained 49 percent. This control of South Africa's largest and only black Sunday newspaper by black owners was bound to revolutionize the Sunday market. Up to that point, Sunday newspapers with high circulation figures had been in the hands of Times Media Limited (*Sunday Times*), Nasionale Pers/Perskor (*Rapport*), and Nasionale Pers (*City Press*).

The change in the print media also mirrored fast changes in the electronic field, where black empowerment made possible the effective "change of the guard" from white to black at the South African Broadcasting Corporation (SABC), in new community and smaller commercial radio stations and in the granting of the first free air-to-air TV channel (e-TV) to a black empowerment group from October 1, 1998 (e-TV, 1998; Golding-Duffy, 1998).

Owing to a tradition of news presentation that was considered to be professionally superior than that of the (earlier more ideologically-orientated) Afrikaans press, the English language press had, up to the mid-1970s, a large number of Afrikaans-speaking readers in the northern provinces. Circulation figures in various regions where the two sections competed directly reflected in the 1990s a steady but gradual loss of these readers to the Afrikaans newspapers. In Pretoria, for instance, *Pretoria News* lost the bulk of its Afrikaans readers to *Beeld*. The English newspapers' steady loss of Afrikaans readers to their own language newspapers, was compensated for by a gain in black readers who preferred English to Afrikaans. For example, *The Star* had more than 60 percent black readers, while statistics compiled in 1989 claimed that it had fewer white readers (300,000) than *Beeld* (346,000).

News Agencies

The South African Press Association (SAPA) is the national news agency (discussed later). It is an independent, cooperative, nonprofit news-gathering and distributing organization that is operated in the interests of the public and its own members. It was formed in 1938 by newspaper owners and replaced the Reuters South African Press Agency. SAPA receives and distributes news in Southern Africa. It has its own correspondents and is supplied with news by members and foreign news agencies like Reuters and Associated Press, though the link with Reuters was broken in the mid-1990s. In the 1990s, AFP gained in prominence as an international news agency, replacing, for instance, Reuters at *Beeld* (discussed later).

METHODOLOGY

From a methodological point of view, one could consider the present research as a quasi-field-and-observation-project (see Stacks & Hocking, 1992). Both myself and a co-researcher were at the time of the project members of the Institute for Communication Research at Potchefstroom University, South Africa. The research methodology was based on typical qualitative measures (Christians & Westley, 1981). The practical implementation of the field and observation research was done on Thursday, September 7, and Friday, September 8, 1995, at the morning newspaper *Beeld* in Johannesburg.

The researchers explained the purpose of their project to Willie Kuhn, the editor of *Beeld*, and were allowed full freedom to observe the editorial process on the particular research days. The editor informed his staff members that the researchers would view the news flow and news selection process. The researchers arrived at 9:00 a.m., attended the first morning news conference and stayed until 8:00 p.m. after the first edition was finalized. The same schedule was repeated on Friday. During this time, they attended all news and other planning conferences as nonparticipating observers. They had taped interviews with key members of the editorial staff. These interviews were for the sole purpose of gaining information. Care was taken during the interviews not to ask questions that could impinge on the news decision-making process. Notes were taken and tape recordings were made throughout the period of observation. The two researchers independently took notes, which they later compared when writing up their first draft report. Throughout the project they endeavored to be as unobtrusive as possible, while at the same time gaining as much relevant information as possible. They could move freely in the editorial offices, but near deadline time on Thursday, and especially on Friday, it was not possible to get full access to the night editor or the staff, due to time constraints placed on the news process and consequently on the senior news staff.

The main concern was to determine how the news agenda or menu of *Beeld* was set, given the general flow of news, while specific attention was paid to international news, and more specifically, news about the UNWC. Consequently, the researchers did not execute a typical gatekeeping analysis, neither did they try to establish the exact reasons (White, 1950) for the use or nonuse of each individual story across the whole news menu for the day. They did, however, ascertain the reasons why specific international news agency stories were used. Obviously, the researchers focused, as per the research questions, only on one specific newspaper, and therefore did not take into account elements such as competition between newspapers (Hardt & White, 1966) or anticipated reader interest as such (Galow, 1973; Stempel, 1967).

Against this background, the main focus of this specific research project was directed toward international news flow and how it interacted with national news flow in setting the news agenda and the selection of actual stories published in the particular newspaper.

THEORETICAL MODEL

News flow and news agendas are influenced by news values (Galtung & Ruge, 1965). For the purpose of this project a theoretical news value model was used (the Distance-Intensity News model, or DIN) developed by De Beer (1977) in a 1970s news flow study of *Beeld* and elaborated by Steyn (1995) and De Beer for an international news flow project regarding South African media coverage of the Olympic Games of 1992 in Barcelona (De Moragas Spá, Rivenburgh, & Larson, 1995). According to the model, the following news values were identified (see De Beer, 1977):

- the distance dimension;
  - distance in terms of timeliness
  - distance in terms of geographical proximity
  - distance in terms of sociopsychological elements
- the intensity dimension;
- changes in the status quo;
- magnitude of the news event both qualitative and quantitative; and
- unusualness/unexpectedness of the event.

RESEARCH QUESTIONS

A number of specific research questions were developed for the bigger international project mentioned previously, and these were then applied to provide six specific research questions for the *Beeld* project against the background of the earlier discussion:

1. What were the main news sources for *Beeld* (international and national)?
2. How was the news agenda constructed?
3. What were the main factors influencing the news agenda in terms of the Distance-Intensity News model; How were these applied in the day's decisions on news stories?
4. What was the nature of the reconstruction of visual and text feeds?
5. What role did electronic and written logbooks play?
6. How was the UN Women's Conference in Beijing covered in terms of the above?

COLLECTION AND ANALYSIS OF DATA

According to the requirements of the international project (Sreberny-Mohammadi & Stevenson, 1995), September 7–8, 1995, were chosen as the two days for the qualitative observation study at *Beeld*. The researchers kept to the schedule on September 7 (discussed later). However, around mid-day on September 8, *Beeld*'s computer system went down for the first time in its 22-year history. While September 7 could be described as a fairly normal and typical news day, September 8 was thrown into a process of crisis management due to the computer breakdown: for example, the news hole was greatly reduced and a large segment of international agency (AP and AFP) news was not received. For this reason, the researchers decided not to use the news flow data gathered on September 8.

The Afrikaans daily newspaper *Beeld* was chosen for this qualitative research project for a number of reasons (see De Wet, 1995; Scholtz, Du Plessis, & De Beer, 1992):

- It is the Afrikaans daily with the highest circulation.
- It is the only Afrikaans daily in the province of Gauteng and the other former Transvaal regions, now separate provinces.
- It is an important roleplayer in the public opinion formation process in the country.
- It has an established record of moving with the times both in a political, technological, but also journalistic sense.
- It was also a rather important period for the newspaper itself, since it celebrated its 21st anniversary a week after the research period.

Beeld is considered very much a professional newspaper, both in its news presentation and on the technical side. It is the main Afrikaans newspaper in the most populated area of the country. Founded in 1974, it soon established itself as a reformist-minded newspaper in a time when apartheid was still the policy of the day (see Scholtz, Du Plessis, & De Beer, 1992, as well as De Wet, 1995).

Beeld is part of the Nasionale Pers group of newspapers (one of four big groups in the country that at that time between them controlled more than 80 percent of all print media). Since its inception in 1915, newspapers of this group have been staunch supporters of the National Party (for example, *Die Burger*, in Cape Town, was for many years the official newspaper *mouthpiece* of the Cape National Party). *Beeld*, on the other hand, was never as closely linked with the National Party, and was seen by many to be the most reformist-minded of the Afrikaans daily newspapers. In its editorials, it campaigned for the dismantling of *petty* apartheid ("Jim Crow-like laws") and for the introduction of a new democratic political dispensation (Scholtz, Du Plessis, & De Beer, 1992).

Perhaps more than any other Afrikaans daily newspaper at the time, *Beeld* paved the way for new liberal thinking amongst Afrikaners regarding the abolishment of apartheid, and nine years before ANC leader Nelson Mandela was released from prison, the then editor of *Beeld* already proposed (see earlier) that the South African government should have discussions with the ANC (Scholtz, Du Plessis, & De Beer, 1992).

With an average July-December 1995 circulation of 111,898, *Beeld* would find itself in good company when compared to same-sized newspapers in America or

Europe, according to criteria usually applied to mainstream daily newspapers. *Beeld* rates itself as an important South African newspaper in terms of bringing the best news in the best possible way (De Wet, 1995).

As no previous research on *Beeld*'s foreign news coverage was available for the purpose of the present research, it was interesting to note that in the commemorative edition (De Wet, 1995), an article on the 21 biggest news stories in the newspaper's history only mentioned two stories with a clear international element, namely the wedding of Prince Charles and Lady Diana in 1981, and the fall of the Berlin Wall in October 1989. Three other stories did have international connections, but the South African focus was more important, namely the failed coup attempt by mercenaries from South Africa in the Seychelles in 1981, the crash of a South African Airlines passenger jet near Mauritius in 1987, and the Rugby World Cup competition in South Africa in 1995. Of the 21 most important newspeople, only three foreigners made it on *Beeld*'s list, namely the USSR leader Mikhail Gorbachev; Princess Diana of Great Britain, and Ian Smith (then premier of Rhodesia-Zimbabwe).

The question thus arose how *Beeld*, as the largest, but arguably also the most influential Afrikaans daily newspaper, would portray the "outside world" to its readers in post-apartheid South Africa?

RESEARCH QUESTION #1: What were the main news sources for Beeld (international and national)?

Beeld places heavy emphasis on national and local news with relative little space made available for international news stories. The main sources of news for what actually appears in *Beeld* are its own editorial staff and own local and national correspondents. There is no foreign desk as such. The news editor (comparable to the city editor at a U.S. metropolitan daily), who is in charge of the news flow from 9:00 a.m. to 6:00 p.m., also checks the incoming international news agency copy.

News agencies

The South African Press Association (SAPA) supplies both national and international news to *Beeld* and other South African subscribers. Until July 1995, SAPA relayed Reuters agency copy from London to its subscribers in South Africa. However, Reuters now runs its own agency from Johannesburg for Southern Africa. SAPA still supplies Associated Press (AP) and Agence France Press (AFP) to subscribers. *Beeld* receives about 95 percent of its foreign agency news for its general news pages from the latter two agencies, while it also subscribes to the Reuters financial news service.

SAPA produces very little news itself, although it does have an editorial team doing some basic reporting, for example, in Parliament. For the rest it receives news from the international agencies (mainly AP and AFP) and from the local press, which it again then puts out to its subscribers. Reuters receives its news from its mother organization, while it has a small staff putting out South African stories.

Unlike English language newspapers such as *The Star* or *Weekly Mail & Guardian*, *Beeld* does not receive international news agency copy such as those of *The Times* of London, *The Guardian*, the *New York Times*, and the *Los Angeles Times*. According to *Beeld*'s editor, it is not very useful for the newspaper to obtain enormous amounts of copy by subscribing to a large number of agencies, if it is not possible to utilize it fully.

Foreign correspondents

Beeld shares with the *Die Burger* and *Die Volksblad* (its two sister newspapers in the Nasionale Pers newspaper group) two full-time foreign correspondents in London and Washington, D.C., as well as part-time foreign correspondents/stringers in: Washington D.C., Amsterdam, Paris, Moscow, Prague, Tel Aviv, Canberra, Harare, and Lusaka. *Beeld* expects them to cover all major breaking stories in their areas that are "significant to South Africa." The three Nasionale Pers newspapers will contact the full-time correspondents on their own for different stories, but once written, the stories are circulated amongst all three newspapers.

Nasionale Pers has a foreign editor that is part of *Die Burger*'s editorial team. However, he does not fulfill the role in the same fashion as the typical foreign editor in British or American newspapers would do. He does not copy-taste the incoming agency stories. This is left to copy-tasters (or wire editors) at the individual newspapers, but he writes background material, a column for *Die Burger*, and indepth analysis of international news trends on a regular basis. According to the foreign editor, there is a definite news policy difference between the three sister newspapers in terms of the emphasis on international news. For instance, *Die Burger* gave much more coverage to the UNWC than *Beeld* did.

According to the foreign editor, the "culture" of his newspaper would influence its use of foreign news. *Die Burger* places a higher priority on international news and this might be attributed to both its broad news culture and the fact that the foreign editor is located at this newspaper. Another reason for *Beeld* to use less foreign copy than *Die Burger* might be found in the fact that foreign news copy from the agencies need to be translated into Afrikaans, and this might place an extra burden on *Beeld*'s editorial staff, though it is quite possible to send copy by electronic means between the sister newspapers once it is translated.

Staff at Beijing

As far as the UNWC is concerned, the Nasionale Pers foreign editor, in a phone interview, indicated that no specific arrangements were made at *Die Burger*, or for that matter, the two other sister newspapers *(Beeld* and *Die Volksblad)* from his side to cover the UNWC. Consequently, they were dependent on news agency copy (or other arrangements made at the sister newspapers). There were also no specific topics or themes that the foreign editor had in mind to cover (discussed later in Research Question #6).

Admitting that maybe they waited too long to give attention to the UNWC, the editor of *Beeld* stated in an interview with the researchers that they did not specifically talk about the UNWC and news coverage thereof as such. Although the editorial board planned to get cooperation from one of the South African delegates to the UNWC to write a story on her impressions of the UNWC on a daily basis, this did not materialize at the time when the research was done. Apart from this, *Beeld* used news agency copy on an *ad hoc* news value basis to cover the UNWC story.

Some pertinent reasons offered by the editor for the scant coverage of the UNWC are discussed under Research Question #6 (for details about the full interview, see De Beer & Steyn, 1996).

Observations

- *Beeld* is not devoting a major portion of the newshole to international news; but is aware of the need to carry such stories.
- A special page is set aside for "international" news each day, but "big" international stories can make it into the general news sections.
- *Beeld* is "satisfied" with the international news feed it receives from AFP and AP, its main sources of international news, and there is a tendency to prefer the former.
- No special editorial interest was paid during the observation period to international news, except for a "knowledge" or "news" sense to be on the lookout for the following "running stories" that might develop into "big" stories: the French nuclear tests, Bosnia, the Middle East, the Simpson trial (though the editor had to remind the particular news staff to keep an eye on the developments), or the British royal family.
- There was an underlying assumption that the international news agencies would "deliver news copy on time" if need be.

Local and national news

Beeld has an extended network of suppliers of national and local news (see De Beer & Steyn, 1996).

RESEARCH QUESTION #2: How was the news agenda constructed?

A comprehensive version of the construction of the news agenda is given in De Beer and Steyn, 1996. Suffice it here to say that the news agenda is basically developed in an *ad hoc* way through a series of four news conferences during the news day for which purpose the news editor kept a written "news menu" that was constantly updated.

Observations

■ Early morning news anticipation did not change very much during the course of the two observation days. However, there was apparently a continuous underlying realization that the news menu might change if something unexpected cropped up.
■ Similar to all morning newspapers, the tempo picked up from 4:00 p.m. and by 6:00 p.m. there was a marked increase in tempo as the first deadline of 8:00 p.m. came nearer.

What follows is a summarization of setting the news agenda for Thursday, September 7, 1995.

On the first day of observation, there were no "big" international, national, or local stories that needed urgent attention. According to the news editor, it was a "very normal day" (see De Beer & Steyn, 1996, for a detailed description). However, some specific international stories were discussed at the early morning news conference as they were considered "worth watching":

French nuclear explosion. Some concern at the 10:00 meeting was expressed because *Beeld* used a rather out-of-focus, vague AP picture of the French nuclear explosion in the South Pacific, "which did not show what was going on," whereas the opposition daily *The Star* carried a better picture. The editor requested a story and picture that would "tell readers what was happening."

Market forces in Cuba. One of the reporters was working on a story on Cuba becoming more market-orientated, but since the reporter was on leave, the topic was put on ice.

Mozambique search for arms. *Beeld*'s Eastern Transvaal (Mpumalanga) correspondent was sent to Mozambique to do a story on the search of arms by Mozambiquen police. (This was a followup on earlier stories about the South African security forces helping the Mozambique authorities to find hidden caches.)

Afrikaans farmers moving to Mozambique. For some time there were news stories about Afrikaans farmers leaving South Africa to settle in neighboring southern African states. A followup story was requested regarding those moving to Mozambique. Some graphics were also requested showing where they will settle. Apparently some 30 families were about to move to Mozambique. They were given citizenship, help in settling in, and land was put aside for them by the Mozambique government.

Hawk 100 fighter planes. A story was put on the news list about British-manufactured Hawk 100 fighter planes coming to South Africa for test flights. A picture was requested.

Miss World 1994 in South Africa. On Thursday morning, *Beeld* carried a color picture of Miss World 1994, Aushwira Rai, visiting South Africa. The possibility of an indepth interview with her was mentioned, but it was decided to rather have an interview with the new Miss South Africa for Friday's edition.

Winnie Mandela/UNWC. *Beeld* carried a front-page story with a color picture of Winnie Mandela in the Thursday edition. A senior editor wrote the story based on an SABC *Agenda/Newsline* interview with her in Beijing. Part of the story related to allegations she made that senior ANC members were involved in so-called subversive Third Force activities. One of the senior political writers was requested to do an indepth background story on Winnie Mandela, especially on her apparent aspirations to become a leader of a secessionist Transkei region. This discussion led to a decision to have the daily cartoon for Friday depicting Mandela in sumptuous clothing as a ruler over a barren country. The bubble would read "Now nobody can fire me" (this is a reference to her sacking as deputy minister by her estranged husband, President Nelson Mandela).

Hugh Grant/Divine Brown. There was a short reference to the fact that *Beeld* did not carry stories or pictures on the sentencing of Divine Brown on account of a sexual conduct charge with British actor Hugh Grant. No followup was planned.

Argentinean woman arrested. An Argentinean woman was arrested at Johannesburg airport with cocaine. This story was put on the local news list.

Neo-Nazi death list. A followup was planned on an exile South African living in Norway, Anthony Hawke, who appears as number one on a death list put out by European neo-Nazis on the Internet.

South African netball team. A story with an earlier international link was that of the South African netball team composition for the Africa Games. Against all odds, the South African team came second in the World Championships, but then the white star performer and five of her white teammates were dropped from the African Games team, to be replaced by "affirmative action" players as part of a then-developing ANC sports policy requiring all national teams to reflect the "true demographic composition" of the country (that is, more than 80 percent of a particular team consisting of "black" players). A followup story and a possible editorial were discussed.

International financial interest in South Africa. The finance editor mentioned that there was an exceptional interest by international bodies such as the IMF and the World Bank on news reports regarding South Africa's poor productivity rate. It was noted for future action.

During the news conference at 1:00 p.m., the news editor rated five main national and international news stories as follows:

- strikes and protest marches by medical staff at South African hospitals;
- the apparent collapse of the Gauteng province's educational structures;
- the apparent collapse of the Performing Arts Council of Transvaal (PACT) due to financial and management problems;

- the Transvaal Agricultural Union were meeting behind closed doors to discuss the prohibition in their constitution on black members; and
- a farmer had his foot cut off by a harvester while trying to repair it; the news editor hoped to get pictures thereof.

There was no apparent "big" international news story that deserved the attention of the editorial staff at midday.

At the final scheduled daily news conference at 4:15, a total of seven stories with an international element to it remained on the news editor's news menu (all stories: N = 92).

These were stories about:

- the Hawk 100 fighter plane;
- the Argentinean woman caught with cocaine;
- aid to Angola;
- the search for military arms in Mozambique;
- President Mandela's reaction while in Botswana on the striking medical workers in South Africa;
- a speech by Deputy President Thabo Mbeki on the stability of Southern African states; and
- a commission of inquiry into charges that South African security forces used ivory as payment during the Angola war.

As the news process gained speed by 7:00 p.m., there was no indication of any main international stories breaking. There was no reference at the 4:15 news conference to the UNWC and at this time there was no indication that the UNWC would make it to Friday's newspaper.

Observations

- The news agenda was constructed in perhaps the same way as in thousands of newspaper offices in the Western world. It is very much a "run-of-the-mill" exercise—there is some planning ahead, news flow into the newspaper's main office, and senior staff go through the process of sorting and selecting news items to be put on the day's news agenda or menu.
- There were no intensive and esoteric debates taking place on the merits of news items. Through a process of "journalistic osmosis" the "best" stories surfaced. Though there was some discussion on the "angle" of certain stories (for example, the medical workers' strike), there was no particular strong indications of any roleplayer trying to push for a specific "agenda."

RESEARCH QUESTION #3: What were the main factors influencing the news agenda in terms of the Distance-Intensity News value scale? How were these applied in the day's decisions on news stories?

The two day observation period did not offer sufficient examples to evaluate the different factors impacting on the news agenda. From personal experience in newsrooms, as well as from the literature, it seems on the surface that *Beeld*'s evaluation process of news is no different than that of any typical morning newspaper in the Anglo-American tradition.

News values

Evaluation of news stories was still articulated in the fashion described by researchers in the early 1950s and 1960s (see, for example, Breed, 1955; White, 1950) by monosyllable sentences like: *Dit lyk na 'n goeie storie* ("This looks like a good story"); or *Dit is 'n lekker storie* ("This is a nice/good story"). The Afrikaans multi-purpose word *lekker*, which is difficult to translate, was used most often (as in "nice" or "good"; also "excellent" for a hard news story, but also "interesting" for a human interest story). This was not only applicable to news stories, but also to news pictures. The other typical word used (*groot/*"big"), although in a negative sense on this particular day, was that there were *geen groot* ("no big") news stories apart from the developing local story of striking medical staff.

Though newsworthiness might consist of different latent attributes on a distance/intensity scale (as was discussed earlier), these values were basically articulated during the news conferences with three adjectives: a *groot* ("big"), *lekker* ("nice/good"), *goeie* ("good; solid") story. *Baie* (very) was also used to denote importance of magnitude.

Breaking stories

The senior editorial staff was continuously aware of the possibility of breaking stories that could impact on the news agenda. During the two research days, there was a particular anticipation that something "big" could happen regarding the medical staff strike. There was also anticipation that President Mandela's call on the striking workers to return to work could have some effect that could change the story within minutes (on the news agenda there was an item of President Mandela's call from Botswana where he was visiting).

Availability of visual material

During the early morning hours there was already an anticipation of the need for good visual material on the strike of medical workers. On this particular occasion, the situation was exacerbated by a feeling that the other Gauteng daily newspapers had some very telling visual material on especially the strike and that *Beeld* should do more than the usual to counteract this. Eventually, *Beeld* did get some pictures of the strike, but there was an apparent lack of finding some really striking photo opportunities through the efforts of the photographic staff in Johannesburg. At

6:00 p.m. on Thursday, the night editor was still awaiting possible "good" pictures from Pretoria.

Ranking of stories

During the research period, the impression gained by the researchers was that the stories were ranked almost through a process of "journalistic/editorial osmosis." On the day news menu, the stories were not yet ranked according to news value priority, but categorized according to the following divisions: Johannesburg office, Pretoria office, "sister" newspapers (*Die Burger* and *Die Volksblad*), "outside" news offices (that is, in other provinces), and possible pictures.

However, during the 4:15 meeting, there was some discussion on the main story of the day and other possible stories that could make it to page 1. Without any intensive discussion, it almost came naturally (*editorial osmosis*) that the story on the striking medical workers ("medical story") and the apparent collapse of the education administration in Gauteng ("education story") would be the important news of the day. On Thursday, the editor suggested that a banner headline should be used should the strike develop into a really "big story." He instructed the night editorial staff to keep a close watch on the story for any possible developments.

Though not articulated by the editorial team in any of the DIN-concepts, the medical and the education stories would rank high (that is, as "page 1" or "big news" material) on this particular scale (none of the international stories were found to be comparable in the same fashion):

- the distance dimension;
- distance in terms of *timeliness*: both were breaking news stories;
- distance in terms of *geographical proximity*: both were in *Beeld*'s immediate proximity;
- distance in terms of *sociopsychological elements*: normally, readers would feel "close" to any serious breakdown of medical or educational structures;
- the intensity dimension;
- changes in the *status quo*: the events involved in both stories could have serious repercussions for the province of Gauteng in general, but also for a big majority of *Beeld*'s readers;
- *magnitude* of the news event, both qualitative and quantitative: both stories were "big" (*groot*) in the normal sense of the word;
- *unusualness* (*unexpectedness*) of the event: though strikes were becoming almost a part of daily South African life, and rumors of bad financial administration were rampant, the magnitude and possible impact on the status quo made these stories unusual.

In this sense, none of the international stories (discussed later) could compare with the two local stories on the DIN-scale.

Form of discussion
During the news conferences chaired by the editor, a rather relaxed atmosphere prevailed, with assistant editors making short comments on different possible stories. There was very little prolonged, serious interaction on whether any particular story should be dealt with in any specific manner. The impression was gained that everybody (instinctively and/or intuitively, and/or by experience gained) knew more or less which stories were "good" and which stories were "not so good" for publication in the newspaper.

On Thursday, much of the discussion on the main story of the day centered around the type of visual material that could/should be used. There was a general agreement that the focus should shift from "toyi-toying" (dancing and chanting) striking medical workers to patients and their plight. During Thursday's photo conference, there was a negative reaction on pictures of the former and an obvious sympathetic view prevailed toward pictures of patients.

While at that stage (5:15 p.m.), it was not yet quite obvious where the story of the striking medical workers was going, it became clear (apart from what was said earlier about editorial members' own manifested agendas or lack thereof) that *Beeld*'s editorial interest was with the patients and the possible effect of a total collapse of the hospital system in the region. One of the typical issues raised at the news conference regarding the strike story was what would the constitutional rights of patients be in damage claims against hospital authorities. A number of different angles to the medical strike story were mentioned by the assistant editors, for example, the moving of patients from one hospital to another and the situation of newborn babies not being taken care of. A point often raised was whether one could really tell how many people were dying due to the strike *vis-à-vis* the death rate in the affected hospitals under normal circumstances.

International stories
No story with an international angle, or with international datelines, were discussed during the late-afternoon news conferences.

However, in the first 24-hour period monitored (Thursday, September 7, 1995), the following international news stories were registered at *Beeld* as incoming copy from SAPA (AFP and AP). These stories were either sent to the editorial staff to be translated in Afrikaans before it could be published on the World page of the newspaper, were kept on ice for possible use in the newspaper, or were sent on to the night editor for publication elsewhere in the newspaper other than on the World page.

The stories (as of 7:00 p.m.) were categorized into two sections (the numbers refer to the attached observation form in the full report [see De Beer & Steyn, 1996]; those stories without numbers were not used):

International stories already "earmarked" to be published on the World page:

(12) Einstein manuscript on relativity sold again

(13)   Civilians killed by UN peacekeeping forces in Bosnia
(14)   Volcanic activity in the Philippines in which 14 people were killed
(15)   Developments in the O.J. Simpson court case in the U.S.
(16)   Toddler in Central Park not allowed to urinate

International stories kept "on ice" for possible use (all AFP/AP, unless otherwise indicated):

(—) Debating competition on the United Nations (*Beeld*'s correspondent in Tohoyando)
(—) Diplomatic row between Russia and Italy over Bosnia
(—) Hillary Clinton's speech in Beijing at the UNWC
(—) Political ghosts (Mbabane, Swaziland)
(—) South African soldier (*Beeld*'s Washington correspondent)
(01) Arabic slogans - West Bank
(02) Seven robbers executed in Saudi Arabia
(04) South African citizen held captive in Thailand for smuggling (received from *Die Burger*)
(06) Big marriage ceremony in southern India
(07) Protest in Tahiti against French nuclear tests
(09) Army members involved in ivory smuggling ring (*Beeld*'s regional correspondent)
(14) Floods in the Philippines
(18) Operation Rachel in Mozambique (*Beeld*'s regional correspondent)
(21) French nuclear tests not condemned everywhere (*Beeld*'s London correspondent)

After 5:00 p.m., the news agenda was amended to include the following international stories:

(03) SA Minister of Health advised by President Mandela to stay on at UNWC in spite of local medical strike (*Beeld*'s Pretoria office)
(05) British Hawk 100 test flights in South Africa
(08) France to test more powerful bomb
(10) South African Secretary of Defense to visit U.S.
(11) King Hussein denies rumors about Iraq
(17) Chancellor Kohl of Germany to visit South Africa
(19) "Affirmative selection" of South African international sports teams (*Beeld*'s Johannesburg office)
(20) Foreign countries storing toxic waste in South Africa
(22) Sports: Tennis results - U.S. Open
(23) Sports: SA Penny Heyns top of world rankings
(24) Sports: Tennis - Sampras and Becker in U.S. Open finals

Eventually, a total of 24 international stories were used.

According to the coding instructions of the international project (see Note #2), the international stories used by *Beeld* on the first observation day could be categorized as follows:

N = 24
8   International military/defense/conflict
4   International politics
4   Sports
3   Oddities/animals/human interest
1   Crime/justice/police
1   National disasters/accidents/weather
1   Entertainment/personalities
1   Energy/conservation/environment
1   UN Women's Conference

The (translated) headlines for these stories, appearing on September 7, 1995, were the following, with page numbers and column width given in brackets. (Because it was not possible to ascertain the reasons for placement of each individual story at the time of publication, an interview was held with the editor the following day, at which time he gave *post hoc* possible reasons why the particular stories were used. These are discussed in the full report [see De Beer & Steyn, 1996], but also see a summary of reasons under "Observations," below.)

Jews burn flag on West Bank (2,2)
Seven men decapitated in Saudi Arabia (2,2)
Zuma stays in Beijing despite strikes (2,3)
Thailand releases South African man, arrests him again (2,2)
British fighter aircraft Hawk 100 tested in South Africa (3,2)
Good heavens! Marriage cost $1 million (3,2)
Airport in shambles after demonstration in Tahiti (4,1)
France about to test a bomb eight times as strong (4,4)
AG says man should keep hands from "secret SADF operation" (4,3)
Court hears: 8 ton ivory in crates (4,5)
Secretary of Defense visits U.S. (4,2)
King denies he wants to be Iraq's leader (8,1)
Einstein's manuscript sold again (8,2)
Four children die in NATO air attacks (8,2)
Fourteen people drowned by volcano (8,2)
Fuhrman refuses to give evidence - certain questions could incriminate him, he said (8,4)
When nature called a toddler, the law called him back (8,4)

Kohl visit a first for South Africa - Nuremberg, economy, politics, and Soweto on
the agenda (10,5)
Hundreds of weapons destroyed in Mozambique (10,5)
Counter-productive (editorial on affirmative action in sports) (12,2)
Handling of dangerous and toxic waste (12,5)
Nuclear test not condemned everywhere - German-French relations more important
than a "small explosion" (13,5)
Results worldwide: Tennis (17,2)
Penny Heyns still on top of world rankings (18,2)
Sampras, Becker through to semi-final (20,1)

The following international stories appeared on September 9 (N = 14):

Opera star Erich Kunz (86) dies (2,2)
O.J. doesn't need to testify - team of lawyers (3,2)
Saddam wants to hold referendum (4,2)
Removal of land mines in Angola probably delayed (4,2)
Weekend television (5,2)
Petula Clark takes over role from Glenn Close in "Boulevard" (7,2)
Tennessee Williams' life and work on NNTV (7,3)
In this way, UNITA wiped out elephants - Breytenbach (10,2)
New Zealand asks that (rugby) tour schedule be revised (16,3)
South African referees to Britain (16,4)
Pete on his way to semi-finals on American Open (16,3)
Heat handicapped South African athletes (16,1)
Penny ready for Africa Games (18,3)
Jim Courier fights back to beat Chang (18,4)

Observations

■ It was difficult to ascertain the main factors influencing each and every item of
news. In the long run, it seemed that the journalists involved "just knew" what
were "good" and were "bad" stories, without discussing the peculiar merits of
each important story in any great detail or depth.
■ However, when the editor was interviewed on the reasons for the selections for
the international stories (N = 24) used on September 8, he gave explanations that
were to a certain extent overlapping with those on the DIN scale (if one looks
at the main reasons given; see the Addendum in De Beer & Steyn, 1996):

N = 24
8   Distance/proximity (South African angle)
7   Unusual/intriguing/interesting/human interest
1   No specific reason, except that copy was needed for "fillers"

2   Present "running stories"
3   Sports
1   Indepth article (French nuclear testing)
1   One international story was used because, apart from the South African angle, it presented the newspaper with an opportunity for an editorial (affirmative selection of national sports teams)

RESEARCH QUESTION #4: What was the nature of the reconstruction of visual and text feeds?

Initially, no specific international news was used combined with visuals, except for the story on the Hawk 100 fighter plane on page 3 (September 8), which was used with a color picture (see De Beer & Steyn, 1996). On the medical workers' strike story on Thursday, there was a continuous interaction between the news editor and the relevant assistant editors on the way the story developed. The night editor and production editor made decisions on how to use visuals and text.

Eventually, the following international news visuals were combined with text feeds in the actual newspaper on September 8 (also see the editor's *post hoc* discussion on each of these stories in the Addendum in De Beer & Steyn, 1996). Numbers refer here to the particular pages of *Beeld* on September 8:

(04) Nuclear protesters at the Tahiti airport
(08) Two pictures of Mark Fuhrman at the O.J. Simpson trial
(08) A single-column picture of Einstein in a story about the selling of a manuscript about his relativity theory
(10) Arms caches found in Mozambique
(13) A graphic front page of the Sydney *Telegraph Mirror* in connection with the French nuclear tests, as well as a one column picture of the foreign correspondent.

The following international news pictures were used with captions and without accompanying stories:

(02) A four-column picture of the British royals
(17) Monica Seles in the U.S. Open tennis tournament
(20) Conchita Martinez throwing her racket on the ground during the U.S. Open tennis tournament

Observations
Very little attention was paid to the process of combining visuals with text, with the exception of a color picture of the British Hawk 100 fighter plane. There was also some specific discussion on the need to get "good colored pictures" of the medical workers' strike that could go with the copy about the strike. In other cases

where pictures were used, they were most of the time used to "break" the monotony of the type in the pages (for example, a single-column picture of Einstein next to a story about the selling of one of his manuscripts).

RESEARCH QUESTION #5: What role did electronic and written logbooks play?

International and national news agency news was received by computer link and the editorial staff worked onscreen from the agencies' news menus deciding what to use and what to discard. The financial editor did not use hard copy printouts of the menu or the stories, but he could supply the researchers with a printout of Reuters' menu if needed. This was also the case with the end editor (which is basically the foreign news editor, in the project's terminology). The end editor just worked through the titles on the screen and decided what to call up for online translation by the group of journalists sitting around him.

The day news editor compiled his own handwritten news menu from local, national, and international sources. For the last afternoon news conference, this was typed out. During the observation period, the research team could not ascertain whether anybody else was making use of set logbooks, nor did they get the impression that there was a strict adherence to news menus sent out by the international news agencies.

RESEARCH QUESTION #6: How was the UN Women's Conference in Beijing covered in terms of the above?

The main focus of the international news flow project was the UN Women's Conference, held September 4–15, 1995, in Beijing. The research team found on the first observation day that the UNWC did not feature a specific news item of any importance at *Beeld*. After attending the news conferences on September 7 and the first part of September 8, an interview was held with the editor, discussing the newspaper's news policy and handling of the UNWC (see the Addendum in De Beer & Steyn, 1996).

From the news conferences attended and general observation, it became clear that *Beeld* did not have a specific news interest in the UNWC. This was illustrated by the fact that *Beeld* did not have a correspondent at the UNWC. They had a loose arrangement with Sheila Camerer, a National Party member of Parliament and a former information official of the party, who attended the UNWC. It was decided that an assistant editor should contact her to get her impressions of the UNWC. Apparently she was asked earlier to write on a daily basis, but this had not materialized up to September 8.

During all news conferences on September 7–8, there was no particular sense of urgency to receive news copy from Beijing, either from the agencies or from Camerer. The editor's point of view expressed to the researchers was that "as the Conference develops, we would see if we could do something about this."

Beeld did plan to use a story on Hillary Clinton's speech in Beijing at the UNWC on September 8, but this story was dropped in favor of a story with a South African angle (see the Addendum in De Beer & Steyn, 1996, on the possible return of the South African Minister of Health from the UNWC).

In the Addendum in De Beer and Steyn (1996), an interview with the editor is given. From his answers and from the research team's observations, *Beeld* did not have a specific news interest at the time of the research project in the UNWC. As the editor put it: "We woke up rather late to this story." This was brought about by a number of factors:

- Little was known beforehand about the conference in South Africa.
- Much of the international news coverage dealt with conflict at and around the conference, which did not entice *Beeld* to search deeper for "better stories." According to the editor, "there was no underlying continuity in the international news reportage, but a rather *ad hoc* emphasis on controversial issues."
- *Beeld* didn't have a correspondent at the conference to deliver news copy, while much of the international news feed did not give serious attention to South African news angles.
- Women journalists at *Beeld* apparently did not go out of their way to bring the importance of the UNWC to the attention of the editor or the senior assistant editors.
- South Africa has been excluded from many international conferences in the recent past, and the newspaper was just not "geared" to turn its attention to an international conference such as the UNWC, while much of its own news coverage focus was, according to the editor, still rather "parochial."
- Plans were made to improve the coverage of the UNWC, for, among other reasons, that China as conference host was also (as is the case with South Africa) just "coming out of a period of isolation and insolation," which could make for interesting stories.

From the above, one can conclude that *Beeld* did not give ample attention and/or coverage to the UNWC, but that this lack could be attributed to inexperience in attending international conferences, after 1994 where the South African media was welcome, rather than to reasons such as a lack of interest in the topic.

CONCLUSION

This project should be viewed as an exploratory qualitative study in news flow and mapping (agenda/menu setting) at a South African Afrikaans newspaper in the post-apartheid era.

As to the general research question, the research team found that:

- *Beeld* was opening a rather small window to its readers on international news, given the total amount of white space available;
- *Beeld*'s international news coverage was based almost exclusively on both its own and Western news agency stories;
- *Beeld* used, in general, news from Africa and the Third World predominantly when there was a South African angle to the stories;
- *Beeld* did not carry news on the UNWC in any depth or detail.

Given the role of *Beeld* as the major Afrikaans daily in South Africa, one could expect that it would in the future open its international news window more and more to Africa.

NOTES

[1] At the time of this writing, the author was a Visiting Professor at the School of Communications at the University of Washington, in Seattle. The research at *Beeld* was undertaken by De Beer and Steyn (1996), while Steyn was at that time a researcher in the Institute for Communication Research at Potchefstroom University, and a media policy student at City University, London. Opinions and comments are those of the author.

[2] For a summary of the international research project, see the conference program of the International Communication Association, 1996, pages 140–141; Sreberny-Mohammadi and Stevenson, 1995, for the coding instructions; and for an overview of a content analysis of foreign news in a number of South African media executed for the same project, see De Beer, Serfontein, and Naudé, 1996.

[3] This section is based in part on Diederichs and De Beer, 1998.

REFERENCES

Atwood, L. E. (1984). International news trends and news maps. *Ecquid Novi, 5*, 3–20.

Barker, G. (1998). Media law - to tread cautiously with newfound freedom. In A. S. De Beer (Ed.), *Mass media - towards the millennium* (pp. 267–285). Pretoria, South Africa: Van Schaik.

Basson, D. (1998, August 7). Die einde van Perskor [The end of Perskor]. *Finansies & Tegniek*, 12–13.

Beukes, W. D. (1992). *Oor grense heen: op pad na 'n nasionale pers 1948–1990* [Across boundaries - towards a national press 1948–1990]. Cape Town, South Africa: Nasionale Boekhandel.

Breed, W. (1955). Social control in the news room: A functional analysis. *Social Forces, 33*(4), 326–335.

Christians, G. H., & Westley, B. H. (1981). *Research methods in mass communication*. Englewood Cliffs, NJ: Prentice-Hall.

De Beer, A. S. (1977). *Nuuswaardes en nuuswaardigheid* [News and newsworthiness]. Johannesburg, South Africa: De Jong.

De Beer, A. S. (in press). The South African media as conflict generator or facilitator of peace in the post-apartheid democratization process. *International Negotiation - A Journal of Theory and Practice* (Kluver Law International).

De Beer, A. S., Serfontein, L. M., & Naudé, A. M. E. (1996, May). *Remapping the world of global news flow in the 1990s.* Panel discussion, 46th Annual Conference of the International Communication Association, Chicago.

De Beer, A. S., & Steyn, E. F. (1996, August). Beeld *as a mirror to the world: A qualitative study of international news flow and news selection at South Africa's biggest Afrikaans daily.* Paper presented at the conference of the International Association of Mass Communication Research, Syndey, Australia.

De Moragas Spá, M., Rivenburgh, N. K., & Larson, J. F. (1995). *Television and the Olympics.* London: John Libbey.

De Wet, J. (Ed.). (1995). Mondig en gereed vir 'n groot toekoms [Coming of age and ready for a big future] [Special issue]. *Beeld, 21.*

Diederichs, P., & De Beer, A. S. (1998). Newspapers - the Fourth Estate - a cornerstone of democracy. In A. S. De Beer (Ed.), *Mass media - towards the millennium* (pp. 85–116). Pretoria, South Africa: Van Schaik.

e-TV. (1998, September 7). Emigrate: Tune in now. e-TV starts on 1 October [Advertisement]. *The Citizen*, p. 5.

Galow, C. F. (1973). *A comparison of one newspaper's editor and subscriber news values.* Unpublished dissertation, Oklahoma State University.

Galtung, J., & Ruge, M. H. (1965). The structure of foreign news. *Journal of Peace Research, 2,* 64–91.

Giffard, C. A. (1993, July). *Africa through the eyes of Africans: Problems and prospects.* Paper presented at the 12th Bi-annual Convention of the World Communication Association, Pretoria, South Africa.

Golding-Duffy, J. (1998, January 31). A new dawn breaks for television. *Saturday Star*, p. 11.

Hagen, H. (1998, August 28). Complaint to HRC "still being studied." *The Citizen*, p. 8.

Hardt, H., & White, M. (1966). Front page news similarities in a.m. and p.m. papers. *Journalism Quarterly, 43,* 552–555.

Hjarvard, S. (1995). TV news flow studies revisited. *Electronic Journal of Communication, 5,* 18–31.

International Communication Association. (1996). *Remapping the world of global news flow in the 1990s: A panel discussion* [Brochure]. Chicago: Author.

Louw, P. E. (Ed.). (1993). *South African media policy. Debates of the 90s.* Bellville, South Africa: Anthropos.

Muller, C. F. J. (1990). *Sonop in die suide* [Sunrise in the south]. Cape Town, South Africa: Nasionale Boekhandel.

Nordenstreng, K. (1995). Media flows and monitoring with focus on racism and xenophobia. *Electronic Journal of Communication, 5,* 1–3.

SANEF. (1998, August). Action at last on media laws. *South African National Editors' Forum Update, 5,* 1.

Scholtz, J. J. J., Du Plessis, T., & De Beer, A. S. (1992). Beeld. In W. D. Beukes (Ed.), *Oor grense heen. Op pad na 'n nasionale pers* [Across boundaries - towards a national press 1948–1990] (pp. 302–326). Cape Town, South Africa: Nasionale Boekhandel.

Sreberny-Mohammadi, A., (1995). International news flows in the post-cold war world: mapping the news and the news producers. *Electronic Journal of Communication, 5,* 7–17.

Sreberny-Mohammadi, A., & Stevenson, R. L. (1995, September). *Project proposal - cooperative study of foreign news and international news flow in the 1990s.* Unpublished paper.

Stacks, D. W., & Hocking, J. E. (1992). *Essentials of communication research.* New York: HarperCollins.

Stempel, G. H. (1967). A factor analytic study of reader interest in news. *Journalism Quarterly, 44,* 326–384.

Steyn, E. F. (1995). *Suid-Afrikaanse mediadekking van die 1992 Olimpiese Spele - 'n kwalitatiewe ondersoek* [South African media coverage of the 1992 Olympic Games - a qualitative research project]. Unpublished master's thesis, Potchefstroom University.

Tomaselli, K., & Louw, P. E., (1991). *The alternative press in South Africa.* Bellville, South Africa: Anthropos.

White, D. M., (1950). The "gatekeeper": A case study in the selection of news. *Journalism Quarterly, 27,* 383–390.

14

South Africa's Miracle Cure: A Stage-Managed TV Spectacular?

P. Eric Louw
University of Queensland, Australia

Naren Chitty
Macquarie University, Australia

In April 1994, South Africa's first one-person/one-vote election took place, followed shortly thereafter by the inauguration of the country's first black president, Nelson Mandela. These elections and inauguration became a world spectacle that rivaled the Olympics in terms of the saturation coverage they received across the globe. Citizens of the world's "global culture" saw the miracle of "democracy" being born. There were the "bad guys" and "good guys." The "goodies" won, the "baddies" lost, and "justice" apparently triumphed. Political violence made the whole transition-spectacle more exciting. What may have been less apparent is that South Africans scripted and stage-managed a "great show" for the world to watch. It became a show/event psychologically analogous to the fall of the Berlin Wall— but whereas smashing the Wall was "spontaneous," South Africa's transition was a

277

deliberately scripted affair. We will suggest that it was scripted (by South Africans) to conform to an emerging globally hegemonic ("liberal") discourse. The 1994 elections were produced to signify a defining moment in the building of a "better" global future (where better equals "liberal").

South Africa's 1994 election drama was "produced" by the then-governing coalition of that country—that is, the African National Congress (ANC), the National Party (NP), and the old (Afrikaner-dominated) bureaucracy. It was a public relations production made, in part, with a global market in mind. Viewed from far afield, there was the appearance of a miracle play, where a cancerous body politic was healed through the intervention of the invisible hand of the world market and electoral therapy. The production characterized some as heroes and others as villains in a gripping spectacle where a visionary fought a repressive state (that robbed him of much of his life through imprisonment) and was finally elected president. That was the appearance. The "reality" was somewhat different. For one thing, the "baddies" were not beaten: they were part of a "deal" and remained centrally involved in writing the "miracle" script. The resultant joint ANC-NP "miracle performance" was designed to "sell" a new, reformed South Africa to the world.

The NP had lacked legitimacy because of their legacy as the inventors of apartheid. By the early 1980s, the NP had already decided to abandon apartheid. However, throughout the 1980s, they were unable to find credible black partners to help them reform the system. In order to stabilize the country, the NP needed "credible" political partners, and who could be more credible than the ANC and Mandela. Hence, behind-the-scenes negotiations were opened with the ANC/Mandela from 1987. From 1991, these negotiations became public. In 1993, a deal was struck, and an ANC-NP ruling coalition was born—Mandela and De Klerk were to rule together. The next stage was to sell the deal to South Africans and the world. For this, a spectacle was choreographed and designed largely by Afrikaner bureaucrats, formerly associated with the NP regime. Their choreography was geared to exploit the televisualization of the late 20th-century world.

The all-encompassing nature of the world market and the international system and the technologies of global culture make it difficult for any country to "democratize" in the late 20th century without the process being presented as an international television event. The forces of the New World Order search for and attempt to destroy vestiges of anti-liberalism, whether that takes the form of Muslim fundamentalism, Serbian nationalism, apartheid, the Inkatha Freedom Party's (IFP) Zulu warriors, or "recalcitrant" governments in Iran, Iraq, Libya, or North Korea. On the other hand, positive liberal spectacles such as the Olympics become fair game in creating a proper agenda for global liberalism. Problem cases like China, Saudi Arabia, or Indonesia—where economic or strategic interests crosscut "liberal truths"—get fudged. This presumably happens because global television news is driven by an Anglo value-system either because of the dominance of American televisual practices among the world's TV crews, or because global events are increasingly choreographed with a global-Anglo audience in mind.

The main players in the South African deal—the NP and ANC—understood the need to project themselves in a way that conformed to the New World Order's "liberal agenda." For the NP, this meant respecting themselves so as to shed their apartheid past; while for the ANC, it meant distancing itself from its pro-Soviet past. Hence, in effect, both the NP and ANC shared a common need to "reinvent" themselves to appear as "liberal" as possible. In part, they collaborated in 1994 to project a joint "liberal" script for the world to watch. So both the NP and ANC reworked their acts in accordance with what global culture considered "appropriate," and by 1993, worked together to maintain the integrity of each other's scripts. If the global community wanted a miracle, they would be given one. Hence, the subtexts and deals that failed to conform to liberal-mythologies could be panned out of the shots. And how would foreign viewers (in distant, gentler contexts) ever know the difference?

VOCABULARIES OF GLOBALIZATION

Naren Chitty's "Vocabularies of Globalization" (1994) framework helps to sketch out a matrix within which we can contextualize the global media's portrayal of South Africa's 1994 election. Chitty's framework, drawing on Wallersteinian political economy and Robertsonian cultural sociology, creates a map of ethnohistorical, administrative, and international spaces linked by ethnohistorical, administrative, and international vocabularies. In Chitty's model, center stage (or the global center) is occupied by a triumvirate of leading players. This triumvirate is made up of the "world market," the "international system," and "global culture," forever seeking to expand and universalize the political, economic, and cultural values of dominant nations. In an inner circle around the global center (or international space) are dominant "national administrations" (administrative spaces) with clusters of appended ethnohistorical spaces. Further afield in outer circles are to be found less globally influential administrative spaces with their systemic ethnohistorical spaces. Administrative actors are linked to the global center by lexical chains (international vocabularies) of science and technology, trade and finance, diplomacy, and media and popular culture. These international vocabularies may be mediated via the global center or based on more direct interpersonal contact.

The ethnohistorical spaces are centered on their own cultures. The further away they are from the global center in Figure 14.1, the more uncomfortable their denizens are likely to be with the nonmaterial values of the "irresistible force." It is, however, possible for ethnohistorical groups to be closer to the global center than their own national administrations. Ethnohistorical groups have both a centrifugal and centripetal relationship to universalizing messages from a global center. They are centered on themselves and hence may be viewed as having a polar relationship

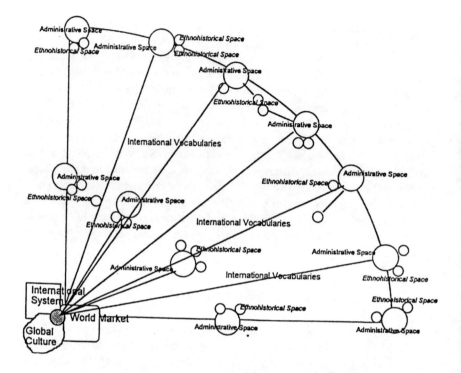

FIGURE 14.1. Vocabularies of Globalization Framework

with the global center. These "ethnohistorical centers" are often critical spaces vis-à-vis global culture, spaces to escape into, or into which one could appropriate, selectively, values from outside.

The vocabularies of different actors may be cast in Lasswellian terms as diplomatic, mercantile and cultural. Diplomatic (regimes/military power), mercantile (market) and ideological (media/academic/cultural/religion) strands of vocabulary are constituent elements in the chain of international vocabulary.

The international vocabularies, which form the lexical chains holding the system together, are a sort of "window" on the world. These vocabularies help to "constitute" the picture of the world within which global players work, by providing the "appropriate" language within which global civilization sees and understands itself. During the 1990s, Anglo-American "liberalism" is very centrally implicated in setting the window's frame. To be "acceptable" players within global culture/the international system/the world market, one now has to work with the lexical framework of the preferred international vocabularies. Failure to do this condemns dissident players to a pariah status—for example, Iraq, Iran, Libya, Serbia, and North Korea. This is an important point for understanding the reforms of South Africa in the 1990s. Essentially, key players within the NP decided that it was easier to mobilize (and work within) the dominant international vocabularies of emergent globalization than to continue to function as pariahs. South Africans learned to play an image game, which conformed to the needs of the ever-hungry image-machinery of global television because they believed that globalized media images were increasingly implicated in the decision-making processes of the global center and that they could not afford not to play along. The South African media-ized transformation consequently raises a number of questions about the nature of the relationship between the global media industry and global political practice.

First, who makes these globally circulating images, and what practices do they use? Are media workers involved in this process so immersed in global culture that they inherently and unproblematically reproduce the discourse appropriate to their global space? To what extent is global culture heavily weighted in favor of the values of one particular ethnohistorical/administrative space (that is, northwest European/liberal-pluralist and its "derivatives" in North America, Australasia, and so on)? In short, is "global culture" merely the result of one particular culture spatially dispersing itself to "global cities" around the world?

Second, is the imposition of global culture's interpretations onto the rest of the world any less imperialistic than was the imposition of Anglo culture onto the inhabitants of the British Empire?

Third, why do certain stories become megastories? Does the global order "need" to manufacture some stories—such as the Olympics, the South African political transition, or a Palestinian settlement—in order to serve as the ideological glue that binds the system together? In other words, do certain events become important globally because they are able to reconfirm and/or rearticulate global cultural values?

Fourth, to what extent are the images circulating in the global network manipulated by public relations initiatives, or the result of "orchestrated spectacles" (Chitty, 1994, p. 19)? There is evidence of U.S. military manipulation of the media during the Gulf War; cities hosting the Olympics engage in huge public relations exercises; and it is suggested that South Africa's political transition was also transformed into a mammoth public relations exercise in which South Africa's "administrative space" was especially concerned with communicating a positive image to the "world market" and the U.S. Mounting a successful public relations campaign would imply familiarity with the rules of the global media game: an ability to successfully mobilize the preferred meanings of global culture so as to stage a "political opera" (1994, p. 19) that global cultural workers would find interesting.

Fifth, what if the process of global image making fails to adequately translate local contexts into global culture's preferred (and increasingly naturalized) codes? What happens when global culture confronts a local "ethnohistorical space" and/or "administrative space" at the margins (such as South Africa), which its preferred codes are simply conceptually unable to grasp? When globality encounters such a problematic "local truth" (Robertson, 1992, p. 166) do global cultural workers (for example, international TV crews and their home-based editors) then merely read their own global understanding into the unfamiliar context? If this is what happens, then political and economic decisionmakers in the global cities would be formulating and executing policies based on secondhand misreadings of local conditions. In other words, perhaps we are seeing the emergence of a new "imperial" decision-making process that, as often as not, may be formulating policies on the basis of media-mediated misreadings (because the global cultural workers are getting it wrong, and perhaps because it is not ever possible for global-actors to adequately read local spaces).

The problem is that a dubious assumption does seem to underpin the thinking of global cultural workers—namely, they see themselves as the embodiment of some sort of "global universal interest" (or "universally valid political truth"), of the sort that Tomlinson (1994, p. 11) scorns. In other words, they operate within an unproblematized "global truth," which they implicitly see as legitimately governing the emerging global "international system." So global cultural workers are simultaneously the agents of producing and circulating the international vocabularies identified by Chitty, as well as ensnared in the lexical chains of this international semiosis. Those in the (dispersed) center of the emerging global order are coming to see themselves as inhabiting some sort of global public sphere—a (media-mediated) space where globally-arrived-at rational solutions to world problems can be found. The way in which the world media handled the "South African problem" and transition is a case in point.

So politically the fiction of some sort of a global public sphere has emerged. American politicians, in particular, seem to think they inhabit such a space—and act as if they are taking decisions in accordance with such a global dialogue. Could it be that many Americans unproblematically accept and internalize the televised images presented to them of "global trouble spots" and, on the basis of these televisual images, form an "emotional position" that is then communicated to their politicians? From these "emotional" responses then flow interventions at the margins such as those in Iraq, Somalia, Bosnia, South Africa, Haiti, or North Korea.

A problem is that for the new "global citizens," decisions taken in accordance with their media-ized experience have the appearance of rational decision making, and of a democratic dialogue. But as both Tomlinson (1994) and Thompson (1993) have noted, what we actually have is a new kind of publicness that is monological and quasi-interactional. Within mass media organizations, the communicator and the medium have been collapsed into one, such that it is now these organizations (centered in the "global cities") that communicate with a generally passive audience. These organizations are both the repositories and the generators of the (supposedly) universal values in terms of which all local contexts are now read (and "measured"). There is little room for dialogue in such a process and the larger (more global) the coverage becomes, the less scope there is for dialogue. No global public sphere is possible—what is feasible is the center taking decisions about the margins in terms of its own media-ized (mis) readings of far away local contexts.

We globally share meaning within this system, but it is not a dialogical sharing. Rather, we share meanings generated by a "global culture." These meanings are generated within mass media organizations located in the "global cities" (the "dispersed center"). These meanings are then circulated to a global audience. The nearer the center one lives, the more the appearance of participation exists. Those on the margins generally only experience the repercussions of the decisions taken within the (dispersed) center: decisions taken in accordance with media-images perceived by the "center" of the "global margins." The margins share the meaning-circulating within this global system, but share on somebody else's (media-ized) terms. However, the margins are not always passive in this process. Hence, in the case of the South African 1994 election, some South Africans learned to manipulate the global media by mobilizing elements of the international vocabulary so as to "play the system" to their advantage (although to do this they had to operate within the preferred meanings of global culture).

BACKGROUND TO SOUTH AFRICA'S
MEDIA-IZED TRANSITION

In 1989, the collapse of the Soviet Union changed the destinies of the NP and ANC. These two organizations faced American pressure to negotiate. They both had to adjust to new global rules and rework their plans and self-images in accordance with an altered global scripting process. A media-ized transition was set in motion when public negotiations began in December 1991 (behind-the-scenes, nonmedia-ized negotiations had been happening since 1988).

Initially, the Kempton Park talks went well for the NP. This reflected a balance of power in which the NP still had greater leverage than the ANC. It also reflected the fact that the NP had learned to mobilize the ("liberalized free market") discourse "appropriate" to the new global order slightly ahead of the ANC. Hence, for the first 16 months, the negotiations progressed largely according to the NP's agenda of a reform process stage-managed and scripted by themselves. Then in April 1993, the assassination of SA Communist Party leader Chris Hani by an East European neo-fascist irrevocably shifted the balance of power (Hani was second only to Mandela within the ANC). The assassination threatened to plunge South Africa into mass violence. For the first time, the NP were unable to control the volatile situation unilaterally. They needed the ANC to calm the situation, which Mandela did. So Hani's assassination empowered the ANC because it ended the NP's capacity to unilaterally stage-manage the process. The NP retained considerable power, but April 1993 saw the balance of power tilt toward the ANC for the first time. The NP never again regained the upper hand—and the ANC began to achieve its major successes during the negotiations. Hence the script, and the PR emerging from the performance, shifted direction. (Also, by 1993, the ANC were far more proficient in mobilizing the sort of "liberalized" discourse appropriate to the preferred meaning structure of a global New World Order.) But even Hani's murder did not end the NP/ANC balance-of-power stalemate (or "interregnum")—it merely altered the power balance; it did not change the fact that the ANC and NP still fundamentally checkmated each other. Mandela and De Klerk still had to work together (whether they liked it or not). But from now on, it would be more on Mandela's (or, more correctly, Ramaphosa's[1] terms than De Klerk's.

So by the time the April 1994 election had taken place, the real transition had already happened—that is, before the negotiations were even finished, the NP and ANC were effectively jointly ruling the country through the Transitional Executive Council (TEC). The elections and Mandela's inauguration were consequently largely public relations hype designed to sell the NP/ANC's Government of National Unity (GNU) deal to the black masses (and, marginally, to the anti-apartheid activists around the world who could now be provided with their emotional payoff). The NP and De Klerk had every reason to feel self-satisfied at Mandela's inauguration. Their stage-managed transitional opera had not gone 100 percent according to plan, but the broad outlines of the script had been adhered to. The election ushered in a GNU that effectively institutionally entrenched the ANC/NP balance of power within a pattern that conformed very much to the NP's original consociational plan. Furthermore, the NP largely succeeded in co-opting the ANC into the old order's "administrative space" in terms of a corporatist settlement. Given the terms of the deal and the existing balance of power, the ANC was left with very little room for maneuver, except to adopt a modified U.S. "affirmative action" program (in terms of which blacks received preferential employment opportunities). This program merely sped up the creation of a parasitic black petit bourgeoisie of the sort described by Franz Fanon (1963). This black middle class would, if the NP's plans came to pass, serve to stabilize South Africa.

PLAYERS IN SOUTH AFRICA'S POLITICAL TRANSITION OPERA

South Africa's political transition had five leading internal players. These five players not only had difficulty in keeping to their ascribed roles, but even had some difficulty in agreeing that they were part of the same operatic scripts. They were the NP, ANC, IFP, Independent Electoral Commission (IEC), and Transitional

Executive Council. Bit players existed like the democratic party (DP), Pan African- ist Congress (PAC), and various right-wing groups in the Freedom Alliance (FA).

The ANC, under Nelson Mandela, had marched to a socialist tune prior to 1990. However, in the 1990s, socialist tunes became "unacceptable" within the emerging hegemony of a "liberalized" global discourse. As a result, the ANC shifted right and began learning a somewhat center-left social democrat set of lyrics (McMenamin, 1992), although with the occasional slippage back to the more familiar sounds of comradely internationalism. But South Africanizing social democratic melodies proved difficult, and increasingly they became intertwined with (and eventually superseded by) black nationalist rhythms (see Louw, 1994). For the ANC, black nationalism proved to be a very functional discourse because first, it proved successful in winning over South Africa's black constituency. Second, black nationalism was easier to harmonize with the liberal discourse (underpinning the emergent global cultural hegemony) than a socialist discourse would have been.

Within South Africa's political opera, the ANC had a distinct advantage over all other players because they began with a good public relations image. Years in exile had taught the ANC to play the PR game. The ANC had learned to mobilize an image of themselves as heroes fighting for a "liberal-democracy" against a brutal fascist regime. Within the preferred discourse of the emerging 1990s Global Order, this was great PR and an image that those South Africans staging the transitional opera were happy to mobilize (despite the fact that only five years earlier many of these people had been constructing anti-ANC scripts for the NP). Similarly, Mandela's image as a benevolent father-figure shielded him from being scrutinized as just another power broker in a rather dirty political opera. Mandela, in a sense, served as the PR lynchpin (prop?) around which the opera was scripted. The Mandela-mystique was, in publicity terms, worth a fortune not only for the ANC, but for all those involved in trying to cobble together the South African corporatist settlement. (Even the leader of the far-right FF, General Constant Viljoen, showed a clear awareness of the value of the Mandela-myth for stabilizing the transitional process.)

The National Party had been responsible for apartheid. From the 1940s to the 1960s, the NP was the party of Afrikaner nationalism and neo-fascism. From the 1980s, the NP began moving left, abandoning Afrikaner and white nationalism in favor of an all-inclusive "South Africanism." By the 1990s, under F. W. de Klerk, the NP occupied a right-of-center position, having rescripted its act, expunging ethnicity from its repertoire, and began learning a nonracial free enterprise set of lyrics (see Louw, 1994). The NP had negotiated a compromise with the ANC over how they could jointly rule the country, and by 1994 had as many "nonwhite" supporters as white. But when it came to the global media, the NP had a serious image problem. Few of the international media corps were equipped with the tools to grasp the NP discourse, its roots, the shifts that had taken place within the NP, or what the NP's real agenda was.

For the purposes of this chapter, it is crucial to understand the NP, its constituency, and their motives, because they mainly scripted the "miracle discourse." Basically, during the 1980s, a "liberal" pro-free enterprise faction assumed control within the NP and successfully purged the NP structures of the far right. By the time F. W. de Klerk became party leader, NP supporters represented center-right opinion. These changes within the NP were tied to shifts within the NP's constituency. During the 1940s, the NP represented a white Afrikaner population impoverished by British imperialism. The NP's national socialist period (1948 to the mid-1970s) represented an "affirmative action" program aimed at uplifting the Afrikaner worker and lumpenproletariat population through state intervention. By the mid-1970s, this affirmative action had produced a large Afrikaner middle class. By 1990, the lifestyles and value system of English and Afrikaans whites were indistinguishable from one another (and indeed indistinguishable from people living in California's Orange County). In short, the NP's policy had been so successful that it had changed the character of its own constituency. By the mid-1980s, NP supporters (unlike their grandparents) no longer needed apartheid or a "national socialist" interventionist state to serve their interests. Instead, by 1990, free enterprise, a liberal-pluralist democracy and deradicalizing society served their interests more effectively. It was this changed NP constituency that drove the 1990s reform process in South Africa, and that then managed the public relations exercise to sell the "miracle discourse" to the world.

Essentially, by the late 1980s, the balance of power within the NP Cabinet tilted away from the "right" and toward the "liberals." Similar shifts occurred in the security establishment. During the 1980s, the "doves" won out over the "hawks" and key officers in the SA Defence Force and Security Police threw their weight behind those in the Cabinet advocating a "negotiated solution." These shifts inside the NP and its support base meant that the NP government was, by the late 1980s, emotionally open to pressures for change coming from local and global business sectors, as well as from the U.S. State Department.

The NP's shift toward negotiation was also built upon a recognition that it had no realistic long-term alternative. First, during the 1980s, white conscripts increasingly failed to report for military call-ups. Second, the cost of the Namibian and Angolan wars looked set to become too great: for example, in Cuito Cuannavale (in 1987) the SA Defence Force, were, for the first time, successfully challenged by a Cuban/Angolan Soviet force. In addition, South Africa's economy was starting to show signs of strain due to the costs of war, sanctions, an accelerating outflow of capital, and mounting white emigration. Effectively, by 1987, the balance of power was such that neither of the two sides (NP versus ANC) could defeat the other. They were trapped in the same boxing ring, slugging it out, but neither side would go down. In Gramscian (1971) terms, by 1987, South Africa was trapped into an "interregnum"—a stalemate born of a balance of power logjam that neither side could break. A militarization of society occurred, the casualties mounted, but neither side could ever win. In the late 1980s, the NP's P. W. Botha and the ANC's

Nelson Mandela began to explore what possibilities existed for negotiating a political dispensation that would reflect the actual balance of power—that is, they explored how they could share power within a GNU (Mandela, 1994).

Furthermore, in the 1980s, key NP intellectuals had begun selling the idea that the NP were strong enough to stage-manage a reform process, which would produce a settlement fundamentally favorable to the NP constituency. Building on Lijphart's (1977) "consociational" model, the NP reformers set about putting into place the groundwork for a negotiated deal between the ANC and NP, which would culminate in a modern etatized corporation. Many of these intellectuals (among whom Afrikaner journalists[2] were very prominent) later became involved in the public relations exercise to script the transition opera and sell the "miracle discourse." It is significant that amongst the most ardent advocates of reform in the late 1980s and early 1990s were Afrikaner journalists, diplomats,[3] and businessmen—all necessarily people exposed to, and able to function with, the international vocabularies of a globalizing world. In a sense, the preferred discourse of the global system/culture began, during the 1980s, to colonize key sections of South Africa's administrative space as well as the Afrikaner ethnohistorical space. This "colonization" was, in part, responsible for the eventual coming of the 1994 media-ized elections—that is, elections as a global public relations event. Effectively, a "global political opera" was staged in which a new reformed South Africa (apparently transformed by a democratizing "miracle") was presented. The aim was to attract global media workers and get them to pick up, package, and distribute an "appropriate" message around the world.

Significantly, this packaging and selling exercise was run largely by diplomats, bureaucrats, and media workers who had served the old apartheid regime. In the past, they had worked to defend their regime against its pariah status. Now, in 1994, they were working within the preferred discourse of the emergent world order communication. This made the 1994 exercise much easier for them—they now had a saleable message.

The NP's reform package, and the deal eventually struck with the ANC, were premised upon the NP's (conservative) desire to stabilize South Africa. In terms of the ANC/NP corporatist settlement agreed to in 1993, the capitalist-industrial state was to be stabilized by an ANC/NP government. The NP realized that they could not stabilize this socioeconomic order alone because they had insufficient "legitimacy." The ANC realized that the only way to access any real power was to do a deal with the NP, because they did not have the strength to beat them. The Kempton Park settlement established a Government of National Unity, in which the ANC provided "legitimacy" (by providing "credible" black faces in government) and the NP delivered "experience in government," a managerial-bureaucratic class, and a security-establishment to run things. The 1994 elections and Mandela's inauguration were little more than a stage-managed public relations exercise that served merely to put a rubber stamp on the 1993 Kempton Park corporatist deal.

The Inkatha Freedom Party represented a mostly pre-modern Zulu constituency living mostly in KwaZulu Natal (Zulus are South Africa's largest ethnic group). The IFP's Chief Buthelezi was head of the KwaZulu black homeland prior to the 1994 election. The ANC's strident urban-based workers' songs as well as its homogenizing black nationalist lyrics struck no chord within the Zulu-traditionalist's heart. Instead, Buthelezi's impis marched to the music of old Africa: they sang the praises of their King, their forefathers, and their ancestral soil. They would fight, if need be, to preserve a federal space for the traditional "Zulu way of life."

When it came to the global media, the IFP faced three problems. First, like the NP, they were automatically classified as "bad." Second, the IFP had no experience of playing the PR game in a global context. The ANC, as seasoned PR operators in the international context, ran rings around the IFP in the image war. Third, the IFP did not conform to the picture of South Africa that global culture wanted to see. Whereas by 1994, the NP had learned to mobilize international vocabularies and had opted to reconstruct itself in accordance with the preferred visions of global culture, the IFP refused to bend. The IFP was concerned with an internal audience, not a global audience—they spoke to the IFP's own constituency in language that jarred the sensibilities of those accustomed to the gentler preferred discourses circulating within global cities. Hence, the IFP presented a discordant note, being largely incomprehensible from within global culture's preferred meaning system. What is more, the personnel driving the image-machinery inside South Africa represented the GNU coalition (that is, the NP and ANC), and so had no vested interest in "clarifying" the IFP's position for the global media crews.

The Independent Electoral Commission, under Judge Johann Kriegler, played a pivotal role in the transition process. The IEC was cobbled together to run the elections from people drawn mostly from nongovernmental organizations (NGOs). These NGOs had been aligned with the UDF/ANC in the 1980s. In reality then, the IEC largely represented an "alliance" of ANC people and liberals who had been sympathetic to the ANC in the 1980s. There was, however, a smattering of government-bureaucrats to appease the NP. That the IEC seemed to hum in unison with the ANC's preferred tunes was one of the reasons the IFP was so hostile to the IEC and Kriegler. Affirmative action plus "politically acceptable" appointees resulted in the employment of large numbers of underqualified and inexperienced pro-ANC people. This, in turn, led to the administrative fiasco (and the irregularities) of the election itself. Ultimately, the IEC's brief was to deliver an election legitimate to enough people so as to stop the civil war. Hence the IEC was, as much as anything else, an exercise designed to "sell" the corporatist settlement and/or "historic compromise" (between the ANC and NP) to black South Africans. Within the transition opera, the global media were to be mobilized to communicate the "miracle discourse" internationally. The IEC was to communicate the same PR message internally by providing an "appropriate" face to the transition mechanism. The IEC was also part of the PR machinery geared up to service "appropriate" ("miracle") images to the global media machine.

The Transitional Executive Council (TRC) became the effective day-to-day government long before the media-ized PR election. The TEC represented the ANC–NP balance of power stalemate, which meant both parties had to work together to get anything done. The TEC represented joint ANC–NP governments before the election (the GNU simply continued this joint rule after April 1994). Within the TEC, the ANC and NP were not only learning to sing the same tunes, they even occasionally sang in tune with each other. In effect, they learned to synchronize their scripts with each other as well as with the ("liberal") global script of the New World Order. The ANC's Cyril Ramaphosa generally acted as choirmaster within the TEC.

Interestingly, the global media crews simply missed the point that the TEC represented an already existing ANC–NP Government of National Unity. That power had already been transferred out of white and NP hands; and consequently the April 1994 elections represented a post hoc PR exercise, not a real transfer of power.

The Freedom Alliance was an early 1990s phenomenon. It was a loose amalgamation of various conservative parties marching to surprisingly disparate songs. The two central parties to this alliance were the IFP and parties representing far-right whites. The latter included parties like the Freedom Front (FF), conservative party (CP), and Afrikaner Weerstands Beweeging (Afrikaner Liberation Movement; AWB)—who had all abandoned the NP as it moved leftward after 1980 (Grobbelaar, Bekker, & Evans, 1989). The far-right's constituency included Afrikaner nationalists, ex-Rhodesians (Anglo-colonials), and East Europeans who had moved to South Africa to "escape Communism." Other parties to the FA were the rulers of some of the "independent" black homelands (like Bophuthatswana and Ciskei) who were concerned at being reincorporated into an ANC-ruled South Africa. What held the alliance together was a shared fear of an ANC government. The FA coalesced around the idea of federalism, as this was seen to guarantee each of the parties a "space" where their constituency could sing their own songs unhindered by others. The FA were, in effect, fighting for the creation of what Mowlana called "ghetto states" (1994, p. 24). However, joint ANC/NP pressure (via the TEC) in March-April 1994 destroyed the FA. Two FA players attracted support in the 1994 election: the IFP won control of KwaZulu-Natal and the FF won about one-third of the white vote.

For the global media, the FA served the role of being identifiable "crazies": the die-hards who did not want to accept the inevitability of sensible change. The AWB, in particular (who actually had very few supporters), served as a very useful televisual symbolic representation of all that was evil in this camp because of their Nazi-ized uniforms. It is unlikely that any of the foreign media corps had the conceptual tools required to decode the FA and its immensely complex discourses. And the FA players had no PR experience on how to mobilize international vocabularies to sell their perspectives to the global media workers. In point of fact, the FA players (especially the AWB and IFP) proved to be extraordinarily inept at playing the global media game—usually succeeding in presenting exactly the images most likely to allow themselves to be portrayed as unidimensional "crazies" and/or to alienate mainstream audiences in the world's global cities. Within the context of the 1994 media-ized election, the FA simply had none of the media-acumen (nor familiarity with global culture) needed to play the game in an appropriate way. In media terms, they were generally their own worst enemies.

The Pan African Congress represented the far-left. It espoused principles that integrated elements of Maoism with a black nationalism of the Kwame Nkhruma variety (Davies, O'Meara, & Dlamini, 1984). But much of the PAC's traditional support-base appeared to vote for the ANC in the 1994 election since the ANC had, by then, learned to sing the songs of black nationalism as well as the PAC. Perhaps the PAC's greatest roles were to frighten the ANC into learning the lyrics of African nationalism and to frighten whites into supporting an ANC-NP ruling coalition (in preference to the PAC). The PAC, like the FA, had no idea how to play the global media game.

The democratic party's liberalism was barely audible on stage. It tried unsuccessfully during the early 1990s to shake off its image inside South Africa of only representing affluent Anglo-whites. Whereas the NP was able to win "nonwhite" support, the DP failed in this regard. To make matters worse, in the 1994 election, most white DP supporters appeared to vote NP, since by then the NP had learned to sing "liberal" free-enterprise songs quite convincingly. Interestingly, the global media machine was fond of quoting DP people (such as Helen Suzman) as a voice of authoritative "reasonableness." Of all South African interest/political groups, DP supporters were the most adept at playing the global media game: the DP's constituency were fully emersed in global culture and were the central South African players in the world market. Consequently, they were the most professional at using the global system's international vocabularies. Not surprisingly then, people like Helen Suzman, Nadine Gordimer, Van Zyl Slabbert, and Alan Paton have slid easily into a symbiotic relationship with global media workers when the global media machine has sought "sensible" people to interpret South African affairs. So ironically, the global media has given such spokespeople far greater credence than one would expect from their limited internal support base.

The cacophony of the above discordant voices became somewhat difficult to hear above the sound of gunfire in early 1994. But slowly two camps of singers emerged. On the one hand, the ANC and NP learned to synchronize their tunes, billing themselves as the center-stage act and jointly set about choreographing the transition to an ANC/NP Government of National Unity. Then there were the IFP, conservative Afrikaner groups and Bophuthatswana and Ciskei black homeland leaders who refused to accept the ANC-NP choreography. They came onto the stage and began singing their own songs. This led to multiple overlapping performances and even the rewriting of the script to include violence between the performers (both on and off stage), which occasionally spilled over into the audience. But by the time Nelson Mandela became president, this messy cocophony appeared to have been stilled and replaced by the now-synchronized ANC-NP script. That's how the global media machine chose to present it anyway, in part because the transition opera had been choreographed that way.

CHOREOGRAPHING A GLOBAL SPECTACLE: THE SABC AS A "HIDDEN" PLAYER

There was another South African player that impacted on the unfolding spectacle. This player, the South African Broadcasting Corporation (SABC), remained "hidden," but nonetheless affected the way the world perceived the transition process. The SABC acted, in effect, as a national public relations agency, making selected information and images available to the world with a view to presenting a positive image of South Africa. The SABC's actions represented, in fact, one section of South Africa's "administrative space" (Chitty, 1994 p. 16) trying to communicate with the "world market" (Chitty, 1994, pp.12–13) and to the U.S. South Africa's Department of Foreign Affairs (still run in April 1994 by the diplomats of the "old apartheid" state) were especially interested in selling the idea of a "miracle transition" to the African Americans—since they believed the African-American caucus could become as important to South Africa as the Jewish-American caucus was to Israel. Hence, South Africa's "administrative space" deliberately set about creating a public relations spectacular, geared up in large measure in accordance with the U.S.'s love of spectacle. So, to a considerable extent, the world watched a South African "show" choreographed with an American audience in mind. It was a public relations exercise launched and executed by media people who fully understood the practices and discourses of the global media, and hence how to tap into these.

By 1994, the SABC mirrored the new ruling alliance in South Africa. In 1993, the ANC effectively "captured" the SABC board (because the TEC controlled the process of appointing a new board). Hence, from 1993, significant staffing changes were set in motion aimed at achieving a mix of pro-ANC and pro-"reform" NP people in the key decision-making positions. SABC staffers who appeared to support the PAC, IFP, or conservative-white groups were marginalized or removed from their posts. This produced discernible editorial effects from early 1994. So although the ANC had not fully captured the SABC's editorial machinery by the April 1994 elections (that sometimes resulted in contradictory messages being broadcast), the ANC's views were clearly dominant within the SABC by April 1994. Hence, in general, throughout 1994, the SABC promoted the ANC/NP alliance and portrayed the IFP, CP, AWB, PAC, and Azanian People's Organization (AZAPO) as "radical crazies." Homeland leaders like Mangope and Sebe were demonized.

This new SABC set up an International Broadcast Centre (IBC) at a cost of $2.7 million, to accommodate foreign journalists covering the election. Most foreign TV crews flew in only for the elections/Mandela inauguration period. Hence, they were unfamiliar with South Africa and would not be in the country long enough to get on top of the situation. Given this, the SABC assumed that professionally produced and canned images, courtesy of the IBC, would be hard to resist in such circumstances. Huge energy was therefore expended by the IBC to create a remarkably comfortable environment in Johannesburg (with branch facilities in Cape Town, Durban, and Port Elizabeth) for the visiting media crews. This would enable them to effectively be tourists and yet still be in a position to file professional-looking feeds to their home bases with minimal effort. Every comfort was available, from onsite laundry, banking, postal, and (multicultural) food facilities to restrooms/lounges, a curio shop, and tourist operators offering special deals on trips to game reserves and other tourist attractions. Each media crew had its own suite of offices, editing suite, and access to an IBC-run decor services and props department. But most importantly, there was an IBC master control (switching) center, which routed an SABC newsfeed directly into the editing area of all foreign crews, and/or to their satellite feeding points. News and actuality material produced by the SABC was automatically pumped into the IBC system with three different soundtracks to choose from: 1) the SABC's actual sound track (which would have alternated between five different languages); 2) "clean sound"; and 3) a "guide-track" (in English) "explaining" the highlights. Thus, foreign TV crews could simply use the "clean" sound and add their own voiceovers, thus giving their home audiences (and bosses) the impression of having collected the material themselves. The IBC also handed out occasional news releases to these media crews, which provided agenda-setting "background" information. In addition, each of the office units was equipped with an agenda-setting teledata TV screen that fed ongoing (SABC-produced) information to the foreign crews. Ultimately, very few foreign media crews did not avail themselves of IBC facilities. In all, 16 TV crews (1,230 newspersons) registered with the IBC. For those who did register with the IBC, it became technically possible to cover the 1994 elections without ever venturing out into the conflict-ridden South African community.

Significantly, the IBC's project manager was Phillip O'Kelly, while his studio manager was Danie Loots. Both O'Kelly and Loots served as officers in SALTIE (the South African Army's public relations/propaganda unit) during the 1980s and were experienced in conducting what SALTIE called "communications operations." During the Namibian and Angolan wars, SALTIE operations were often very "political" and involved working out of uniform with nonmilitary branches of South Africa's "administrative space"(for example, foreign affairs). This experience was well-suited for choreographing the "miracle discourse," since it combined knowledge not only of media/PR but also of working with other sections of the state bureaucracy.

The SABC person who took the key editorial decisions on the news material that was fed via the IBC to the foreign crews was Andre Le Roux, a veteran of the old (NP-controlled) SABC. Le Roux, as Executive Editor of Television News Productions, worked very closely with the IEC and other sections of South Africa's "administrative space" in constructing images of the transition opera. The material fed into the IBC system was, in part, tailored to try and improve South Africa's rather battered international image. South Africa desperately needed capital to regenerate its shattered economy and social infrastructure. The election (and Mandela's inauguration ceremony) was seen to offer a unique public relations opportunity for talking to the "world market." It also projected an image of "a miracle" in which South Africans had "found each other" through negotiation and in the process created a social order worthy of foreign investment. Mobilizing and expanding the Mandela myth was seen as a central component of any discourse targeting the global audience (particularly the African-American component of this audience).

What seems clear is that the IBC achieved its purpose. As a result of SABC/IBC intervention, it appears that few people in the global audience were ultimately not exposed to the self-same "pooled" images of South Africa's transition. The foreign media performed as expected and by the end of the April 1994 period, the global community was convinced that a miracle had indeed taken place in South Africa. Had a global public relations coup been pulled off?

CONCLUSION

The curtain came down on South Africa's political opera, and the TV crews went home—or off to Rwanda—having filed their stories. Their global audiences were content that the "South African miracle" had taken place. With the TV crews gone, South Africa largely slid off the world's news agenda. For people in New York, London, or Sydney, the post-1994 decline of news about South Africa could presumably be interpreted as an indication that things had been "normalized." And even when post-1994 problems have been covered by the global media, they are reported as "normal" tensions within a society transforming itself into a liberal-democracy. In reality, all is not well. For most South Africans (except for the minority onboard the black, middle-class "gravy train") the transition has failed to deliver the promised "miracle." The gap between the PR image and reality is a large one.

What is fascinating about the 1994 South African transition is what it seems to reveal about the manufacture and circulation of global discourses/myths within the emerging network of globalized-televisual image making. South Africa's transition opera showed the way in which global myths emerge out of a complex interaction between the needs of regional "administrative spaces"/regional "ethnohistorical spaces" and the needs of the global media machine (and the global culture this machinery serves). The reportage of the South African 1994 elections hence raises a number of questions.

First, can this election be seen to tell us about emergent preferred discourse(s) within a globalizing world? If there is a 1990s pattern, it seems that to be "acceptable" within the new global system, players need to either be "liberal" or able to create the appearance of operating within a broadly liberal discourse. Whether appearance and reality need to coincide is debatable. But certainly the symbolic glue ("international vocabularies") binding the post-1990s global system together now serves to frame the world within a rather narrowed range of symbolic possibilities. (Interestingly, there seems to be a rather close correspondence between this new hegemonic global discourse and the preferred/hegemonic discourse of the Anglo world—that is, North America/U.K./Australasia). So to be successful, global media workers (whether CNN or BBC TV crews or South African PR strategists trying to "sell" their country) presumably now need to work (either consciously or unconsciously) within a somewhat narrowed vision of the world. Global culture is consequently developing a rather predictable set of self-images and symbolic-tools in terms of which it "measures" all the players within the global system. It would also seem to increase the danger of naive interpretations of certain contexts (for example, Eastern European/Balkans, South Africa, China, Iran, and/or Iraq)—because such places and "ethnohistorical spaces" seem incomprehensible to global cultural workers, since their preferred (Anglo-"liberal") meaning-structures have insufficient symbolic-capital to deal with such complex contexts.

Second, did the elections of 1994 reveal anything about 1990s global myth-making? Two major global myths emerged from 1990s South Africa, namely the "miracle" transformation myth and the supportive and crosscutting constructs, both of which serve to confirm the preferred global/"liberal" reading of South Africa. They were myths that seemed to have serviced some deep "psychological need" (the desire for a "good news" story) and somehow "stabilize" the beliefs and hopes of millions of people living through the turmoil and insecurity of a globalizing and postfordizing world.

South Africa's "miracle" and myths about Mandela seemed to give hope amidst an otherwise unstable set of signifiers. Not surprisingly, these myths have the greater credence outside the country than within South Africa itself—because they are myths that are only really believable to audiences with little or no knowledge of the immense complexity of South Africa's past and present. But having been manufactured by a PR machinery serving the needs of South Africa's new (GNU) rulers, these myths took on a life of their own—they have subsequently fed into an external (global) industry, which now recirculates and embellishes on the original myths to create an amazingly complex set of globally circulating signifiers (increasingly with little grounded referential connection to the contemporary South African context). In a sense, the "miracle" and "Mandela" myths have served to demonstrate how signifiers and the signified can be decoupled within the contemporary global media industry.

Third, the elections of 1994 revealed something interesting about the power of the "global center" to direct global discourse/culture. In a sense, the South African elections both simultaneously confirmed and negated the notion of a global center able to control the peripheries. On the one hand, South Africa's PR functionaries demonstrated a capacity to manipulate the messages received by a global audience.

This seems to suggest that players living in the "margins" are not powerless (and merely manipulated) within the emerging manufacture and circulation of global meanings. But, on the other hand, the South African case also demonstrated that to have an impact, the GNU's PR operatives who were never able to sell apartheid's mythologies, were spectacularly successful when given a "saleable" liberal-sounding discourse to present to the global machinery of news-making.

Tuchman (1980) described news as a "window" on the world. The position and size of the window are all important in deciding the view of the world received. The coverage of South Africa's elections, presidential inauguration, and post-election period raise a number of questions about the practices of global media workers and the agendas underpinning the worldview they choose to present. Perhaps more work needs to be done examining "gaps" that may exist between events on the ground and the global media's portrayal of these events in places like South Africa, North Korea, Haiti, the former Yugoslavia, and Russia. It may just be the global media machine either deliberately or unintentionally misreads local situations around the world in accordance with the needs of the global center. The propensity for intercultural misreadings increases dramatically, the greater the gap between the global and local cultures. Such misreadings may be exacerbated by the interventions of skilled public relations operators at the margins, who learn to play along with "the center's" discursive needs and so "deliver" appropriate material to feed the global media's voracious appetite. If this is the case, it raises questions not only for communicologists, but also for foreign policy analysts. Perhaps there is some need to recognize the limitations of the tools possessed by the global media machine to adequately report on all contexts. Furthermore, by extension, there may be value in exploring the possibly dangerous repercussions global myth-making may be having within the global system's policymaking machinery.

NOTES

[1] Cyril Ramaphosa (not Nelson Mandela) was the ANC's chief negotiator at the Kempton Park talks. Ramaphosa was also the chair of the TEC. So while Mandela served largely as the PR figurehead, or nodal point around which to construct a credible transition myth (both internally and globally), Ramaphosa played the role of real ANC power broker and strategist.

[2] Significantly, among the journalists promoting reform was the brother of F. W. de Klerk. Wimpie de Klerk had been the editor of *Rapport* newspaper, and had then become professor of communication at the Rand Afrikaans University.

[3] The man credited with playing perhaps the most important role of advocating reform within the NP was the Minister of Foreign Affairs, Pik Botha. Significantly, he began strongly advocating abolishing apartheid while serving as South Africa's ambassador to the United Nations—that is, after he learned to work within the preferred international vocabularies of the global system. After returning to South Africa to join the Cabinet, Botha became the nodal point for reformers within the NP.

REFERENCES

Chitty, N. J. (1994). Communicating world order. *The Journal of International Communication, 1*, 100–120.

Davies, R., O'Meara, D., & Dlamini, S. (1984). *The struggle for South Africa*. London: Zed Books.

Fanon, F. (1963). *The wretched of the Earth*. New York: Grove Press.

Gramsci, A. (1971). *Selections from prison notebooks*. London: Lawrence & Wishart.

Grobbelaar, J., Bekker, S., & Evans, R. (1989). *Vir volk en vaderland: A guide to the white right*. Durban, South Africa: Indicator SA.

International Broadcasting Centre. (1994). *Facilities guide: International Broadcasting Centre*. Johannesburg, South Africa: IBC/SABC.

Lijphart, A. (1977). *Democracy in plural societies*. New Haven, CT: Yale University Press.

Louw, P.E. (1994). Shifting patterns of political discourse in the new South Africa. *Critical Studies in Mass Communication, 11*, 22–53.

Mandela, N. (1994). *Long walk to freedom*. Randburg, South Africa: MacDonald Purnell.

McMenamin, V. (1992). Shifts in ANC economic policy. In G. Howe & P. Le Roux (Eds.), *Transforming the economy: Policy options for South Africa* (pp. 245–254). Durban, South Africa: Indicator SA.

Mowlana, H. (1994). International communication in the twenty-first century. *Journal of International Communication, 1*, 14–32.

Robertson, R. (1992). *Globalization*. London: Sage.

Thompson, J. (1993). The theory of the public sphere. *Theory, Culture and Society, 10*, 173–189.

Tomlinson, J. (1994). Mass communications and the idea of a global public sphere. *The Journal of International Communication, 1*, 57–70.

Tuchman, G. (1980). *Making news*. New York: The Free Press.

IV

Transnational Perspectives

15

Constructing the Global, Constructing the Local: News Agencies Re-Present the World

Oliver Boyd-Barrett
California State Polytechnic University

In this chapter, I consider a number of interrelated questions pertaining to what I want to argue is the dual role of the global news system—comprising "global" or transnational agencies and their junior national or regional partners—in simultaneously constructing "national" identities while facilitating the development of a transnational consciousness and contributing to an intensity of transnational activity that is said to constitute a process of "globalization."

I address the following:

What does the discourse of "globalization" add to our knowledge of the relationship of news agencies to the global framework of nation states; in particular, what does it provide that the older concept of "media imperialism" did not?

Inasmuch as "globalization" is facilitated by information "superhighways," how far should we expect new communications technologies, including the Internet, to influence the mediation of news agencies, global activities, and national identities?

Much of globalization theory concerns the relationship between global forces and nation states. How well do the agencies fit into this discourse; in particular, in what ways do news agencies "construct" the "national" and the "global"? In the context of agency construction of the "national," what has happened to the debate about news agencies and national "development"?

NEWS AGENCIES AND THE "GLOBALIZATION" THESIS

There are two principal discourses about globalization. One is the sociological, best epitomized in the work of Giddens (1990), which locates globalization in relation to modernization as a process that has developed over several hundred years. I have argued (Boyd-Barrett, 1997) that study of the major news agencies reveals how international media activity was well-established by the mid-19th century, well organized and disciplined on international markets, and also commodified. News agencies are a part of modernization and link it with globalization. Modernization is in part constituted by the development of nation-states, nation-state rivalries, and the struggle for additional territories. It is further constituted by the hegemony of scientific rationalism, industrialization, and trade links between industrial centers and sources of raw materials. Other factors include urbanization, and the development, among other things, of services of mass information and entertainment. These processes of nation-state formation, industrialization, and urbanization created the conditions for a systematization of demand for transnational political and economic intelligence that came to be known simply as "news."

News agencies represent a form of communication appropriate to the informational and relational needs of state, capital, and civic society in modernity. They emerge from modernity and reinforce it through simultaneous construction of global and national "imagineries." They do this in a variety of ways:

- They consolidate information networks within national boundaries through support for and endorsement of powerful national institutions, contributing to the rationalization of communication between state and people.
- They contribute to internationalization, constructing influential international news agenda that act upon retail media, governments, and finance.
- They develop and/or exploit technologies to improve global communications networks.
- They bring the global to the local and incorporate the local within the global in their day-to-day news-gathering and news-dissemination practices, selling international news to national and local media, and using local and national media as sources of news for global distribution.
- Reuters and other financial agencies facilitate global financial transactions, and even create the means to conduct international negotiations in equities, money

markets, and many commodities (from money markets to oil to advertising space).

■ They routinely provide the data that enable news commentators to think globally, by identifying parallel processes within different nation states and relating these to actors and events at a global level.

■ They define "globalization" as synonymous with "Westernization" by: embedding Western news ideologies—which they themselves had helped to form in the second half of the 19th century—as the determining criteria of news selection; by taking "Western-interests-as-norm" through their adoption of particular news frames (for example, "cold war frame"); and by their unequal distribution of attention and selection between different countries and world-regions.

■ They contribute to the homogenization of global culture in their distribution of certain influential kinds of political, economic, and sports discourse, while greatly multiplying (through their "wholesale" services for "retail" clients) the quantity of such texts that are available within these commodified discourses.

A second model of globalization is the neo-liberal prescriptive model represented by Reagan's "World Order" and taking concrete form through GATT and the WTO: this model advocates deregulation of trade and open markets, and the progressive extension of deregulation to services and cultural industries. It is claimed that this will lead to greater competition, healthier economies, and more cultural diversity (through the commodification of cultural products and population mobility), and that it will promote the interests of the citizen as consumer, once liberated from protectionist nation-state bureaucracies.

CONVERGENCE, DIVERSITY, AND THE INTERNET

How far does the evidence of the global news system support the neo-liberal model of globalization? Transnationalization of the global news business has intensified generally, in response both to technological development and to deregulation. This is most of all evident in the development of satellite television news, but also in the activities of news entrepreneurs such as Murdoch, Black, and O'Reilly. Nonetheless, as I previously noted, it has not so far led to a significant increase in the number of "wholesale" players in international news, the ones who typically have the largest networks of correspondents and resources for news-gathering. There has been *some* increase, and there has certainly been an increase in the number of "retail" television news media that are operating internationally. The key providers of international news, however, are still predominantly associated with the U.S., the U.K., and France/Europe. Nor have processes of deregulation introduced a more "global" news agenda to national news systems: "national" news generally dominates "national" news media, and the coverage of most other nations of the world is unequal and extremely patchy.

It can be argued, nonetheless, that processes of digitization, convergence of communications technologies, and the "information superhighway" in effect make available a much greater diversity of texts from all over the world to private citizens. Through the Internet, it is possible to access the text of newspapers and broadcast media electronically from most countries of the world—access that could theoretically facilitate the establishment of new services or simply offer alternative spaces for consumption. In practice, however, access to such sites, even in countries of the first world, is slow, often subject to interruptions or nonarrival. The news services that can be accessed are sometimes slim selections of the full editions that are available in hard-copy counterparts in domestic markets. For some of these, a registration and/or subscription charge is imposed (for example, the *New York Times*). Users who do not have access through their employment need to pay access costs to Net servers, as well as time charges. Many users find such access frustrating in contrast to traditional skimming of hard-copy versions.

There are, of course, many unique facilities that the Internet does offer, like being able to move directly from one news story to a related news story in a previous edition, through links that have been created on the website. The foreign or international news carried by national media that can be accessed through the Internet often derives in whole or in part from the major news agencies. But electronic access, even to versions of newspapers from a variety of different countries, does at least provide a source of news of countries as reported directly from domestic media of those countries. Through the Internet, private individuals can achieve direct access to some news agency services they would normally see only after such sources have been mediated by "retail" media. These readers may conclude that the quality of news agency news is often very good relative to the mediated or transformed versions that are available in retail media. However, the proportion of news agency output that is available through such online connections is usually only a small proportion of the total that is available to major retail clients. I strongly suspect that as far as news is concerned, the Internet is mainly used for accessing mainstream news services that provide composite national and international news services. The possibility of going further afield, to access, say, the comprehensive services of EFE (the Spanish news agency) or Argentina's *La Nacion* newspaper, from the United Kingdom, for instance, is doubtless a significant new communications facility, but one that is likely to be of practical value to a tiny number of users. The most important value of such facilities is for mainstream news media who can access original sources of foreign news much more easily, and can reformat that news for their own news services. Within the international "wholesale" market, the value of direct sources of national news is limited by the particular constraints, often political, on their credibility, or reliability, in contrast to the greater credibility which is generally enjoyed by established major news agencies with their own extensive networks of correspondents.

A substantial majority of all Internet sites are American and European, the predominant language is English. In his address at a conference in March 1997, U.K. sociologist Peter Golding (see Golding,1998) argued that users are disproportionately male, middle-class, middle-aged, and managerial. Only a relatively small number of people were regularly accessing the Internet in 1996 (for example, 10 percent of the population in California, and 7 percent of the adult population in the U.K., although regular access in the U.S. had increased to approximately 30 percent by 1999). Internet access divides by social class, and I believe will continue to do so for quite some time: it requires considerable outlay, generally speaking a minimum 386 computer, a modem, telephone line, registration with a gate server, and possibly timed calls. Internet access not only requires money, but it also requires time. Time is at a premium for precisely those news consumers most attractive to commercial news providers on account of their simultaneous appeal to advertisers, and these are the people who, for want of time, will be likely to depend on mainstream, "proven" news services.

A measure of skepticism is due with respect to whether the Internet has broadened diversity of mainstream news services in a way that is likely to undermine the existing global news system, especially once we take into account actual penetration rates of the Internet and uses of the new technology.

May it not be argued that the development of the Internet has greatly reduced the costs of entry to the global news market—providing a medium of global communication that is extremely cheap in distribution costs, relative to previous forms of production, and offering cheaper access to news sources, thus reducing the costs of news gathering?

Both arguments have weight. But neither cheaper news-gathering nor cheaper distribution can in itself secure a market of actual readers or consumers. Indeed, precisely because costs are lower there is the potential of an increase in the number of suppliers, further fragmenting the market available for "alternative" news sources. A service that depends primarily on secondary sources (for example, existing news sources on the Internet) has to resolve problems of copyright and attribution. It faces problems of credibility in the eyes of influential consumers— retail media, business, and government communities, especially in media-rich first world markets—who are accustomed to receiving skillfully integrated and refined news services that benefit from global networks of on-the-spot foreign correspondents who are "in tune with" the news appetites and demands of their best-paying clients. Dependence on secondary news services reduces the degree of possible evaluation and corroboration of such sources. Such a service will not be regarded as a safe or sufficient basis for decision-making by powerful clients.

The Internet will most likely improve the viability of some "alternative" and specialized news agencies; by mere dint of their easy Internet availability, it is possible that major agencies and retail media will, over time, begin to take more routine notice of these, quoting them as sources, perhaps occasionally being influenced by their agendas, even commissioning them for certain kinds of coverage.

Whatever advantages the Internet makes available to new players, they are also available to the major players who are better positioned to capitalize on them: for example, in the case of Reuters, through the addition of customized news services to company or private network "intranets," or through its part ownership of services such as Yahoo!, to which it also supplies an advert-carrying news service.

Among news agencies, therefore, there is more competition than there was, especially if we extend beyond the traditional "wholesalers" to those who operate both as "wholesalers" and "retailers," but this is mainly a form of competition among the already powerful in the already powerful countries. Most of the names are familiar (for example, Reuters Television), and some of those that are relatively new, like CNN (now part of Time-Warner) belong to established media or nonmedia conglomerates or have close affiliations with them (such as Bloomberg with Merrill-Lynch, Yahoo with Reuters, NBC with Microsoft).

In 1997, the founder and proprietor of Bloomberg's financial news service, in response to those who predicted that the Internet will displace the need for his service, offered this view:

> Why can we charge $1,200 a month and these other idiots can't get away with anything? The fact of the matter is that on the Internet, when you try to charge for anything, usage goes to zero. The data that we have is publicly available, but the value added is in the categorization, the scruffing and the utilities that let you do something with it. (Napoli, 1997)

NATIONAL AGENCIES AND NATION CONSTRUCTION

For the major players the important consequences of internationalization, deregulation, and privatization have to do mainly with enlargement of opportunities in video and financial news, and the opening up of many national markets, which before were relatively closed or controlled. Are there any implications for the way in which the national news agencies operate? As in public service broadcasting, deregulation has in some cases undermined claims to monopoly national status for established "national" media, with retail news media starting up rival agencies. Old protected agreements between global and national news agencies are being circumvented where global agencies prefer to deal directly with local media, in some cases supplying local news services in direct competition with national agencies. Weakening of national agencies, like the weakening of public service broadcasters, may undermine the capacity of the state to harness the media for the development of nationalist iconography and agendas, and contribute to the fragmentation of audiences.

This is an appropriate moment, therefore, to consider at greater length the relationship of the national agency to the state and to the role of "national" construction. There are several reasons for doing so. In the first instance, the role of national news agencies is not highly visible within media research, yet it has clear and important implications for processes of national formation and globalization. A second reason has to do with the "development" ideology, which supported the emergence of many national news agencies during the major waves of decolonization. Yet the actual "developmental" role of news agencies is somewhat obscure.

I shall first look at some of the ways in which national agencies, with their global partners, help to "construct the nation," taking as an example the case of the Athens News Agency (ANA). I do not want to argue that ANA is "typical"; it does illustrate several features of how agencies can contribute to national formation, while at the same time it also has features that are not common to all, or even to any other news agencies.

This concept of "constructing the nation" draws on the seminal work of Scannell and Cardiff (1991) in their study of how the BBC helped to construct a sense of "Britishness." The formation of a national iconography as a basis for cultivating the experience of national identity is not a one-off event or even a consistent process. The "nation" that has to be constructed is a dynamic and fluid entity, very much subject to the changing projects and fortunes of major power-holders and institutions within society. In the case of news agencies, major changes may be marked by changes of institutional title. The nationhood of France, as constructed by Havas prior to World War II, was doubtless very different to that which its successor, AFP, constructed from 1945, although only a comparative content analysis could demonstrate such a shift.

My brief exploration draws on information culled in response to a 1996 questionnaire survey (see Boyd-Barrett & Rantanen, 1997), an unpublished 1995 MA study of the Athens News Agency (ANA) (Kamaras, 1995), and an interview by the author with the agency's managing director in 1997. While the ANA has certain unique characteristics, it also conforms in many respects to the features of other national agencies that emerged within the global news system when this was still controlled by an overt global cartel up to the 1930s. I want to argue merely that national agencies play a significant role in the construction of a national identity. This need not mean that the identity that is constructed necessarily commands the sympathies and affections of all or even most of the people who live within the territories controlled by a nation-state (in this respect, it could be a counter-productive ploy—especially in countries where the image of the nation is an image cast in the likeness of a dominant ethnic group within a pluri-ethnic context). It merely indicates that the national agency is a tool, often a powerful tool, within the cultural armory normally available to the state or to leading media interests within the capital city of the state, for the promotion of the image of the nation, a nation whose "natural" center and "brain" is usually, though not always, its capital city.

In itself, a news agency is a statement to the proposed "nation" that the "nation" coheres, physically and culturally: that is to say, that there is shared interest inside the state borders in a range of discourses that are marked as being of special interest to the inhabitants, and that a single organization can competently collect and process information relating to those discourses from all points of the nation and distribute it back to the nation, by way of its national and local media.

Writing about the Spanish national news agency, Schulze-Schneider (1998) indicates how there have been periods when the symbolic value of the news agency as expression of national coherence counted for little in some of the major regions of this pluri-national state. For much of its history, the agency was owned by a "multinational media company"—the French agency, Havas. While this may have done no harm in a capital whose culture and state formation had been much influenced by the French, it was certainly a limiting feature for any broader call to national allegiance. None of this alters the fact that the "national" agency was an important "centering" device, promoting the power of Madrid through Spain, and representing state interests to both capital and provinces.

Established in 1895 as a private company, the ANA passed to the public sector in 1906. Similar to many national agencies, it started life principally as a vehicle for receiving, translating, and retransmitting news items from international news agencies to Greek newspapers. Initially, the ANA was incorporated within the Havas sphere of influence as determined by the multilateral pacts agreed by leading members of the "ring combination," the news cartel then controlled by Reuters, Havas, and Wolff. In 1922, it also signed a contract with Reuters. Later, it came to depend exclusively on Reuters, although now in the 1990s it draws on a wider variety of sources than heretofore: mainly AFP, DPA, and Reuters.

The Greek state is the company's sole shareholder, but in common with many national agencies (and like AFP), the ANA also has a seven-member board of directors that is chaired by the general director of the ANA, who is designated by the Minister for the Press and Media for a period of five years and is renewable. Other members include two from the field of communications and mass media designated by decision of the Minister for the Press and Media. Two others are elected representatives of journalist unions, one by the Union of Athens Daily Newspaper Publishers, and one by ANA employees. Because the agency is dependent on the state for more than 75 percent of its finance, the influence of state representatives on the board carries considerable weight. The relatively favorable weighting of journalist organizations, as opposed to publishers or proprietor organizations, is not typical, however, of all such agencies.

In a recent study of the ANA, Kamaras (1995) talks of "the absence of competition at national level—due to the fact that no private agency could compete in a small market without the state subsidy ANA enjoys" (p. 50), indicating the importance of the agency for the numerically prolific but economically weak sector of Greek newspapers and broadcasters. Content analysis of ANA client newspapers shows that ANA news material is extensively used in the press, although it is often not credited. In the provincial press, entire issues are sometimes built around ANA reports (Kamaras, 1995). The most important daily news stories in the provincial front pages are those distributed by the ANA, with very few exceptions to the rule. Almost all important daily foreign news stories distributed by the ANA (mainly originating from global agencies) are used by the Athens press, although only two out of seven mainstream Athens dailies regularly refer to the ANA as a source for their supply of foreign news. The provincial press is at least three times more likely to use ANA news than the Athens press, for domestic as for foreign news.

In his study of ANA news selection, Kamaras (1995) argued that the importance of news, either domestic or international, is determined first by the effect it might have on Greek society, and second, in terms of its interest for certain specific markets. A third criterion is geographical proximity. For secondary news items, the degree of "peculiarity," novelty, and unusualness is a criterion, followed, fifth, by the "personality" factor, when a well-known figure is involved in a newsworthy issue or event. Such "human interest" news (typified by the fourth and fifth criteria) is a device by which the agency tries to increase the presence of ANA credits in subscriber newspapers. Kamaras notes that established sources play a prominent role in newsmaking: that is, press offices of ministries, political parties and businesses. The agency's first priority remains the transmission of all official views of the government, political parties, and "establishment" organizations and institutions.

In addition to its own domestic correspondents, often client newspaper editors, the agency maintains four overseas offices in Brussels, Nicosia, Istanbul, and Bonn, thus reflecting Greek national interests (the Turkish question, Cyprus, and the EC). There are correspondents (not necessarily full-time) in 14 other locations, of which 10 are European (three in the Balkans), three are North American, and one Australian. The agency takes international news principally from AFP, DPA (by satellite), Reuters (by leased lines), and ITAR-TASS and Xinhua by Telex. (AP distributes direct to most mainstream Athens media.)

The ANA annual budget came to $1.4 billion in 1995, of which more than 75 percent was paid by a subsidy from the Press and Media Ministry. Until 1994, provincial newspapers did not pay any subscriptions at all, but today all recipients pay subscriptions, and ANA's goal is to cover 40-50 percent of its expenditures by subscriptions. Despite heavy reliance on the state for revenue, the agency is required, under presidential decree, to maintain "full political and ideological autonomy with respect to any legal, natural, public, or private entity, while its journalistic and specialized personnel is obliged to process and evaluate news items with objectivity, without discrimination and with respect to the rules of journalistic ethics."

The "public service" mission of the agency, therefore, is squared with state patronage through the composition of the governing board and its legislated charter.

Services include the "Athens Service" supplying "national media" with international news items and reports from ANA correspondents abroad (most of whom work for several other Greek media). ANA foreign correspondents are required to report mainly on news of interest to Greek media or media of the Greek diaspora. In a somewhat unusual arrangement with the principal journalists' union in Athens, the agency does not supply Athens news to Athens newspapers, but does supply them with provincial news. Kamaras (1995) remarks that this illustrates the extent to which Athens journalists depend on official sources: they fear that if their newspapers rely on ANA to do the official reporting, there will be nothing else left for them to do.

Other than the agency's own correspondents, international items come mainly from the major international news agencies, in particular Reuters, AFP, DPA, and from ITAR, Tass, and Xinhua. Because they are generally first, more succinct, more "Western," and because they also quote the agencies of Russia and China when dealing with Russian and Chinese news, the Western news agencies are invariably the only ones that are used directly. A small percentage of news derives from exchange relationships that the ANA, in common with many such agencies, maintains with dozens of other national agencies. Kamaras writes:

> Thus it is more than obvious that, even for news originated in the East or elsewhere besides the Western world, it is the western agencies' discourses which are predominantly used as a source of information in the Athens News Agency, as far as international news are concerned.
>
> If news originates in countries where the agency employs a correspondent, then western agency reports are cross-referenced with those sent by the ANA correspondent. Bilateral agreements between ANA and other national agencies "do not alter the heavy usage of the major established news agencies as predominant suppliers of international news. (1995, p. 63)

The Provincial Service supplies approximately 130 provincial newspapers with domestic and international news items. There is the Greeks Abroad-Cyprus Service for all Cyprus media and many overseas Greek media, and this carries domestic and international news items. A radio-television service provides continuous transmission of news to dozens of radio and television stations in Greece. Additionally, there is a sports service; a special "English service" (supplying the most important domestic news items to foreign subscribers in Greece and abroad); an Internet service in Greek and English; an audio text service; photographic service; an ANA English-French bulletin for foreigners in Greece and abroad; a monthly magazine that "aims to present the Greece of today and its creative aspects" for distribution to persons in key positions throughout the world; and a "PR service" for organizations and corporations, which circulates subscriber announcements to mass media on the ANA network.

The agency provides online access to six data banks: the Greek-language News Bank, the English-language News Bank, the Elections Bank (containing data on all the Greek governments since 1833 and analytical electoral data since 1926, and analytical data on European Parliament elections in Greece), the Biographies Bank (containing the biographies of approximately 4,000 Greek politicians, and 500 foreign politicians); the Sports Bank (including details of Greek soccer championships, and Greek basketball championships); the Photo-Bank, covering photos of Greek and international news since 1996.

The "national" itself is in permanent development, sometimes in radical transition. In recent Greek history, for example, there has been a remarkable change since the end of the 1970–1980 military dictatorship: before the 1980s, the ANA was principally a conduit for government ideology but it now plays a more subtle role, borrowing from the public service traditions of editorial independence typified by the BBC and similar media institutions, but nonetheless continuing to construct the "national" primarily in terms of establishment sources and national-bounded news categories.

In summary, ANA "constructs the national" in its self-designation as a national agency. Unlike many national agencies, it bears the name of the nation's capital city, Athens, but like most national agencies it reinforces the status of the nation's capital by electing the capital as its hub, and as the "natural" center of news gathered throughout the territories governed by the nation state. The agency's correspondents primarily communicate their news to the capital not to one another, although many of them may work for or own media that are in receipt of the agency's services. The very institution of "national" agency, therefore, bestows additional legitimacy on the capital city, the key national institutions, and their people, based in the capital.

The agency serves as a means by which the media are fed a diet of "national" new—which is the news that ANA determines should be regarded as "national." Simultaneously, it serves as a conduit for the distribution of important state news, and the views and concerns of establishment sources, throughout the nation's territories (although not supplying Athens news to Athens newspapers, in deference to the interests of Athens journalists). It thus functions as an agency of legitimation of the nation state, which is also its owner and principal source of finance.

In some countries this function has a separate institutional existence, taking form as a Government Information Service, thus leaving the national news agency greater leeway, in theory, to formulate its own agenda. Many content studies of both national and international news agencies, however, attest to heavy reliance on "official" sources (see Harris, 1977). ANA's news and other services are literally representations of the state's version of "Greekness"—Greek language, Greek interests, proximity to Greece, the Greek diaspora—as well as a guide to what "visitors" to Greece or Greek culture will need to know about Greece and "Greekness." The agency's foreign correspondents are primarily Greek journalists working for other Greek media, and reporting on issues considered being of interest to Greeks. The agency selects, translates, and retransmits stories that it has edited from many of the world's giant agencies, so acts to filter and interpret outside news in favor of the news interests of its owner, the state, and clients. This project of

"Greekness" has a strong taken-for-granted character, which is the hallmark of ideology (Hall, 1982).

The news of ANA, as is the case with most national and international news agencies, may be described as "informational" in contrast to the "info-entertainment" needs, which are increasingly what is required by deregulated and commercialized news media. The ANA makes concessions to this need in the supply of "human interest" stories, and in the routine application of Anglo-American news criteria (which favor negative over positive, urban over rural, elite over nonelite, event over process, and so on). There is a certain "solemnity" of output, which is appropriate to the function of national institutions representing the nation to itself and, through links with international media, including international news agencies, to the rest of the world. News is largely restricted to a narrow range of key categories. Excessive solemnity, however, could have a counter-productive effect, where, as is the case with many news agencies of relatively new African nations, agency news is no more than "protocol" news, strong on diplomatic form, empty of substance. Such news services command little interest among the international news agencies and other news media, and are not, therefore, a very effective vehicle for the presentation of the nation to the international community (Boyd-Barrett & Thussu, 1991).

In legitimating the notion of "Greekness" and the Greek nation state, the agency also plays a role in articulating a model of the world as formed principally through similar nation states—for example, in its exchange relationships with other national news agencies—even while it takes news from international news agencies (in this case, principally AFP, DPA, and Reuters), much of whose news is the news of other nation states selected by the international agencies as "national," the composition of which is, in turn, often influenced by the agendas and services of the national news agencies of those nation states, especially where those services, like those of the ANA, adhere in certain respects to the canons of Anglo-American journalism.

GLOBAL AGENCIES CONSTRUCTING THE NATIONAL

The services that international news agencies provide to "retail" media are primarily constituted by a mixture of "national" news of different countries around the world and of news about the relationships between nation states or between significant players of different nation states. The content of the news tends to be about topics that privilege elite national institutions or players, or about their interrelationships at transnational levels, primarily within the spheres of politics, military affairs, business and economics, intergovernmental organizations, and sports.

There has been a dearth of recent studies of the print news agencies (which need to be distinguished from studies of international news in "retail" media such as newspapers). But studies across the period from 1950 to 1985 identified a number of outstanding consistencies, and it is unlikely that these will have changed dramatically within the last decade or so. The International Press Institute (1953) looked at the five major agencies then transmitting news into Europe. At that time the news wires were dominated by a relatively small number of countries: the U.S. (between 17 percent and 63 percent of the total), the U.K. (29–43 percent), France (31–51 percent), and Germany (1.9 percent and 6.6 percent). Content tended to focus heavily on politics, economics, foreign relations, defense, and war, which accounted for between 63 percent and 78 percent of all news.

Adams (1964) looked at the AP trunk wire in the United States. Politics, war, and economics accounted for 51 percent of all non-U.S. stories. Coverage concentrated on certain countries as well as certain regions; the most heavily represented were the United Kingdom, Germany, the USSR, and the Vatican City, accounting for 33 percent of the whole. Hester (1971), also looking at non-U.S. coverage of AP service in the U.S., found the major content categories were military and defense, foreign relations, and domestic government politics: these accounted for over half the news about developed nations and 84 percent of the news of the developing countries. Looking at the news sent to AP from its South American bureaus (1974), Hester noted that most of the stories were about single nations; in only about 15 percent of all items were there international linkages.

Boyd-Barrett (1979, 1980), on the other hand, analyzed AFP, UPI, Reuters, and AP wires for the U.K., Europe, and Southern Africa. On the Reuters wires, between 35 and 47 percent of the news was news of single nations, between 45 and 62 percent was international, and between 3 and 8 percent was mixed. There was a tendency for particular dateline sources to dominate in any given region. Datelines were generally capital cities (between 61–76 percent on Reuters and AP wires). Political and economic news categories dominated AFP and UPI wires (50–60 percent), and close to 50 percent of AP and Reuters wires. Agencies gave significantly more emphasis to stories that dealt with two or more countries directly than with stories that were primarily about just one country.

Leung (1979) studied the content of UPI news to Asia, and news sent from Asia for UPI's U.S. wires. Of news sent from the U.S. to Asia by UPI, 55 percent was accounted for by five categories: international politics (25 percent), domestic politics (6 percent), military-defense (7 percent), international economy (7 percent), and domestic economy (10 percent). Of UPI news going from Asia back to the U.S., 50 percent was accounted for by four categories: international politics (24 percent), domestic politics (12 percent), international economy (8 percent), and crime/violence/justice (6 percent).

Boyd-Barrett (1980) observed that in order of volume importance, the local region (to which any given wire was directed) came first, then North America and Western Europe. The next cluster of regions to be represented were Asia, the Middle East, and Latin America, with Africa, the Soviet Union, and Eastern Europe trailing a long way behind. In Rimmer's (1981) study, "foreign" stories dominated on UPI's U.S. "A" wire, with 23 percent of foreign items, while a similar percentage was accounted for by the next four countries together—the U.K., USSR, Uganda, and

Israel. UPI's foreign world picture was dominated by the Americas (41 percent—over half of this originating from the U.S.) and Europe (22 percent—over half of this originating from the U.K.), followed by the Middle East and North Africa (11 percent), then by the rest of Africa (8 percent), Eastern Europe (6 percent), and India, Pakistan, Indochina, and Asia (10 percent).

On the basis of their studies of several wires, Weaver, Wilhoit, Stevenson, Shaw, and Cole (1980) concluded:

> These rankings, averaged across all eight wire services, suggest that Western Europe was the most heavily covered region of the world, with the Middle East a close second, followed by Latin America, North America, Africa and Asia. Eastern Europe and the General World (news not occurring in one of the seven regions, or news of international organisations that are not clearly tied to a single region) were the two consistently least-covered regions. (p. 62)

Stevenson and Cole (1980) examined the wires of AP, UPI, Reuters, and AFP going to Latin America; they also considered the Arab-language Reuters file for the Middle East, the AFP wire for Francophone Africa, and the regional domestic wires of AP and UPI for smaller U.S. media. They concluded: "Across all nations, regions, political and economic systems, one pattern emerges: politics is news. Between one quarter and one half of all foreign news in all of the countries and wire services in the study dealt with either domestic affairs in other countries or with international relations" (p. 12). Stevenson and Cole noted further that "a second cluster of three topics, each averaging about 10% of the total, concerns economics, defense material (including war) and the less serious topic of sports" (p. 12). Domestic and international politics, economics, and defense, therefore, accounted for between 45 and 70 percent of the contents of these wires.

Rimmer (1981) studied foreign news coverage on UPI's "A" wire in the U.S. He reported that the foreign news was drawn mainly from government sources, and was overwhelmingly concerned with political material, most of it in the area of foreign relations and diplomacy. Three categories accounted for 74 percent of the total number of foreign news for six days in 1977: politics (65 percent), economic activity (6 percent), and war and the armed services (3 percent).

Mokekwu (1982), studying the slow-speed IB wire of AP for smaller U.S. members, found that the top three categories of international news were diplomatic and political activities between countries, internal conflict, and armed conflict. Boyd-Barrett (1980) makes reference to an early report by Schramm and Atwood (1981), a study of news coverage in Asian news media. This study showed that 66–75 percent of each agency's Third World news coverage was committed to the categories of foreign relations (36 percent), military/violence, domestic government, and economics.

Kang (1997) reports a study of uses of AP, AFP, UPI, and Reuters in four major Korean newspapers, which found that the most important categories were political-government (34 percent); military/defense (18 percent); human interest (16 percent); domestic (14 percent); economics, business, and labor (12 percent); entertainment and culture (4 percent); and science and technology (2 percent); crisis/accident (0.4 percent); health and media (0.3 percent); and education (0.1 percent). Although studies of agency usage are unreliable indicators of news agency provision, the pattern of usage here largely reflects the findings of older studies of agency services, except that it excludes sport, and has a very low rating for crisis/accident news.

In Boyd-Barrett (1980), it is noted that after the major categories of politics, military/defense, and economics, there are two others that tend to rank prominently in many studies: crime/legal and sport. In Schramm and Atwood (1981), crime/judicial accounted for only 3.3 percent of the Third World news supplied by the "Big Four" (as the majors then were called) to Asian news media, but sports accounted for 14 percent and accident/disaster for a further 6 percent. Crime/legal accounted for between 6 and 9 percent on the different wires studied by Stevenson and Cole (1980), while sports accounted for a wider range, from 0 to 23 percent, and natural disaster from 0 to 4 percent. In their study, sports was high on the Latin American wires and low on the wires for the Middle East and Africa. Sports accounted for 22 percent of the news sent by UPI to Asia in Leung (1979), while in Rimmer's (1981) study, 4 percent of the news fell into a "crime, disaster, and public safety" category of foreign news carried on UPI's U.S. "A" wire, but, exceptionally, there was no sports at all.

Boyd-Barrett (1980) argues that there is little scope for large percentage scores on any other categories of news once the aforementioned categories have been taken into account. And this observation is borne out by the more recent studies. In Schramm and Atwood (1981), for instance, science and health score 0.7 percent, culture 0.7 percent, education 0.4 percent, and human interest 1.99 percent. Using a wide range of categories, Stevenson and Cole (1980) reported very low scores for such headings as social services (0–1 percent), culture (0.8 percent), religion (0–2 percent), science (0–3 percent), ecology (0–2 percent), student matters (0–1 percent), and so on. Rimmer (1981) reported 4% for science and 1% for culture and entertainment.

Both Schramm and Atwood (1981) and Rimmer (1981) refer to the high dependence of all wires on news from official or government sources; that is, sources that are quoted within news stories, more often than not, are official or government sources (although the initial "tip" for many such stories will very likely have been the national news media of the countries concerned).

Recent content analysis of the output of Associated Press Television (APTV) and of CNNI, by Clare (1998) and Cavagnero (1998), respectively, show that the services of these international television news agencies/broadcasters demonstrate a strong emphasis on politics and conflict, on the First World, and a tendency for the emphasis on violence and conflict to be exacerbated in the case of Third World coverage. Cavagnero's study of CNNI (distributing outside the U.S.) identified a tendency to focus on stories of war/conflict/military and politics (52.6 percent of all stories). Major geographical sources of stories were from the U.S. (45.7 percent), Western Europe (17.7 percent), and the Middle East (14.3 percent), trailed by Eastern Europe, Asia, Africa, Central and South America, and Australasia. Western Europe accounted for 64 percent of CNNI revenue.

Clare (1998) found that only 8 percent of APTV stories were contextualizing features and backgrounder stories, 19 percent were soft news features, and 73 percent were hard news. Europe accounted for 28.1 percent of stories, the U.S. for 22.9 percent, Asia for 18.9 percent, with other world regions trailing behind. International relations was the most common topic (29.1 percent) followed by internal politics (25.6 percent); these two categories together accounted for well over half of all stories. The next most important categories were culture and art (8.8 percent) and internal law and order (7.7 percent). Clare also identified an overwhelming reliance on government sources. Private citizens were second only to governments in the table, featuring as vox pops (brief comments from members of the public), giving opinions, or as demonstrators.

Stories from elite nations outnumbered nonelite nations by more than two to one. Furthermore, items from nonelite areas such as Africa, parts of Asia, the poorer countries of the Balkans and the former Soviet Bloc nearly all concerned conflict, violence, and disasters. Only among the nonelite countries of Latin America was there a balance of hard and soft news and items other than conflict. Clare (1988) concludes:

> Elite nations are portrayed as having strong leaders constantly flying around the globe trying to broker peace deals and further the cause of international brotherhood. Their citizens, meanwhile, appear to be able to choose from a number of cultural pursuits, supported by stable business and innovative technology, while being allowed to make peaceful protests about important matters.
>
> Non-elite nations, in contrast, appear to be constantly embroiled in, or on the point of, violent conflict, either within or across their borders, while at risk from natural disasters. They have crisis-hit governments, untrustworthy leaders, volatile populations and when they do have elections, they do not meet the democratic standards of the west and are characterised by vote-rigging and violence. (pp. 62–63)

In his study of the Bosnian crisis by the television news agencies, Paterson (1997) concluded:

> Despite an increase in news channels worldwide, ownership of TV news institutions is highly concentrated. While agencies promote themselves as global services, my research demonstrates the manner in which broadcaster priorities in the U.S., Britain, and Western Europe are privileged, even though these are often assumed. (p. 61)

What is it, overall, that such studies tell us about the construction of what is "national" and "international"?

a) the global agencies privilege affairs that relate to relations between nations, or between prestigious sectors of those nations, often involving matters to do with national iconography and pride (such as in the case of sports and national politics);

b) they privilege news of domestic political events;

c) their major sources are official or government sources, so that in representing nations to other nations they give pride of place to prestigious "national" actors;

d) this tends to marginalize "oppositional" voices, except in extreme circumstances such as uprisings or violence;

e) many facets of life that map less readily onto notions of the "nation," such as religion, science, ecology, culture, and so on, rank very low;

f) in the distribution of datelines, as of the news itself, global agency coverage favors elite nations, and capital and big cities. This urban or capital bias, already evident in the coverage of national news agencies, is merely intensified in global news coverage, further reinforcing associations of the "nation" with images of the "capital" or of the urban.

ISSUES OF "NATIONAL DEVELOPMENT"

From the 1950s, the United Nations and its sister agency, UNESCO, were important sponsors and advocates of the setting up of national news agencies, a seemingly appropriate part of the process of decolonization that marked the 1950s and 1960s. It was considered that the establishment of national news agencies and, later, in the 1970s, regional news cooperatives would contribute to the "free flow of information" and would contribute to national and economic development. Exactly how this contribution would be realized was less than precisely articulated.

Explicitly or implicitly the following rationales were at play: It was thought that news agencies would promote mutual awareness among the constituent provinces of the new nation, consolidating a "news map" that corresponded with the physical boundaries and divisions of the nation state itself. News agencies would constitute part of an infrastructure of communications resource, both in terms of hardware and people. Central government would be better informed about its provinces and would benefit from control over a valuable tool for the dissemination of information, campaigns, and propaganda. News agencies could transmit news, much of it foreign, to local as well as national media. This information—political, economic, agricultural, and so on—could directly assist development, helping to overcome barriers of distance. Improved circulation of information in the public sphere would help inform the citizenry and contribute to democratization. News agencies would create a "national" voice to counteract the voices of Western media, both domestically and internationally, and this would improve the nation's standing and influence in international contexts.

If such reasons were indeed influential in the setting up of national news agencies, then the reality was to be disappointing, especially where agencies were subsumed within the existing structures of power to sustain corrupt or ineffective national elites and practices.

In considering the functioning of one European news agency, ANA, we have seen an example of how a national news agency might very well fulfill some of these objectives and expectations. I have argued that such an organization can indeed contribute to an image of nationhood, but by itself this is unlikely to be especially effective in commanding sentiments of patriotism and loyalty. Construction and maintenance of positive sentiment requires many additional ingredients. The "national" news agency of the old Yugoslavia, Tanjug, was widely reputed for its work in establishing cooperative exchange links between news agencies of the non-aligned nations. Domestically, of course, Tanjug could do little to withstand the disintegration of Yugoslavia. Another limitation is that of resource. Musa (1997) has chronicled the resource limitations faced by the national news agency of Nigeria in covering the provinces largely with city staff lacking command of the local languages necessary to communicate directly with rural populations. For him, the national news agency was less a state agency that served developmental purposes, than an agency functioning to support a national, capital-based elite, which had been co-opted into the system of international finance.

For this news agency, "development" news was defined as the "observable activities of elite groups, especially government representatives and some corporate personnel, in activities like "mobilization" campaigns, official launches, speeches at conferences or seminars, or the inauguration of new schools" (Musa, 1997, p. 137). Even the lack of provision of essential items such as telephones and Jeeps for coverage of the countryside can be significant obstacles to progress in poorer countries. Where news agency journalists are also civil servants, and sometimes when they are not, there are severe limitations to the range and objectivity of the information that they feel is safe or prudent to report. Claims for the relevance of news agencies to development often commit the same error as modernization theorists such as Lerner (1958), Schramm (1964), and others in the 1950s and 1960s, who believed that mass media *per se* were a good thing for development, yet who did not take proper account of what or how these media could be used in practice. Content is vitally important, in terms of subject matter and in terms of language and mode of address. Some national news agencies have been criticized for dealing mainly in "protocol" news of the superficial comings and goings of members of the government and diplomats (Harris, Malczek, & Ozkol, 1980); others, those more likely to apply criteria of Western journalism for news selection, may deliver interesting or entertaining information, while the "development" connection remains obscure.

If we do accept that news agencies are contributing to a sense of nationhood, that is not the same thing as saying that they contribute to "development," unless we also argue that the process of national formation in itself is a force for development.

If so, that is a definition of development in which the particular character of any given state, or the particular usefulness, veracity, or relevance of any particular news services, is regarded as of only secondary importance to the achievement of some kind of basic enabling infrastructure. In the case of highly repressive, corrupt, or ineffectual states, however, this is a developmental luxury that ordinary people might be happy to forgo.

More radical definitions of development that have emerged over the past few decades talk of development in terms of the articulation of needs and wants, emerging from among the people—as the proper beneficiaries of "development"— through participatory structures of decision making (Servaes, 1996). The traditional national news agency, however, is a centralized top-down information transmission system and arguably most unsuited to an egalitarian concept of development. Indeed, this model is a tortured combination of a) Western ideas about the need for a news agency to provide a relatively cheap source of "national" news for the benefit of national and provincial media, helping them to rationalize news-gathering costs while providing them with copy that will help sell newspapers; and b) a concept similar to a machinery of government information services for the dissemination of public service information and propaganda—official, worthy, and not to be trusted.

To some considerable measure, the NWICO debate of the 1970s was fueled by concerns about the role of the international news and news-film agencies. Its concerns were fed by the growing realization that the establishment of national news agencies as contributory countervailing forces in the global flow of news had not, as expected, brought about a more equitable flow. Rather, they had served as conduits through which "international" news from the Western-dominated news agencies could be efficiently distributed to state and media clients. They were also means by which "national" news could be collected and placed at the disposal of the global agencies for global agencies to select or to supplement as they chose, through the prism of western news values, for the purposes of global distribution (but principally for consumption by wealthy news media of the United States and Western Europe).

From both UNESCO and the Non-Aligned Movement came various expressions of dissatisfaction of Third World leaders about Western news agencies. In essence, the complaints were that news flow was unidirectional, from "north" to "south"; that news was dominated by the Western countries, and that it was dominated by "coup and earthquake" coverage, thus misrepresenting and stereotyping the countries of the developing world (Boyd-Barrett & Thussu, 1992).

What was the background to those complaints? I consider that the answer to this question lies in two factors: "face" and the demands for a NWEO (New World Economic Order), which preceded and then ran in parallel with demands for a NWICO. It is hardly surprising that newly independent nations would object to their dependence on Western-based agencies for the supply of global news and for the distribution of their own national news to the rest of the globe. What would the

U.K. have said if its main news media were dependent on services from organizations based, say, in Cairo, Manila, and Buenos Aires? But in the case of Third World or nonaligned nations protesting the dominance of the world news system by a few Western news organizations, was such protest any more than a matter of hurt feelings or national pride?

These new nations lacked the resources to offer serious competition to western media in order to influence world markets. Representation of media-poor countries in the rest of the world's media, in effect, was out of the control of the poor countries themselves, and in their reliance on Western media they were obliged to consume western misrepresentations of themselves. Behind postcolonial rage against the continuation of cultural dominance was growing realization of the importance of "national image" to attract and to influence the "right" kind of inward investment; yet these countries were powerless to exert control over that image, at the mercy of Western news values, which had real consequences for investment flows. Such connections were not new. Not much more than half a century earlier, Russia had squirmed beneath its dependence on the German agency, Wolff, which at that time exercised a monopoly, on behalf of the cartel, of the supply of news of Russia to the rest of the world. The cause of Russian concern was expressly linked to Russian attempts to attract inward investment (Rantenen, 1990).

The strength of evidence in support of NWICO charges against the major agencies was mixed (see Boyd-Barrett & Thussu, 1992, for a summary of the arguments). With respect to imbalance of flow it was clear from research, including UN research, that the major news agencies indirectly represented First World interests; they gathered news from most countries and distributed it to most countries; there was very little "reverse flow" of news from the media of developing countries to the global news agencies, other than that which the news agencies themselves filtered. The extent to which the services of these major agencies were actually dominated by Western countries had diminished by the 1970s, however. The agencies had begun to "regionalize" their services, reduce the dominance of U.S. and Western European news, and to tailor news services for the postcolonial era. In the distribution of news space across the different world regions, the highest proportion now went to the region to which a news wire was destined (and only then followed in importance by the U.S. and Western Europe). As for "coup and earthquake" coverage, this was true in part, but was merely the product of the application of Western news values, which tended to favor the negative over the positive.

Other than through the NWICO debate itself, UNESCO's response to the continuing imbalances of the global news system was to foster the development of regional news cooperatives, such as the Non-Aligned News Agencies Pool or the Pan-African News Agency (PANA). In their original form, these initiatives are now generally acknowledged to have been failures (Boyd-Barrett & Thussu, 1992). They were inadequately resourced, hampered by poor training and technical resources, subject to interference from member news agencies (mostly government owned or controlled), overly dependent on "protocol" news, lacking the resources and credibility to compete against the major news agencies or to attract clients from media-wealthy countries, dependent on aid from intergovernmental bureaucracies, crippled by irregular payment or nonpayment from their members, their news services dominated by a relatively small number of countries. Some of the blame should be laid at the door of UNESCO and other aid sponsors for their failure to properly theorize the relationship between news agencies, news flow, and national or economic development. Even the evidence against the major agencies was less compelling than UNESCO itself had originally believed (Boyd-Barrett, 1980; Boyd-Barrett & Thussu, 1992). But without a clear sense of what it was that national agencies were for, how precisely they were going to improve the fortunes of the majority of the populations that these agencies were set up to serve, it is hardly surprising that the results were disappointing. There was no proper assessment of the nature of the relationship between the state, "public" information, democracy, and development. While it may have been difficult to predict a potential for nonstate initiatives in media-poor countries, any success at all in this sphere has been related to an element of independence and economic enterprise—as in the case of those agencies that have operated economic news services, or that, like IPS (based in Rome) or Gemini (based in London) have established distinctive ideologies of news gathering and distinctive networks of clients, operating internationally, free from direct political control and self-sustaining.

CONCLUSION

In this chapter, I have argued that both the major global agencies and national or regional news agencies have contributed, in parallel, and as part of a coherent global news system, to the construction of "national" identities, and of a global world that is constructed principally on the basis of nation states. While the global agencies are and have always been prime examples of transnational business activities, sometimes working to subvert the interests of nation states, it can also be said that in their constructions of news they have primarily delivered a national image. In this sense, therefore, the economics of the global news system runs at apparent odds with the nature of its product.

REFERENCES

Adams, J. (1964, Autumn). A qualitative analysis of domestic and foreign news on the AP TA wire. *Gazette, 10*, 285–295.

Boyd-Barrett, O. (1979). *The world-wide news agencies: Development, organization, competition, markets and product*. Ph.D. thesis, Open University, Milton Keynes, U.K.

Boyd-Barrett, O. (1980). *The international news agencies*. London: Constable.

Boyd-Barrett, O. (1985). *Assessment of news agency and foreign broadcast monitoring services as information sources.* Hague, Netherlands: NATO.

Boyd-Barrett, O. (1997). Global news agencies as agents of globalization. In A. Sreberny-Mohammadi, D. Winseck, J. McKenna, & O. Boyd-Barrett (Eds.), *Media in global context: A reader* (pp. 131–144). London: Edward Arnold.

Boyd-Barrett, O., & Rantanen, T. (1997). News agencies in europe. In A. Briggs & P. Cobley (Eds.), *The media: An introduction* (pp. 52–64). London: Longman.

Boyd-Barrett, O., & Rantanen, T. (Eds.). (1998). *The globalization of news.* London: Sage.

Boyd-Barrett, O., & Thussu, D. K. (1992) *Conta-flow in global news.* London: John Libbey.

Cavagnero, L. (1998). *CNNI.* Master's thesis, University of Leicester, UK.

Clare, J. (1998). *Town criers in the global village.* Master's thesis, University of Leicester, UK.

Giddens, A. (1990). *The consequences of modernity.* Stanford, CA: Stanford University Press.

Golding, P. (1998). Worldwide wedge: Division and contradiction in the global information infrastructure. In D. K. Thuss(Ed.), *Electronic empires* (pp. 135–148). London: Edward Arnold.

Hall, S. (1982). The rediscovery of ideology: Return of the repressed in media studies. In M. Gurevitch, T. Bennett, J. Curran, & J. Woollacott (Eds.), *Culture, society and the media* (pp. 56–90). London: Methuen.

Harris, P. (1977). *News dependence: The case for a new world information order.* Unpublished report.

Harris, P., Malczek, H., & Ozkol, E. (1980). *Flow of news in the gulf.* Paris: UNESCO.

Hester, A. (1971). An analysis of news flow from developed and developing nations. *Gazette, 17,* 29–43.

Hester, A. (1974). The news from Latin America via a world news agency. *Gazette, 20,* 82–91.

International Press Institute. (1953). *The flow of news.* Paris and Zurich: Author.

Job, P. (1997, July 22). The Davidson interview. *Reuters Business Briefing.*

Kamaras, D. (1995). *News production in Greece with special reference to the Athens News Agency.* Master's thesis, City University, London.

Kang, M. (1997, May). *Foreign news in four Korean newspapers.* Paper presented at the conference of the International Communication Association, Montreal.

Lerner, D. (1958). *The passing of traditional society.* Glencoe, IL: Free Press.

Leung, W. (1979). *News flow between the United States and Asia.* Ph.D. thesis, University of Minnesota, Morris.

Mokekwu, M. (1982). *The Associated Press and the flow of international news into Indiana: A study of content and editorial practices.* Ph.D. thesis, Indiana University, Bloomington.

Musa, M. (1997). From optimism to reality: An overview of Third World news agencies. In P. Golding & P. Harris (Eds.), *Beyond cultural imperialism* (pp. 117–146). London: Sage.

Napoli, L. (1997, April 29). Profile: Bloomberg, a man and his information machine. *New York Times.*

Paterson, C. (1997). International television news agency coverage of conflict. *Journal of International Communication, 4,* 50–66.

Rimmer, T. (1981). Foreign news on UPI's "A" wire in the USA. *Gazette, 28,* 35–49.

Rantanen, T. (1990). *Foreign news in imperial Russia: The relationship between international and Russian news agencies 1856–1914.* Helsinki, Finland: Suomalainen Tiedeakatemia.

Scannell, P., & Cardiff, D. (1991). *A social history of British broadcasting.* Oxford: Basil Blackwell.

Schramm, W. (1964). *Mass media and national development.* Stanford, CA: Stanford University Press.

Schramm, W., & Atwood, E. (1981). *Circulation of news in the Third World.* Hong Kong: Chinese University Press.

Schulze-Schneider, I. (1998). From dictatorship to democracy: Agency and state in Spain. In O. Boyd-Barrett, & T. Rantanen (Eds.), *The globalization of news* (pp. 108–124). London: Sage.

Servaes, J. (1996). *Media and development: Alternate perspectives.* Leicester, UK: Centre for Mass Communications Research, University of Leicester.

Stevenson, R., & Cole, R. (1980). *Foreign news and the "new world information order" debate. Part 2: Foreign news in selected countries.* Washington, DC: Office of Research, International Communication Agency.

Weaver, D., Wilhoit, G., Stevenson, R., Shaw, D., & Cole, R. (1980). *The news of the world in four major wire services.* Paris: International Association for Mass Communication Research, UNESCO.

16

Development News Versus Globalized Infotainment

Daya Kishan Thussu
Coventry University, United Kingdom

As the mainly Western-based international media corporations expand and consolidate their operations in the "emerging markets" of the developing world, questions about the role of the mass media for development and imbalances in global newsflow have once again assumed significance.

The media landscape in the South has been transformed in the 1990s under the impact of neo-liberal, market-oriented economic policies that encourage privatization and deregulation. With the imposition of structural adjustment programs run by the World Bank and the International Monetary Fund (IMF), Southern governments have been obliged to open up their media industries to profit-seeking transnational companies, more interested in entertainment than public service.

With post-Cold War globalization, U.S.-made or -inspired news and entertainment programs have come to dominate the mediascape of much of the world. Game and chat shows are rapidly replacing more stolid but educational public-service programs, especially in the developing world. Increasingly, the news itself is becoming mere spectacle. What could be termed "globalized infotainment" is acquiring new audiences everyday.

While this has revived debates about cultural imperialism and information imbalances and inequalities, the resulting competition has, at the same time, created opportunities for developing a diverse and plural media culture in the South, hitherto dominated by the State. However, given the emphasis on entertainment-oriented programming, which characterizes private media and their profit-driven ideology, this supposed plurality may also be responsible for undermining the public-service role of the mass media for development and education.

Supporters of media globalization welcome the changes and consider them necessary for democracy, for a pluralistic world citizenry and an evolving global public sphere. Recent academic writing, especially emanating from the United States, has hailed the supposed diversity brought by the expansion of the U.S.-dominated Western media, as enriching media culture by such phenomenon as "transculturation, hybridity and indigenization" (Lull, 1995, p. 153). The general tenor of these arguments is that the expansion of the media transnationals and the "modernity" they are supposed to promote is a positive development for the democratization of information and communication.

Opposed to this is the neo-Marxian view, which sees the rapid growth of "global" media empires as a manifestation of what Herbert Schiller (1989) has called the "corporate takeover of public expression" driven by powerful corporate interests and supported by an ideological shift from state-centered, public service-based media and communication industries, to a privatized, deregularized, and liberalized regime with an eye toward the global market.

Schiller (1996) argues that the fundamental policy and institutional shifts in international organizations—from a state-supported role for communications to adherence to a free market dogma—have made this possible. Such multilateral fora as the United Nations, International Telecommunication Union, UNESCO, and the former Centre for Transnational Corporations, have "either been bypassed, restructured, weakened or neutered" (p. 123).

With the rapid developments in communications technologies and the resulting expansion of Western satellite and cable television in the developing world, key issues in the 1970s debates about the New World Information and Communication Order (NWICO) (Masmoudi, 1979; McBride, 1980) may again be relevant. What impact has globalization had on the imbalances identified then between the information-rich North and the information-poor South, and the need for development-oriented journalism?

While NWICO has been all but forgotten, the "free flow of information," which the West insisted on at the time has, in fact, increased tremendously as transnational information and media conglomerates—multibillion dollar enterprises driven by profit, such as Time-Warner, Disney, Microsoft, Reuters, and News International—consolidate their electronic empires in the South. As the full implications of the recently agreed General Agreement on Tariffs and Trade (GATT) come into effect, these hugely powerful media conglomerates are set to tighten their hold and accelerate the commodification of global information and communication.

Such mostly Western corporations dominate all spheres of global communication and the resultant information imbalance is seen by critics to be detrimental to the interests of Southern countries (Hamelink, 1997). In their 1997 study, Edward Herman and Robert McChesney identify key transnational media players and conclude that "the global media market is dominated by ten or so vertically integrated media conglomerates, most of which are based in the United States" (p. 104).

Not only do these conglomerates have the power, reach and influence to set and then build the global news agenda that reflects Western geo-strategic and economic interests, they also have become the vehicles for promoting infotainment to a global audience. In the process, they have contributed to the eclipsing of public-sector broadcasting in the South, where the state monopoly over broadcasting has been challenged by transnational media players such as Hong Kong-based STAR (Satellite Television Asian Region), BBC World, and the Atlanta-based Cable News Network (CNN).

The growing commercialization of national media in the South, it can be argued, is undermining the public-service ethos, however limited, of broadcasting. The increasing emphasis on entertainment in news programs contributes to the trivialization of vital public concerns and undermines the Habermasian concept of a public sphere in which the media helps to create a forum for public discourse and the articulation of public opinion. In a Southern context, "development" is central to the public debate and a responsible journalism should reflect this concern. But is there a distinct kind of journalism called "development journalism," and how is it relevant in the market-led media environment of the 1990s?

THE ORIGINS OF DEVELOPMENT JOURNALISM

Development journalism has been one of the key concepts informing the evolution of the media in the South since the 1970s. It emerged as a response to the debates over the NWICO, which voiced Southern grievances about the perceived dominance of a "one way flow of information" from the North to the South, which had contributed to the misrepresentation of the South in the global media (Masmoudi, 1979).

In addition, many analysts, especially in the so-called Third World, believed that the media could be harnessed to promote social and political development by contributing to the creation of a civil society and in nation-building. This was consistent with the dominant communications paradigm advanced by Western, mainly American communications scholars, which urged that the mass media could play a crucial role in society and, by implication, could be an agent in the "modernization" of the "Third World."

One of the key early texts of this modernization thesis was Daniel Lerner's *The Passing of Traditional Society*, published in 1958. The book, based on an extensive survey of social and cultural attitudes in the Middle East, became the "bible" of the modernist creed, which saw enormous potential of the mass media for development. Later, theorists such as Schramm (1964) viewed the mass media as a "bridge to a wider world," as the vehicles for transferring new ideas and models from the North to the South and within the South from urban to rural areas (pp. 41–42).

Critical analysts such as Vincent Mosco saw the developmentalists in a different light: "The theory of modernisation meant a reconstitution of the international division of labour amalgamating the non-Western world into the emerging international structural hierarchy" (1996 p. 121). They argued that, in the name of modernization, the West was trying to create an elite in the South, which followed the capitalist model of development.

Historically, the press in the developing world formed part of the anti-colonial nationalist movements. In India, the forerunner of the anti-colonial movements, the press played a prominent role in articulating and disseminating the nationalist message. Most nationalist leaders were involved in activist, campaigning journalism, none more than Mahatma Gandhi, who realized the importance of the written word and used Gujarati, his mother tongue, as well as English, to spread the message of freedom from colonial rule (Desai, 1976).

The legacy of anti-colonialism continued to influence journalists after independence, many of whom in India, as elsewhere in the developing world, had taken part in the nationalist movement, and, consequently, the anti-colonial press assumed, by and large, a supportive attitude toward the State. Most developing countries inherited from their colonial rulers a tradition of a private press and a government-controlled broadcasting system, which the leadership was keen to use for what came to be known as "nation-building."

Since the majority of the newly independent peoples were illiterate, the ruling elite considered radio as a crucial instrument of state communication. In many cases, such as India, where independence was achieved after large-scale violence, radio was given a key role in integrating ethnically, linguistically, and religiously diverse regions of the country. The broadcasters' task was to develop "national consciousness," to help in overcoming the immediate crisis of political instability that followed independence and to foster the long term process of political modernization and nation-building that was the dominant ideology of the newly emergent and activist State (Chatterjee, 1991).

The leaders found it difficult to relinquish political control over broadcasting, the most potent instrument of propaganda, trying to justify this in terms of the need to use broadcasting for "development" purposes. It was also argued that an uncontrolled broadcasting system could destabilize the newly independent countries. Consequently, the public broadcasting organizations became little more than propaganda services for the government. Like other public-sector departments, they were over-bureaucratized and their performance was generally dull.

When television arrived in the South in the 1950s, governments followed more or less the same pattern. On paper, television's objectives were to help in "nation-building," but in practice it was used for serving the ruling party or dictatorship, which applied to most of the political leadership in the South.

Many of the norms dictated by the early, congenial relationship between the media and the state continued to govern the nature of Southern journalism for several decades after independence. There was an implicit acceptance of what represented the "national interest." Most developing countries agreed that it was the role of the mass media to create national unity and foster development. Many governments in the developing world took total control of the mass media through nationalization, making journalists civil servants and government spokespeople. Journalists were even offered senior positions in the newly formed governments, especially in Africa, where the leadership viewed the media as "largely a political weapon" (Okigbo, 1995, p. 380).

This raised the issue of the independence of the media. Since development policy was decided by governments, were journalists to accept their governments as the sole arbiters of what was to be communicated? Given that in much of the South, newspapers and the electronic media were wholly or partly controlled by the state or the ruling parties, it was hardly surprising that the news Southern agencies put out—reports about state visits and the opening up of mega "developmental" projects, sometimes referred to as "protocol news"—was seen as government propaganda.

In addition, government interference restricted journalists' freedom to critically examine state policies. Where direct control was not exerted, pressure was put on journalists to follow the government's line, especially in reporting foreign affairs, by threatening to lift newsprint supply, disrupting electricity to newspaper offices and introducing draconian censorship laws (Bhattacharjee, 1972).

Such uses of the media found little favor in the Western media and among most Western analysts, who have generally been opposed to the concept of development journalism. During the 1970s and 1980s, in the ideological fervor of the cold war, Western media analysts, especially in the U.S., equated development journalism with Communist efforts to control the media: "Moscow could champion the Third World while winning UN support for state control of the domestic press, television and foreign correspondents" (Rosenblum, 1993, p. 273).

It is now accepted even by pro-development journalists that Southern governments tried to hijack the idea of development news to highlight their achievements and suppress critical evaluation of their failures. In addition, by complying with the government and using their handouts as news, Southern journalists were compromising their professionalism.

Phil Harris, an advisor at Inter Press Service (IPS), a key Southern news agency, observes:

Unfortunately for those of us involved in the business of communicating to and with others on development issues, "development journalism" has been done so sloppily for so long by so many people. That does not mean the concept of and need for development journalism is no longer valid, but it does mean taking care to provide information in a way that avoids hackneyed phraseology and says something interesting and intelligent. Above all, it means discarding the myth that development reporting accentuates the positive—but it doesn't accentuate the negative either. (1997, p. 161)

However, one positive outcome of the NWICO debate, generally considered to have been a failure by most commentators, was the emergence of a new perspective on development journalism in the South. It argued that though development news should not be identical with "positive news" and government propaganda, there was still a need for an alternative form of journalism, with an active role as an agent for social and political change.

The most widely used definition of the concept was advanced by Narinder Aggarwala at the height of the NWICO debate in 1978, and since cited by most writers on the subject: "Development journalism is the use of all journalistic skills to report development processes in an interesting fashion" (1979, p. 181).

Aggarwala (1979) believed that the key difference lay in the news agenda, rather than in professional practice. Development news is not different from regular news or investigative reporting, but what distinguished it from Western notions of "objective reporting" was that it took a proactive role in following development issues and providing a critique of the development process.

In covering the development newsbeat, a journalist should critically examine, evaluate, and report the relevance of a development project to national and local needs, the difference between a planned scheme and its actual implementation, and the differences between its impact on people as claimed by government officials and as it actually is. (p. 181)

The agenda tended to reject the reliance on immediacy and drama for newsworthiness. This shift toward long-term issues found a more appropriate format in news features. Typical stories for the development journalist would be about an agricultural breakthrough, a successful literacy program, or the impact of large-scale projects on local communities—topics that have relevance in many developing countries.

Many Southern journalists argued that a new style of journalism, one that asserted that good news is just as newsworthy as bad news, was essential to promote national development. Some, like senior Indian journalist Dilip Mukerjee, went so far as to demand a complete break with the Western philosophy of journalism:

Our need is urgent and acute: we belong to societies which are in the process of restructuring and reshaping themselves. In our environment there is, and there will be for a long time to come, much that is ugly and distasteful. If we allow the Western norm, we will be playing up only those dark spots, and thus helping unwittingly to erode the faith and confidence without which growth and development are impossible... (cited in Legum & Cornwell, 1978, p. 35)

According to this view of "positive" journalism, reporters have to do more than react to events by observing and writing about them. This implies a far-reaching reassessment of the established Western definition of "news," redefining it in conventional terms of "objectivity" or newsworthiness.

One key aspect of development news is the emphasis it places on investigating the process behind a story rather than simply recording the news event itself. The mainstream news media thrive on immediacy and interest of "action" or "spot" news, and tend to ignore "soft" or "development" news; economic and social development is a slow and almost imperceptible process. For example, a development journalist would cover drought not simply as a shortage of water, but as a struggle for control of resources and conflict between competing sections of society.

NEWS AND THE MARKET

In an increasingly commercialized global media market, news is becoming a commodity that can be bought and sold like any other commercial transaction. Reporters sell their "exclusives" throughout the world as "properties"—the more gruesome the story, the more likely it is to make to the foreign pages of newspapers or fiercely competitive slots of the networks. News values are increasingly market-led, which assumes a ready audience for sensationalist stories. Such stories get prominence, and journalists and editors are tempted to reject other kinds of news in their favor.

Southern critics have argued that because news is a commodity, there is a built-in discrimination against news events that cannot be "sold." This results in a distorted presentation of events "to make them more marketable." Western journalists see "aberrations" as "news," which in turn "obliges" them to "sensationalize" (Masmoudi, 1979; Somavia, 1976).

The result of this commodification process, according to this argument, is that most reporting of serious issues in the South is reduced to a simplistic version of often complex realities. With scant space to cover news from developing countries, these are often stereotyped into shorthand media clichés—Thailand is known for child prostitution, Columbia for cocaine, Ethiopia for famine, and so on.

While covering "news" of wars, disease, corruption and disasters in the South—the "coups and earthquake syndrome"—international journalists are seldom encouraged by their editors to probe how the situation developed, how the event in question was related to its socioeconomic and political environment, or to explore alternative viewpoints. As a result, there is a steady underreporting of the cultural, economic, and political progress being made by developing countries.

Moreover, it is not simply what the international media say, or how they say it, that creates stereotypical perceptions of the South. Equally important is what they choose to ignore. One kind of absence is the entire "blanking out" of vast areas of experience and life—how more than 80 percent of the world's population live, their social and economic interests, their cultures and traditions—which are very rarely represented in the mainstream international media. Another kind of absence in international media output stems from the tendency among journalists to conform to dominant economic and political interests whereby they leave several crucial questions unasked and explore and investigate news stories on the basis of dominant perceptions of what constitutes news and deeply ingrained assumptions about the "Third World."

These "absences" in international media content, and the distorted views of the South that result from this, affect understanding of the developing world in the North as well as among the countries of the South, since most of news flow continues to be from North to South and very limited South-to-South news exchange takes place.

As in most of the developing world, the press generally caters to the requirements of the urban readership and has little contact with the villages where a majority of the population live. Although women account for half of the world's population, gender-related concerns, especially from the South, are generally not considered good copy. When such questions do draw the attention of the media, there is a tendency to either sensationalize, trivialize, or otherwise distort the story. Bringing in a "women's perspective" on global, national, and local issues—and not simply those that have traditionally been seen as "women's concerns"—is another facet of development news.

A development journalist would look beyond the "lipstick beat"—coverage of fashion and food and celebrity profiles—to focus on such issues as violence against women and their subordination in society. They would explore, for example, how neo-liberal policies have affected the lives of women in the South. Such reporting would help to empower women by informing them about legal and political rights.

DEVELOPMENT NEWS IN PRACTICE

Widening the news agenda to include such concerns and offer a Southern perspective on events in the South was behind the move to establish international and regional news-exchange mechanisms (NEMs), with support from UNESCO, as a result of the NWICO debates. However, the NEMs' success in achieving these aims has been very limited.

One major international program was the Non-aligned News Agencies Pool (NANAP), designed to promote news exchange among the nonaligned nations. However, it dismally failed to make any impact on news flow among nonaligned nations, primarily because it was little more than an exchange of official information among member countries, most of which opposed a free and independent media. In the post-cold war world, the movement, which was supposed to steer newly independent nations of Asia, Africa, and Latin America from East–West ideological confrontation, has lost much of its relevance and, with that, nonaligned governments' interest in the news pool. Ironically, the Yugoslav newsagency Tanjug, which for many years was a nodal point in NANAP, is now a vehicle for Serb nationalism.

Similarly, regional news-exchange programs such as the Pan African News Agency (PANA), the Caribbean News Agency (CANA), and the Organisation of Asian News Agencies (OANA) have largely failed to develop a Southern news agenda or make any visible difference to global news flow (Boyd-Barrett & Thussu, 1992). Development news is scarcely visible even in Asian or African newspapers, which continue to print most of their foreign news from Western news agencies, such as Associated Press (AP), Reuters, and Agence France Presse (AFP).

Specialized Southern-oriented news agencies, such as IPS, comparatively a smaller actor in the global news arena, tended to be used more by nongovernmental organizations than mainstream media. A not-for-profit organization, it continues to run into financial difficulties, though heavily subsidized by donor support from Northern governments and international organizations. IPS defines itself as an agency that "focuses attention on the countries of the South, and the marginalised in the North, and goes behind the scenes to examine and analyse what is happening, so that people can begin to understand the complex processes that lie behind day-to-day events" (see the IPS website on the Internet at http://www.ips.org).

IPS has more than 250 journalists covering over 100 countries and serving 1,000 subscribers worldwide. In addition to its main services in English and Spanish, delivered via satellite, news bulletins are produced in other languages, including Bahasa Indonesia, German, Hindi, Kiswahili, Mandarin, and Swedish.

Despite higher professional standards than NANAP, IPS has limited presence, even among Southern publications. This is primarily because it tried to compete with much better resourced, managed, and marketed transnational news agencies such as AP and Reuters into the area of spot news. However, its Spanish language service continues to be an important player in South America, a region with which the agency has a special relationship—IPS was started in 1964 by a journalists' cooperative in South America.

Other small-scale media actors—such as Third World Network based in Penang, Malaysia—have found a niche, especially among Asian newspapers. But it only puts out features, and more often than not these are what conventional journalists would call "opinion pieces."

CASE STUDY: GEMINI NEWS SERVICE

More successful has been a London-based small news features agency, Gemini News Service, which has kept the concept of development news on the global agenda. This section analyses Gemini's contribution to reversing the imbalance in global news flow and assesses how far this tiny agency has been able to meet its aims against heavy odds. It also looks at the constraints on its operation in terms of its funding, technology, and market.

Gemini News Service is a not-for-profit international news features agency, supplying topical news features to about 100 subscribers in 80 countries around the world. Although based in London, it covers very few stories about Britain and is particularly strong in Africa and covering parts of the globe such as the South Pacific, often not written about in the mainstream international press. The agency, with a special connection with the Commonwealth, occupies a unique niche in the English-speaking world and plays an important role in the education of journalists in the South, and in broadening and deepening the concept of development journalism. It has succeeded where government-to-government, South to South news-exchange mechanisms, such as the NANAP, have failed, primarily because unlike them, it has had high journalistic credibility.

The Gemini News Service was established in 1967 by Derek Ingram, a British journalist and former deputy editor of the London *Daily Mail*. The philosophy behind the move was what Ingram called "decolonization" of news:

> The theory behind Gemini was simply this. By the mid-1960s the colonial age was dead, and in the new age of non-alignment and the desire to recreate separate national identities many newspapers no longer wanted the kind of material that had been flowing to them from the big agencies and from the syndicated services of the Western, mainly British and American, newspapers. For one thing, most of this copy was written for Western readers (qtd. in Bourne, 1995, p. 9)

One key factor that distinguished it from other Western-based news organizations was its emphasis on using a worldwide network of local journalists. As one of the commemorative articles put it in 1987: "Rather than reporting Third World disasters and coups solely from a Western viewpoint, most Gemini correspondents are from the region they are writing about, providing a continuing and topical perspective on the countries they know best" (qtd. in Bourne, 1995, p. 35).

A global agenda defined Gemini from its inception. Though, with its limited output of 12 features per week, it could never be an international player on a par with transnational news agencies, its presence has been felt from the Caribbean to Africa and Asia, and from the Middle East to the South Pacific. Unlike many Southern news agencies, which require journalists to become government propagandists, promoting only the good news about progress in their countries, Gemini argued that development journalism could not be a one-dimensional affair. The agency tried to free the concept of development news from the clutches of news bureaucrats by reporting, with critical objectivity, small-scale and community efforts, as well as major international issues of trade and debt.

The emphasis is on readability without sacrificing the substance of the story. It urges its correspondents to file reports that have depth, local color, and people in them, full of quotes rather than dry statistics. In this way, it can cover stories that have meaning for other states in the South and contribute to a horizontal South to South news flow as against the dominant, vertical North to South, or more accurately, West to South news flow.

Reporting Development News

Gemini produces a weekly package of 12 news features, each between 600 and 1,200 words long, with accompanying graphics. Gemini's graphics, the services' strongest point, appear in scores of newspapers everyday. Many newspapers use Gemini graphics on their own and sometimes even with stories provided by transnational news agencies.

What makes the features stand out is the fact that they try to provide a different perspective on global news to the mainstream Western news agencies and to encourage reporting of positive development stories. This attitude gives it credibility and since the agency cannot be identified with any particular country and its contributors are drawn from many developing nations, its reports are perceived in the South as accurate and objective. For a number of smaller newspapers, virtually the entire foreign coverage is provided by Gemini.

Over the years, the agency has established a unique niche by seeking out stories and angles neglected by the mainstream media. The emphasis has been to reflect local perspectives rather than the outsider's view, which is provided by most of the transnational news agencies. It has covered virtually every subject under the sun and tries to write about development in "an interesting way," as Aggarwala (1979) would say. Subjects range from elections to sports, from personality profiles to World Bank and IMF-sponsored structural adjustment policies, to gender, militarism, media, and culture.

Its features are widely used, which means that each story may appear scores of times in newspapers around the globe. Unlike transnational news agencies reports, which are often cut, edited, and merged, Gemini articles are usually run as they stand by subscribing newspapers. Yet Gemini is not in a position to compete with international news agencies in spot news and its stories are placed on features rather than "hard news" pages. Many pieces with strong opinion or commentary quality make it to the Op/Ed pages of newspapers in the South.

Gemini has also helped promote development news by its emphasis on rural reporting. It recognizes that a majority of people in the developing world live in the countryside and most have to eke out a living by subsistence farming. Gemini was among the first of the international news agencies to popularize issues such as sustainable development and the environment, long before they became fashionable in the mainstream international press.

In the 1980s, it launched its Village Reporting project, in an attempt to recognize the reality that so many people in the South live in rural communities, with needs, stories, and interests of their own, which are often ignored by journalists based in their capitals, let alone by the international media.

Under the rural reporting initiative, funded by Western donors, Gemini sent its reporters to live in villages for three months and then write about problems of rural life. More than 15 reporters in almost a dozen countries, ranging from India to Fiji to South Africa, took part. Their copy was edited and a training manual, entitled *Views from the Village*, filled with practical advice for making stories more interesting, treating statistics with discretion, and putting the focus on the human and the village rather than the national and international agencies, was produced (McParland, 1988).

Unlike the development news agendas of the information departments of Southern governments, which are aimed to put the government's rural development programs in the best light, Gemini's reports were often critical of governments or international organizations, such as the World Bank, in their failure to reduce poverty. Such reporting, where the emphasis was to "tell it as it is," has contributed to improved environmental coverage and brought to life such macro-level issues as impact of debt crisis or structural adjustment programs on the rural poor.

Subscribers

In 1997, Gemini had 100 subscribers from around the world. Among the main newspapers receiving the service were: *The Guardian Weekly* and *Scotland on Sunday* in Britain; *The Ottawa Citizen* in Canada; the *Miami Times* in the United States; *Gulf News* and *Oman Daily Observer* in the Arab world; *China Daily* in Beijing; the *Hong Kong Standard*; the *New Straits Times* in Malaysia; the *Dawn* in Pakistan; the *Deccan Herald* in India; *The Herald* in Harare; and *The Standard* in Kenya.

The range and quality of its subscribers vary. Some, like the *Hong Kong Standard* and the *New Straits Times*, are premier newspapers in their respective countries with access to all major online news services, equipped as they are with state-of-the-art technology. For many others, often small circulation newspapers in Africa or the South Pacific, Gemini is often the only source of foreign news. In the South Pacific, for example, the agency played a unique role especially during the formative years of the news media in the region in the 1970s and the 1980s. David Robie, Gemini's correspondent in the South Pacific, recalls:

> Most of the media in the smaller Pacific countries were unable to afford paying for wire services and the Gemini service was a godsend—it provided international articles on major issues and development dilemmas backed up with strong graphics

tailor-made for their needs. Also, it provided far more refreshing perspectives on world and Commonwealth events than were usually available through the wire services. (qtd. in Bourne, 1995, p. 67)

In addition, some Northern NGO publications and UN organizations involved with development work, such as UNICEF and UNDP, also subscribe to the service. In the late 1980s, as the end of the cold war freed up media in the former Soviet bloc, Gemini acquired several new subscriptions in Eastern Europe. Yet Africa continues to be the stronghold of the agency. The regional news services in the South—CANA in the Caribbean, PACNEWS in the Pacific, and PANA in Africa—have never challenged the niche service provided by Gemini and it also fought off direct competition from the well-resourced Compass features service, backed by the Aga Khan, and which expired in the early 1990s after seven years of losses (Bourne, 1995, p. 8).

Gemini was not founded as a charity or an NGO, but with the aim of operating in a free market, depending on subscribers for its survival. However, almost from its inception, it had to live with a precarious financial situation as income from subscriptions alone could never be sufficient to cover running costs. One of the problems is that most of its subscribers are in the South, where many countries have restrictions on foreign exchange transfers, even if they can afford to pay the subscription.

Funding from international agencies such as the Canadian International Development Agency, Canada's International Development Research Centre, the Swedish International Development Agency, and the United Nations Children's Program (UNICEF)—effectively subsidize the news features service, although Gemini ensures that it is not too dependent on one particular source so that it does not compromise its independence. However, it is questionable how long this system can survive, especially at a time when interest in development-related subjects is waning among international donors.

Training For Development News

Another key contribution of Gemini toward development journalism has been its record in the field of educating journalists in the South. Development education through the media along with professional advancement of Southern journalists are key aims for Gemini and the main rationale for financial support of international agencies.

Its policy is to give international exposure to journalists in the South. Several journalists who got their first foreign stories published by Gemini are now in positions of authority in their own country's media. Some have started their own media businesses and others work for governments or for international organizations. Under one scheme, development country journalists visit the Gemini office in London for three months and get hands-on experience of working in a small but very busy office and are exposed to international news concerns.

From its inception, Gemini has looked for local correspondents and encouraged them to contribute. Postal delays and the modest rates paid by Gemini to its contributors—£60 ($100 U.S.) per article in 1997—do not deter contributors from filing. Gemini's policy of paying the same rate wherever the correspondent is based—£60 in Dhaka or Dakar could equal a month's salary but less than a day's wage in London—encourages a kind of democratic culture in the organization.

Gemini aims to provide a training and development element in its day-to-day relationship with correspondents. Gemini editors encourage correspondents to look for on-the-spot topical reports, seek out fresh angles on old stories, and cover issues that have been dropped off the agenda of the international media. Its *Guidance for Correspondents* offers regular advice and encouragement, especially to help journalists for whom English is a second or third language. Often stories need rewriting, researching, and reinterpreting. Sometimes the lead may be buried in the 10th paragraph, or subsequent events may have necessitated a drastic change in the focus of the piece to suit a global readership.

Gemini also has an educational role in the developing world. Training journalists in writing internationally accessible and readable copy has been a key contribution of Gemini in promoting development news. Its training and educational projects are supported by international funders. Every year it runs at least two workshops on development journalism for Southern journalists.

These workshops, organized with funding from various sources such as the United Nations Development Program (UNDP), UNICEF, and agencies connected with the European Union and Canadian and Swedish governments, have been organized to develop professional skills of Southern journalists, especially to improve their coverage of subjects such as the environment. The agency has also produced practical guides to environmental and rural reporting (Ingram, 1992).

In addition, the workshops, often bringing together journalists from a particular region of the developing world, contribute to the exchange of ideas on communications and thus promoted regional journalist-to-journalist exchange.

Technology

Since it started, Gemini has depended on the mail system. A package of six stories are sent out on each Tuesday and Friday by airmail. This mode of delivery obviously constrains the service to only produce features that have a shelf life of at least a week because that is the average time it takes for Gemini features to reach newspapers in most places. Correspondents mail, fax, and, since 1993, file stories onto modem. The features are edited, printed, and then photocopies are mailed to subscribers.

That Gemini continues to be used widely, despite these technological constraints, demonstrates that newspaper editors across the developing world are keen to find a fresh perspective on global issues. If they decide to use a Gemini feature, they have to key it in again, unlike the transnational news agencies whose stories can be downloaded from computers. Therefore, the Gemini story has to be sufficiently different in emphasis to warrant use.

Being dependent on this primitive technology has limited Gemini's operations. Sometimes a story that has been issued from London can be overtaken by events, although the editors make sure that in such instances an update is issued immediately. But in the age of digital media, this delivery system cannot be competitive. Gemini experimented with Presslink, a computerized service for distributing its feature packages, but the cost was prohibitive. Since 1996, however, Gemini is available on the Internet on the OneWorld Online, a "supersite" for alternative news agencies and NGOs (http://www.oneworld.org).

For Southern newspapers, Gemini is unique in its commitment to development coverage. In his account of the agency, Richard Bourne (1995) sums it up well:

> The Gemini News Service is a triumph of hope and hard work over adversity. All
> media enterprises must expect competition and many new ones are short lived. But
> the Gemini news feature agency based in London has had several additional handi-
> caps: its service has always been seen as optional for newspaper subscribers, rather
> than essential, like a news agency supplying up-to-the-minute news; it has aimed to
> cover events in some of the poorest countries of the world, and from their viewpoint;
> it has always been under-capitalised; it remains very small, part of the price it pays
> for independence; and it has always lived on the edge of crisis. (p. 7)

So what future is there for such small, alternative news agencies as Gemini in this age of market-driven journalism? Has its availability on the Internet gained new subscribers in the South or among the Northern media? Evidently not. If anything, it has been losing subscribers as many who download its stories do not pay for use. In addition, its deteriorating financial situation makes it extremely difficult to compete in an increasingly crowded international market, dominated by media conglomerates.

Yet Gemini's global agenda has made a small difference in the way journalists in less-developed countries perceive news. It has contributed to popularizing a grassroots journalism. Given that media in Africa are still largely untouched by media globalization—declining incomes in Africa does not make it a promising proposition for transnational conglomerates—and given that multi-party democracy is growing on the continent, it is possible that Gemini will continue to be a presence, at least in its traditional stronghold. Elsewhere in the South, though, its prospects seem bleak as visual media take priority and entertainment becomes the norm.

DEVELOPMENT NEWS AND GLOBALIZATION

What then is the relevance of development news in the market-led, entertainment-oriented media of the late 1990s? If the U.S.-dominated global media fails to cover it adequately, does it mean that issues of development have ceased to be relevant?

The challenge that agencies such as Gemini have to grapple with is how to market development news without compromising its essence. As noted earlier, the development news agenda deals with economic, social, and political processes, which take time to unfold, an almost imperceptible process, given the short attention span of media producers and consumers. There is a need to broaden development news to take account of complex sociopolitical changes in the evolving civil societies in the South.

Partially freed from the control of government dictates, Southern journalists have a greater scope to take a more active role in covering stories that affect ordinary lives, going beyond the official development beat and using the opportunities offered by the competitive private media, spurred by globalization. As Harris (1997) comments:

> Development writers have often been told: don't touch coups, earthquakes and disasters—they are told that is for the event-oriented Northern wire services. This is nonsense. The task of the journalist should be to report the process, the common citizen's gripes which feed the collective national frustrations that periodically erupt in military mutinies. (p. 161)

If development news is to be effective, media personnel and policymakers in the South will need to recognize that a key task of journalism is to extend the scope of reporting to cover issues of relevance to the majority as part of the development of democracy and the evolution of a public sphere. They also have to work toward acting as watchdog, an "early warning system" to preempt a natural or man-made disaster. This would entail a fundamental shift in emphasis in news values—from individual to society, from urban to rural, from powerful to impoverished, from elitist to ordinary.

The unquestioning acceptance of the Western definition of what constitutes news by the majority of journalists, both in the North and the South, has hitherto affected the coverage of development issues directly and adversely. Most development issues do not fit into the traditional concepts of what constitutes news. The poor, who are supposed to be the subject matter of development news, are neither affluent nor in positions of authority. In addition, in writing about the dispossessed, the journalists get little in return except perhaps some moral satisfaction and professional pride. In contrast, while covering celebrities and members of economic and political elites, they rub shoulders with the rich and famous and that proximity to power is what gives journalism much of its professional appeal.

The impact of neo-liberal market "reforms" on the people of the South is hardly discussed in the mainstream Western media. Nor are the policies of such international organizations as the World Bank, the IMF, and the World Trade Organization, adequately reported or analysed in the mainstream Southern media—though their prescriptions often dictate government policy in many developing countries.

Few Southern journalists are trained in the economics and political sociology necessary for writing with insight about economic and social development. Even fewer are competent in dealing with corporate journalism, a discipline that is still in its infancy in much of the South. They need to develop expertise to make sense of and interpret, in an accessible way, the complexity of, for example, global electronic data exchanges, electronic funds transfers, the commodity price fluctuations, and foreign-exchange mechanisms, which have an enormous impact on the day-to-day lives of their fellow citizens.

In less developed parts of the South, such as sub-Saharan Africa, where an independent media has contributed to the establishment of multi-party democracy, this need is especially pressing. With declining incomes, low literacy, and small populations, many African countries have no economies of scale to sustain independent media, which have been supported by foreign donors and often abused by local business elites and unrepresentative politicians. In addition, strict press laws and censorship make their survival difficult. "Unless the independent media take root and prosper," warns an analyst, "Africa's current multi-party experience would be short-lived. The continent could revert to dictatorship" (Kasoma, 1995, p. 553).

These fears are well-founded, yet, there are also perceptible signs, emanating from some developing countries, notably India, which defy the proposition that development news is doomed. Unlike other developing countries, the press in India is independent and has contributed significantly to political education in the world's largest democracy. At the same time, multi-party politics has ensured a tradition of adversary and investigative journalism. One example of this is in the work of award-winning journalist Palagummi Sainath, who published a series of stories between 1993 and 1995 in the country's premier newspaper *The Times of India*, covering the lives of people inhabiting India's poorest districts.

"The reports," writes Sainath in the introduction of a book based on his journeys and interestingly titled *Everybody Loves a Good Drought* (1996), "are on the living conditions of the rural poor. The idea was to look at those conditions in terms of processes. Too often, poverty and deprivation get covered as events. That is, when some disaster strikes, when people die. Yet, poverty is about much more than starvation deaths or near famine conditions. It is the sum total of a multiplicity of factors" (p. ix).

Sainath's stories brought to life the problems of extreme poverty and the struggle for survival among some of the world's poorest people, and covered topics rarely reported by metropolitan journalists, such as malnutrition, education, literacy, rural exploitation, and debt. His subject, he says is "beyond the margin of elite vision.

And beyond the margins of a press and media that fail to connect with them" (1996, p. xiii).

Yet, the fact that the *Times of India*, a privately owned newspaper, sponsored Sainath's study, which meant traveling 44,000 miles over a 14-month period, shows that development news has not fallen altogether off the news agenda in the mainstream Indian press, despite commercial pressures.

There are other positive signals. Media globalization has hit India at a time when the country has witnessed an extraordinary growth in the vernacular press and regional language television channels, in many ways a more authentic and democratic voice of the people. The changing contours of national politics, with regional parties taking center-stage, has given a new impetus to newspapers in Indian languages, which now sell four times as many copies as the English language publications. Analyzing data from the Annual Report of the Registrar for Newspapers, Robin Jeffrey (1997) comments that in 1961, the circulation of Hindi dailies by the most generous estimate was 750,000 copies and of English, 1.3 million—1.7 English dailies for every one in Hindi. By 1992, Hindi dailies claimed sales of 11.2 million to 3.9 million for English—a ratio of 2.9 Hindi dailies for each one in English.

As literacy grows and the purchasing power of readers of such regional language newspapers increases, journalists from these publications and broadcasting organizations are more likely than their Westernized metropolitan counterparts to cover with greater insight the issues that impact on the everyday lives of people. This should end the ghettoizing of "development news," and contribute to making it a more marketable product.

Another challenge for Southern media professionals and policymakers will be how to harness the potential of new information technology, especially the Internet, to disseminate alternative perspectives on development to a growing community of Net-surfers and contribute to a North to South and, perhaps more significantly, South to South dialogue on such issues as inequalities in global trade and debt, gender and ethnic discrimination, human rights, and environmental protection. However, skeptics consider the enthusiastic support for new information technologies by the prophets of modernization as a "revisionist version of the developmentalist view" (Mosco, 1996, p. 130).

Although the question of access obviously limits the potential of the new technology—a majority of the people in the world have yet to make their first telephone call—the Internet has opened up a new window on the South. Already, scores of Southern newspapers are accessible to Web-surfers, many of them media personnel. Organizations such as the U.K.-based OneWorld Online, which provides a forum for alternative media, including Gemini, and nongovernmental channels, offer the opportunity to develop an egalitarian global space where international development, in all its dimensions—political, economic, and cultural—can be discussed.

However, the forthcoming debates are likely to be about control of the airwaves, as visual media comes to dominate journalism and any sense of optimism has to be balanced against the growing power of entertainment-oriented multimedia moguls. In Asia, potentially the biggest market for media products, the advent of STAR, the pan-Asian satellite service launched in 1991, has bought Western entertainment-oriented programming to traditional societies of this diverse continent, necessitating a rethinking of public-service broadcasting norms (Chan, 1994).

The explosion of private, commercial television has made the state broadcasters' role of education and public information more difficult, since they now have to provide popular entertainment to remain competitive. As a result, the percentage of public-service programs have gone down. The Indian national broadcaster, *Doordarshan*, for example, has increased its channels from 2 in 1991 to 19 in 1997 (one of the new channels is, in fact, called "infotainment"). While the Satellite Instructional Television Experiment (SITE), India's effort to use television as an educational tool, was aimed to educate the masses, STAR is there to "tickle the public," to use an old expression.

Although technological improvements mean that the problems of reaching remote areas have been overcome, and, with the help of the Indian Satellite System (INSAT), the number of TV transmissions has phenomenally increased, yet there are few viewers of educational and developmental programs (Sinha, 1996).

In Africa, the state-run media have been starved of funds, while an entertainment-rich media is mushrooming across the continent. In Latin America, the region's both main players, Brazil's *Globo* and Mexico's *Televisa*, are thriving on a diet of commercial programming (Sinclair, 1996).

What future is there then for the journalism that purports to highlight the problems of the powerless and the marginalized? As globalized infotainment strengthens its hold over more and more Southern media and the commodification of news and information grows apace, it is likely to further undermine the scope for development news in national and international media. It is yet to be seen whether the potential of new spaces and opportunities created by new media technologies and diversification will deliver any significant or effective alternatives.

REFERENCES

Aggarwala, N. (1979). What is development news? *Journal of Communication, 29*, 180–181.
Bhattacharjee, A. (1972). *The Indian press: Profession to industry.* New Delhi, India: Vikas.
Bourne, R. (1995). *News on a knife-edge.* London: John Libbey.
Boyd-Barrett, O., & Thussu, D. K. (1992). *Contra-flow in global news.* London: John Libbey/UNESCO.
Chan, J. M. (1994). National responses and accessibility to STAR TV in Asia. *Journal of Communication, 44*, 112–131.
Chatterjee, P. C. (1991). *Broadcasting in India.* New Delhi, India: Sage.

Desai, A. R. (1976). *Social background of Indian nationalism* (5th ed.). Bombay, India: Popular Press.

Hamelink, C. (1997). International communication: Global market and morality. In A. Mohammadi (Ed.), *International communication and globalization* (pp. 92–118). London: Sage.

Harris, P. (1997). Communication and global security: The challenge for the next millennium. In P. Golding & P. Harris (Eds.), *Beyond cultural imperialism: Globalisation, communication and the New International Order* (pp. 147–162). London: Sage.

Herman. E., & McChesney, R. (1997). *The global media: The new missionaries of corporate capitalism.* London: Cassell.

Ingram, D. (Ed.). (1992). *Environmental reporting handbook.* London: Gemini News Service.

Jeffrey, R. (1997, January 18). Hindi: "Taking to the *Punjab Kesari* line." *Economic and Political Weekly,* 77–83.

Kasoma, F. (1995). The role of the independent media in Africa's change to democracy. *Media, Culture and Society, 17,* 537–555.

Legum, C., & Cornwell, J. (1978). *A free and balanced flow: Report of the Twentieth Century Fund Task Force on the international flow of news.* Lexington, MA: Lexington Books.

Lerner, D. (1958). *The passing of traditional society.* New York: Free Press.

Lull, J. (1995). *Media communication, culture: A global approach.* Cambridge, England: Polity.

Masmoudi, M. (1979). New International Information Order. *Journal of Communication, 29,* 172–185.

McBride, S. (1980). *Many voices, one world: International Commission for the Study of Communications Problems.* Paris: UNESCO.

McParland, K. (1988). *Views from the village.* London: Gemini News Service.

Mosco, V. (1996). *The political economy of communication.* London: Sage.

Okigbo, C. (1995). Africa. In A. Smith (Ed.), *Television, an international history* (pp. 358–380). Oxford, England: Oxford University Press.

Rosenblum, M. (1993). *Who stole the news?* New York: John Wiley.

Sainath, P. (1996). *Everybody loves a good drought.* New Delhi, India: Penguin.

Schiller, H. (1989). *Culture Inc.?* New York: Oxford University Press.

Schiller, H. (1996). *Information inequality.* New York: Routledge.

Schramm, W. (1964). *Mass media and national development.* Stanford, CA: Stanford University Press.

Sinclair, J. (1996). Mexico, Brazil, and the Latin world. In S. Cunningham, E. Jacka, & J. Sinclair (Eds.), *New patterns in global television: Peripheral vision* (pp. 33–66). Oxford, England: Oxford University Press.

Sinha, A. (1996). Development dilemmas for Indian television. In D. French & M. Richards (Eds.), *Contemporary television: Eastern perspectives* (pp. 302–320). New Delhi, India: Sage.

Somavia, J. (1976). The transnational power structure and international information. *Development Dialogue, 2,* 15–28.

17

Flows of News from the Middle Kingdom: An Analysis of International News Releases from Xinhua

Charles W. Elliott
Hong Kong Baptist University

Xinhua, the news agency of the People's Republic of China, "is not quite like any other news agency in the world" (Parker, 1975, p. 32; Schramm & Atwood, 1981, p. 111). It is an apparatus of a coordinated government effort to control internal and external information flows. Parker notes that it operates in such an alien way for the Western mind, that to understand the magnitude of the difference between Xinhua and its Western counterparts, one would have to imagine what it would be like if "Reuters were part of the Foreign Office, as if Agence France Presse were hand-in-glove with the Quai d'Orsay, as if the United Press International were the State Department's most valuable section" (p. 32). As such, it is a national news agency that "resists being thought of as a national or 'internal' news service" (Schramm & Atwood, 1981, p. 111). Rather, it consistently considers itself the paramount source of news in China, about China, and from China's perspective. It not only exists to be the chief supplier of China news to China's domestic media, it seeks to enlighten and "distribute news to the length and breadth of the world..." (p. 111).

Xinhua is noteworthy in any discussion of international news for several reasons. In the context of the debates over how and what information is distributed, China's news agency exists as an important alternative to the "Big Four" news agencies that dominate world information flows. Xinhua can also be considered as an international news provider that structures information in a way that exemplifies the national and cultural concerns of the Chinese nation and people. Thus, news is structured with concern for consistency from a unique sociocultural basis that differs greatly from other news perspectives.

To understand the characteristics that make Xinhua distinctly unique as a purveyor of international news, this chapter has been organized into three sections. The first section considers the identity of Xinhua as a news agency and explores its unique character and role. The second section offers an examination of the background in which Xinhua is considered a unique source of international news by considering two theoretical approaches. This section begins with a brief consideration of the problems raised concerning international flows of communication that have led to a demand for alternate news voices in the world marketplace of ideas, a role that Xinhua seems to play. The other theoretical area explores how Xinhua's national and cultural vantage point have an impact on the news it produces by looking at the literature developing the theory of news as narrative and national myth. Finally, in the last section of this chapter, an empirical examination of the international news content of Xinhua is offered to identify how the agency has produced international news, how this changed over time, and the implications this has for an understanding of the evolution of the agency itself and its flow of international news to the world.

THE NEWS AGENCY

Xinhua is the biggest news organization in China. It is directly subordinated to the State Council and is supervised by the Culture Education Office. The content of the agency is carefully controlled by the Chinese Communist Party through its propaganda department (Markham, 1967; Yao, 1963). The agency's headquarters is located in Beijing and is headed by a director general and five deputy directors (Markham, 1967). The directors, along with subordinate department chiefs and their senior executives, comprise the editorial board, which administers the agency. They supervise the General Editorial Office, which in turn controls the day-to-day operation of the agency (Chang, 1989). Personnel in the editorial office are divided into a hierarchy of 30 ranks (Yao, 1963), where each individual is responsible to that director that is superior to him or her in this stratification of organization.

The head office in Beijing has several departments that handle the administration of the organization. These are specific departments that handle the management of the agency as well as its technology. They deal with nonnews-gathering activities and tend to coordinate the operational structure of Xinhua on a domestic basis as well as for the large number of international bureaus the agency maintains. The management of the agency's staff, which numbers more than 5,000, is administered through these departments (Chang, 1989).

Other departments have been designated to administer the content and the flow of the news. In this regard, particular types of news are the responsibility of specific departments. News is segmented into domestic, international, domestic news for international release, and visual or photographic information (Chang, 1989; Howkins, 1982; Yao, 1963). Different departments structure domestic news for international release in a way that is different from the way domestic news is structured for domestic release. This is due to the assumption that foreigners will need the explanatory background that China's own people are quite familiar with from their day-to-day experience with the news (Sinclair, 1986). A department in the agency also exists to deal with foreign news agencies. It coordinates the information from 47 different news organizations that have agreements with Xinhua to provide information (Bishop, 1989). This department primarily gathers news for internal reference. A special department also exists to serve an evaluative function, operating to monitor the performance of the agency in its news operations (Chang, 1989).

Xinhua has several spheres of operation under its control. It has a domestic news-gathering organization as well as an international one (Markham, 1967). The domestic news organization is a hierarchy structure of branches that extend from the national headquarters to the broad based correspondent service at the grassroots level in towns and rural areas (Howkins, 1982).

Internationally, Xinhua's structure is built to enable the Party to have access to current and important information and, historically, to "release news to the whole world in order to compete with the Western capitalist news agencies, break off their news monopoly and blockade, and expand our country's influence" (Yao, 1963, p. 84). From one foreign bureau in 1948, Xinhua has expanded its foreign news network to 90 bureaus with a staff of 400 workers operating outside of China (Lee, 1985). These foreign branches fall into two categories. One type of branch is in countries with which China has diplomatic relations. The other type is in those countries that do not recognize the People's Republic of China or have diplomatic relations with it. In the latter cases, the agency has an important role in acting as the Party's "official" unofficial representative. Bishop (1989, p. 126) notes that all Xinhua correspondents hold diplomatic passports and often "will be found in countries where every other agency has been expelled."

The Function of Xinhua

The role relegated to the Xinhua is one quite different from that which a Western news agency fulfills. Xinhua is considered as fundamental to the survival of the nation as the army (Yao, 1963). In fact, in certain periods of China's history, it has been described as "an army engaged in the ideological struggle" (Markham, 1967, p. 371). Another common metaphor for the agency is that it is the Party's "eyes and tongue" (Yu, 1964, p. 120). This is a description given to the agency's two-fold imperative of coordinating information from the masses to the masses. As the eyes of the Party, it observes what is important to the masses; as the tongue, it takes the Party's message to the masses. Zheng Tao, a former Xinhua director, noted that the agency acted as "a bridge between the Party, the government and the people. It should tell the masses about the Party's policies and also should report to the Central Committee immediately the struggle, the experiences, the demands, and the voices of the masses" (Markham, 1967, p. 21).

Xinhua is commissioned to serve other basic functions internally as well. One role it plays is an informative one: to tell the Chinese people what is happening in the world and in China. As well, the agency is responsible for educating the masses. For example, preparing them to understand the changes that took place in the former Soviet Union to prevent this from affecting Communism in China (Lam, 1991). The agency is also responsible for inspiring the population to strive for the prosperity and development of the nation (Chang, 1989). Xinhua has functioned internally as a potent political tool to be used to gain or regain power at times in China's modern history. While examples of this abound, one telling episode saw Mao using the media to discredit Liu Shao-chi "and to mobilize the masses to seize power from him..." (Liao, 1984, p. 211). All these responsibilities have, at times in recent history, become confusing as journalists within the agency sought to resolve conflicting responsibilities, especially between acting for the Party and for the masses (White, 1979). Yet, when there was any doubt, it was devotion to the Party's interests that always was given the highest priority.

Externally, Xinhua's role is defined somewhat differently. Historically, the external function of Xinhua was "explaining to the world what is happening in China" (Sinclair, 1986, p. 2). In this regard, the agency does take great pains to explain to a world unfamiliar with its particular mindset what is being done and why it is being done. This goes beyond the political to incorporate all aspects of the Chinese world—economic, cultural, and social (Chang, 1989). The agency is also important as a means to express the Chinese position on world affairs. When the changes in Eastern Europe and the Soviet Union influenced the world's interpretation of the Chinese response to a similar attempt at democracy in Tiananmen Square in 1989, China found the agency invaluable to define the events in the world according to its unique perspective. This has been important as China attempts to protect its right to be what it is politically and culturally, and improve its international image as well (Fan, 1990).

China holds to the general mistrust of the Western news agencies expressed by the Third World. The basic concepts of a lack of concern for developing countries and overemphasis of negative events that culminated in the development of the New World Information Order are another *raison d'etre* for Xinhua. China tries to use Xinhua as a balance for the perceived heavy influence of Western news agencies. This has been particularly true in China's coverage of the developing world, which has been enhanced over the years (Parker, 1975). Lee (1985) notes in this regard that:

> China subscribes to the belief that the Western-dominated media distorts the image of developing nations. To balance this distortion Xinhua, for instance, gives heavy coverage to reports on the economics of African countries while the *People's Daily* prints far more news about the Third World and Eastern Bloc nations than it does about Western countries.... (p. 46)

So China acts as an alternate voice in a world it sees as dominated by Western concepts implicit in the news of the Big Four news agencies. And with the collapse of communism in the USSR and Eastern Europe, it appears China's Xinhua will increasingly be unique among all the press agencies delivering news to the world.

A more recent indication for the role of Xinhua that has developed with the increased efforts for modernization is the objective to become a world news agency in the same league with the major agencies of the West (namely AP, AFP, Reuters, and UPI). This is a natural outgrowth of the need for balanced news in the world as expressed in the sentiments noted above. And while efforts to create an agency of international standing began as early as 1957, it was not until Deng Xiao-ping's vision of modernization dominated in Chinese policy that movement toward this type of agency gained momentum. In 1983, Xinhua submitted a report to the Party Central Committee with suggestions that it envisioned would make the agency a worldwide news service with Chinese characteristics in the 1990s. This international news agency would purvey news guided by Marxist-Leninist-Maoist thought that would serve the world's masses, balance the flow of the news, and present greater accuracy of the world's reality (Chang, 1989). While the retrenchment after the Tiananmen incident and the changes in Communism abroad have set back this effort, there is no indication that it will be scrapped altogether.

The Output of Information by Xinhua

What does Xinhua produce? It would be quite easy, and relatively accurate, to say that almost all the mass-mediated news in China is produced by Xinhua. In its early years, the centralized control it presently assumes did not exist (Yu, 1964) and there was much greater diversity in news collection and publication. However, this resulted in problems, as much of what was gathered at the lower levels was inappropriate to the needs of all China as set by the Chinese Communist Party.

Those contributing articles for nationwide publication did not realize "the main function and duty of Xinhua is to engage in propaganda for the whole nation" (Yu, 1964), and most contributions did not meet this criteria. Only about one third of all the material contributed in these early years was usable, the rest served only for reference (Yu, 1964). This inefficiency was eliminated when the relative autonomy of the branches ceased in 1950. Since then there has been, with few exceptions, a flow of news considered appropriate for publication throughout the entire nation. The resulting material is the core of most news publications, which results in a conformity among the media unlike anything in the Western press (Houn, 1958–59; Markham, 1967; White, 1979). In terms of foreign news, regional bureaus have a bit more flexibility. News from parts of a geographical area have only to be cleared through Xinhua's regional desk before being directed to clients. However, in the case of sensitive information, caution dictates that key information goes to Beijing for its approval before being released (Bishop, 1989).

Inside China, Xinhua provides the news to its people but has traditionally defined news much differently than the West does. Timeliness is based on political demands, not proximity to the date of occurrence. This is as much a condition of structural circumstances as political ones, since it is almost impossible to be timely when news has to be approved by authorities before publication (Yao, 1963). In the past, researchers have found the content of the domestic news service tends to move more toward analysis and explanation of events rather than straight presentation of fact. This is not to say that all the elements of Western journalism are absent in the domestic service of Xinhua. They were used, but with much less frequency than in the West and, more importantly, they were used for much different reasons. For example, a hard news approach and timeliness were all part of the trial of the Gang of Four reporting because both these elements were appropriate for the political needs of the time (Chang, 1989). Investigative journalism likewise is employed when reforms of the system that have gone wrong are needed (Chang, 1989).

In general, an important news criterion has been that most news must be devoted to achievements of the nation and be positive in tone. The percentage commonly called for is 70–80 percent success and 20–30 percent critical/negative news (Chang, 1989; Hu, 1986). The stress is on the positive because China believes that there is more of this type of news to publish anyway and it acts to encourage rather than to tear down the system in the minds of the masses. Another reason is to maintain harmony. It is believed that while negative-oriented news may serve to warn of danger or mistakes to be avoided, it may also create havoc in society as it causes the public to panic (Chang, 1989). The idea of harmony and consensus is also important in the concept of democratic centralism, which affects domestic news service. This principle holds that while public policy can be discussed, public support is required for it after a decision has been reached. So, it is important that the news reflects this by the content it presents being one of agreement rather than dissension. Though channels still exist for dissent (for example, letters to the editors of newspapers), once policy is decided the news agency acts as the announcer of the fact. As such, Xinhua reports "have a much greater impact among the people than the Western agencies have among their people" (Chang, 1989, p. 71).

The concept of unity is taken one step further in press releases from Xinhua in that China has consistently portrayed itself as a friend to peace-loving countries who need to take a united stand against the threats to peace posed by other powerful nations (Schramm & Atwood, 1981). Therefore, potential allies against the "warmongers" should not be alienated through any presentation of the news. Schramm and Atwood (1981) note this united front concept permeates Xinhua's press releases. This is another clear example of how unity and harmony are prime news values for Xinhua.

Xinhua's domestic news service has historically presented slightly more domestic information than international news to the people of China. In the past, this has meant about 32,000 words per day of domestic news and 30,000 words per day of international news (Yao, 1963). However, this may be misleading because the qualitative difference may well exceed these quantitative figures. China spends more effort explaining the news of the world to its own people because it assumes that a lack of access to the world at large by most of its people precludes a context from which to understand international news. Similarly, it expends more effort explaining news of China to the world because it does not assume foreign audiences have the context and background to understand China. The principle of assumed ignorance about the processes behind the news in both these cases is the root of the motivation here. This would mean that while the number of words per day of international news to the Chinese public may be similar to the domestic count, in reality the proportion of explanation in the international news to the Chinese masses may cut down the true amount of news allowed to pass through. Parker (1975) seems to indicate this when he notes that very little information from China's correspondents finds its way into the domestic press through Xinhua. He believes this is not due to any widespread effort to keep out foreign information, but rather based on the "genuine assumption that the Chinese population at large has better things to do than get involved in the rest of the world's problems" (p. 32). The interpretative element, which not only explains international news but considers what is appropriate for the people of China to be involved in, takes its toll on the amount and type of foreign news available to domestic receivers of Xinhua information.

Chang Won Ho (1989) gives a complete overview of the foreign news selection in China, breaking it into four basic components: gathering news, selecting news, translating news, and releasing the news. Gathering the foreign news by Xinhua takes the same style and form as it does in any news agency. Xinhua journalists attend press conferences and conduct interviews to gain information like any of their Western counterparts would do. This material is then sent to local subscribers as well as sent back to Beijing (Sinclair, 1986). The criteria that motivates the way a reporter determines what is news, however, is different than that used by a reporter from AP or Reuters. Chang (1989) notes four basic Xinhua criteria:

1. **Precedent**—what was considered newsworthy in the recent past. ("Recent" is a key concept here, as political situations can change the criteria in this regard even overnight.)
2. **Instruction**—what types of news the journalists are told to gather by their superiors.
3. **Specialized topics**—news specific to the needs of a particular department, such as sports or science, may give guidelines for what is important news on a more detailed basis.
4. **China-related news**—information about other countries' relationship to China is always considered newsworthy (Chang, 1989, p. 74).

News coming into Xinhua headquarters is checked by junior editors and then sent on to editors who cover specific topics or geographical regions. These gate-keepers make the major decisions as to what news is published. These editors also consider whether the news item will be of interest to those subscribing to the Xinhua service, whether it fits the standards set by the government in each evening's editorial meeting, whether it fits the nature of news Xinhua has set as the official guardian of Chinese policy, and whether other editors would agree it meets a high level of newsworthiness (Chang, 1989).

Some of the information China needs about international conditions cannot be obtained from their own correspondents. While the agency does have a sizable number of journalists stationed throughout the world, it doesn't have the resources for broad coverage like the Big Four news agencies. As a result, Xinhua has had to use the press releases from the foreign news agencies from which they make their own translations (Boyd-Barrett, 1980). In addition to receiving information from the Big Four, Xinhua has also taken information from agencies such as DPA, ANSA, PTI, Kyoto, MENA, and Tanjug. The Chinese agency also subscribed to Tass, but this source of news, while significant in China's early years, decreased in importance over time (Markham, 1967). Translations from all these sources are a major part of Xinhua's responsibility in the Chinese news system. Data from all the sources of information is often consolidated to create a news item that is unidentifiable from one source but rather "reflects the opinion of the Xinhua News Agency" (Chang, 1989, p. 75). Even in the process of translation, the news becomes a conscious reflection of policy set from above for Xinhua.

Finally, all the news, foreign and domestic, is released in two basic forms. One is through the wire service that operates 24 hours a day. The wire service distributes the news to domestic subscribers and releases it to Xinhua branches all over the world as well (Chang, 1989). News is transmitted via a Chinese-language general wire (for domestic and international news for the major publications within China) at a rate of about 50,000 words per day (Chang, 1989; "Fifty Militant Years," 1981; Howkins, 1982). Another Chinese-language wire provides domestic and international news to media at the provincial or regional level at a rate of about 30,000 to 40,000 words per day (Yao, 1963). A wire carrying foreign-language news for overseas clients delivers 60,000 to 100,000 words per day (combined) in English, French, Russian, Spanish, and Arabic (Chang, 1989; Howkins, 1982). A photo service issuing many pictures through the wire and an overseas feature service are also part of Xinhua's transmitted news service (Chang, 1989; "Fifty Militant Years," 1980; Markham, 1967).

The other basic form by which the news is released through Xinhua is by means of a publication service. Xinhua news bulletins are published in Beijing once daily in six languages (Chang, 1989). Xinhua produces other publications that are also quite important. *Reference News* is a tabloid newspaper that carries translations of foreign news dispatches and is available only to authorized Chinese citizens (Rudolph, 1984). Another important publication is called *Reference Materials (Cankao Ziliao)*. It is a much more restricted publication for the use of upper-level Party members and government officials. This report is much more candid and provides more representative information from foreign news services (Markham, 1967; Rudolph, 1984). A top secret news sheet, called *Internal Reference*, is the most restrictive of all Xinhua news documents and is provided to high ranking members of the leadership of China. While little is definitely known about this publication, most scholars believe that Xinhua is behind its production because no other organization is equipped with the structure or access to create such a thing (Markham, 1967; Yao, 1963). Besides these publications, Xinhua also produces a newsphoto magazine, an economic magazine, several political periodicals, a general information publication, and a general photographic magazine (Chang, 1989).

With the rise of Deng Xiao-ping, the style and content of the press releases of Xinhua, both foreign and domestic, saw many changes. Efforts have been made to remedy the ill effects that the Cultural Revolution wrought on the agency and establish greater credibility for the official voice of the People's Republic of China. One of the more positive changes was that the form of the writing became less pedantic. Releases in general tended "to be better written, more concise, free of party dogma, and comparably straight-forward when covering the bread and butter issues of the day" (Sinclair, 1986, p. 2). One commentator noted this change by observing that "while its output couldn't be described as 'racy,' it is at least readable" (Lewis, 1985, p. 13). In content, changes have been made to provide more accuracy and objectivity than in the past (Bishop, 1989; Chang, 1989). Now, material included in Xinhua releases includes topics that "never would have seen the light of day before the open door policies of Deng Xiao-ping swept away the old bans" (Sinclair, 1986, p. 2).

Yet while great strides in the output of Xinhua have been made, some problems remain. Observers note that despite reforms that were initiated in the 1980s, some problems of the Cultural Revolution era still haunt the agency. Factual errors continue to be rationalized in order to promote a perceived greater good of unity and collectivism (Mulligan, 1988). Despite the commitment China and Xinhua express toward dealing with potentials of the Third World (Chang, 1989), the press releases are often found to use creative news writing in order to save face or maintain harmony. For example, Faison (1991) reported the case of an African student who was amazed to read in the Chinese press that he had apologized for creating racial tensions when he was a university student in China. The African denied both his guilt and the alleged apology, saying that he had never spoken to a Xinhua reporter. Other problems in factual reporting include the deliberate undercounting of figures related to disaster information and the rewording of news to create heroic impressions of people involved in events transpiring in Chinese news (Mulligan, 1988). More subtle manipulation is found in the changing of dates of news from foreign news sources, restructuring headlines, and selectively presenting foreign news reports to fit propaganda themes (Rudolph, 1984).

THEORETICAL BACKGROUND

Flows of Information

In order to understand the significance Xinhua has as a news source, it is important to examine the context in which it operates as an alternate source of international news. The call for alternate news voices is generally traced to the period following World War II when an increasingly vocal group of developing countries asserted that Western media had created a one-way flow of news from the developed countries to the developing world. This group of developing countries petitioned UNESCO for the establishment of domestic news agencies in order to protect their local cultures and provide a better balance of information. The developing countries' complaints were summarized in a United Nations document called the MacBride Report, which noted that while many developing countries did have their own national news agencies, "they often have meager resources—material, technical or staff—so that their supply of news must be supplemented by outside material. For this reason...the mass media in such countries still depend mainly on news selected and transmitted by larger, outside agencies" (*Many Voices, One World*, 1980, p. 97). This was a sore point.

Basically, the developing countries' resentment originated from three main issues concerning this inequity in the flow of information. The first issue was that the developing countries claimed the Western news agencies were disrupting the flow of news. "News flows tend towards a north-south direction and inhibit development of exchanges between developing countries themselves" (*Many Voices, One World*, 1980, p. 144). The developing countries wanted the flow of news to flow *from* it as evenly as it flows *to* it. This then was seen as a problem of *distribution*.

The West historically has dominated the flow of international news. In this regard, four Western news agencies carry the bulk of the world's news. Between them, the four agencies send out "34 million words per day and claim to provide nine-tenths of the entire foreign news output of the free world's newspapers, radio, and television stations. The AP alone claims to reach one-third of the world every day"

(Smith, 1980, p. 73). As one observer puts it, U.S. news agencies possess the means "to submerge the entire press of the Third World" (Gauhar, 1981/82, p. 172). The developing countries found themselves in the awkward position of looking to Western nations for stories about other developing nations as seen through the eyes of journalists and gatekeepers in New York, Paris, and London (Rosenblum, 1979).

Examples of imbalance abound. Developing countries, with 68 percent of the population, receive 10–30 percent of the total news devoted to them (*Many Voices, One World,* 1980). UPITN news transmits 150 stories to Asia each month, yet it takes only an average of 20 from this region (*Many Voices, One World,* 1980). "AP sends out on its general world wire service to Asia from New York an average of 90,000 words daily. In return, Asia files 19,000 words to New York for worldwide distribution" (*Many Voices, One World,* 1980, p. 146). Historically, the data on news flows has justified the developing world's criticism of unbalanced news flows.

The second issue raised by the developing countries was the claim that the West was distorting the realities of the developing world, both to the world as a whole and to the developing nations themselves. The distorted image comes from a stereotyped presentation. This complaint considered the impact of the *effect.* Evidence supporting this notion can be seen in the fact that the transfer of media from one culture to another has been found to exert a significant impact on lifestyles (Katz, 1977), the family (Kent, 1985), personality (Balbontin-Arteaga, 1982; Granzberg, 1985; Knoll, 1981; Newton & Buck, 1985), and acculturation (Iverson, 1976; Rada, 1978), to name but a few areas. In addition, work on cultural indicators also demonstrates the impact of media flows on cultural standards (Pingree & Hawkins, 1981; Tan, Tan, & Tan, 1987; Zohoori; 1988).

As well, the impact of incoming media products on the domestic media can be seen in the literature. Anderson (1981) notes the Chinese reaction to Western advertising was to copy it almost immediately. Guback (1969) and Tunstall (1977) both illustrated how the historical development and the spread of the film industry affected local filmmaking in countries around the world. Varis (1984), by implication, notes the impact of television due to the flow of American programming that inexpensively fills broadcast time.

The final issue raised by the developing countries was the assertion that the West was presenting a negative image of underdeveloped countries. The developing countries wanted to see a balance of good news with bad news. The focus in this regard was on the *content.* The developing countries found that too much emphasis was placed on events instead of the context of the situation and most of the news was negative in its focus. Instead, they said, there should be more consideration given to the presentation of progress.

News of development is something Western news coverage by definition does not do. The Western definition of news "...tends to oblige Western journalists to seek the aberrational rather than the normal as the main criterion for selection; Western news agencies are, therefore, on the lookout for information concerning violence, war, crime, corruption, disaster, famine, fire, and flood" (Smith, 1980, p.

70). A former head of the Associated Press says that the Western press situation traditionally emphasizes "the dramatic, the emotional, and the amusing—the 'coups and earthquakes syndrome'—[and this] is seen not only as unbalanced but detrimental to the development process" (Rosenblum, 1979, p. 245).

Another complaint by developing countries along these lines was that the Western press tended to portray them in a bad way. This kind of news is dangerous for the developing country because it tends to strip them of their self-worth and national identity (Skurnik, 1981). Often this is done by means of negative stereotypes (Rubin, 1977). Studies of the contents of mass media flows have addressed this to a limited degree. Stressing media literacy to correct the problems of negative stereotypes, Gumbert and Cathcart (1983) note that teaching people to interpret media images of foreigners is as important as direct contact with foreigners.

There seems to be a growing awareness that media cannot legitimately be transferred from one culture to another without regard for cultural considerations. Mayo, Oliveira, Rogers, Guimaraes, and Morett (1984) considered the trouble with creating a Latin American Sesame Street and determined that basics of education could not simply be transferred directly because of the differences in educational methods, value priorities, and lifestyle varieties in the cultures among the nations of Latin America. Katz (1979) echoes this concept as well when he writes, "There is a need to link media with other arts, traditional and modern, from which ideas will flow" and do so in a manner that accommodates social and national backgrounds and traditions (p. 80).

Given this overall situation, many suggestions were offered to create greater equity in the global flow of information. One method put forward to resolve this was to strengthen alternate voices providing information about the world to the world through the establishment of cooperative news organizations (Many Voices, One World, 1980). Another solution proffered was to establish national news agencies for developing countries that did not have them. It was believed that "strong national news agencies are vital for improving each country's national and international reporting" (Many Voices, One World, 1980, p. 255).

In this regard, a great deal of attention was placed on those countries with well-established information organizations for the transmission of international news. Many countries looked to the People's Republic of China as an example of a country providing news from an alternate perspective to the dominant West. Yet how much different was the news distributed by China's news agency, Xinhua? How did this provider of news evolve over time and what was the impact of that evolution on the news of the world it offered? These questions require a closer look at Xinhua to determine how this particular voice of international communication operates and the contribution it makes to providing an alternate perspective on the world's news.

News as National Myth

The concept of news carrying more than simply facts has been evolving in the area of study that evaluates news as narrative. Key to this perspective is the idea that "Journalists do not write articles. They write stories" (Bell, 1991, p. 147). As a story, news presentations exhibit "a structure, direction, point, and viewpoint (p. 147). Scholars considering the news from a narrative perspective have found that the news is "orienting, communal, and ritualistic" (Bird & Dardenne, 1988, p. 70), but above all, it is not a natural but a cultural formulation.

Seeing news as stories created in a cultural context allows two important insights to be gained from an examination of Xinhua as an international news source. The first links to the discussion of news flow, specifically to the question of the appropriateness of news constructed in one culture transmitted to another. While news as storytelling is universal, there is growing evidence that different cultures retell stories in quite different ways (Bartlett, 1932; Bird & Dardenne, 1988; Mander, 1987; Rice, 1980). So, not only the content of the news, but its very context as well may be flowing from one country to another.

Considering news as narrative is also valuable to apply to the consideration of Xinhua because, as seen in the discussion of this news agency's structure and function, it has a unique nature and position as the national voice of the People's Republic of China. This role creates an organization that produces news for external distribution to explain "not only what has been going on in China, but also to give the Chinese perspective on world events" (Chang, 1989; Fan, 1990; Sinclair, 1986). Xinhua can be examined as creating news stories that instruct the world of its interpretation of events by the way it tells its news stories.

The study of news as narrative is an area of research that is increasingly important among communication scholars who are asking deeper questions about journalism and its practice (Zelizer, 1997). Narrative has moved from the domain of "literary specialists or folklorists borrowing their terms from psychology and linguistics...[to]... become a positive force of insight for all branches of human and natural sciences" (Mitchell, 1981, p. ix). From this perspective comes the insight that news is not just a recounting of facts or a "neutral conveyor of reality," but a retelling of current events "through the aid of enduring folklore" (Berkowitz, 1997, p. 323). Viewing news as narrative "casts media in the role of myth-constructor, selectively forming a coherent narrative from journalists' reading of events" (Carey & Fritzler, 1989, p. 2).

Fitting current events into the form of a story is not without its problems. The story form has requirements that may be artificial for events covered as news. White (1981, p. 23) notes in this regard that there is a "desire to have real events display the coherence, integrity, fullness and closure" that real life does not always allow. The real world does not fit neatly into story form. Stories, for example, have definite endings and putting news into story form, some scholars note, often forces an artificial type of closure on the news being reported. Researchers studying the narrative nature of the news show this by noting that "at the heart of the practice of reporting the news, of translating real events into narrative, lies a moral impulse" (Mander, 1987, p. 54). White (1981) affirms this, saying, "The moral makes the story complete [and]...distinguishes a narrative from a chronicle" (pp. 5–6). Examining this process of creating news in a story form reveals not only how the tale is told, but also tells a great deal about the narrator of the story. For, while news reports may purport to reflect or mirror the world at large, in reality they represent a selected consideration of particular facts (Mander, 1987) that define reality and make it comprehensible to the audience (Gans, 1979; Gitlin, 1980; Tuchman, 1978).

The study of news as story can enhance the understanding of international news in many ways. Understanding the retelling of stories provides insights into the legitimacy of the narrator (Zelizer, 1993). As well, it informs of the efforts at consistency taken to provide news that is consonant with the pervasive ideology of the social context as well as the underlying philosophy of the publication itself (Carragee, 1990; Lentz, 1989; Seeger, 1989). Finally, it provides insights about the current state of conditions in which the narration takes place. As Zelizer (1997) notes, "Narrative helps us explain journalism by stressing elements that are formulaic, patterned, finite, yet mutable over time. In this sense, news as narrative offers analysts a way to account for change within predictable and defined patterns of news presentation" (p. 26).

While storytelling is one of the "most universal means of representing human events" (Bennett & Edelman, 1985, p. 156), certain narratives have been found to occur more frequently than others (Smith, 1997). Bennett and Edelman note that a list of common narrative plots in the U.S. media have included the treachery of lying Communists, the immorality of criminals, and the aversion to work found in welfare recipients. Not only are some themes more prevalent than others, but narrative themes differ in different contexts as well. Pisarek (1983) found that in the socialist press, themes surrounding work, organization, nationality, and planning were most prevalent, while in capitalist contexts, the focus was on money, government, business, and the market. So, the stories that are created as news and told most often reflect the specific characteristics of the people and place in which they are constructed.

News as narrative comes in many formats, and can include types such as "fairy tales, fables, parables, gospels, epics, and sagas" (Bell, 1991, p. 147). One form of narrative that is particularly relevant to the understanding of news production is the myth. From a narrative perspective, myth is defined as a distinctive form of expression referring to "any real or fictitious story, recurring theme or character type that appeals to the consciousness of a group by embodying its cultural ideas or giving expression to deep commonly felt emotions" (Chapman & Egger, 1983, p. 167). Myths have a reassuring effect on a specific people "by telling tales that explain baffling frightening phenomena and provide acceptable answers" (Bird & Dardenne, 1988, p. 70).

Myths are appropriated based on relevancy. As Chapman and Egger (1983) note, mythical content emerges as it fits the interactional needs of a people. Myths vary in content from one culture to another, based upon one particular group of people's particular need to retell the deep meaning of a particular myth (Chapman & Egger, 1983). Not only is a theme recast in terms appropriate to the cultural group (Silverstone, 1988), it must also have relevance to that group's needs at that particular time in order to be appropriated at all. So, myths, like other symbolic configurations, are valuable "to find an entrance point into a culture" (Bird & Dardenne, 1988, p. 75), and to open up an understanding of that people.

Media have been identified as carrying a national mythology in its context. In an essay along these lines, Auge and Callan (1986) relate that the common basis of Western civilization gives rise to a mythology in mass media products to which nations sharing the same civilization heritage can readily relate. By looking at the mythic aspects, the dominance of capitalistic and imperialistic emphasis is reduced. Breen (1986) also considered this in terms of the Australian audience. In this study, it was the unique mythology of Australia that separated it from the products of other English-speaking countries. The Australian audience had their own myths that were meaningful to them. Mediated communication that incorporated those myths was found to be more popular with this local audience than the foreign imports. Hamilton (1975) used this means to examine children's books and found myths that embodied important Australian themes. Dorfman and Mattelart (1975) also considered mythical elements and themes in their classic study of comic books. Drummond (1984) looked at myth in movies and focused on it as a "metaphorical device for telling people about themselves, about other people, and about the complex world of natural and mechanical objects which they inhabit" (p. 27).

News, as a mediated form of communication is particularly relevant to study from the mythic perspective. Since it contains potentially volatile information, news is easier to accept and digest when "journalists use myths as a 'skeleton on which to hang the flesh of the news story,' casting new occurrences around the frameworks they have learned in the past" (Berkowitz, 1997, p. 322). News provides not mere fact, but "reassurance and familiarity in shared community experiences" (Bird & Dardenne, 1988, p. 70). Mythical narratives of news hold all the characteristics of narrative approaches considered previously. Myths "facilitate and constrain the telling of social narratives" (Berkowitz, 1997, p. 323). They create reality as they strive not to "tell it like it is," but rather to "tell it like it means" (Bird & Dardenne, 1988, p. 71). News is thus a unique type of "mythological narrative with its own symbolic codes that are recognized by its audience" (p. 70–71). Myths do not start from scratch when needs arise, but rather are maintained in a cultural storehouse to be withdrawn when they are needed (Berkowitz, 1997; Bird & Dardenne, 1988). Archetypal stories are evident as journalists cloak each day's news in forms that resonate with the audience (Bird & Dardenne, 1988).

Therefore it is important in the study of international news to examine the way media carry national mythology in context. From this perspective, what is revealed is how a particular group of people embody the themes and values important to them at a particular point in time in their news representations. This concept of national myth has been defined as the way human history is recast to represent a nation's self image and its place in the world (Starr, 1973). Kluver (1996) further develops the idea of a national mythology as a form of narrative that informs and upholds a people's social sense of themselves. Along these lines he notes:

> The national myth provides a national and social identity for a nation and its people, thereby establishing the transcendence necessary for legitimation. The myth establishes identity for a people based on their most salient values, an identity distinct from other nations. (pp. 18–19)

Kluver uses the concept of the national myth to explain the social changes in China since the mid-1970s. He illustrates how the national myth of liberation has been reworked in recent times from a political basis to a more economic basis. For, "in order to implement reform policies, the Chinese Communist Party had to reconstruct the dominant political myth to a version that would allow room for the nation to experiment with quasi-capitalistic practices" (p. 21). Throughout the modifications to the national myth, it retained two key features: "the inevitable progression of history and epic characters who serve as authorizing figures" (p. 32).

Kluver's (1996) research considers national myth by examining documents from the Chinese Communist Party and makes a compelling case for the importance of the narrative in understanding the context of contemporary China. The same arguments might also be made in consideration of the news from China. For the way that international news is constructed by Xinhua will not merely present facts, but the themes and values embodied in the structure of the stories that are relevant to China at different points in its history.

INTERNATIONAL NEWS IN XINHUA'S PRESS RELEASES

How then can we understand the contribution Xinhua makes to the distribution of international news? This descriptive research effort seeks to understand the international news content in the press releases of Xinhua of the People's Republic of China and to understand how this content has evolved over time. In this regard, it seeks to fill a gap in the literature on the news of China by looking at a broad picture of evolving journalism instead of specific and limited periods, as has been the case in much of the previous attempts in this vein. Much of the research conducted in the past has drawn its analysis from periodicals or publications that in turn take their information from the dominant well of news information in the PRC: Xinhua. This research goes directly to that source for its analysis of news because it represents the full range of information considered acceptable, given the news selection criteria in effect at different times in China. By examining the releases from Xinhua, the widest range of news is available for examination before the gatekeeping processes of specific publications weed through to select that which they need to publish and that which is optional. Press releases then give the potential to gain a more realistic picture of what is considered international news from China's perspective.

This study sought to determine if there was consistency or evolution over time in the way international news was deemed worthy for presentation by China's news agency. Historically it is important to evaluate how a country's news evolves and to consider the implications on the flows of information to the rest of the world. Important as well is the consideration of the major story themes and patterns and how they develop over time to provide evidence about the national mythology of China. The news to be analyzed in this particular study comes from the international press releases (in English) of China's Xinhua News Agency. Xinhua is considered to be the ultimate definer at any particular time of what is considered to be news from a Chinese context and by what standards that news should be selected. To examine this over a period of time will exhibit the direction in which these standards have moved and thus a better understanding of the press of China.

Several assumptions informed this research. As the official news agency of China, Xinhua was believed to represent the official priorities of the State and the Party. Also, it was assumed that there is a logical and reasonable method for the selection of news in China and that given proper methodological safeguards and cultural sensitivity, this process of cross-cultural communication could be understood. Given these assumptions, this research was deemed possible to accomplish with constant advice and consultation with Chinese news experts in order to avoid as much Western cultural bias as possible.

As the literature review indicates, there is much to be learned about China from its media output, since it is officially controlled and therefore reflects the official viewpoints of those in control. This research sought to examine how international news concepts have evolved from the beginning of the People's Republic of China through the decade of the 1980s. It was believed that this 40-year period contained periods of transition that will be reflected in the press content. With this in mind, the basic research questions that inform this research are:

RQ1: What is the nature of international news content from China from 1949 to 1989?
RQ2: How does this change over time?
RQ3: How was the national myth defined in the news stories over time?

Method

Ten content categories were used to examine international news releases for four time periods representing two years from each decade of China's first 40 years. In addition to providing basic descriptive information to answer the research questions, the data collected was also used to understand something about

Xinhua as a news agency distributing international news, and how China through this agency provides an alternate voice to the other major sources of global information.

Content analysis was the method selected as appropriate to these research goals. As an empirical method of research, content analysis assigns "numerical values to various characteristics of individuals, objects, or events through the use of a set of criteria called measurement" (Budd, Thorpe, & Donohew, 1967, p. 31). For consistency, reliability, and generality, the areas of quantification must be clearly defined. In this regard, two units of measurement must be carefully delineated: the unit of analysis and the unit of enumeration.

In this research, the unit of analysis selected was the individual news item presented in the English press releases of Xinhua. Xinhua releases the news each day through a wire service that operates 24 hours a day. The wire service distributes the news to Xinhua branches all over the world. The news item is the individual story carried in the press release each day. The numbers of these news items varies over time. In the early years of the People's Republic, the individual news items were fewer in number than in more recent years. A complete collection of Xinhua press releases in English from 1949 to the present is contained in the University Service Center at the Chinese University of Hong Kong. The unit of enumeration used in this research was frequency.

To understand how China constructed its international news in concrete form and how this news fits in the international context, basic information was gathered about what was presented in the press releases of Xinhua over time. Categories that identified key characteristics defined in the literature were selected from previous research in order to upgrade reliability and validity measures as well as to enable comparisons in the findings. In some cases, categories were created from the literature to measure simply whether a concept was apparent in the press release or not. The content categories used in this research were employed to determine content traits such as time orientation, positive/negative orientation, objectivity, conflict orientation, function, contextualization, dominant actor, topic of the story, and the primary country of origin. As noted in the literature review, all these concepts help define aspects of the news that are considered vital by different news systems or have been at the heart of the criticism regarding international news flows. The content categories were used to measure these factors in order to describe what China's international news has contained in these categories for a better under-standing of how it compares and contrasts to other world services and how it has changed over time.

The sample for this study was defined as all press release items dispatched in English for international distribution by Xinhua during the period from January 1, 1950, to December 31, 1989. Because large time blocks of press releases (1960–1966; 1969–1976) were unavailable for sampling, two years' worth of press releases from each decade were randomly sampled to examine for this study. These years were 1957–1958, 1967–1968, 1977–1978, and 1987–1988. While it was recognized that these two-year time periods could not possibly represent the dynamics of the entire decade from whence they were taken, they were considered valuable indicators for the longitudinal analysis of this study.

Given the extent of the evaluation in this research, 4 percent of the sample was selected as a manageable proportion that still provided an adequate sample size for the classification of this material. This represents approximately 15 days per year to be considered. According to Stempel (1952), as few as six days in a sample to represent a year was sufficient for legitimate generalization and "that increasing the sample sizes beyond twelve does not produce marked differences in the results" (p. 333). However, 15 was the number selected for each year, despite Stempel's assertion that smaller numbers of randomly selected subjects were legitimate because, as Kerlinger (1973) notes, larger numbers allow randomness the opportunity to work. Random sampling was employed to select the dates in which the news items transmitted would be analyzed.

This research, focusing only on international news from Xinhua during these time periods, was part of a larger study that examined China's total news picture. International news releases were identified and isolated from that larger study for analysis in this study. A total of 4,764 international news items were evaluated from the four time periods. Out of a total of 9,298 news items, this represented about 51 percent of all news items presented by China's national news agency in the four periods studied.

Krippendorff (1980) notes there are three kinds of reliability that must be considered in regards to content analysis: stability, reproducibility, and accuracy. *Stability* is consistency by the same coder over time. Changes may occur in the coder (Weber, 1990) due to many factors, such as ambiguous coding rules, ambiguous text, changes in the thinking of the coder, or simple errors. *Reproducibility* is consistency of coding by more than one coder. This is often referred to as *intercoder reliability*. In order to establish reliability of this study, intracoder and intercoder reliability were evaluated. As a result of this evaluation, both intra- and intercoder reliability levels exceeding the standard .80 level of acceptability were established.

Validity is a concept that demands researchers ask the question: Are you testing what you think you're testing? Budd, Thorpe, and Donohew (1967) note that this consideration is vital, and that "whoever is concerned with scientific inquiry, and not mere purposeless exercises, must give considerable attention to methods of validation" (p. 69). Validity for content analysis can be assessed by a variety of means. This research used the jury method, whereby the material for both the method and the categories of assessment were submitted to a panel of judges for their consideration of whether the means used to study values and content were appropriate, accurate, and comprehensive.

After their consideration of these areas, the comments from the panel of judges were implemented into the research method and categories. To further insure that the categories were indeed testing what was intended, a test of the coding sheet was conducted on a press release not included in the sample. Problems discovered in this exercise were noted and changes to the categories or method were then implemented. A guide book with each content category and a detailed definition was constructed for training and reference of the coders.

Findings

Evolution of Xinhua's international news content
This research sought to explore the content of the international news from Xinhua over a 40-year time period. To do this, a total of 4,764 press releases were considered across the time frame of this research. Table 17.1 indicates the number of press releases for each decade. The first decade of the People's Republic of China shows a large number of press releases were issued on the topic of international news. During the 1950s, 71 percent of all items released were about international news events. This figure dropped dramatically in the 1960s when international news represented 47 percent of all news items. The 1970s showed an increase once again when 64 percent of all stories had an international focus, but dropped once more in the 1980s to 41 percent of all news items, the lowest percentage of all four periods.

Ten content factors were considered. These were: currency of the news item (measuring how soon after the event the news was transmitted), time orientation of the news (whether the news was predominantly about the past, present, or future), geographical orientation (what region of the world the news was from), positive/negative orientation of the news, harmony/conflict orientation of the news, function of the news, context (whether the news was set in context or an isolated incident), major topic, dominant actor, and whether an outside source was cited. Each of these factors was compared across the four periods examined in this study

TABLE 17.1.
Number of Press Releases by Decades

	1950s	1960s	1970s	1980s
Total number of press releases sampled	2058	661	1328	5251
Number of internat'l news items	1467	309	849	2142
Average number of news items per day	76	23	47	219
Average number of internat'l news items per day	54	11	30	89
Internat'l news items % of the total	71.3%	46.7%	63.9%	40.8%

to explore changes that have taken place in the transmission of international news from Xinhua. Differences statistically significant at the .001 level of probability were discovered on each variable across all four time periods.

Currency of the news was defined as the amount of time between the news event and the news report. A number of interesting findings appear when a comparison of the concept of currency across these periods is made. First, in all periods, most of the international news issued by Xinhua came two days after the event. This fluctuated across periods, but never dipped below one third of all news items and in two periods accounted for 43 percent of all international news releases. When combined with items that came three days after the event, an even greater proportion of all international news reports is accounted for in these findings. In the 1950s, 71 percent of all international news reports were released 2 to 3 days after the event occurred. This number decreased to 61 percent of all international news in the 1960s. The percentage rose slightly in the 1970s and continued to rise to 79 percent of all international news items in the 1980s.

Another important finding was that while very few news items of international news were released in each period the day after the event (less than 3.5 percent in each period, and as low as .3 percent in the 1970s and 1980s), some news was reported the very day it occurred. Again, this varied in frequency by period (9 percent in the 1950s, 16 percent in the 1960s, 14 percent in the 1970s, and 10 percent in the 1980s), but there is evidence that some of the news from the world was considered important enough to publish without the process of passing through the system of gatekeepers to slow it down.

Finally, most news was transmitted within five days of its occurrence. In all periods, the percentage of international news released five days after the event decreased dramatically. Interestingly, eight days after the event in all periods except the 1980s, there is a slight jump in the frequency of news items released. This is especially true for the 1960s, when 7.4 percent of all international news items were released at this time. It is almost as if one week passed after the event and then the proper spin could be determined for it to fit in the news mix established during this time. It must be remembered too that this period of the 1960s represents a time beset by problems of the Cultural Revolution. As such, this time lag might be due in part to changing political contexts from which to structure the news.

Another factor considered in this research was whether international news was oriented on the past, present, or future. In all periods, as might be expected, the international news was oriented toward the present. This was the highest in the 1970s period (95 percent of all cases), but then dropped to a low for all periods of 69 percent in the 1980s. During the 1980s period, there was a greater percentage of international news that was linked to the past (21 percent of all items) or linked to the future (9 percent of all items) than in other periods. This time period was one of relative stability in China and thus would allow the luxury of considering news in a broader sense rather than simply the events of the day. The 1950s were somewhat similar in this orientation to different times, but not to the extent of the

TABLE 17.2.
Geographic Regions in China's International News

	1950s	1960s	1970s	1980s
Africa	11	16	141	231
Asia	703	150	310	674
E. Europe	244	39	53	161
W. Europe	122	18	109	270
S. America	36	11	83	115
Mid-East	220	16	80	218
N. America	76	45	27	250
Oceania	9	8	13	51
Multiple	46	4	33	132
N/A	0	2	0	40
Total	1467	309	849	2142

n=4767

1980s. The 1960s and 1970s, however, show a different result. The 1960s did not have international news stories that looked forward. There was, however, a large proportion of international news coverage that considered past events (18 percent of all cases). This once again might be explained by the tenor of the times. Criticism of the past was a part of the Cultural Revolution and world events were no less victim to this process as well. This situation decreased dramatically in the 1970s, where the attention was turned almost exclusively to the events of the present.

Where in the world did China turn its attention in international news over these four decades? Table 17.2 illustrates this by considering the frequency of international news by region across the four periods examined. What is readily apparent is that when China covered the world, it did so most frequently by looking in its own backyard. Of all the regions where news was covered, Asia consistently received the highest frequency of news attention from Xinhua. However, this coverage decreased consistently in each decade from the 1960s, when it was at an all-time high. During the 1960s, almost half of all the international news was from Asia. This dropped to a little more than one third in the 1970s and a further five percentage points in the 1980s. While proximity still is important in the coverage of international news, it decreases after the 1960s. This seems to indicate that Xinhua is broadening its horizons geographically in its presentation of the world news.

The patterns of coverage of other regions fluctuate across time. Some areas (Africa and Latin America) show a continual increase from the 1950s to the 1970s and then drop off in the 1980s. Perhaps this is due to China's role as a leader of the Third World and then growing emergence as a contender with the other major

TABLE 17.3.
Positive/Negative Orientation in China's International News

	1950s	1960s	1970s	1980s
Positive	788	121	686	1141
Negative	588	163	155	641
Neither	91	25	8	360
Total	1467	309	849	2142

n=4767

powers that it may have competed with in the 1980s. Other regions (like North America, Oceania, and Western Europe) go up and down over time. News from the Middle East fluctuates, decreasing from the 1950s to the 1960s, then gradually increasing over the next two decades.

What is most interesting about the findings on this variable across time is the consistency in spreading the news coverage across geographical areas. In contrast with the distribution by area of the major international news agencies, this is a relatively even distribution across areas. The complaint, going back to before the MacBride Report, but clearly stated within it, said that the Third World, with 68 percent of the population, received 10–30 percent of the total news devoted to them (*Many Voices, One World*, 1980). UPI TV news transmitted 150 stories to Asia each month, but took only an average of 20 from this region (*Many Voices, One World*, 1980). Thus, to see North America and Western Europe in the 1980s receive less than a quarter of all news story focus from Xinhua, while Asia, Africa, and Latin America received almost half the news attention is a stark contrast. Granted, some parts of the developing world, like Latin America, still receive less coverage than the countries of the West, even in this distribution. But there is not the traditional overwhelming inattention to vast portions of the globe evident in the Big Four news agency releases.

Another variable studied in this research was whether the news was predominantly positive or negative in tone. This was considered important since the Western definition of news "...tends to oblige Western journalists to seek the aberrational rather than the normal as the main criterion for selection" (Smith, 1980, p. 70). A former head of the Associated Press says that the Western press situation traditionally emphasizes "the dramatic, the emotional, and the amusing—the 'coups and earthquakes syndrome'..." (Rosenblum, 1979, p. 245). How the Chinese news agency contrasted in this regard was considered an important area to explore.

The findings on this variable show a great deal of fluctuation over the time period considered in this research, as Table 17.3 indicates. In the 1950s, the balance was almost 60/40 for positive/negative news. This reversed in the 1960s, so that positive news was the orientation for 40 percent of the international press coverage, while just over half the stories were negative. The turmoil and uncertainty of the Cultural Revolution surely must be credited with giving China a dark view of the world at this point in time.

The 1970s had the highest percentage of positive news. Eighty-one percent of all international news stories had a positive orientation compared with less than one-fifth of stories with a negative orientation. This was the era when China opened its doors to the world once again and therefore this dramatic, positive orientation may reflect overcompensation in doing that. It can be seen that by the 1980s, this positive orientation had dropped to just above half of all international news stories presented. This is still a large proportion, especially in comparison with Western news agencies. In the 1980s, it is interesting to note that a large number of stories were not found to emphasize either a positive or negative orientation. Almost 17 percent of all international news stories released by Xinhua in this time period were either not concerned with either of these orientations, or balanced so that neither was dominant. This represents a significant change in the way Xinhua structured its content in the distribution of world news. Also interesting is that only one of these periods (the 1970s) had the prescribed balance of 80 percent positive orientation (Chang, 1989) achieved in the international news releases.

Similar to the concept of positive/negative orientation to the news was the variable in this research that considered the concept of harmony versus conflict. As this research explored an Asian context, this variable was included because the importance of harmony in the Asian culture is generally recognized to be a powerful force. In China, this has a long tradition of being an important part of the way news is determined. In 1936, for example, one scholar (Lin, 1936) noted that of four values that were used to determine the selection of the news, one of importance was "friendly"—not reporting information that would damage international relations. While all the values Lin reported had the basic concept of maintaining harmony at their heart, this one dealt specifically with international news. In this regard, this research attempted to understand if the need for harmony permeated the presentation of the world's events as constructed by Xinhua. Table 17.4 illustrates the findings.

The element of harmony and consensus was measured to determine how this traditional Confucian value was used and to check for changes over time. What was found in this regard was that the conflict element was highest in the 1960s and lowest in the 1970s. The change between these decades was a decrease of 36 percent. In the same two decades harmony increased even more, rising from 26.2 percent of all international stories to almost 54 percent of all stories. Also important to note is the fact that by the 1980s, the category of international stories that were neither conflict oriented or harmony-oriented rose to a high of 44 percent of all stories released. This means that Xinhua was presenting more straightforward news rather than focusing on friction in the international news world on the one hand or highlighting equanimity among nations on the other. This indicates that Xinhua has

TABLE 17.4.
Conflict/Harmoney Orientation in China's International News

	1950s	1960s	1970s	1980s
Conflict	607	172	168	554
Harmony	516	81	457	646
Neither	344	56	224	942
Total	1467	309	849	2142

n=4767

changed quite substantially in its role as a purveyor of international news, providing more information, not drama or diplomacy-building exercises.

As a form of government that upholds a system with the Marxist-Leninist philosophy of media, China's press would most likely be oriented to a very subjective presentation of all news (Siebert, Peterson, & Schramm, 1963). The Marxist-Leninist approach takes a definite position or point of view in the recording of the events, in contrast to Western journalistic philosophy, which strives for balanced, fair, and neutral reporting that does not take a position but states the facts for the reader. Subjectivity is slanted in such a way so "all reports must be cast as well understood—it is like one vast and continuing commercial in support of the regime" (Markham, 1967, p. 150). Journalists working in this particular system are required to take a position on matters and that position has to align with the government's stance. International news coverage was explored in this regard and the findings are presented in Table 17.5.

What is evident across time is an increasing tendency toward the objective reporting of international news. This confirms findings in earlier studies, noting greater accuracy and objectivity in China's reporting than in the past (Bishop, 1989; Chang, 1989). About 40 percent of all international news reported by Xinhua in the 1950s was objective. During the 1960s, this decreased dramatically to 16 percent of all international news stories. Again, the Cultural Revolution probably created

TABLE 17.5.
Objective/Subjective Orientation in China's International News

	1950s	1960s	1970s	1980s
Objective	595	50	373	1864
Subjective	872	259	476	278
Total	1467	309	849	2142

n=4767

an environment in the reporting of news that promoted subjectivity. Perhaps Siebert and his colleagues' (1963) ideas about the influence of the political realm on the content of news needs to be refined to consider the extent of the political situation. In this case, the Cultural Revolution represents an extreme emphasis of political philosophy impacting on the news environment. As such, subjectivity in the 1960s is found in a very high percentage of press releases about international news, but not in all periods to the same extent. Siebert, Peterson, and Schramm's work is a good starting place for considering the impact of the political structure on the content of news but, as these results show, it must not be overgeneralized to cover all countries at all times. To do so is misleading.

Charles Wright (1959) established a functional inventory to evaluate mass communication's impact on various levels of society. That inventory of four basic functions was adapted for this research by adding other categories the literature indicated were appropriate for the context of China. While surveillance, transmission of culture, and entertainment were kept from Wright's original model, the correlation function was divided into linkage for instructional purposes and linkage for ideological purposes. In addition, two other functions were added. These were a propaganda function (defined as actively pushing forward a point of view, or ideology) and mobilization (a call to stimulate the public to an action, movement, or way of thinking).

What purpose, then, did international news serve over the period from the 1950s to the 1980s? Generally speaking, the basic functions of a controlled press to carry the government's line seemed to peak in the 1960s and then steadily decline over the next two decades. This can be seen in Table 17.6, in the way that international news for the purpose of ideological or propaganda purposes decreases from 44 percent of all international news items holding a propaganda function in the 1960s to only 4.8 percent in the 1980s. Correlational ideology likewise decreased from

TABLE 17.6.
Function of China's International News by Period

	1950s	1960s	1970s	1980s
Surveillance	627	59	458	1770
Instruct	53	16	99	131
Ideology	86	47	14	14
Cultural Trans	82	43	13	67
Entertainment	11	0	0	46
Propaganda	576	137	262	103
Mobilization	213	5	3	7
Other	9	2	0	4
Total	1467	309	849	2142

n=4767

15.2 percent of all international news stories in the 1960s to just .6 percent in the 1980s.

Also interesting in these findings is the fact that the surveillance function increased dramatically from the 1950s to the 1980s. Once again, the 1960s represents a time period when international news from China was a chance to put forward the official line rather than publish basic information and so the percentage of this function is low during this time. This changed in the 1970s to reflect the changes in China itself. The 1970s represent a time when China opened to the world. But, as can be seen in these findings, it is also a time when the world was opened up by China in its news. International news served to inform about world events rather to interpret them to fit the current political stance of the government. By the 1980s, 83 percent of all China's international news was informative, a substantial change from the situation 20 years earlier.

A frequent criticism of Western news is that it isolates news events by reporting them out of context (Smith, 1980). This study evaluated the international news from China to determine if this same situation existed in the Xinhua's reporting or if the news from this agency provided an alternative way of presenting the news from that which was offered by the Big Four news agencies. The findings related to contextualization of Xinhua's international news are found in Table 17.7.

Except in the 1960s, China's international news offerings were most likely to be reported as isolated events rather than in the context of an ongoing situation. This was the case for two-thirds of all international news stories in the 1950s and the 1980s, while in the 1970s, more than three-quarters of these stories were without context. The period of the 1960s diverges from the rest on this variable by having more than half of its international news items presented in context. Typically then, China's press is not providing the contextualized alternative to the Western press in its international news coverage. Perhaps China holds to the same philosophy in its presentation of world news to the world that it holds in its philosophy of domestic news to its own people: no explanation is needed for those who already live in the international context.

The topics of international news from China were explored in this research to assess the nature of how China was contributing to the information available about

TABLE 17.7.
Context Orientation of China's International News

	1950s	1960s	1970s	1980s
Context	469	161	188	735
No Context	988	143	658	1395
N/A	10	5	3	12
Total	1467	309	849	2142

n=4767

the world. Consistent across the periods examined, the most frequent international news stories dealt with military or diplomatic events. Military events reported by Xinhua were most frequent in the 1960s period. This may be the result of the coverage of the Vietnam War, a military news event that was right on China's border. Thirty-one percent of all international news stories during the 1960s period were about military topics. This figure dropped to 5 percent in the 1970s, when China turned its attention to a broader variety of other news events. Foreign relations and diplomacy was frequently the topic of international news stories in both the 1950s (46.1 percent of all stories) and the 1970s (51.9 percent of all international stories). This topic of stories was consistently one of the highest in frequency offered by Xinhua.

China's modernization made the topic of economics in international news increasingly important over time. From a low of 2.3 percent in the 1960s, economics in China rose to account for 16 percent of all news stories issued by Xinhua in the 1980s. This is matched, on the other hand, by a consistent reduction in the percentage of stories from the world about Communism. From a high of 10 percent of all international stories in the 1960s, a steady decrease in the number of stories about Communism is apparent up until the 1980s, when it dropped to 1 percent of all news accounts.

What is apparent in Table 17.8 is the fact that in the 1980s, Xinhua was producing a much greater variety of international news than in any previous time. Though the 1950s gives indications that there was diversity in the early international news offered by Xinhua, typically in the 1960s and 1970s very few categories had percentages of inclusion over 2 percent of the total. Indeed, in the 1970s, just five categories account for more than three-quarters of all news types in international news. The same is basically true in the 1960s.

However, by the 1980s, Xinhua expanded its coverage to areas not covered, or covered infrequently, in the past. These included areas such as environmentalism, population, legal matters, religion, sports, and telecommunications. And the coverage is well-distributed across the categories, not as bunched together as in some of the earlier decades. The 1980s is the only decade in this study in which every category included in the measurement of this variable had news items in it. All the others had some categories that were not found in a review of the content.

Who were the actors that appeared in the international news releases from Xinhua? What international figures receive the most attention in Xinhua's news releases? The three types of actors that consistently get the most attention are individuals, organizations, and governments, as seen in Table 17.9. These three types consistently had double-digit percentages of representation (except for government in the 1960s period). While these types were the most frequent of actors found in China's press releases of international news, the extent of their inclusion in the news fluctuated over the four periods examined. The individual, for example, was the dominant actor in one third of all news items in the 1970s, but in other periods the frequency hovered around 20 percent of all items. Governments as the

TABLE 17.8.
Topic of China's International News by Period

	1950s	1960s	1970s	1980s
Military	203	94	42	284
Diplomacy	677	91	441	543
Population	2	0	0	12
PRC Gov't	122	26	41	156
Labor	36	12	13	19
Economics	85	7	59	351
Agriculture	14	2	17	29
Science	15	2	21	85
Education	15	4	9	26
Industry	18	4	18	20
Accidents	6	5	3	51
Legal	23	3	2	99
Environment	11	0	7	34
Housing	6	2	2	21
Telecom	6	0	9	34
Sports	22	0	80	124
Arts	49	7	21	45
Religion	3	0	1	2
Ideology	2	11	4	3
Communism	34	30	20	3
Society	28	3	11	28
Commentary	40	1	10	3
Safety	0	0	0	4
Memorial	28	3	10	15
Other	22	2	8	151
Total	1467	309	849	2142

n=4767

focus of news from abroad decreased in frequency of inclusion as the dominant actor from 1950s to the 1960s, but then increased from the 1970s to the 1980s. Organizations as a primary actor in the news consistently received high percentages of inclusion in China's press releases across all periods. This figure fluctuated between one quarter and one third of all news items, with organizations as the primary focus in the international news coverage, but still represents a large constant emphasis in presentation of a news figure type.

Also important to see here is what types of actors did not merit attention. Least apparent in the news is the family. This is logical, given the previous indication of the type of news topics covered. If the predominant topic in the news is diplomacy and military events, families would not figure prominently into this. What is

TABLE 17.9.
Dominant Actor in China's International News

	1950s	1960s	1970s	1980s
Individual	329	55	293	446
Organization	474	83	269	503
Party	64	·19	29	14
Society	73	25	49	77
Government	399	77	175	790
Family	1	0	0	2
Nature	2	1	0	103
Military	6	5	3	113
Total	1467	309	849	2142

n=4767

surprising is the low emphasis on the military as the primary actor. What appears to be the case in this regard is that while the topic may be about a military event, the actor that is the focus is the power behind the military, which is a government or a head of state. A third actor infrequently appearing in China's news releases was nature. This did not appear to any noticeable degree until the 1980s, when about 5 percent of all releases had this as the predominant actor.

Two other types of actors in the news were found to a very modest extent. Society as the main actor in international news was seen to be dominant in 4 to 8 percent of all stories. It was found at the upper limits of this range in the 1960s and at the lower end in the 1980s. Why was society emphasized more in the 1960s? A check on the function the stories with society as the dominant actor in the 1960s shows that most were very subjective, used to teach ideology and put forward propaganda for the most part, or to teach or transmit culture. Only 20 percent of all stories with society as the primary actor were strictly for information purposes. Topically, these stories were about official relations of one group with another or had to do with communism and ideology. So society was the collective actor used to tell the world about important ideas about the political agenda of the People's Republic of China.

This changed in the 1980s, when society as dominant actor was at the lowest frequency of all four periods. The dominant function of these stories is for surveillance purposes (80 percent of all stories). The topic of press releases with society as the dominant actor is quite low in the diplomatic area and spreads across a wide range of topical categories from agriculture to telecommunication. Therefore, society as an actor is used for political purposes in the 1960s and as such is higher in frequency than in the 1980s, when it was found to be mostly for informative purposes.

Another dominant actor in the news, one that is interesting to note because of its modest representation, is the political party. Once again, this actor was most frequently found in the 1960s, when 6 percent of all international news had this type of actor. If internal priorities give a rationale for external priorities, the political situation within China during this time period may have resulted in this period receiving the highest amount of attention toward political parties of all the periods considered. The decrease in attention to political parties is dramatic over the next two decades. By the 1980s, the frequency of political parties as primary actors in the news is found in less than 1 percent of all news releases. Another factor that may explain this is the breakdown of Communist parties in the world, which begins to show itself in the late 1980s (from whence this data for the 1980s was gathered). China itself was in the midst of turmoil and thus would be unlikely to focus attention on potentially sensitive areas.

The final variable explored in this research considered outside sources of information cited in China's international news. This variable was considered an important indicator of China's ability to gather news from abroad itself and its reliance on other sources of information. The findings are presented in Table 17.10. In the past, Xinhua's ability to send correspondents to other countries was limited by both financial and manpower constraints. International news was taken from foreign news services and interpreted from the official position of Xinhua before being transmitted on to clients. The problem with this, despite the reorientation to the Chinese view of things, was that a foreign gatekeeper had already marked the international news by their selection of the event and inclusion of specific details to the exclusion of others.

The results of the findings regarding this variable indicate a growing tendency for Xinhua to gather its own international news. In the 1950s, 41 percent of all global information transmitted by Xinhua originated from other international news agencies, predominantly the Big Four (AP, UPI, AFP, and Reuters). This decreased in the 1960s and remained stable in the 1970s and 1980s, at 26–28 percent of all stories. While still more than one quarter of all China's international news was coming through foreign gatekeepers, the tendency was still a lower frequency than that of the previous periods.

TABLE 17.10.
Outside Sources Cited in China's International News

	1950s	1960s	1970s	1980s
Outside sources cited	599	100	219	593
No outside sources cited	867	209	630	1547
N/A	1	0	0	2
Total	1467	309	849	2142

n=4767

Xinhua's News Stories and China's National Mythology

Another objective of this study was to consider how national mythology was defined in the news stories over time. In this regard, Kluver's work (1996) on the national mythology of China was used to focus the analysis on two concepts found vital in the context of China: actor and topical theme. Kluver suggests that China's dominant mythological theme was liberation and that important individuals were vital to carrying that theme forward in the national consciousness. Therefore, to begin to understand how international news was embodying national mythology over the four decades this study considered, topical themes were compared with dominant actors in the news.

One observation that was readily apparent in the consideration of how news stories were constructed over time was the fact that the individual actor never accounted for the highest frequency of news coverage. In the 1950s, 22 percent of international news featured individuals and this declined in the 1960s to 18 percent of all news items. The 1970s found a bit more than one third of all news items featuring individuals, but this again dropped to 21 percent of all news items in the period of the 1980s. In constructing their international news, group actors (organizations, political parties, governments, social groups, and so on) were found more often than individuals. This is a logical representation, given the fact that China held to a collectivist perspective from both a political and cultural standpoint.

When individuals were presented in China's international news, they tended to be prominent individuals. In the 1950s period, 71 percent of all individuals presented in international news items were well-known people. This percentage rose in the 1960s to 87 percent of all individuals and reached a peak in the 1970s period at 94 percent of all individuals. In the 1980s, 77 percent of all the individuals were well known. International newsmakers in every period were not common folks, but rather from the elite realms of politics or society.

What does this tell us about the way China was embodying important concepts into its news items? If, as Kluver (1996) suggests, China held individuals important in its national mythology, then this finding shows how that concept varied over time as China presented news about the international scene. It is interesting to note how the importance of the prominent individual increases from the 1950s through the 1970s. It is during this time period that Mao became an increasingly dominant mythological figure internally and therefore it is logical to see this feature grow in importance as China looks outward at other news figures as well. By the 1980s, this was in decline, moving back down toward the figure found in the 1950s, in tandem with the de-emphasis of the cult of Mao under the reforms initiated by Deng Xiao-ping.

Yet all this is tempered by the fact that collective actors, rather than individuals, were the focus of international news in all periods. If China held prominent individuals so important in its own mythology, why did it not focus on these actors in the international news it distributed? China may have been observing the world through its cultural perspective and thus leaned more toward the collective actor than the individual one. Or, to stand apart from the news philosophy of the West, Xinhua's style of journalism may have focused on collectives and group processes. This indeed may be a remnant of the Soviet press philosophy that was implemented after the 1949 revolution. More research is needed in this regard to understand how the actor in the news fits into China's evolving national myth.

When the dominant actor is considered with the general topic presented in the international news items presented by Xinhua over these periods, other interesting indications about the national mythology are discovered. In all periods, individual actors in the news are found in stories with news themes concerning diplomacy and foreign relations. Indeed, this category is found in all periods to have the most news items, exhibiting a consistency across time in the way China created its news. This is logical, given the fact that this represents China's international news items. Yet, while China did consistently give the most attention to foreign relations in its news presentation, the degree of concentration of this area changed over time. Xinhua's press releases weigh heavily in the international political realm in the 1950s, while in the 1960s, it decreases to shift to a balance of this area and military news. However, once again in the 1970s, the percentage of news items in this area increases to include more than half of all the news presented. In the 1980s, the focus on foreign relations drops to a low of 25 percent of all news items. This is the lowest of all four periods investigated here, but it still represents the news theme most prominent among all the news topics in the 1980s.

Two things are evident here about China's sense of priorities when presenting international news. One is the consistency with which this news agency found international relations the dominant theme in all periods. While on one hand, since this study focuses only on international news, foreign relations as a dominant area of coverage is logical; on the other, it fits well with the revolutionary concept of a new China arising after 1949. Mao declared, with the initiation of the People's Republic, that "the Chinese people had stood up" (Kluver, 1996, p. 28). So it is natural when China is presenting the news about the rest of the world that it considers the relationships countries have with each other as it endeavors to stand with them. To see that interest in international relations slump in the 1960s is again reasonable, given China's isolation from the rest of the world and its focus on military threats it perceived at that time. As China reenters international relations with the open door policies of Deng in the late 1970s, international relations regain importance. The declining figure in the 1980s does not mean a lessening of the importance of the international context, but indicates Xinhua's more catholic, topical approach to international news coverage.

This broader consideration of international news is the second important point to be noted about Xinhua's emphases in news topics across time. In the 1980s, the themes of the news are more inclusive. China is not just presenting news about the workings of governments, but is considering a variety of subjects in more detail. This indicates that China as a nation is looking beyond the political in this era to consider other aspects of life. Especially evident is the greater attention given to economics and business news internationally. This reflects China's own increased attention to this area domestically. What is evident in China's presentation of international news is reflective of the evolution of its national consciousness from newly emergent Communist republic through the isolation of the 1960s and the reemergence in the world community in the 1970s, to the openness of the country to new concepts and ideas in the period preceding the Tiananmen incident.

One additional consideration of the international news from Xinhua was made to better understand how press releases represented the national mythology in stories over time. An effort was made to identify story types used frequently by Xinhua in each of the periods examined. To do this, all international news items were crosstabulated by dominant actor and topic and controlled by the dominant function of the story. By controlling for the function of the news items and then looking at the dominant topic and actors, a clearer picture of the types of news stories Xinhua was creating was evident. Tables 17.11–17.14 list the dominant patterns of actors and themes by function for each of the four periods explored in this study.

Table 17.11 shows the major story themes for the period of the 1950s. Basically, three kinds of stories were predominant styles of news during this period. The most frequent story type was about foreign relations or military activities and was used for either informational or propaganda purposes. The actor was typically a government, organization, or an individual, though for propaganda purposes, political parties and social groups were also used. Therefore, in Table 17.11, the first four story structures can be collapsed into one general pattern.

Two other story models are evident. One recurring pattern of a news story is how a government or individual was involved in matters involving the People's Republic of China. This was typically international diplomacy stories recounting the coming of foreign officials to China or China's leaders being welcomed in other countries. Conversely, it might also tell how international individuals or governments had antagonized the domestic or foreign policies of China. The key to the distinctiveness of this story is the international focus, which has domestic implications and is written to inform rather than propagate a particular political point of view.

The other type of story found in Xinhua's press releases was another informational one, though in this case one in which a foreign government or organization was reported to act in economic or financial activities. While this pattern of news story was found to occur least frequently of all those noted in Table 17.11, it is interesting to note its presence in this early period of the People's Republic of China. While economic reforms are an important part of the recent priorities in China, it can be seen that even in the late 1950s, this type of news recurred in the storytelling patterns used to convey what was considered news of the world.

In comparison with the 1950s, an evolution in the pattern of telling news stories is evident in the 1960s. For, while the first basic pattern seen in the previous period is maintained, it is augmented by other patterns that give the news story a distinctly

TABLE 17.11.
Function by Actor and Topic in China's International News in the 1950s

Function	Actor	Topic
For propaganda	A government	Foreign relations, political, or diplomatic activities
	An organization	
	An individual	
	A political party	
	A society	
To inform	An individual	Foreign relations, political, or diplomatic activities
	An organization	
	A government	
For propaganda	An organization	Military, defense, war, intelligence operations, or political violence activities
	A government	
	Other actors	
To inform	An individual	Military, defense, war, intelligence operations, or political violence activities
	An organization	
	A government	
To inform	An individual	China's national political affairs
	A government	
To inform	A government	Economic and business activities
	An organization	

Note: Accounts for 60 percent of all stories by topic and function.

different nature. Seven specific story patterns are found occurring most frequently in the 1960s period, but there are certain threads that tie some of these together in ways that are revealing. Apparent at first glance is the increased use of news stories for propaganda purposes. For example, in Table 17.12, the first three news story patterns account for about one third of all news stories issued during this time and each functions for propaganda purposes. Two themes found important in the previous period are again important in this regard: foreign affairs and military activities. Additionally, however, is the inclusion of international Communism as a frequent topic of the news. The dominant actor in these stories was most frequently an individual or an organization, though governments, political parties, or other actors were found in specific story types, as noted in Table 17.12.

One major news story type that was important during the 1960s was the propagation of a particular point of view through the news. Views, not news, have been noted in the news of China in this period in previous research (Yu, 1979). In terms of content, Chang (1968) noted that the newspapers were filled with "long speeches, or pronouncements, political editorials, slanted reports passing as news stories, and

TABLE 17.12.
Function by Actor and Topic in China's International News in the 1960s

Function	Actor	Topic
For propaganda	An individual	Foreign relations, political, or diplomatic activities
	An organization	
	A government	
For propaganda	An individual	Military, defense, war, intelligence operations, or political violence activities
	An organization	
	Other actors	
For propaganda	An individual	Communist activities
	An organization	
	A government	
	A political party	
To teach ideology	An individual	Military, defense, war, intelligence operations, or political violence activities
	An organization	
	Other actors	
To inform	Other actors	Military, defense, war, intelligence operations, or political violence activities
	An organization	
To inform	An individual	Foreign relations, political, or diplomatic activities
	An organization	
To transmit values	An individual	Military, defense, war, intelligence operations, or political violence activities
	An organization	
	Other actors	

Note: Accounts for 56 percent of all stories by topic and function.

even full texts of articles written by Mao Tse-Tung many years previous. These texts frequently take up the whole front page" (p. 23). Chang finds that especially during the Cultural Revolution, the Western concepts of good journalism—objectivity, detachment, integrity, accuracy, investigation, and truthful reporting—were all condemned. So it is not surprising when considering China's international news that the same approach to telling news stories would be evident.

Another thread that runs through the patterns of news stories during the 1960s is the focus on military, war, intelligence activities, and political violence. This theme is presented frequently in Xinhua's international news for a variety of functions. As previously noted, this theme was used for propaganda functions in numerous press releases. But military news is also used in this era to teach ideology and to provide basic information, as well as to transmit values. A great deal of mileage was gained by China's news agency from the coverage of the world's wars during this time period.

What does this indicate about China's mythology at this point in time? China in the 1960s was caught up in the furor of its own domestic struggles in the Cultural Revolution. Perhaps it was the revolutionary focus internally that fixed China's attention on this type of conflict internationally. Certainly it can be seen as consistent confirmation of Mao's ideas of ongoing revolution in the big context. The predominance of international conflict in war and political struggle mirrors the national context of China at this point in time. As well, there were increasing threats on its borders that commanded China's attention. Skirmishes with Russia to the north and U.S. involvement growing in Vietnam to the south were ready sources of international news in this area. So a convergence of both internal and external conditions change the focus of the stories, shifting them to include a militaristic theme. This remains consistent with a national myth based in liberation, however, the perspective of liberation changes from the previously exclusive diplomatic point of view to one that adapted to the military focus of this period.

In the 1970s, the militaristic bent to the news in patterns of storytelling virtually disappeared. While the format of foreign relations as information and propaganda (apparent in Table 17.13) remained a solid fixture in this time period, two other story patterns were evident during this time period as well. One pattern is completely new. It relates information about an international news topic that formerly received scant attention: sports. In this recurring new form of telling the news, foreign individuals or organizations are reported as they are involved in sporting events. These press releases were still hard news-oriented, for the function of these items was informational rather than for entertainment purposes. But the prominent focus on a story that deals with a nonpolitical area is a development that shows a change in the way China was seeing and reporting the world to the world.

The final story format in this period is one that harks back to the 1950s in the consideration of international economic and financial topics. The difference in the 1970s is that this international news format focuses only on governments as the actors, not international organizations, as was the case in the 1950s. Two things may explain this. One was the external condition of the time. Much of the world was in an economic recession and governments were struggling to recover in ways that generated a great deal of news. A second reason may be found in the context in which China was operating during this period. In the late 1970s, China was making leadership transitions after the death of Mao. These transitions focused not only on changes that were taking place in the government itself, but also on the philosophy toward economics held by that government. While Deng Xiao-ping was making overtures toward the West for economic openness, the Gang of Four was holding fast to the traditional communist line. So internally there were struggles in the area of economics and this would naturally turn attention to this topic as it played itself out in the international context. And, unlike the 1950s, the approach to economics and finance in the international realm was not generally restricted to

TABLE 17.13
Function by Actor and Topic in China's International News in the 1970s

Function	Actor	Topic
To inform	An individual	Foreign relations, political, or diplomatic activities
	An organization	
	A government	
For propaganda	An individual	Foreign relations, political, or diplomatic activities
	An organization	
	A government	
To inform	An individual	Sports activities
	An organization	
To inform	A government	Economic and business activities

Note: Accounts for 62 percent of all stories by topic and function.

examples of exploitation of the masses. Rather, China was adapting to new conditions in which it would become a major force in the international marketplace. It is here that a definite shift in the national mythology is evident as Xinhua's news stories show the gradual change in emphasis from political liberation to economic liberation. The image of China standing up among the nations of the world, invoked by Mao at the founding of the People's Republic, also begins to become evident in China's international news during this era.

The last period under consideration in this study was the 1980s, and it is significant in terms of the way news stories were constructed, in that all the dominant patterns served the function of informing. This is quite a shift from the past, when the propaganda function was prominent. Indeed, the Marxist-Leninist perspective of news philosophy confirms that a propaganda function is a vital part of the role journalism should play in the political context. So, this change is noteworthy, for it shows that the dominant storytelling patterns of news is reflecting a new consciousness.

In the period of the 1980s, individuals, organizations, or governments are prominently found as the actors in reports about foreign relations, economics, the military, China's national affairs, sports, and legal matters. As seen in Table 17.14, one pattern in this is consistent with all the previous periods and that is the one in which news items were used to present information about relations between foreign nations. This story pattern was the one used most frequently to tell news in the 1980s.

Second in frequency was a storytelling format in which information about economics and finance was reported. This development demonstrates that this theme's newsworthiness has progressed from minor to major status in the presentation of international news. This basic story format was first seen in the 1950s, but

TABLE 17.14
Function by Actor and Topic in China's International News in the 1980s

Function	Actor	Topic
To inform	An individual	Foreign relations, political, or diplomatic activities
	An organization	
	A government	
To inform	An individual	Economic and business activities
	An organization	
	A government	
To inform	An individual	Military, defense, war, intelligence operations, or political violence activities
	An organization	
	A government	
	Other actors	
To inform	An individual	China's national political affairs
	An organization	
	A government	
To inform	An individual	Sports activities
	An organization	
To inform	An individual	Judicial and legal affairs
	An organization	
	A government	

Note: Accounts for 61 percent of all stories by topic and function.

was not evident in the 1960s. It reappears as a story format in the 1970s, but was minor when compared to other formats that accounted for a greater proportion of news items. Yet in the 1980s, this storytelling theme moves to a place in the pantheon of storytelling modes that is second only to foreign relations. This reflects the growing importance of this theme in the scheme of things in China overall. It was during this time period when Deng's open door policy modified the former political context in China, allowing a more pragmatic stance while pushing for economic reforms. As was seen in Kluver's (1996) analysis of national myth, news as a way of telling stories is found to be reflective of the interests of the storytellers themselves. Thus, the increased attention given to economics at the international level clearly shows the shift toward a priority of this theme within China itself. Indeed, news stories with this prominent theme send a signal to the world community of the changes in China as it takes its place in the international sphere.

Two other observations about storytelling patterns in the international news from China in the 1980s can be made. The first is the continuing importance on sports, which is found in the frequent use of this topic as a news theme. This confirms earlier research, which found a high amount of sports information in the early 1980s flowing from Xinhua's press releases (Schramm & Atwood, 1981). China was creating linkages to the rest of the world community; in the 1980s, sports was a means to accomplish this effort outside the typical diplomatic means of the past. Indeed, relations with the United States had greatly improved through what had been termed "ping-pong" diplomacy in an earlier period. Thus, sports takes on a linking function for a Chinese society looking for a means of integration with the community of nations.

The second observation that can be made here is the rise of legal themes as a form of storytelling. In times past, this topic was not a frequent focus in telling international news. Indeed, Schramm and Atwood (1981) noted at the beginning of this decade that news dealing with crime was relatively nonexistent in Xinhua international news flows. The presentation of this topic of news is interesting because, typically, this is a feature important in Western constructions of news stories. With its focus on the "the aberrational rather than the normal as the main criterion for selection; Western news agencies are, therefore, on the lookout for information concerning violence, war, crime, corruption, disaster, famine, fire, and flood" (Smith, 1980, p. 70). Crime news is thus a significant part of what is constructed as news in Western contexts. To see this type of news expanded in the news formulas of China in the 1980s may be indicative of the evolution of the overall news story format in China to a style that is more competitive with other international news purveyors. As well, it may simply represent the natural evolution of journalism in China. More research is needed to understand this situation.

The consideration of national myth embodied in Xinhua's news stories is touched upon in this study by considering how actors and topics of the news were used in recurring patterns when isolated by specific news functions. Much more detailed analysis from this perspective is needed to probe further the patterns of stories created by Xinhua as it constructed its news. While this study does not purport to analyze indepth the narrative of China's news, it begins to reveal important concepts by considering the frequency by which news story patterns existed over time. These patterns fit neatly with Kluver's (1996) assessment of China's adaptation of its national myth to accommodate the increasingly important economic element while maintaining the consistency of the traditional liberation myth. The news patterns also show the changing ways in which modern China, taking its place among the other nations of the world, stands up.

CONCLUSION

This research sought to understand Xinhua in the context of the ongoing exploration of flows of information research. As a long-standing national news agency with a unique form and mission, this agency provided a valuable context in which to consider how alternate voices of international communication report the news. To understand this, three basic questions were posed. These questions probed the nature of international news content from China in the period of time from 1949 to 1989 and how that nature appeared to change over time. Across 10 content variables, a picture of how China reported the world became apparent as a result of this research. While there was a great deal of fluctuation from one period to the next, a basic evolutionary development was hinted at in the data. There seemed to be a movement across time from a stance of international news reporting that was unique to China to a reporting style and content that was more competitive with an international standard.

This must take into consideration the fact that the 1960s appears to be an aberration in this development process. The Cultural Revolution not only impacted on the news *in* China, it appears, but also on the news *from* China. It is this time period that stands out as very different from the others. News in the 1960s is marked by differences in approach, content, function, and actors that make it unique from other periods. News from abroad during this time was used to serve political goals. Events were examples to uphold the ideas and ideology of the times. This fits in with the concept that Xinhua is the tongue of the Party, an idea that is usually considered when looking at domestic news, but not typically when international news is considered.

If there is another time period that is striking in its presentation of international news it is the 1970s. In some ways it appears that this period is a reaction to the 1960s era, a time when the pendulum swings in the opposite direction. The changes between the two periods on the variables explored are sometimes dramatic. Looking across all four periods, this is clearly seen as the 1950s findings and the 1980s findings often settle close to each other in frequency. However, the 1960s was found to be one extreme, while the 1970s represented another. The 1970s reaction appears, at this point in time, to be extreme in the general direction things seem to be moving in the 1980s. Whether this evolutionary development is actually the case requires more research over time to determine if the 1980s findings remain consistent and the 1960s and 1970s are indeed exceptions to the rule.

An important point to be seen here is that China has changed. Often lost in the political rhetoric that surrounds international assessments of China is the fact that there is definite movement toward change in this new country with an old culture. That change was one that moved closer to the way news was covered by the rest of the world instead of maintaining an immovable independence and an attitude that the world become more like China. In basic news philosophy, like timeliness, for example, one can see more of an orientation to get the news out quickly rather than to ponder the implications in light of the overall political context and thus delay coverage. Perhaps this is linked to the increased availability of alternate forms of communication with which Xinhua must now actively compete.

Another important finding in this work is to show that China did seem to have a specific niche in the reporting of international news. Its primary emphasis was in focusing on the international news of Asia and a secondary emphasis was on the developing world as a whole. In this regard, it did fill a gap that the literature indicates Western news agencies create with their particular news focus. Topically and geographically, Xinhua remains one news provider that does cover parts of the world that have historically been overlooked. Whether that is attractive to consumers or not is another area of study that requires more research.

An examination of the storytelling forms used predominantly by Xinhua to report international news over four decades reaffirms these ideas from the perspective of China as a storyteller behind the news. China consistently used one particular story format across all four periods and that was one in which the coverage of foreign relations and military matters was presented for informational purposes. That this form of telling a news story would occur frequently in all periods is reasonable, given the focus in this study on international news. In addition, other formats of stories were apparent and varied across the time periods evaluated in this research. An evolution of storytelling is apparent from the ebb and flow of these variations, which indicates the changes from political persuasion to political and economic information processes. This confirms the overall findings regarding national myth found by Kluver (1996) in his examination of the changes from Mao through Deng's leadership. News as a form of telling stories reveals different priorities of the storyteller and in this case, the change to a balance of political with economic themes is readily apparent.

Another major evolutionary change is seen in the opening of China's international news to a greater variety of topics for purposes of information rather than propagation of political ideas. China in the 1980s was reintegrating itself in the community of nations after a period of relative isolation followed by a period of political transition. The stories it told about the world's events show an increased interest in the way of life of the world, rather than just the formal political and diplomatic stance it had traditionally taken in the past. While foreign relations is still seen to be a high priority, indications through the story patterns in the 1980s give evidence of a different storyteller than in previous periods. This is particularly evident in the presentation of sports and legal news items, areas that deviated from the typical governmental orientation of the past. Thus, examining the news as stories illuminates the changes in China as it conceptualized and legitimated itself in the international realm through the content and style of its news representations.

This study of Xinhua offers an interesting portrait of how an organization presents international news and gives some indications of how that process changes over time. Xinhua is seen to hold a definite identity in the way it presents the news of the world to the world. It has a role to play in Asia and a role to play in the developing world. However, China is also taking its place as a major power in the world and that role takes it into another realm. In the international sphere, China's communication serves another function and correspondingly it must operate in another way, making its presentation and content increasingly consonant with the way the rest of the major information purveyors present the news while remaining true to its own character.

REFERENCES

Anderson, M. H. (1981). China's great leap toward Madison Avenue. *Journal of Communication, 31*, 10–22.

Auge, M., & Callan, H. (1986). Teleculture heroes, or a night at the embassy. *Current Anthropology, 27*, 184–188.

Balbontin-Arteaga, I. (1982). Participation, socialization and youth. *De Juventua-Revista de Estudios e Investigaciones, 7*, 153–168.

Bartlett, F. C. (1932). *Remembering.* Cambridge, England: Cambridge University Press.

Bell, A. (1991). *The language of news media.* Oxford, England: Blackwell.

Bennett, W. L., & Edelman, M. (1985). Toward a new political narrative. *Journal of Communication, 35*, 156–171.

Berkowitz, D. (1997). *Social meanings of news: A text-reader.* London: Sage.

Bird, S. E., & Dardenne, R. W. (1988). Myth, chronicle and story: Exploring the narrative qualities of news. In J. W. Carey (Ed.), *Media, myths and narratives: Television and the press* (pp. 67–86). Newbury Park, CA: Sage.

Bishop, R. L. (1989). *Qi Lai! Mobilizing one billion Chinese: The Chinese communication system.* Ames, IA: Iowa State University Press.

Boyd-Barrett, O. (1980). *The international news agencies.* Beverly Hills, CA: Sage.

Breen, M. P. (1986). *National mythology on television: The Australian experience.* Unpublished manuscript.

Budd, R. W., Thorpe, R. K., & Donohew, L. (1967). *Content analysis of communications.* New York: Macmillan.

Carey, J. W., & Fritzler, M. (1989). News as social narrative. *Communication, 10*, 1–92.

Carragee, K. M. (1990, February). Defining solidarity: Themes and omissions in coverage of the Solidarity trade union movement by *ABC News. Journalism Monographs, 119*.

Chang K. S. (1968). *A survey of the Chinese-language Daily Press.* Hong Kong: Asia Press.

Chang W. H. (1989). *Mass media in China: The history and the future.* Ames, IA: Iowa State University Press.

Chapman S., & Egger, G. (1983). Myth in cigarette advertising and health promotion. In H. Davis & P. Walton (Eds.), *Language, image, media* (pp. 166–186). Oxford, England: Blackwell.

Dorfman, A., & Mattelart, A. (1975). *How to read Donald Duck.* New York: International General.

Drummond, L. (1984). Movies and myth: Theoretical skirmishes. *American Journal of Semiotics, 3*, 1–32.

Faison, S. (1990, November 13). Attack on Hong Kong publications. *South China Morning Post*, p. 10.

Fan, C. W. (1990, November 13). Hostile media singled out. *Hong Kong Standard*, p. 12.

Fifty militant years. (1981, November 23). *Beijing Review, 24*, 20–21.

Gans, H. J. (1979). *Deciding what's news: A study of* CBS Evening News, NBC Nightly News, Newsweek, *and* Time. New York: Pantheon Books.

Gauhar, A. (1981/82). Third World: An alternate press. *Journal of International Affairs, 35*, 165–177.

Gitlin, T. (1980). *The whole world is watching: Mass media in the making and unmaking of the New Left.* Berkeley, CA: University of California Press.

Grantzberg, G. (1985). Television and self-concept formation in developing areas: The Central Canadian Algonkian experience. *Journal of Cross-Cultural Psychology, 16,* 313–332.

Guback, T. (1969). *The international film industry.* Bloomington, IN: Indiana University Press.

Gumbert, G., & Cathcart, R. (1983). Media stereotyping: Images of the foreigner. *Communications, 9,* 103–111.

Hamilton, A. (1975). Snugglepot and Cuddlepie: Happy families in Australian society. *Mankind, 10,* 84–92.

Houn, F. W. (1958–59). Chinese Communist control of the press. *Public Opinion Quarterly, 22,* 435–448.

Howkins, J. (1982). *Mass communication in China.* New York: Longman.

Hu Y. (1986). On the Party's journalism work. In B. Womack (Ed.), *Media and the Chinese public: A survey of the Beijing media audience* (pp. 174–198). Armonk, NY: M. E. Sharpe.

Iverson, P. (1976). *The Navahos: A critical bibliography.* Bloomington, IN: Indiana University Press.

Katz, E. (1977). Can authentic cultures survive new media? *Journal of Communication, 27,* 113–121.

Katz, E. (1979). Cultural continuity and change: Role of media. In K. Nordenstreng & H. Schiller (Eds.), *National sovereignty and international communication* (pp. 65–81) Norwood, NJ: Ablex.

Kent, S. (1985). The effects of television viewing, A cross-cultural perspective. *Current Anthropology, 26,* 121–126.

Kerlinger, F. (1973). *Foundations of behaviorial research* (2nd ed.). New York: Holt, Rinehart, and Winston.

Kluver, A. R. (1996). *Legitimizing the Chinese economic reforms: A rhetoric of myth and orthodoxy.* Albany, NY: State University of New York Press.

Knoll, J. H. (1981). Social ethical standards in youth-oriented magazines. *Communications, 7,* 187–213.

Krippendorff, K. (1980). *Content analysis: An introduction to its methodology.* Beverly Hills, CA: Sage.

Lam, W. W. L. (1991, July 16). Alarm over Soviet changes. *South China Morning Post,* p. 10.

Lee, M. (1985, November 14). News of foreign devils. *Far Eastern Economic Review, 130,* 46.

Lentz, R. (1989). The prophet and the citadel: News magazine coverage of the 1963 Birmingham civil rights crisis. *Communication, 10,* 5–28.

Lewis, M. (1985, November 17). The rise and the rise of Xinhua. *Asia Magazine,* 12–16.

Liao, K. S. (1984). *Antiforeignism and modernization in China* (Rev. ed.). Hong Kong: The Chinese University Press.

Lin Y. T. (1936). *A history of the press and public opinion in China.* Shanghai: Kelly and Walsh.

Mander, M. S. (1987). Narrative dimensions of the news: Omniscience, prophecy, and morality. *Communication, 10,* 51–70.

Many voices, one world. (1980). New York: UNESCO.

Markham, J. W. (1967). *Voices of the red giants.* Ames, IA: Iowa State University Press.

Mayo, J. K., Oliviera,. J., Rogers, E., Guimaraes, S., & Morrett, F. (1984). The transfer of Sesame Street to Latin America. *Communication Research, 11*, 259–280.

Mitchell, W. J. T. (1981). *On narrative.* Chicago: University of Chicago Press.

Mulligan, W. A. (1988). Remnants of Cultural Revolution in Chinese journalism of the 1980s. *Journalism Quarterly, 65*, 20–25.

Newton, B. J., & Buck, E. B. (1985). Television as significant other: Its relationship to self-descriptors in five countries. *Journal of Cross-Cultural Psychology, 16*, 289–312.

Parker, D. (1975, June 20). Keeping the news in the national interest. *Far Eastern Economic Review*, 31–32.

Pingree, S., & Hawkins, R. (1981). U.S. programs on Australian television: The cultivation effect. *Journal of Communication, 31*, 97–105.

Pisarek, W. (1983). "Reality" East and West. In H. Davis & P. Walton (Eds.), *Language, image, media* (pp. 156–164). Oxford, England: Blackwell.

Rada, S. E. (1978). Ramah Navajo radio and cultural penetration. *Journal of Broadcasting and Electronic Media, 22*, 361–371.

Rice, G. (1980). On cultural schemata. *American Ethnologist, 2*, 152–171.

Rosenblum, M. (1979). Reporting from the Third World. In K. Nordenstreng & H. Schiller (Eds.), *National sovereignty and international communication* (pp. 237–274). Norwood, NJ: Ablex.

Rubin, B. (1977). *International news and the American media.* Beverly Hills, CA: Sage.

Rudolph, J. M. (1984). *Cankao Xiaoxi: Foreign news in the propaganda system of the People's Republic of China.* Baltimore, MD: School of Law, University of Maryland.

Schramm, W., & Atwood, E. (1981). *Circulation of the news in the Third World.* Hong Kong: The Chinese University Press.

Seeger, A. (1989). An unreported class war: Ideology and self-censorship on the Berkeley Barb. *Communication, 10*, 31–50.

Siebert, F. S., Peterson, T., & Schramm, W. (1963). *Four theories of the press.* Urbana, IL: University of Illinois Press.

Silverstone, R. (1988). Television myth and culture. In J. W. Carey (Ed.), *Media, myths and narratives: Television and the press* (pp. 20–47). Newbury Park, CA: Sage.

Sinclair, K. (1986, May 27). Changing face of a "party mouthpiece." *South China Morning Post*, p. 2.

Skurnik, W. A. E. (1981). A new look at foreign news coverage: External dependence or national interests? *African Studies Review, 14*, 99–112.

Smith, A. (1980). *The geopolitics of information: How Western culture dominates the world.* New York: Oxford University Press.

Smith, R. R. (1997). Mythic elements in television news. In D. Berkowitz (Ed.), *Social meanings of news: A text-reader* (pp. 325–332). London: Sage.

Starr, J. B. (1973). *Ideology and culture.* New York: Harper and Row.

Stempel, G. H. (1952). Sample size for classifying subject matter in dailies. *Journalism Quarterly, 29*, 333–334.

Tan, A. S., Tan, G. K., & Tan, A. S. (1987). American TV in the Philippines: A test of cultural impact. *Journalism Quarterly, 64*, 65–72.

Tuchman, G. (1978). *Making news, A study in the construction of reality.* New York: The Free Press.

Tunstall, J. (1977). *The media are American: Anglo-American media in the world.* London: Constable.

Varis, T. (1984). The international flow of television programs. *Journal of Communication, 34,* 143–152.

Weber, R. P. (1990). *Basic content analysis* (2nd ed.). Newbury Park, CA: Sage.

White, H. (1981). The value of narrativity in the representation of reality. In W. J. T. Mitchell (Ed.), *On narrative* (pp. 1–23). Chicago: University of Chicago Press.

White, L. T., III. (1979). Local newspapers and community change, 1949–1969. In G. C. Chu & F. L.K. Hsu (Eds.), *Moving a mountain: Cultural change in China* (pp. 78–112). Honolulu, HI: University of Hawaii Press.

Wright, C. R. (1959). *Mass communication: A sociological perspective.* New York: Random House.

Yao, I. P. (1963). The new china news agency: How it serves the Party. *Journalism Quarterly, 40,* 83.

Yu, F. T. C. (1964). *Mass persuasion in Communist China.* New York: Praeger.

Yu, F. T. C. (1979). China's mass communication in historical perspective. In G. C. Chu & F. L. K. Hsu (Eds.), *Moving a mountain: Cultural change in China* (pp. 27–56). Honolulu, HI: University of Hawaii Press.

Zelizer, B. (1993). American journalists and the death of Lee Harvey Oswald: Narratives of self-legitimation. In D. K. Mumby (Ed.), *Narrative and social control: Critical perspectives* (pp. 189–206). London: Sage.

Zelizer, B. (1997). Has communication explained journalism? In D. Berkowitz (Ed.), *Social meanings of news: A text-reader* (pp. 23–30). London: Sage.

Zohoori, A. (1988). A cross-cultural analysis of children's television use. *Journal of Broadcasting and Electronic Media, 32,* 105–113.

18

International Agencies and Global Issues: The Decline of the Cold War News Frame

C. Anthony Giffard
University of Washington

THE COLD WAR FRAME

The end of the cold war has resulted in major changes not only in international relations, but in the way global affairs are covered by the news media. Prior to 1985, when Soviet Premier Mikhail Gorbachev began his policies of *perestroika* and *glasnost*, much reporting on international events was characterized by what scholars have termed a "cold war frame"—a means of selecting and presenting information that emphasized the superpower rivalry between the United States and the Soviet Union (Herman & Chomsky, 1988). As Hallin (1986) puts it, the cold war frame "explains all international conflicts in essentially the same, familiar terms, sparing the public the burden of mastering a new set of political intricacies each time a crisis erupts" (p. 110). Larson's (1984) study of news broadcast on U.S. television networks between 1972 and 1981 showed that the Soviet Union was the most frequently mentioned foreign country. This emphasis was not limited to media in the United States. Hester (1991), for example, in an analysis of shortwave radio

389

news from 20 nations during the 1980s, found that the Soviet Union and the United States were mentioned far more frequently than any other nations. Servaes (1991) determined that newspapers in Great Britain, France, Germany, the Netherlands, Spain, and Switzerland all construed the U.S. invasion of Grenada as primarily a confrontation between East and West.

The existence of the cold war frame did not necessarily mean that news media worldwide paid more attention to the United States and the Soviet Union than to other nations. Sreberny-Mohammadi, Nordenstreng, Stevenson, and Ugboajah (1985) found that the "consistent newsmakers" were the United States and Western Europe, while the socialist countries of Eastern Europe were part of the area of "invisibility." A study by Gerbner and Marvanyi (1981) showed that "the world of the Third World newspapers was the only one in which the Soviet Union loomed large, in fact the largest among all regions." Weaver and Wilhoit (1984) found that in one three-month period in 1979, the Soviet Union was the foreign nation mentioned most frequently by the Western agencies, but it was in the fourth position during another period that year. These discrepancies may be attributable to news events at the time the studies were undertaken.

In addition to the cold war frame, researchers have found that the wealthy, powerful "core" nations generally feature prominently in international news coverage, while those on the periphery attract little attention, unless something dramatic happens there (Galtung & Ruge, 1965; Schramm, 1964). Hester (1978) suggests that there is a hierarchy, or "pecking order," of nations and that more information will flow from high-ranking nations than from those ranked "low" in the hierarchy. Wall (1995) argues that media frames still exist, but that the cold war frame has been supplanted by others.

During the 1990s, however, East–West tensions have eased considerably, with the disintegration of the Soviet Union and the apparent triumph of the capitalist/democratic system. No longer is international reporting concerned primarily with East–West tensions. The attention now is on specific trouble spots—areas plagued by political or armed conflict, or by famine, flood, or other natural disasters. However, various issues that transcend national or regional boundaries have come to the fore. Since 1992, a series of major conferences organized by United Nations agencies has focused the world's attention on such shared concerns as the environment, human rights, population, social development, and women. Each conference was attended by high-level delegations from almost every nation. These delegates, in theory at least, had an equal chance of presenting their views and of being reported. News agency coverage of these conferences therefore offers a unique opportunity to determine, in the abeyance of cold war tensions, which nations and regions are perceived as being the major protagonists on the world stage when global concerns are at stake.

RESEARCH QUESTIONS

This chapter seeks to determine:

■ which nations/regions figure most prominently in international news agency reporting of global issues;
■ whether the national/regional coverage varies from issue to issue, or whether the same countries usually dominate the coverage; and
■ whether international news agencies with divergent regional perspectives differ in the amount of attention they pay to various nations.

METHOD

The study uses computerized content analysis to examine news agency coverage of five large international conferences organized by the United Nations this decade:

Conference on Environment and Development (Rio de Janeiro, June 1992);
Conference on Human Rights (Vienna, June 1993);
International Conference on Population and Development (Cairo, September 1994);
World Conference on Social Development (Copenhagen, March 1995); and
Fourth World Conference on Women (Beijing, September 1995).

The news agencies were selected to represent three different perspectives: those of North America, Europe, and the developing world. They are:

■ the Associated Press, the major U.S.-based international agency;
■ Inter Press Service, the largest international agency specializing in Third World news; and
■ Reuters, the largest European-based international agency.

Reports about the five conferences filed by each agency were collected from two weeks prior to their official opening until the day after they finished. For AP and Reuters, the reports were transmitted to full-service newspaper clients in North America. According to editors consulted on the international desks of these agencies, the feed to other regions of the world would have been similar. IPS coverage came from its English-language World Service, which goes to all regions.

Each of the conferences had not only the main event, attended by representatives of governments, but a large and vociferous side-show organized by nonprofit organizations (NGOs) seeking to influence their outcomes. The analysis includes coverage of these "alternative" summits as well as the official meetings.

The sample comprised a total of 1,236 news reports from the three agencies for all five conferences. It included 325 reports from the AP, 375 from IPS, and 536 from Reuters. The Beijing women's conference drew the most extensive coverage, with a combined total of 472 reports (38 percent of the all-conference total). The Rio Earth Summit, with its stellar cast of heads of state, was second with a combined total of 354 reports (29 percent). The population conference in Cairo had the third largest number of reports at 194 (16 percent). Then came the Vienna human rights conference at 123 reports (10 percent), and finally the Copenhagen social development summit at 93 reports (7 percent). The rank order of the number of reports for each conference was similar for all three agencies.

The reports were analyzed using the TEXTPACK PC content analysis program (Mohler & Zuell, 1990). The frequency of mention of individual countries was determined by constructing a dictionary of all nations and territories. It included both noun and adjectival forms of reference (Brazil and Brazilian, France and French, and so on). Individual nations also were tag-coded into geographic regions (Africa, Asia, Europe, and so on) and by level of development.

Conference on Environment and Development

The UN Conference on Environment and Development that took place in Rio de Janeiro in June 1992 was at the time the largest international conference ever held. It was attended by more than 100 heads of state from both developed and developing nations. Tens of thousands of people attended the Earth Summit itself, or the parallel nongovernment organization conference called Global Forum. Hundreds of NGOs were represented at the Global Forum, ranging from well-known international organizations like Greenpeace to little-known local groups in Third World countries. An estimated 8,000 journalists reported on the event for individual media organizations or for the news agencies that provided the bulk of coverage (*USIA World*, 1993).

This was the first major international conference since the end of the cold war. East–West tensions had largely faded into history: the former Soviet Union, preoccupied with its own internal problems, was not a major player. The meeting had two broad goals: to focus the world's attention on environmental concerns, and to set forth an agenda to achieve sustainable development (Hansen, 1993). It was the first summit to articulate the concept that many problems facing mankind—human rights, peace, social justice, and environmental concerns like global warming, deforestation, and loss of biodiversity—are planetary in scope and cannot be solved by traditional diplomacy that pits one region against others. However, despite the realization that cooperation rather than competition was required, there was debate between the wealthy industrialized countries and the relatively poor nations of the developing world about how such environmental concerns need to be tackled.

For countries from the South, the environment had emerged as a potential lever for developing nations to obtain the levels of aid, investment, and access to rich-country markets to which they felt entitled. For the North, protection of the environment—particularly saving tropical rainforests to absorb carbon dioxide produced mainly in the industrialized countries, and as a genetic reservoir—was the major goal. The Southern nations, however, asserted they had a right to make economic use of their resources, and should not have to make sacrifices to compensate for excessive growth and consumption in the North (Petesch, 1992). Their concern was development, and the extent to which the North was willing to pay for measures taken in the South to mitigate global environmental degradation (Hurrell & Kingsbury, 1992). These key differences on environmental issues were reported as dividing the United States and the Third World.

The aggregate coverage by the three news agencies was dominated by the United States, which had a high-level delegation, including President George Bush, and was mentioned more often than any other nation. The conference also drew attention because it became a political issue during the 1992 United States presidential election campaign. The image presented of the country was not always favorable. The United States was singled out as being obstructive and isolated for resisting specific limits on carbon dioxide emissions, and for refusing to sign the Biodiversity Treaty. Brazil had the second-highest number of mentions, by far the majority of them being in the context of its role as host nation for the conference. It also was reported as opposing limits on its sovereign right to burn down Amazon jungles, and particularly for human rights violations against indigenous Indians. Brazil, along with India, China, and Malaysia, was depicted as being the most obdurate in opposing any curbs on logging in tropical forests without adequate compensation from the industrialized world.

Japan was the focus of a large number of reports, but received a very mixed press. Some depicted it as an environmental outlaw, indifferent to endangered species and environmental destruction. But Japan also drew praise for its pledge of $7.7 billion to help the developing world overcome environmental problems. Great Britain and Germany, along with three other industrialized countries—Canada, Norway, and the Netherlands—were praised for their pledges to increase development aid and to curb the emission of greenhouse gases.

The former Soviet Union was 13th overall in the ranking, with one-twentieth as many references as the United States. Most had to do with pollution in the Baltic Sea, and the appointment of former President Mikhail Gorbachev as chairman of a new environmental group, International Green Cross. The former Soviet republics also were depicted as being in competition with the Third World. They wanted favored financial treatment for "countries in transition to a market economy"—a concept opposed by the developing nations.

All three agencies had a similar ranking of nations, typically the United States followed by the host country Brazil, then some combination of Japan, India, Germany, and Great Britain. IPS, however, paid proportionately less attention to European and North American nations than did the others, and more to developing countries in Asia, Africa, and Latin America.

Conference on Human Rights

The UN Conference on Human Rights took place in Vienna in June 1993. The meeting drew more than 8,000 delegates from 168 nations. In addition, about 3,000 people representing over 2,000 NGOs with an interest in human rights attended a parallel conference, held on a different floor of the same building. The aim of the Vienna talks was to review progress since the adoption of the Universal Declaration of Human Rights in 1948, and to affirm fundamental human freedoms and ways to strengthen their enforcement (Reoch, 1993). The intention was to shape a new global approach to human rights after the changes in the political framework in a number of countries in Africa, Asia, Eastern Europe, and Latin America, which in the past decade had undergone transitions from military or authoritarian to civilian and democratic governments.

The conference did not generate as much news agency coverage as the Rio Summit, partly because most nations were represented by lower-level government ministers rather than heads of state. Agency reporting again tended to highlight the rift between developed and developing nations, and more specifically between the United States and China, which was characterized as the leader of the group of mainly Asian and Middle Eastern states that rejected Western concepts of freedom and also the right of the international community to enforce them. Instead, these nations were reported as favoring collective rights (such as food, clothing, shelter, and political stability) over individual civil and political rights, and their own cultural history above Western traditions. They spurned efforts by the West to impose its human rights standards on other nations. The developed countries, led by the United States, Great Britain, and Germany, but supported also by Russia, argued for a universal standard of human rights, enforced by a global court. Developing nations, and particularly China, Colombia, Cuba, India, Indonesia, Mexico, Pakistan, Sudan, and Yemen, argued that protection of human rights must be insured without damaging the principles of national sovereignty and without interference in their domestic affairs. Japan wanted to link human rights to development assistance.

The United States and China dominated the coverage on all three agencies. Bosnia was third, with numerous reports of human rights violations during the civil war raging there at the time. The war overshadowed the talks when the 51-nation Organization of the Islamic Conference, led by Pakistan, insisted that the arms embargo against Bosnia's Muslim-led government be lifted. Fourth place went to host nation Austria, whose foreign minister, Alois Mock, also was chairman of the conference and was reported as being pivotal in blocking China's efforts to bar Tibet's exiled Dalai Lama from addressing the meeting. Japan, India, Gerat Britain, and Malaysia all were ranked in the top dozen at both gatherings.

Several nations that did not get extensive coverage at the Rio Summit did attract attention in Vienna. India and Pakistan figured prominently in reports about its disputes over rights violations in Kashmir. Human rights violations by Indonesia, particularly in East Timor, and by Turkey against its Kurdish minority, drew attention to those nations. Cuba was mentioned in several AP and Reuters reports that dealt with human rights violations there.

Russia was in ninth place overall, with one-seventh as many mentions as the United States. Many stories dealt with Russia's siding with the Western nations in their efforts to set up a United Nations high commissioner for human rights. Russia's domestic politics also intruded on the summit: there were reports of its dispute with Baltic states over discriminatory citizenship laws against Russians stranded in Latvia and Estonia after the breakup of the Soviet Union.

As in the case of the Rio Summit, the three news agencies had a similar ranking of nations. All three played up the clash between the United States and China. Reuters' references to China depicted that nation as being hostile to Western concepts of fundamental human rights, and singled it out as one of the world's top human rights abusers. Reuters and the AP also made much of China's effort to prevent the Dalai Lama from attending the conference. IPS reports mentioned China as arguing for noninterference and national sovereignty in the face of efforts by Western governments to impose universal standards. Austria's role as host nation and disputes between India and Pakistan over Kashmir put those nations in the top half-dozen on each agency after the United States and China. Reports on rights violations in Cuba, Indonesia, and Iran drew attention to those nations.

Conference on Population and Development

The Conference on Population and Development, which took place in Cairo in September 1994, was attended by more than 15,000 people, including representatives of 150 nations, with 19 of the delegations led by heads of state or government. More than 1,200 NGOs from around the world sent delegates to a forum that ran in parallel with the official government meeting. The primary aim of the conference was to draft a 20-year plan to slow population growth, limiting the world's population to 7.27 billion in 2015—up from 5.67 billion in 1995.

The proposed Program of Action sought to curb population growth by making family planning available worldwide and by giving women more power over their own lives, especially on childbearing, through education and social change. The document stressed the importance of gender equity and empowerment of women as the cornerstone of population and development-related programs. To keep population growth within acceptable limits, the United Nations wanted a three-fold increase in spending from current levels to $17 billion a year by the end of the century.

Included in the Program of Action was a wide range of controversial subjects: abortion, birth control, women's rights, family structures, and extramarital sex. It soon became apparent that these issues would divide the proceedings into four main blocks of delegates: rich industrialized nations, the Vatican and its Catholic allies, Muslim states, and developing countries.

Western nations, led by the United States, emphasized the need to stabilize the global population. To achieve this, they endorsed the view that women and men should be able to freely choose what kind of contraception to use. Muslim countries were concerned about what they saw as Western campaigns to promote birth control in the Muslim world, whose rapid population growth the West considered as a threat to global security. And they argued that the program opened the door to accepting homosexuality and other forms of sex abhorrent to Islam, which approved of sex only between husband and wife. Iran, Pakistan, and Egypt were the primary spokesmen for a more moderate Muslim point of view. Libya, Yemen, Algeria, Syria, and Afghanistan said they put Islamic law first and attacked the concept of individual rights in sexual matters. Four Muslim countries—Iraq, Saudi Arabia, Sudan, and Lebanon—announced they would boycott the conference.

The Vatican, which had observer status at the conference and sent a 17-member delegation to Cairo, campaigned against proposals it believed would promote abortion and artificial contraception, and would have the effect of undermining family values and encouraging promiscuity. Together with its Catholic allies—Argentina, Ecuador, Peru, the Dominican Republic, and Malta—the Vatican held up the conference for five days until language was changed to stress that abortion could not be promoted as a means of population control. The Vatican was reported to have sought an alliance with Muslim nations, including Iran and Libya, in opposing some of the conference's goals.

Third World nations saw increased funding as a key factor. They were concerned that decreases in their populations without simultaneous economic development could have grave social repercussions in societies where parents depend economically on their children. They wanted Western donors to allocate 20 percent of their aid budgets to basic social services. Also at issue was an impasse between the North and the South over whether immigrants have an absolute right to bring their families to join them.

Clashes between Catholic, Muslim, and secular Western views on sexual rights, gender, and the family dominated reporting from the conference. In the combined coverage by the three agencies, the Vatican was mentioned more often than any nation state. Many of these references were condemnations of its intransigent stand and accusations that it was trying to "hijack" the meeting. Second was Egypt, which was prominent largely because of its role as the host nation and due to concerns about domestic terrorism and threats to security from Muslim fundamentalists who had warned foreign participants to stay away.

The United States, as leader of the Western group, was third, with one-third as many references as the Vatican. It attracted attention through the prominence of the delegation leader, Vice President Al Gore, and its role as the primary backer of the conference's draft document and as the largest donor to population-control projects in the developing world. But several reports cited critics of the United States who, among other things, accused it of "demographic imperialism." Pakistan ranked fourth in the overall coverage, as a nation having one of the fastest population growth rates in the world, but one that was trying to promote family planning. Prime Minister Benazir Bhutto was cited for her positive contribution, and her decision to attend despite domestic pressure to boycott the talks.

India was fifth—referred to as a country that, despite efforts at family planning, was likely to have the world's largest population in the next 40 years. Iran, often portrayed in the West as intransigent and uncooperative, was described in some reports as having played a constructive role. Iran sat with the U.S., Great Britain, and Germany in a working group on reproductive health and rights, and surprised the Westerners by negotiating in good faith. The resulting media attention moved it up to sixth place. Germany, in seventh place, drew attention for its offers of financial aid to promote family planning, and for its efforts to limit immigration from the Third World. Saudi Arabia was referred to primarily as having boycotted the talks.

Russia was all but invisible in the agency reports, occupying 35th place in the rankings. Three of the four references to Russia were in one AP interview with a Russian delegate who was looking for guidance on establishing a national population program, but was frustrated by the way abortion had come to dominate the summit agenda.

The three agencies displayed some similarities in their rankings. All three had more references to the Vatican and Egypt than any other nation, followed (with some variation) by the United States, Pakistan, India, Iran, Germany, and Canada.

Conference on Social Development

The Social Summit that took place in Copenhagen in March 1995 was attended by delegates from 182 of the UN's 185 member states, including, for the final session, more than 100 heads of state or government. An alternative summit, NGO Forum '95, was attended by hundreds of charity, aid, peace, and religious organizations. The purpose of the conference was to fight poverty, unemployment, and social injustice, and to narrow the gap between the world's rich and poor nations.

The 90-page summit declaration spoke of the need to cut the debt burden of developing countries, particularly in Africa. It said plans drawn up by the World Bank and International Monetary Fund should take more account of possible social consequences of radical economic reform plans. It also called for providing women with equal access to productive resources and reducing their workloads.

The alternative summit, NGO Forum '95, presented its own resolution urging world leaders to close the gap between rich and poor. It called for full and equal rights for women, cuts in military spending, and an immediate cancellation of the debts of developing countries. Christian and Muslim groups at the NGO Forum announced a plan to organize joint relief and development projects. At the close of the official summit, the Forum issued a counter declaration saying the meeting had been a failure and would do little for the poor.

As in the case of the previous summits, the debates were characterized by news reports as conflicts between the developed and developing worlds. Reports stressed differences between rich and poor countries over the wording of clauses on trade, debt reduction, and labor laws. The poor nations wanted a global commitment to debt forgiveness. Some leaders of developing nations (among them several accused by Western countries of human rights violations and corruption) blamed the West for failing to assist countries it had once colonized and exploited. The donor countries argued there should be no blanket proposals to deal with aid and debt. These should be handled on a case by case basis.

Despite the attendance of high-level delegations from more than 180 nations, the Social Summit resulted in fewer agency reports than any of the three major UN conferences that preceded it. Expectations were not high: according to Reuters' reports, the organizers conceded in advance that little or nothing concrete might emerge from the deliberations. Over time, the novelty of UN summits seems to have worn off for media gatekeepers, particularly since the results appeared to have been meager.

In the aggregate coverage by all three agencies, Denmark was the nation cited most often. It was the host country, and the Danish government grabbed the spotlight with an announcement that it was writing off $180 million in government loans to six developing nations in an attempt to inspire other rich countries to do the same. The United States had a large delegation led by Vice President Al Gore. First Lady Hillary Rodham Clinton attended the conference and announced a $100 million U.S. aid package to provide enhanced educational opportunities for women in Africa, Asia, and Latin America. Cuba was third, chiefly because of the presence of President Fidel Castro, who clashed with Gore over the relative merits of market and nonmarket economic systems. India was cited as an example of a nation trying to relieve the miseries of abject poverty.

The AP coverage focused primarily on just two nations, the United States and Denmark. No other nation was mentioned more than 10 times. Reuters' profile was similar to that of the AP, focusing primarily on Denmark, the United States, and Cuba. IPS had a more even distribution. India ranked first, as a result of several dispatches that detailed the nation's problems and efforts to overcome them, followed by Japan, which was reported as being the world's largest source of development aid, and as seeking an expanded role in world affairs. Then came China, Mexico, the United States, and Cuba. Russia was 23rd in the ranking, being mentioned in passing in one report from the AP and two from Reuters.

Fourth World Conference on Women

The Fourth World Conference on Women that took place in Beijing in September 1995 drew 17,000 participants, including 6,000 delegates from 189 countries, a host of international civil servants, and more than 4,000 representatives of accredited NGOs (Boutros-Ghali, 1996). More than 20,000 people participated in the parallel

NGO Forum on Women in 1995 in the Beijing suburb of Huairou to establish contacts, discuss a wide range of issues affecting women, and to lobby the official conference. These events were covered by more than 4,000 media representatives. A primary purpose of the conference was to assess how women's lives have changed over the past decade and to keep issues of concern to women high on the international agenda. The intention was to review the progress made since 1975— the International Women's Year and the year of the First World Conference on Women—to determine how women have fared in the areas of health, education, employment, family life, politics, and human rights.

The agenda for the conference can be found in the Platform for Action—an agenda for empowerment of women—that called for the removal of all obstacles to women's active participation in public life. The platform evolved from previous events, including the United Nations Decade for Women, and the Third World Conference on Women that took place in Nairobi in 1985. That conference called on governments to improve conditions for women in areas such as employment, education, industrial investment, housing, transportation, and the environment. The Beijing conference adopted the platform, which analyzes obstacles to women's advancement and recommends steps for overcoming them. The platform focused on a dozen critical areas of concern: poverty, education, health, violence against women, the effects of armed or other kinds of conflict, economic participation, power-sharing, mechanisms to promote women's advancement, human rights of women, women and the mass media, the environment and development, and the girl-child.

The Beijing events spawned more coverage by the three news agencies than any previous UN summit. More than 130 nations were mentioned at least once by one or more of the agencies. IPS referred to the largest number, with a total of 123, followed by Reuters with 90, and the AP with 81. The nations mentioned most frequently by all three agencies were China, the United States, and the Vatican, which, while not technically a nation, had observer status at the conference, and drew attention particularly for its opposition to birth control and abortion.

China alone accounted for more than half the references to all nations on both AP and Reuters. Most of these references were in the context of China as the host nation for the conference, especially criticisms about inadequate facilities and intrusive security at the NGO Forum site in Huairou. Many had to do with issues only indirectly related to the conference, for example, criticism by the United States and other Western nations of China's human rights abuses and repressive policies in Tibet. In the weeks preceding the conference, coverage was dominated by China's arrest of activist Harry Wu on charges of spying, and a subsequent debate on whether Hillary Clinton should go to Beijing as planned. The IPS team paid less attention to these topics, choosing to focus instead on coverage of issues in the Platform for Action. Consequently, the references to China on IPS comprised less than 10 percent of its references to all nations.

The United States ranked second in the number of references, with just under 20 percent of the total. The U.S. had a high-profile official delegation, led by Hillary Clinton, and American women's rights organizations and activists like Bella Abzug featured prominently in coverage of the NGO Forum. The Vatican was third (8.5 percent), largely because of controversy over its opposition to reproductive rights for women, including contraception and abortion. Japan was fourth, partly because of reports that, as the biggest source of foreign aid for developing countries, it planned to target its largess on women's needs and social development, and partly because of reports about Japan's use of sex slaves to entertain soldiers during World War II. Iran was fifth in the ranking, with reports on protests about its seeking to roll back the clock on progress made toward equality for women. Iran opposed passages in the Platform of Action that appeared to support abortion and sexual freedom for women, and was depicted as a leader of Islamic nations in this regard. Peru, on the other hand, achieved prominence in the coverage when President Alberto Fujimori assailed the Catholic Church for attacking his drive to bring birth control to all Peruvians. Coverage of Russia was sparse—it ranked 18th, with about 4 percent as many references as the United States.

AGGREGATE COVERAGE OF NATIONS

The combined coverage of all five conferences by the three agencies included 14,168 references to 132 nations (including multiple mentions). Just six nations account for nearly 50 percent of the total (China 19.1 percent, the United States 14.3 percent, the Vatican 5.7 percent, Brazil 5.1 percent, Japan 3.2 percent, and Egypt 2.4 percent). Add India, Germany, Great Britain, Pakistan, Canada, and Iran, and the top dozen account for almost 60 percent (see Table 18.1, Column A). No other nation accounts for more than 1 percent. Nearly 90 percent of the references to China were in coverage of the Beijing conference, but it also was among the top 10 nations mentioned at the environmental, human rights, and population conferences. The United States had a consistently high ranking across conferences. It was among the top three nations mentioned at every meeting. The Vatican's third ranking was based largely on its coverage at two of the five conferences—the population summit in Cairo and the Women's Summit in Beijing. Its coverage was minimal at the other three. Ninety-three percent of the references to fourth-place Brazil were in connection with the Rio Earth Summit. Sixty-six percent of Japan's coverage came as a result of its prominent role at the Rio Summit, and another 16 percent at the Women's Summit. India featured prominently in the population, human rights, and environmental conferences. Egypt (2.4 percent) was in seventh position, largely because it was mentioned frequently as the host for the Cairo population conference. Germany (1.5 percent) drew attention at Rio and in Cairo. Great Britain (1.4 percent) was in 10th place, largely because of its prominence at the environmental

TABLE 18.1.
Rank Order of Nations (Combined News Agencies)

Column A (all references)			Column B (host nations omitted)		
Rank	Nation (n=14,168)	Percentage	Rank	Nation (n=10,921)	Percentage
1	China	19.1	1	U.S.	18.6
2	U.S.	14.3	2	Japan	4.2
3	Vatican	5.7	3	China	2.9
4	Brazil	5.1	4	India	2.3
5	Japan	3.2	5	Germany	1.9
6	Egypt	2.4	6	Britain	1.8
7	India	1.8	7	Pakistan	1.8
8	Germany	1.5	8	Canada	1.7
9	Britain	1.4	9	Iran	1.7
10	Pakistan	1.4	10	Cuba	1.3
11	Canada	1.3	11	Peru	1.2
12	Iran	1.3	12	France	1.1
13	Cuba	1.0	13	Indonesia	1.1
14	Peru	0.9	14	Russia	1.0
15	France	0.9	15	Norway	1.0
16	Indonesia	0.9	16	Bosnia	0.9
17	Denmark	0.8	17	Mexico	0.9
18	Russia	0.8	18	Malaysia	0.8
19	Norway	0.8	19	Sweden	0.7
20	Bosnia	0.7	20	Argentina	0.7
21	Mexico	0.7	21	Philippines	0.7
22	Malaysia	0.6	22	Thailand	0.7
23	Austria	0.6	23	Netherlands	0.6
24	Sweden	0.6	24	Kenya	0.6
25	Argentina	0.5	25	Egypt	0.6
26	Philippines	0.5	26	Israel	0.6
27	Thailand	0.5	27	Iraq	0.5
28	Netherlands	0.5	28	Colombia	0.5
29	Kenya	0.5	29	Australia	0.5
30	Israel	0.4	30	Saudi Arabia	0.5
31	Iraq	0.4	31	Brazil	0.5
32	Colombia	0.4	32	Chile	0.5
33	Australia	0.4	33	Kuwait	0.4
34	Saudi Arabia	0.4	34	Vietnam	0.4
35	Chile	0.4	35	Turkey	0.4
36	Kuwait	0.3	36	Denmark	0.4
37	Vietnam	0.3	37	Venezuela	0.4
38	Turkey	0.3	38	Italy	0.4
39	Venezuela	0.3	39	Palestine	0.4
40	Italy	0.3	40	Switzerland	0.4

TABLE 18.1.
Continued

	Column A (all references)			Column B (host nations omitted)	
Rank	Nation (n=14,168)	Percentage	Rank	Nation (n=10,921)	Percentage
41	Palestine	0.3	41	Jamaica	0.3
42	Switzerland	0.3	42	Yugoslavia	0.3
43	Jamaica	0.3	43	Portugal	0.3
44	Yugoslavia	0.3	44	Austria	0.2
45	Portugal	0.2	45	El Salvador	0.2
46	El Salvador	0.2	46	Panama	0.2
47	Panama	0.2	47	Uganda	0.2
48	Uganda	0.2	48	Guyana	0.2
49	Guyana	0.2	49	Haiti	0.2
50	Haiti	0.1	50	Spain	0.1
	Other nations	76.5		Other nations	59.8
	TOTAL	100.0		TOTAL	100.0

and human rights conferences. At the same level as Britain was Pakistan (1.4 percent), which featured in the population and human rights coverage, then Canada, Iran, Cuba, Peru, France, Indonesia, Denmark, and Russia (18th in rank, with 0.8 percent of all references). The remaining 114 nations that were mentioned were depicted as bit players, with less than 1 percent of the total number of references each.

The overall profile is skewed, however, by the fact that nations that hosted the various conferences—Brazil, Austria, Egypt, Denmark, and China—received a disproportionate amount of coverage on those occasions. Overall, about 40 percent of the mentions were substantive—actions or positions taken by the host nations with respect to the conference agenda, or references to conditions in their countries. The rest tended to be nonsubstantive references to their being the venues, including datelines on reports.

If one omits references to nations during the conferences they hosted (for example, references to Brazil are omitted from the Rio Earth Summit; those to China from the Women's Summit), and references to the Vatican are omitted because it is not a typical nation state, the rank order of those nations changes markedly (see Table 18.1, Column B). China drops from first to fourth position,

Egypt from seventh to 26th, Denmark from 17th to 35th, and Austria from 23rd to 44th. The pecking order for the top 20 then becomes the United States, Japan, China, India, Germany, Great Britain, Pakistan, Canada, Iran, Cuba, Peru, France, Indonesia, Russia, Norway, Bosnia, Mexico, Malaysia, Sweden, and Argentina.

Six of the seven top industrial nations (members of the group of 7) are included in the list. Missing is Italy, which was not reported as playing a leading role at any of the conferences. The prominence of the United States, Japan, Germany, Great Britain, Canada, and France, as traditional elite nations, could be anticipated. China, India, and Pakistan are more surprising. Russia, which as the Soviet Union rivaled the United States in the cold war frame of media coverage, has diminished to 14th position, below many developing nations.

Just three African nations—Egypt, Kenya, and Uganda—were among 50 countries mentioned most often. South Africa made an appearance at the later conferences, after majority rule was achieved in 1994 and the republic was readmitted to the United Nations. Only three Eastern European nations made the top 50: Russia, Bosnia, and Yugoslavia—the latter two only because of reports at the human rights conference about wartime conditions there. Asian nations in the top 50, in descending order, were Japan (mainly as a major donor nation), China, India, Pakistan, Indonesia, Malaysia, Thailand, and the Philippines. There were five Middle Eastern nations on the list: Iran (mainly at the human rights and population summits), Israel, Iraq, Saudi Arabia, and Kuwait—the latter in the context of environmental damage after the Gulf War, and the treatment of women. Western European nations in the top 50, in descending order, were Germany (particularly at the environmental, population, and women's conferences), Great Britain and France (environment and women), and Norway and Sweden (environment, population, and women). These were followed by the Netherlands, Turkey, Denmark, Italy, Switzerland, Austria, and Portugal.

VARIATIONS ACROSS AGENCIES

The rank order of nations across the three agencies was similar. However, while all three gave more prominence to the United States than any other nation, this emphasis was much less pronounced in the case of IPS, where 11.2 percent of all references were to the U.S., compared with 21.8 percent for the AP and 25.8 percent for Reuters (see Table 18.2). The IPS coverage was generally more evenly distributed, and across a greater range of countries, than the other two agencies. Thus, almost 50 percent of IPS mentions were to nations that did not appear among the top 50 (virtually all were in the developing world), while the corresponding figure for the AP was 65 percent, and for Reuters 70 percent.

TABLE 18.2.
Frequency of Mention by News Agency (Percent)

Nation	Total (n=10,921)	AT (n=3,200)	IPS (n=4,523)	Reuters (n=3,199)
1. US	18.6	21.8	11.2	25.8
2. Japan	4.2	3.3	3.9	5.6
3. China	2.9	2.2	3.3	2.9
4. India	2.3	1.7	3.2	1.8
5. Germany	1.9	2.8	1.0	2.3
6. Britain	1.8	1.9	1.0	2.8
7. Pakistan	1.8	1.8	1.9	1.6
8. Canada	1.7	1.6	1.7	1.9
9. Iran	1.7	1.6	0.9	2.9
10. Cuba	1.3	1.1	0.9	2.1
11. Peru	1.2	2.3	0.7	1.0
12. France	1.1	1.2	0.6	1.8
13. Indonesia	1.1	0.3	1.9	0.8
14. Russia	1.0	1.6	0.7	0.9
15. Norway	1.0	1.2	0.9	0.9
16. Bosnia	0.9	1.9	0.2	1.0
17. Mexico	0.9	1.0	1.1	0.6
18. Malaysia	0.8	0.6	1.0	0.9
19. Sweden	0.7	0.6	0.6	1.0
20. Argentina	0.7	1.1	0.7	0.2
21. Philippines	0.7	0.4	1.1	0.3
22. Thailand	0.7	0.3	0.9	0.7
23. Netherlands	0.6	0.5	0.8	0.6
24. Kenya	0.6	0.8	0.6	0.3
25. Egypt	0.6	0.6	0.5	0.7
26. Israel	0.6	0.4	0.1	1.3
27. Iraq	0.5	0.5	0.4	0.8
28. Colombia	0.5	0.6	0.5	0.5
29. Australia	0.5	0.4	0.3	0.9
30. Saudi Arabia	0.5	0.5	0.6	0.3
31. Brazil	0.5	0.7	0.5	0.2
32. Chile	0.5	0.7	0.5	0.3
33. Kuwait	0.4	0.5	0.2	0.8
34. Vietnam	0.4	0.3	0.7	0.2
35. Turkey	0.4	0.4	0.5	0.4
36. Denmark	0.4	0.6	0.2	0.5
37. Venezuela	0.4	0.3	0.8	0.0
38. Italy	0.4	0.5	0.2	0.6
39. Palestine	0.4	0.3	0.4	0.5
40. Switzerland	0.4	0.7	0.1	0.4
41. Jamaica	0.3	0.1	0.7	0.0

TABLE 18.2.
Continued

Nation	Total (n=10,921)	AT (n=3,200)	IPS (n=4,523)	Reuters (n=3,199)
42. Yugoslavia	0.3	0.4	0.2	0.4
43. Portugal	0.3	0.6	0.1	0.3
44. Austria	0.2	0.4	0.2	0.2
45. El Salvador	0.2	0.1	0.2	0.4
46. Panama	0.2	0.5	0.0	0.3
47. Uganda	0.2	0.3	0.3	0.1
48. Guyana	0.2	0.2	0.3	0.1
49. Haiti	0.2	0.1	0.4	0.1
50. Spain	0.1	0.2	0.0	0.3
Other nations	39.8	35.4	50.6	29.0
TOTAL	100.0	100.0	100.0	100.0

REGIONAL VARIATIONS

Again omitting references to nations during the conferences they hosted, Asian countries collectively accounted for the highest proportion—24 percent of the combined agency coverage (see Table 18.3). Although the United States was the single nation mentioned most often in the overall coverage, North America as a region was in second place at 20.5 percent—chiefly because only two nations, the

TABLE 18.3.
Rank Order of Regions by News Agency (Percentage)

Nation	Total (n=10,921)	AP (n=3,200)	IPS (n=4,523)	Reuters (n=3,198)
1. Asia	24.0	17.8	29.7	21.8
2. North America	20.5	23.0	13.8	27.3
3. Western, Europe	17.0	21.8	14.2	16.4
4. Africa	13.0	11.3	17.5	8.2
5. Latin America	9.5	10.8	11.3	5.7
6. Middle East	5.6	5.3	4.4	7.8
7. East Europe	4.1	5.7	2.0	5.7
8. Caribbean	4.1	2.0	5.5	4.5
9. Oceania	2.2	2.3	1.6	2.6
TOTAL	100.0	100.0	100.0	100.0

United States and Canada, were included in this category. Then came Western Europe, Africa, Latin America, the Middle East, Eastern Europe, the Carribean, and Oceania (Australia, New Zealand, and the Pacific island states). It is evident that the AP and Reuters paid proportionately more attention to North America and Western Europe than did IPS—about 44 percent in each case—compared to 28 percent for IPS, which spotlighted Asian, African, Latin American, and Caribbean countries. The former Soviet Union and other Eastern European nations ranked at the same level overall as the Caribbean islands; only Oceania drew less attention.

THE DECLINE OF THE DOMINANT NEWS FRAME

These data suggest that the cold war frame for reporting international affairs is largely a thing of the past, at least when it comes to issues of global concern. Eastern Europe, including the former Soviet Union and its client states in the Warsaw Pact, has almost disappeared from the information map. Russia ranks 14th in the list of nations mentioned across all five conferences. Where Russia does feature, at least in the context of these global issues, it is not depicted as being in conflict with the West. Rather, its positions are reported as being congruent with those of the developed world and often in conflict with the developing nations. Cuba, which was cited more often than Russia, has become the main remnant of cold war tensions, and that is largely because of Western concerns about Castro's human rights record. Only 3.5 percent of references are to the former Warsaw Pact nations as a group. The AP had the highest proportion at 3.9 percent; Reuters was 3.5; and IPS was a scant 3 percent.

The decline of East–West rivalry as a news frame does not mean that international issues are no longer reported in terms of conflict. The conflictual frame remains, but the protagonists have changed. There are new principal actors in addition to such traditional industrial powers as the United States, Great Britain, Canada, France, Germany, Japan, and Italy. The major change is the emergence of newsmakers of Asian or Pacific Rim nations—China, India, Pakistan, Indonesia, Malaysia, and the Philippines. Less prominent are Africa, Latin America, the Middle East, and the Caribbean.

East–West controversies have largely given way to a North–South divide, a clash of ideologies and economic interests between the have and have-not nations. No doubt this was present in the past, but was overshadowed by superpower rivalry. However, qualitative analysis of the agency reports suggests that, while developing nations now feature more conspicuously, they often are defined in terms of their support for or opposition to Western policies and values. Most often, with the exception of IPS, the relationship is conflictual: they are depicted as chainsaw-wielding despoilers of the rainforests, exploiters of child labor who deny women equal rights and allow their populations to spiral unchecked (or worse, enforce abortion), as undeserving supplicants for debt relief or bigger handouts. Now that the developing nations have the attention of the international media, the challenge will be to achieve correspondingly more sympathetic coverage.

REFERENCES

Boutros-Ghali, B. (1996). Translating the momentum of Beijing into action. In *The Beijing declaration and the platform for action*. New York: UN Department of Public Information.

Galtung, J., & Ruge, M. H. (1965). The structure of foreign news. *Journal of Peace Research, 2*, 64–91.

Gerbner, G., & Marvanyi, G. (1981). The many worlds of the world's press. In J. Richstad & M. Anderson (Eds.), *Crisis in international news: Policies and prospects* (pp. 184–196). New York: Columbia University Press.

Hallin, D. (1986). Where? Cartography, community and the cold war. In R. Manoff & M. Schudson (Eds.), *Reading the news* (pp. 109–145). New York: Pantheon Books.

Hansen, A. (Ed.). (1993). *The mass media and environmental issues*. London: Leicester University Press.

Herman, E. S., & Chomsky, N. (1988). *Manufacturing consent: The political economy of the mass media*. New York: Pantheon Books.

Hester, A. (1978). International information flow. In H. Fischer & J. C. Merrill (Eds.), *International and intercultural communication* (pp. 242–250). New York: Hastings House.

Hester, A. (1991). *A comparative analysis of external service shortwave radio news broadcasts from the 1st, 2nd and 3rd worlds*. Athens, GA: University of Georgia.

Hurrell, A., & Kingsbury, B. (Eds.). (1992). *The international politics of the environment: actors, interests and institutions*. Oxford, England: Clarendon Press.

Larson, J. (1984). *Television's window on the world: International affairs coverage on the U.S. networks*. Norwood, NJ: Ablex.

Mohler, P., & Zuell, C. (1990). TEXTPACK PC, Release 4.0 [Computer software]. Mannheim, Germany: Zentrum fuer Umfragen, Methoden und Analysen.

Petesch, P. (1992). *North–South environmental strategies, costs and bargains*. Washington, DC: Overseas Development Council.

Reoch, R. (1993). *Rights or privileges? An independent guide to the World Conference on Human Rights*. Rome: Inter Press Service.

Schramm, W. (1964). *Mass media and national development*. Stanford, CA: Stanford University Press.

Servaes, J. (1991). European press coverage of the Grenada crisis. *Journal of Communication, 41*, 28–41.

Sreberny-Mohammadi, A., Nordenstreng, K., Stevenson, R., & Ugboajah, F. (1985). *Foreign news in the media*. Paris: UNESCO.

USIA World, 11(4). (1993). Washington, DC: U.S. Information Agency.

Wall, M. (1995). *Post cold-war media frames in coverage of Third World conflicts: Case studies of Cambodia, Northern Iraq and Rwanda*. Master's thesis, University of Washington, Seattle.

Weaver, D., & Wilhoit, G. C. (1984). Foreign news in the Western agencies. In R. Stevenson & D. Shaw (Eds.), *Foreign news and the New World Information Order* (pp. 153–185). Ames, IA: Iowa State University Press.

APPENDIX

Discussion Questions and Assignments

PART I: THEORIZING NEWS

1. What is the role of television news as a mediator of modernity and postmodernity in national and global terms? Discuss with examples from different countries.
2. Are the forces of transnationalization (as seen in the development of certain narrative genres) overtaking those seen in national media?
3. Is the concept of "international media echo" applicable to other cultural and national contexts?
4. How has the "New World Order" and global media events such as the Gulf War changed how news operates?
5. Using examples from other national and comparative contexts, construct a matrix model for different national news media contexts.

PART II: COMPARATIVE PERSPECTIVES

1. Does media support the status quo in its coverage of international news? Critically evaluate the claims made by Huang and McAdams, Lozano and colleagues, and Acosta and Lester.

2. Discuss the relevance of the dependency and cultural imperialism argument as they relate to news. Speculate as to possible similarities found by Lozana and colleagues with other parts of the world, Asia and Africa in particular.

3. In methodological terms, what are the advantages of doing comparative news research? What are its disadvantages? Draw on the three studies here to make your arguments.

4. Discuss the relevance of national versus regional frame of cultural referencing in terms of news. To what extent does the chapter by Acosta and Lester help us make sense of how each national and regional culture influence news coverage?

5. Design a project to study news comparatively. Provide a rationale for your choice of countries and the theoretical questions you wish to address.

PART III: NATIONAL PERSPECTIVES

1. From your reading of the chapter on North American news coverage of the Peruvian hostage crises and the Jihad model of journalism, discuss whether such news coverage is typical of coverage of all such events of terrorism. Identify stories where alternative news frames appeared.

2. From your reading of the comparative national frameworks of Israeli and Indian news, discuss whether each country has a specific cultural basis to their national news framework.

3. Based on your reading of the chapter on CCTV news, discuss whether state controlled windows on international news is fundamentally different from market based windows on international news.

4. Based on your reading of the chapters on South African and Bulgarian news media, what general model for emergent news media exists in contemporary conditions of media globalization? Is it possible to have "national" media in the traditional sense anymore?

5. What are the methodological advantages of doing textual analysis of news texts? What kinds of messages are gleaned from this method, that traditional quantitative analysis does not yield? Conversely, what are the disadvantages of textual analysis and the results that it does not yield?

PART IV: TRANSNATIONAL PERSPECTIVES

1. Log on to a website for one of the major news agencies and take a sample of news stories over a week. What patterns of globalization best fit the flow and appropriation of news as related to news agencies? Discuss with examples.

2. Is it possible to think of "development" and the public service function of news under current conditions of capitalism?

3. What new global frames for news coverage have emerged to replace the cold war news frame? Discuss with specific examples.

4. What other national news agencies might approximate Xinhua's pattern of development of news coverage? Discuss with examples drawn from specific national news agencies.

Author Index

Subject Index

About the Editors

Abbas Malek is a professor in the Department of Radio, Television, and Film in the School of Communications at Howard University, in Washington D.C., and is the president of the International Communication Association.

Anandam P. Kavoori is Associate Professor of Broadcast News and Telecommunications in the Henry W. Grady School of Journalism and Mass Communication at the University of Georgia, in Athens.

About the Contributors

Carolina Acosta is Assistant Professor in the Henry W. Grady School of Journalism and Mass Communication at the University of Georgia, in Athens.

Charles Quist-Adade teaches in the Department of Communication Studies at the University of Windsor, in Canada.

Gina Bailey is a doctoral candidate in the School of Communications at Simon Fraser University, in Canada.

Arnold de Beer is director of the Institute for Communication Research, Potchfestroom University, in South Africa, and Editor of *Ecquid Novi: Journal for Journalism in South Africa*.

Oliver Boyd Barrett is a professor at the College of the Extended University at California State Polytechnic University, in Pomona.

Kalyani Chadha has a doctorate from the School of Journalism at the University of Maryland, College Park.

Tsan-Kuo Chang is Associate Professor in the School of Journalism and Mass Communication at the University of Minnesota-Twin Cities.

Naren Chitty is director of the graduate program in International Communication in the Media and Communication Studies Department at Macquarie University, in Australia. He is also Editor of the *Journal of International Communication* and secretary general of the International Association for Media and Communication Research.

Anelia Dimitrova teaches in the Department of Communication Studies at the University of Northern Iowa, in Cedar Falls.

Charles Elliott is Assistant Professor in the Department of Communication Studies at Hong Kong Baptist University, in Kowloon.

Anthony Giffard is a professor and the director of the School of Communication at the University of Washington, in Seattle.

Li-Ning Huang is Assistant Professor at Central Connecticut State University, in New Britain.

Krishna Jayakar is a doctoral student in the Department of Telecommunications at Indiana University, in Bloomington.

Ritu Jayakar is a doctoral student in the School of Journalism at Indiana University, in Bloomington.

Christina Joseph is Adjunct Assistant Professor of Cultural Anthropology at the University of Georgia, Athens.

Karim H. Karim is Associate Professor in the School of Journalism and Communication at Carleton University in Ottawa, Ontario, Canada.

Elizabeth Lester is Associate Professor in the Henry W. Grady School of Journalism and Mass Communication at the University of Georgia, in Athens.

Eric Louw is a senior lecturer in the Department of Communications at the University of Queensland, in Australia.

Jose Carlos Lozano is a professor in the Department of Communication at the Instituto Tecnologico y de estudios superiores, in Monterrey, Mexico. His co-authors are **Edgar Gomez** (Instituto Tecnologico y de estudios superiores de Monterrey, Mexico), **Alejandro Matiasich** and **Alfredo Alfonso** (Universidad Nacional de La Plata, Argentina), **Martin Becerra** (Universidad Nacional de Quilmes, Argentina), **Ada Cristina Machado Silveira** (Universidad Federal de Santa Maria Rio Grande do Sul, Brazil), **Magdalena Elizondo** and **Jorge Morroquin** (Tecnologico de Monterrey, Mexico), and **Luciane Delgado Aquino** and **Franciso-Javier Martinez** (Universidad Autonoma de Barcelona, Spain).

Katherine McAdams is Associate Professor at the College of Journalism and Mass Communication at the University of Maryland, in College Park.

Peter Oehlkers is Assistant Professor in the Department of Communication at Emerson College, in Boston.

Daya Kishan Thussu is a senior lecturer in the Department of Communication, Culture and Media at Coventry University, in the United Kingdom.

Chen Yanru is a doctoral candidate in the School of Communication Studies at Nanyang Technological University, in Singapore.